THE EARLY ENGLISH THEATER

John Gassner, in his preface to this anthology, writes:
"Medieval drama offers us a varied and rich experience
of theatre rooted in a living society, in a world spiritually and culturally more unified than any we have
known since then in the West." Strolling players, monks
and priests, members of medieval guilds, schoolmasters
and their pupils—all participated actively in the writing,
staging and performance of plays in pre-Elizabethan
England.

MEDIEVAL AND TUDOR DRAMA

includes twenty-four plays from this vital period in English dramatic history, extensively annotated by Professor
Gassner. The language of the earliest plays has been
modernized, and plays composed in Latin have been
translated by Sister Mary Marguerite Butler of Mercy
College.

JOHN GASSNER, late Sterling Professor of Playwriting
and Dramatic Literature, Yale University, was the author
and editor of numerous books, including **Form and Idea
in Modern Drama, Theatre at the Crossroads**, and **Ideas
in the Drama.**

MEDIEVAL
AND
TUDOR
DRAMA

Edited and with introductions by

JOHN GASSNER

APPLAUSE
NEW YORK • LONDON

Medieval and Tudor Drama
Edited and with Introductions by John Gassner
© 1963, 1987 Mrs. John Gassner

Library of Congress Cataloging-in-Publication Data

Medieval and Tudor Drama.
   Bibliography: p.
     p.   cm.
  ISBN 0-936839-84-8
   1. English Drama- Early modern and Elizabethan, 1500-1600. 2. Drama, Medieval.
3. Passion-plays 4. Liturgical drama. I. Gassner, John, 1903-1967.
PR1262.M43   1987
822'.2'08

87-18836

British Library Cataloging-in-Publication Data

A catalogue record for this book is available from the British Library.

Applause Theatre & Cinema Books

19 West 21st Street, Suite 201
New York, NY 10010
Phone: (212) 575-9265
Fax: (212) 575-9270
Email: info@applausepub.com
Internet: www.applausepub.com

Applause books are available through your local bookstore, or you may order at
www.applausepub.com or call Music Dispatch at 800-637-2852.

Sales & Distribution:

North America:
  Hal Leonard Corp.
  7777 West Bluemound Road
  P.O. Box 13819
  Milwaukee, WI 53213
  Phone: (414) 774-3630
  Fax: (414) 774-3259
  Email: halinfo@halleonard.com
  Internet: www.halleonard.com

Europe:
  Roundhouse Publishing Ltd.
  Millstone, Limers Lane
  Northam, North Devon
  EX 39 2RG
  Phone: 01237-474474
  Fax: 01237-474774
  Email: roundhouse.group@ukgateway.net

ABNER HENRY KERN (1915-1961)

Atque in perpetuum, frater, ave atque vale.

CONTENTS

PREFACE

A vagabond performer, frowned upon by the Church and having no more claim to social status than a mountebank, appears in a village square and attracts a crowd with pantomime, jugglery, and comic recitation. A village bustles with "mumming," dancing, and local playmaking. A procession moves from place to place in honor of the Virgin, of some saint, or of some event. Monks or priests are giving a performance in a monastery, church, or cathedral in the midst of antiphonal singing; they chant and sing in Latin under the mystic light of the stained-glass windows, while moving from station to station or taking positions around an altar. They perform perhaps outside the church walls in the churchyard, or in the square in front of the west portal of the church or cathedral on a platform adjoining the steps, and the actor or cleric impersonating God goes in and out of the church.

A large town, enriched by industry and divided into craft associations, or "guilds," holds a great summer festival lasting several days outdoors, each craft accounting for a dramatized biblical episode. In an English town, the community presents a cycle of these biblical plays on double-decker pageant wagons that follow one another at specified locations while the public congregates in front of the wagon-stage. In a French city, the playgoers, standing in the town square, face a stationary stage consisting of simultaneously viewed little scenes, or "mansions," representing different localities ranging from Heaven to Hell. A cycle composed of numerous little plays dealing with miracles attributed to the Virgin Mary is given on these "mansions," episode by episode, scene by scene. A single play, consisting of one or more episodes, celebrates the martyrdom or the miraculous deeds of a popular saint on his name day. An allegory of good and evil is performed on some religious or public occasion on stationary platforms in some town or city. A farce is played by professional actors on an improvised stage in a castle, public building, or town square.

A comic debate on a popular subject is staged in some banquet hall for the edification or, rather, amusement of the guests. A classic Latin comedy or an imitation in the vernacular, written by a gifted schoolmaster, is staged by students at their school or college.

These and sundry other dramatic presentations stirred or enlivened the medieval world of Western Europe and the British Isles from the time the West emerged out of the disorder of the "Dark Ages" in the tenth century to the time it achieved a new order or synthesis in the thirteenth and fourteenth centuries—and later, when a new synthesis began to appear in the Renaissance world of the fifteenth and sixteenth centuries.

The strolling players, the monks and the priests, the worthy citizens of the medieval guilds who put on and paid for the production of the biblical plays, and the schoolmasters and their scholars vanished five hundred or more years ago. The colorful processions stopped moving a long time ago. The stationary stages of wood and the richly painted pageant wagons, as well as the lavishly constructed edifices on which allegories were presented, mostly in pantomime, on the occasion of such public events as the arrival of a royal personage or his noble representative crumbled away centuries ago. But for surviving verbal descriptions and pictures, we would not even know what they looked like. The flourishing cities that once supported a cycle of biblical plays that took several days to perform—Wakefield, Norwich, York, Chester, Coventry, Newcastle, Beverley, Lincoln—lost much of their wealth and population or dwindled into relative unimportance, while new cities began to overshadow them centuries ago.

The plays remain. Their authors' names are forgotten, if indeed their authorship was, in most instances, ever identifiable. Many liturgical plays have not been exhumed from monasteries or were lost in rubble. The scriptural cycles and the Passion plays of many medieval cities, including that of London itself, are lost to us. Time took its toll of much medieval drama. The surviving cycles are not entirely intact, and some cycles and individual episodes are mere fragments. But the plays remain in sufficient number to preserve the memory of the ample and varied theatre that belonged to the Church and the people of the Middle Ages. They also remain in a sufficiently satisfactory state of preservation to provide us with the richest store of folk drama that has come down to us. Along with the epic material of ancient times and the romances, ballads, and songs of the Middle Ages, the extant plays preserve for us the voice of common humanity with persuasive simplicity and amusing directness, as well as

with realism and wonder, homely detail and religious trans-
cendence. Without constituting great dramatic literature,
medieval drama offers us a varied and rich experience of
theatre rooted in a living society, in a world spiritually and
culturally more unified (despite the fragmented character of
feudal society) than any we have known since then in the
West.

It is my privilege and pleasure to present a subject close
to the heart of anyone who has a passion for the theatre. Anyone who persists in the opinion that the worth of a play as
drama rather than as a purely literary composition is closely
associated with its theatrical vitality, and that this vitality is
essentially communal rather than private, is bound to be
interested in the medieval drama. His interest, moreover,
cannot be limited to academic study even after the passage
of half a millennium, since many so-called miracle ("mystery")
plays of the Middle Ages have been produced successfully on
the twentieth-century stage. Anyone interested in the Renaissance or in Shakespeare is also bound to take early Tudor
drama into consideration, and in this instance, too, academic
interest can no longer be divorced from a lively sense of
theatre—at least in the case of the Tudor comedies.

This volume is intended to serve the dual purpose of intro-
ducing the general reader to the drama of the Middle Ages
produced in England and at the same time to acquaint him
with its international character. One cannot, indeed, do the one
thing without doing the other, for medieval plays written and
produced in different parts of Europe had many features in
common, including origins, subject matter, and point of view.
The reader is therefore introduced in this volume to the
beginnings of English and Western European drama simultaneously. Although the emphasis of most sections of the book
is on England, the liturgical drama that precedes the popular scriptural cycles of the English cities belongs to all of
Western Europe. The scriptural cycles of England share about
half their content or about half the number of their individual plays—those representing the New Testament—with
the Passion play cycles that appeared in many parts of continental Europe during the Middle Ages and still survive as
living theatre in the town of Oberammergau in southern
Bavaria. The other half of an English cycle consists of episodes based on the Old Testament, but the subject matter is
inevitably neither foreign to the European theatre nor unre-

lated to the Passion, the Old Testament events forming the groundwork and foreshadowing the advent of the drama of the redemption of sinful humanity by Christ the Redeemer.

Since the scriptural drama of the English cycles and the continental Passion plays is the major achievement of the medieval theatre, it receives fuller representation in the present volume than any other type of play. Drawing upon the various cycles written in Middle English, the book presents the outlines of a complete cycle itself, the individual plays comprising, as it were, a sacred history of the world from the Creation to the Last Judgment. But other types of drama prevalent in the Middle Ages also require, and receive, representation here. Among these are relics of pagan performances, early Christian imitations of Roman comedy (by the nun Hrotsvitha), liturgical drama in medieval Latin intended for performance by the clergy, and moral allegory written in the vernacular, a type of drama of which *Everyman,* in Middle English and Dutch, is the best-known example. The rich field of medieval farce is also represented here by a transitional composition known as an "Interlude," developed in England during the early Tudor period. The rest of this volume is given over to other Tudor works blending medieval and Renaissance elements. Two of these plays, *Ralph Roister Doister* and *Gammer Gurton's Needle,* carry the art of comedy in England beyond its medieval limits; while the third work, *Gorboduc,* a sedulous imitation of Roman—that is, "Senecan" —tragedy, shows serious drama in a new, nonreligious, guise.

.It remains to be noted that in spite of a tendency to take a generalized view of the medieval stage we may not overlook its variety. The various facets of medieval theatre acquired different degrees of emphasis in different regions. Thus a study of the German stage would assign importance to comic and grotesque elements derived from indigenous pagan ritual, as in the case of a carnival play, a so-called *Fastnachtspiel* (later performed at any other season as well), which developed in the fifteenth century. Carnival plays constituted the bulk of secular drama, and they reflected the relatively unsophisticated taste of a country that lacked large metropolitan centers like Paris and London in differing from the French *"soties"* and English "interludes"—that is, in lacking the satirical acuity of the former and the conversational charm and intellectualism of the latter. Folksy vigor was preponderant also in other parts of Central Europe, as in the Austrian farce known as the *Neidhartspiel*, named after the courtly minne-singer Neidhart of Reuental, who is tricked, while elegantly attempting to celebrate spring and love, by coarse-humored and hostile peasants. A central figure in German farce was the *Narr*, or fool, either a congenital dolt or a sly character who assumed obtuseness to his advantage. In Germany, the trade guilds, especially the guild of the so-called Master-singers in the south, made a specialty of farce; best known among the writers of farce was Hans Sachs (1494-1576), the master-cobbler of Nuremberg, who provided the city's annual carnival play. Later drama (including translations into Latin from the Greek of Euripides) acquired a vogue in the learned, humanist circles of the fifteenth century; and somewhat later, in Protestant-influenced Germany and Switzerland, medieval religious drama became transformed into coarse anti-Catholic satire.

In France, humor developed finesse as early as the thirteenth century and became incorporated in the early medieval re-ligious drama. Strident amateurs, organized into the society of *Enfants sans souci*, promoted intellectual humor. The secular farce, of which the masterpiece is the late-fifteenth century *Master Pierre Pathelin*, came to be supplanted to a degree by the *sotie*, a form of dramatic entertainment in which plot invention was secondary to satire and wit. In Italy, the drama outgrew its liturgical phase rather slowly, but religious plays of a popular character, known as *sacre rappresentazioni*, ac-quired much vogue in the fifteenth century, especially in Florence. They were episodic dramatizations of Old and New Testament matter and of the lives of the saints (Siena, for example, had a sequence of episodes based on the life of Santa Caterina). The *sacre rappresentazioni* attracted atten-tion primarily as "theatre"—that is, as spectacle and pag-eantry, apparently with musical accompaniment. In Spain, after the early rise of rudimentary religious and farcical pieces, the festival of Corpus Christi, established in 1264 in honor of the Holy Sacred, became the occasion for numerous devo-tional and allegorical Corpus Christi plays later known as *autos sacramentales*. The *auto* was given a first performance in the principal chapel of the local cathedral and was then brought in a processional to various predetermined sites for performance. Popular entertainment and religious theatre were characteristically inseparable in Christian Spain.

Some general comments on medieval staging may be ap-propriate here. The staging of the plays varied from extreme simplicity to considerable complexity. There is, however, one unifying principle to be noted, until the late development of banquet-hall "interludes." In all the important cases of medieval drama except that of the literary plays of the Saxon nun Hrotsvitha, the governing principle is simply that of *festival theatre.* This means that even after the early drama left the church building, the main objective was to make a ceremony of playgoing and play-production such as prevails in ritualistic performances. The public and the players were involved in acts of communion, though not necessarily solemn ones from start to finish. The tendency in staging the religious plays was to unite the playgoer with the actor instead of separating the one from the other, as we do in producing plays behind a proscenium arch, and seating the playgoer at a psychological distance from the stage.

There were several ways of relating the audience to the stage production. One way was to present the play in a "round" or a raised earthen (or occasionally stone) amphitheatre, the perimeter of a central plain known as a *platea* in the Latin stage directions, or "place" in English. The inward side of the mound, except where the *tenti* or raised scaffolds were located, served as a sort of grandstand for the public, which could also overflow into the central area of *platea.* This area, when kept free from the crowd, and the elevated structures or *tenti* at the perimeter, accommodated the stage action.

An arena with multiple stages—that is what the "round" was, and it was used more frequently for performances in England than many accounts of the medieval stage have suggested. It is known that they were used both for some biblical "mystery" plays, such as the English *N. Town* or *Hegge Plays* (miscalled the *Ludus Coventriae*) and the three-day Celtic cycle of *The Creation of the World, The Passion,* and *The Resurrection* in Cornwall, and for moral allegories or "morality plays" such as *The Castle of Perseverance.* Some English saint plays, such as *Mary Magdalene,* also occupied these "rounds," as did non-religious, topical "moralities" such as the Scottish poet Sir David Lindsay's *Pleasant Satire of the Three Estates* (*Estaits*), which was produced in 1540 at the royal court of Scotland. Some "rounds" have survived to this day in Cornwall; one earthen "round" remains in Perranzabuloe and another, made of stone, in the village of St. Just. It also appears that performances were given in Roman theatres that were still more or less intact in France—at Arles, Orange, and Nimes.

A second mode of stage presentation is illustrated by the late sixteenth-century production of a Passion Play at Lucerne, a two-day Easter festival using acting areas, scaffolds and stage properties on the level ground of the market square. The various structures or playing areas were scattered about the square, instead of being formally arranged in a straight line, circle, or semi-circle. The result was a multiple stage that used the entire square for the production of a Passion Play, plainly dispensing with a formal separation of the townspeople from the play. Whether at Frankfort in Germany or Lucerne in Switzerland, the town square was the theatre!

A third type of medieval theatre consisted of an arrangement of a number of "mansions" or "houses" in a semi-circle or straight line on a long elevated platform. This is the style of production associated with the passion plays of Valenciennes and Mons in France before the middle of the sixteenth century. In the Valenciennes cycle, the "houses," which were arranged in a straight row facing an open acting area, served to localize actions in a palace, temple, Hell, and other places. Other localities were indicated by doors and turrets in a back wall extending behind the main houses. The "sea" or "lake" was on the floor of the stage platform with a "prop" ship floating on it; and "Hell-Mouth," set beside a prison or "house of torture" at one end of the lengthy stage platform, was a sculptured set piece, the "dragon's head." Out of its "mouth," devils issued amid appropriate brimstone, while into it filed, no doubt with abundant prodding by devils, the reluctant damned. About a dozen scenes or locations were on view simultaneously at Valenciennes in 1547. *The Mons Passion Play* in 1501 that lasted for eight days appears to have used sixty-seven or more different *loca* or scenes. In front of these collectively visible settings comprising the multiple or polyscenic medieval stage sat and stood the public—the well-to-do seated on a grandstand, the common spectators, like the groundlings in Shakespeare's theatre, closely planted on the ground, where, it would appear, some of the dramatic action, overflowing the stage platform, was apt to have collided with the public. "Devils," in particular, could provide the Passion Play productions with ample "audience participation" by running into the crowd.

Finally, we come to the so-called pageant system of production, consisting of performances on wagons with the scenery, the "mansions" or "houses," mounted on wheels, which was most prevalent in England, but also had some vogue in Italy

and Spain, where the pageants were known respectively as
edifizii and *carros*. It was the system considered typical for the
English theatre because it was followed in the productions of
the great York and Chester cycles. Play followed play, each an
episode in a cycle starting with the beginning of the world
and ending with the Last Judgment, as pageant wagon followed pageant wagon and came to a stop at appointed places
in the town. And this type of stage production, too, belongs to
the great festive occasion for a significant part of the medieval
drama.

A peoples' theatre in the fullest sense—a festival lasting
several days or longer inspired by epic or "universal" matter
and unifying belief, the faith of the Universal or Catholic
Church, and an open-air theatre of large casts and of a vast
semi-participating public (many of the performers, the non-
professional ones, were themselves members of the public in
being members of the medieval trade or craft associations or
"guilds" responsible for many of the productions)—this is the
medieval theatre in its most impressive manifestations.

A radically different type of theatre, however, takes shape
by its side before the end of the fifteenth century, achieves
especially neat and sometimes witty concentration in the clever
English "interludes," and then attains classical features associated with Roman Comedy and Senecan Tragedy initiated by
the humanist schoolmasters and the young intellectuals or law
students of the Renaissance. This is no longer universal drama
and theatre; but almost coterie theatre presented "privately"—
the Interludes in Tudor halls where the rich hold their
banquets, and the domesticated variants of Roman Comedy,
such as *Ralph Roister Doister,* in the schools largely devoted
to classical studies.

In the case of the "Interlude" type of theatre, which may
be defined as a special extension of the medieval comic stage,
perhaps best known for its French examples, we encounter a
distinct example of contraction. Instead of the large epic
cycles of religious drama, we now have very short plays with
small casts. The performances are indoors and require hardly
any scenery. The action is largely mental, employing hardly
any external plot other than the conflict that revolves around
some notion or opinion. For this type of drama there is no
need for the great open-air spectacles contained in the medieval "rounds" and town squares, exhibited in front of the
"mansions" or "houses" of the Valenciennes production, or
displayed on the pageant wagons of some of England's flourish-

ing cities. The hall of a Tudor gentleman's house was sufficient for the Interludes, the performance being given at one end in front of a wooden screen while at the other end on a dais, sat the owner of the house and his guests, while tables for other guest-spectators could be set at the other two sides of the hall. The survival of over seventy Interludes from the Tudor period attests to the vogue of this non-spectacular entertainment. In the case of the "school-play" theatre represented by *Ralph Roister Doister*, written by a schoolmaster for his pupils, and an "inns-of-court" or, as we would say, a law-school play such as the "Senecan tragedy" *Gorboduc*, or an Italianate comedy such as Gascoigne's *Supposes*, the production is also private. There was little call for spectacle while the play unfolded the more or less unified action of a single story or anecdote and, as in *Gorboduc*, telescoped many events by means of Messengers, who substituted reports for extensive or drastic actions. All told, then, the expansiveness of medieval religious drama is followed by the contracted comic and pseudo-classical drama of that period of transition from the medieval to the modern world that is called loosely the Renaissance.

Nevertheless, England does not subside into a strictly circumscribed non-medieval theatre until about half a century after Shakespeare's death. Nor does France until about the same time (the sixth decade of the seventeenth century), with the rise of a courtly and circumspect "neo-classic" drama during the Age of Louis XIV. The Spanish theatre does not lose its effervescence until also about the same period, while in the theatre of the Germanic lands and Italy nothing much happens to concern us until we move on to the late eighteenth century. The fact is that, for all their renaissance and baroque attributes, the prodigious ages of Elizabethan and Spanish theatre during the late sixteenth and early seventeenth centuries (that is, Shakespeare's and Lope de Vega's theatres) retain at least some of the medievalism of the preceding centuries that gave us the communal Christian drama of Europe that is most memorably represented by the English "mystery" cycles and *Everyman*.

The proliferation of theatre, we can only conclude, was a remarkable phenomenon throughout Western Europe. This development took place under the auspices of both the Roman Catholic Church (in sharp contrast to the long suppression of the drama in Russia, where the Greek Orthodox Church was in power) and the medieval towns. The English theatre, from which most examples of medieval drama are drawn in the present volume, manifested the same flourishing state of affairs with especially noteworthy literary-dramatic results. And this is perhaps a suitable occasion for remarking, too, that to a considerable degree the early Tudor drama included in this anthology is still medieval. This is so not only in the fairly obvious case of the disquisitory Interludes (and how can we overlook the prepotency of argument and reasoning in the cultural life of the Middle Ages), but in the "humanist-renaissance" comedies *Ralph Roister Doister* and *Gammer Gurton's Needle,* so replete with folksy details, and even in the quasi-classical *Gorboduc,* patterned after Senecan drama but dramatically alive only in so far as this play originally performed for the intellectual Inns of Court public of lawyers possesses the blunt vigor of medieval folk theatre.

JOHN GASSNER

Note: As this compilation is not intended for the specialist, the Latin texts are given in English, and all the plays originally written in Middle English are presented in more or less modernized versions. No liberties, however, have been taken with the content, the characters, and the sequence of events.

The Classical Heritage

There is no external evidence that the six plays written by Hrotsvitha, the tenth-century Saxon nun of the monastery of Gandersheim, were ever performed in her time, although several of them were staged in our own century; two by the present translator, Sister Mary Marguerite, at Mercy College. (See *Hrotsvitha: The Theatricality of Her Plays*, by Sister Mary Marguerite Butler, New York, Philosophical Library, 1960.) Apparently resolved to counteract an interest in pagan authors and eager to serve Christianity with examples of piety, chastity, and martyrdom (an inexhaustible medieval subject), Hrotsvitha wrote moderately didactic plays. But taking Terence for her model, this evidently well-educated Benedictine nun utilized characterization, dramatic conflict, and various degrees of humor as well as emotional interest; and it is entirely possible that she may have intended her plays for the stage and may perhaps have seen them performed at Gandersheim. And if that is the case, the stage might well have consisted of the cloister walk, with the arcades providing the background. In any case, Sister Mary Marguerite has proved these short plays to be entirely stageworthy, except perhaps in the case of certain requirements for scenes of torture (boiling the martyrs in oil, and the like) which do not actually have to be presented to the audience.

Gandersheim was an important cultural center in northern Saxony and was administered by abbesses of noble rank. Hrotsvitha herself (*circa* 935–1001) was evidently of noble birth and had more access to the world than "regular" Benedictine nuns were likely to have; Sister Mary Marguerite surmises that the nun-playwright was a "canoness," not wholly set apart from the world by her vows. It is not surprising, therefore, that Hrotsvitha should have revealed an interest in the dramatic and literary artistry of Terence, the last of the distinguished writers of Roman comedy, who is believed to have died about 159 B.C. Since her work also reflects the theatrical tradition of the wandering players, or *mimes*, whose improvisatory comic art survived from the debris of the Western Roman Empire despite the disapprobation of the Church, she was also distinctly aware of the mainstream of popular theater during the early Middle Ages. She wrote, moreover, at a time when a new Christian type of drama was starting in the *tropes,* the little dramatic or semi-dramatic compositions (see page ix) that were being introduced into the wordless sequences of the Mass at Christmas and Easter. It may be said, therefore, that her dramatic work is related to *three* streams of actual or potential dramatic and theatrical development—the classical influence, the vogue of the *mimes* and *jongleurs* who provided popular entertainment, and the evolving liturgical drama in Latin.

Hrotsvitha is especially important in a historical survey as the main link between medieval and classical drama. Although her themes and sentiments are inviolably Christian, she has wit, humor, and theatricality in her work. And in the case of *Dulcitius,* which follows, it will be seen that she also employed the farcical elements of popular theater. (Among her other plays are *Gallicanus,* in which a woman converts her suitor; *Paphnutius,* also presented here, an early version of the Thais story dealing with the conversion of a courtesan by a pious hermit who comes to her disguised as a would-be lover; and *Sapientia,* an allegorical but not actually abstruse drama.) One authority has written that the *Dulcitius* "contains comic elements worthy of Terence." Perhaps not, but its effective theatricality is especially evident in the first part dealing with the discomfiture of the comic villain, Dulcitius.

The *Paphnutius* is added to the *Dulcitius* in this section not only for its intrinsic interest as an early treatment of the Thais story, but as a precursor of a genre of medieval drama which has been designated as the Saint Play. Extant examples of this type of drama in England are few and not particularly distinguished. The best-known specimens are *The Conversion of St. Paul,* a longish late-fifteenth-century work in East Midland speech, apparently intended for production in a village on three "stations," or platform stages (an extant liturgical play antecedent in medieval Latin, *Conversio Beati Pauli Apostoli,* survived in a thirteenth-century manuscript in Fleury, France) and a lengthy *Mary Magdalene,* also from the Midland section of England and plainly intended for production on little platforms arranged in a circle. "Miracle" or "saint" plays were particularly abundant in France, where the miracles of the Virgin Mary and of post-biblical saintly figures actually formed dramatic cycles. *Paphnutius,* however, is not the "archaic" predecessor of this type of drama, but perhaps the most poignant example. The conversion of the courtesan Thais, her confinement in a narrow cell, and her death are moving little scenes conceived with simplicity and truth. It is interesting to know that a marionette production of *Paphnutius* inspired Anatole France to write his novel *Thais*, which in turn inspired Massenet's opera.

Dulcitius

Hrotsvitha

TRANSLATED BY
SISTER MARY MARGUERITE BUTLER, R.S.M.

THE ARGUMENT OF THE PLAY

The Martyrdom of the Holy Virgins, Agape, Chionia, and Irena

The Governor Dulcitius, with evil intent, goes to seek the girls in the silence of the night. But, upon entering the apartment where they are imprisoned, acting as if he were demented, Dulcitius begins kissing the kitchen pots and frying pans, thinking he is embracing the girls. His face and clothes are covered with soot and dirt. Later, by order of the Emperor, he releases the young girls to Sisinnius for punishment. Sisinnius, the victim of supernatural powers, finally succeeds in having Agape and Chionia put to death by fire, and Irena killed by a soldier's arrow.

Characters

DIOCLETIAN, the Emperor	SISINNIUS
AGAPE, CHIONIA, IRENA[1]	SOLDIERS
CHRISTIANS	PORTERS
DULCITIUS, the Governor	WIFE OF DULCITIUS

SCENE 1[2]

DIOCLETIAN. The renown of your illustrious family, your noble birth, and the brilliance of your beauty de-

---

[1] AGAPE means Love; CHIONIA, Purity; IRENA, Peace. The play is based on the legend of the martyrdom of three young women during the reign of Diocletian, *c.* 290 A.D. But the farcical element is the invention of Hrotsvitha.

[2] The translator in staging the play used a Romanesque arcade motif for the setting.

mand that you be united in marriage to the highest
rank in our court. This we will not oppose, if, at our
command, you will deny Christ and offer sacrifice to our
gods.

AGAPE. Be not concerned with us, nor with the prepa-
rations for our marriage, for nothing in the world can
force us to renounce a Name that we are called upon to
defend, nor to sully our virginal purity.   10

DIOCLETIAN. What does this mean, this folly which
impels you?

AGAPE. What sign of folly do you detect in us?

DIOCLETIAN. A sign clearly evident.

AGAPE. In what manner?

DIOCLETIAN. Is it not folly for you to renounce the
practice of our ancient religion and follow this new
Christian superstition?

AGAPE. You rashly attack the majesty of Almighty
God. That is dangerous.   20

DIOCLETIAN. Dangerous! To whom?

AGAPE. To you and to the state which you govern.

DIOCLETIAN. She is mad. Take her away.

CHIONIA. My sister is not mad but justly reproves your
folly.

DIOCLETIAN. This girl raves more violently than the
first; remove her likewise from our presence, and we will
question the third.

IRENA. You will find the third equally rebellious to
your orders and ready to resist you.   30

DIOCLETIAN. Irena, since you are the youngest, show
yourself the eldest in dignity.

IRENA. Show me how, I beg of you.

DIOCLETIAN. Bow your head to the gods; and in this
deference, be an example to your sisters that they may
be freed.

IRENA. Let those who wish to incur the wrath of the
Most High bow before idols; as for me, I will not dishonor my head, which has been anointed with kingly
oil, by abasing myself at the feet of idols.   40

DIOCLETIAN. The worship of the gods brings no dishonor; on the contrary, it brings the greatest honor.

IRENA. What baser shame, what greater disgrace to
venerate slaves as if they were princes or lords?

DIOCLETIAN. I do not ask you to venerate slaves but
the gods of the leaders and princes.

IRENA. Is not that which can be purchased cheap in the market place a slave?

DIOCLETIAN. Enough of this presumptuous talk; let these girls be taken away and put to the tortures. 50

IRENA. That is what we most desire: to bear the cruelest torture for the love of Christ.

DIOCLETIAN. Let these stubborn girls who defy our orders be bound with chains, be cast into a prison, and be examined by Governor Dulcitius.

SCENE 2

DULCITIUS. Soldiers, produce the girls whom you hold in prison.

SOLDIERS. See, these are the ones you ask for.

DULCITIUS. Wonderful! What beauty, what charm, how extraordinary these girls are! 60

SOLDIERS. They are truly beautiful.

DULCITIUS. I am captivated by the very sight of them.

SOLDIERS. We are not surprised.

DULCITIUS. I am thrilled. Do you think they will return my love?

SOLDIERS. We do not believe you will have any success.

DULCITIUS. And why not?

SOLDIERS. Because their faith is steadfast.

DULCITIUS. No matter, I will persuade them with a little flattery. 70

SOLDIERS. They despise flattery.

DULCITIUS. Then I shall treat them to punishment.

SOLDIERS. That matters little to them; they will suffer punishment without yielding.

DULCITIUS. Then what can we do?

SOLDIERS. That is for you to determine.

DULCITIUS. Lock them up in the inner workroom near the porch, the one in which the serving pans are kept.

SOLDIERS. And why in that place?

DULCITIUS. Because I can visit them easily and often. 80

SOLDIERS. It shall be as you command.

SCENE 3

DULCITIUS. What are the prisoners doing at this time of night?

SOLDIERS. They are singing hymns.

DULCITIUS. Let us go nearer.

SOLDIERS. Now we hear their shrill voices in the distance.

DULCITIUS. Take your lanterns and guard the doors without; I will go inside and enjoy their embraces which I greatly desire.

SOLDIERS. Enter and we will await your return.

90

SCENE 4

AGAPE. What is that clattering noise outside the door?

IRENA. That wretched Dulcitius has come in.

CHIONIA. May God protect us!

AGAPE. So be it.

CHIONIA. What is this clashing of pots and kettles and frying pans?

IRENA. I will look out.

IRENA. Come, I beg you and peek through this small crack.

100

AGAPE. What is it?

IRENA. Look, the foolish fellow must be out of his mind; he thinks he is embracing us.

AGAPE. What is he doing?

IRENA. Now he hugs the kettle, now the frying pans, and now he hugs the pots, caressing them with soft kisses.

CHIONIA. How ridiculous!

IRENA. His face, his hands, his clothes! They are soiled and dirty. With the soot clinging to them he looks like an Ethiopian.

110

AGAPE. That's fine, his body should turn as black as his soul which is possessed by the devil.

IRENA. He seems to be going. Let us see what the soldiers who are waiting for him are going to do when he goes outside.

SCENE 5

SOLDIERS. Who comes here? one possessed by the devil? or more likely the devil himself? Let us get out of here.

DULCITIUS. Soldiers, where are you going? Stay, wait for me; light the way to my home with your lanterns.

SOLDIERS. It is the voice of our master but the face of the devil. Let's not stay here, let's run away; this monster will destroy us.

120

DULCITIUS. I will go to the palace. I will tell the court what insults I have suffered.

Scene 6

Dulcitius. Porters, admit me to the palace, I wish to speak privately with the Emperor.

Porters. Who is this vile, disreputable creature who comes here in these filthy rags? Let's cuff him and pitch him down the steps; don't let him come any closer.

Dulcitius. Woe is me! What has come over me? Are 130 not my clothes splendid, am I not neat and clean in my appearance? Yet everyone who meets me shows disgust, just as if I were some horrible monster. I shall return to my wife and learn from her what has happened to me. But look, here she comes, her hair disheveled, and her whole household follows her weeping.

Scene 7

Wife of dulcitius. Alas, alas, my lord! What has happened to you? Are you out of your mind? You have become a laughingstock to the Christians.

Dulcitius. Now at last I know; these Christians have 140 made a fool of me.

Wife of Dulcitius. What troubles me more than anything, and makes me very sad, is that you are ignorant of what has happened to you.

Dulcitius. I'll order these insolent girls to be dragged forth and stripped of their clothes in public, that they may experience the mockery to which I have been subjected.

Scene 8

Soldiers. Here we are, sweating and laboring in vain. Look how their clothes stick to their virginal bodies like 150 their very skin. And he who ordered us to strip them sits here before us snoring, nor are we able in any way whatever to rouse him from sleep. Let's go to the Emperor and report to him what has happened.

Scene 9

Diocletian. I am grieved to hear of the outrageous manner in which Governor Dulcitius has been tricked and insulted. But these mere children will not boast of having freely made a mockery of our gods and of those who worship them; I shall direct Count Sisinnius to wreak our vengeance.   160

SCENE 10

SISINNIUS. Soldiers, where are these insolent girls who must be put to the torture?

SOLDIERS. They are bound in prison.

SISINNIUS. Keep Irena there and bring the others here.

SOLDIERS. Why do you make an exception of one?

SISINNIUS. We'll spare her youth. By chance, she may be more easily influenced if she is not frightened in the presence of her sisters.

SOLDIERS. That's very true.

SCENE 11

SOLDIERS. Here are the girls whose presence you demanded.   170

SISINNIUS. Agape and Chionia, be sensible and take my advice.

AGAPE. And if we do?

SISINNIUS. You will offer a sacrifice to the gods.

CHIONIA. We offer a continual sacrifice of praise to the Eternal Father and to His Son coeternal with the Holy Spirit.

SISINNIUS. I do not recommend this sacrifice; I forbid it under pain of severe punishment.   180

AGAPE. You have no right to forbid us, nor will we ever offer sacrifice to false gods.

SISINNIUS. Do not be stubborn, but offer the sacrifice. For if you do not, I shall, by order of the Emperor Diocletian, be forced to put you to death.

CHIONIA. You must obey the order of your Emperor and put us to death; we know of his decree in our regard and scorn it. If you were to delay and spare us, you too would die.

SISINNIUS. Do not delay any longer; soldiers, seize these blasphemers and throw them alive into the flames.   190

SOLDIERS. We will build a pyre at once and cast them into the raging flames which will put an end to their contemptuous insults.

AGAPE. O Lord, we know Your power, it would not be unusual if the fire forgot the violence of its nature and obeyed You. But we are weary with delay. So we beg of You, dissolve the bonds that bind our souls, so that, by destroying our bodies, our spirits may rejoice with You in Heaven.   200

SOLDIERS. A marvel, a tremendous miracle! Behold, their souls have left their bodies and there is no sign of any injury. Neither their hair, nor their clothes, much less their bodies, have been touched by the flames.

SISINNIUS. Go and bring Irena here.

SOLDIERS. Here she is as you commanded.

SCENE 12

SISINNIUS. Fear your sisters' death, Irena, and be on your guard lest by their example you too will perish.

IRENA. I desire to follow their example by dying, that I may merit eternal happiness with them.   210

SISINNIUS. Give in to my persuasion.

IRENA. I will not give in to any evil persuasions.

SISINNIUS. If you do not yield, I will not promise you a quick death, but I shall drag it out and multiply new torments each day.

IRENA. The more I am tortured, the greater will be my glory.

SISINNIUS. You are not afraid of punishment, but I shall use such torture as will make you shudder.

IRENA. With the help of Christ I shall escape whatever   220
torture you shall propose.

SISINNIUS. I can send you to a brothel, where your body will be shamefully violated.

IRENA. It is better that my body should be defiled than that my soul be dishonored by offering sacrifice to idols.

SISINNIUS. If you live among harlots, you cannot, because of this disgrace, be numbered among the virgins.

IRENA. Pleasure brings punishment, suffering merits the crown; nor is there guilt unless the soul consents.

SISINNIUS. In vain I spared her; in vain I pitied her   230
youth.

SOLDIERS. We foresaw this; you can do nothing to force her to worship your gods, nor can her spirit be broken by terror.

SISINNIUS. I shall show her no further clemency.

SOLDIERS. Right! Give your orders.

SISINNIUS. Take her without mercy, and drag her with utmost cruelty, and in dishonor take her to the lowest brothel.

IRENA. They will not take me there.   240
SISINNIUS. Who will be able to prevent them?
IRENA. He Whose Providence rules the world.
SISINNIUS. We shall see!
IRENA. Yes, sooner than it will please you.
SISINNIUS. Soldiers, do not be frightened by the false prophecies of this blasphemer.
SOLDIERS. We will not be frightened, but we will hasten to carry out your orders at once.

SCENE 13

SISINNIUS. Who are these men who are coming toward us? They resemble the soldiers who took Irena away.   250
Yes, it is they. Why are you returning so soon? Why are you panting for breath?
SOLDIERS. We are hurrying to reach you.
SISINNIUS. Where is she whom you took away?
SOLDIERS. On the crest of the mountain.
SISINNIUS. Which mountain?
SOLDIERS. That one close by.
SISINNIUS. O stupid and insensate men, have you lost your reason?
SOLDIERS. Why do you reproach us with such threaten-   260
ing words and looks?
SISINNIUS. May the gods destroy you!
SOLDIERS. What have we done to you? How have we injured you? And in what manner have we disobeyed your orders?
SISINNIUS. Did I not order you to drag to that infamous place the girl who rebelled against our gods.
SOLDIERS. Yes, you did order us to do so and we were complying with your command when two young strangers came up and assured us that you had sent them to lead   270
Irena to the summit of the mountain.
SISINNIUS. I know of no such thing.
SOLDIERS. So it seems.
SISINNIUS. What were these strangers like?
SOLDIERS. They were richly dressed, and their manner and bearing were very respectful.
SISINNIUS. Did you not follow them?
SOLDIERS. Yes, we did follow them.
SISINNIUS. What did they do?
SOLDIERS. They placed themselves one on the right and   280

one on the left side of Irena and told us to come here and tell you what had taken place.

SISINNIUS. There is nothing left for me to do but mount my horse and seek out those who made sport of us so freely.

SOLDIERS. We will go with you.

SCENE 14

SISINNIUS. I don't know what has happened to me. I am bewildered by the evil deeds of these Christians. I keep wandering around this mountain finding again and again this narrow path; I can neither follow it nor re-   290
trace my steps.

SOLDIERS. We all are the victims of some extraordinary spell, and we are exhausted as if from a great weariness of mind and body. If you let this insane wretch live any longer, we shall all perish.

SISINNIUS. Any one of you who can, quickly bend a bow and shoot an arrow that will pierce this wicked girl.

SOLDIERS. We shall do it.

IRENA. Unhappy Sisinnius, blush for shame and admit   300
your defeat, since you are unable, without force of arms, to overcome the strength of a little child.

SISINNIUS. Whatever shame there is, I accept it gladly since I am sure now of your death.

IRENA. Death for me is reason for great joy, but death for you is great grief. For the severity of your cruelty you will be damned in Tartarus. I, moreover, shall receive the martyr's palm and the crown of virginity; I shall enter the heavenly home of the Eternal King, to Whom be glory and honor forever.   310

Paphnutius

Hrotsvitha

TRANSLATED BY
SISTER MARY MARGUERITE BUTLER, R.S.M.

THE ARGUMENT OF THE PLAY

The Conversion of Thais by the Hermit, Paphnutius

Dressed in the disguise of a lover, the hermit Paphnutius goes
in search of Thais, a harlot, that he may recall her from her
evil ways. Moved by his pleading, Thais is converted.
Paphnutius imposes a penance which confines her to a narrow cell for five [sic] years.

Thais, by this worthy expiation, is reconciled to God, and
fifteen days after the completion of her penance, she goes
to sleep in Christ.

Characters

PAPHNUTIUS, the Hermit   YOUNG MEN, Lovers of Thais
THE DISCIPLES OF PAPHNUTIUS   ANTHONY and PAUL, Hermits
THAIS, the Courtesan   AN ABBESS

SCENE 1[1]

DISCIPLES. Why are you so unhappy, why not the
serene countenance to which we are accustomed, Father
Paphnutius?

PAPHNUTIUS. He whose heart is sad wears a sorrowful
countenance.

DISCIPLES. Why are you so sad?

PAPHNUTIUS. Because of the ingratitude shown to my
Creator.

DISCIPLES. What is this ingratitude of which you
speak.   10

PAPHNUTIUS. That which He suffers from His own
creatures, creatures made to His image and likeness.

---

[1] The place of the action of each scene is indicated in the dialogue and
action of each scene. But the rapid changes of scene suggest that the author
did not have any realistic scenery in mind but an essential neutral acting
area.

DISCIPLES. You frighten us by your words.

PAPHNUTIUS. It is understood that the eternal majesty of God cannot be injured by any wrong, nevertheless, if it were permitted to transfer by a metaphor the weakness of our frail nature to God, what greater wrong could be conceived than this—that while the greater part of the world is subject to His will, one part rebels against His law?   20

DISCIPLES. Which part rebels?

PAPHNUTIUS. Man.

DISCIPLES. Man?

PAPHNUTIUS. Yes.

DISCIPLES. What man?

PAPHNUTIUS. All men.

DISCIPLES. How can this be?

PAPHNUTIUS. It so pleases our Creator.

DISCIPLES. We do not understand.

PAPHNUTIUS. All of us do not understand.   30

DISCIPLES. Do explain it to us.

PAPHNUTIUS. Listen then, to what I say.

DISCIPLES. We are listening.

PAPHNUTIUS. Accordingly, the greater part of the world is made up of four contrary elements, but by the will of the Creator, the contraries are adjusted according to harmonious rule, and man possesses not only these same elements, but has more varying components.

DISCIPLES. And what then is more varying than the elements?   40

PAPHNUTIUS. The body and the soul, because one can understand that they are contrary, yet they are both in one person; the soul is not mortal like the body, and the body is not spiritual like the soul.

DISCIPLES. So!

PAPHNUTIUS. If, moreover, we follow the logicians, we will not admit these to be contrary.

DISCIPLES. And who can deny it?

PAPHNUTIUS. He who can argue logically; because nothing is contrary to Essence, for she is the receptacle of all   50
contraries.

DISCIPLES. What did you mean when you said "according to harmonious rule"?

PAPHNUTIUS. I meant that, as low and high sounds are joined together harmoniously to make a certain music, thus discordant elements, being brought together harmoniously, make one world.[2]

* * *

DISCIPLES. Where did you acquire all this knowledge with which you have just wearied us?

PAPHNUTIUS. I wish to share with you the small drop   60 of knowledge which flowed from the full well of learning; this I found, passing by chance rather than by seeking it.

DISCIPLES. We appreciate your goodness, but we are terrified by the word of the Apostle saying: "God chooses the foolish of the world to confound the wise."

PAPHNUTIUS. Whether a foolish man or a wise man does wrong, he deserves punishment from God.

DISCIPLES. Indeed he does.

PAPHNUTIUS. Knowledge does not offend God, but the   70 wrong doing of him who has knowledge offends Him.

DISCIPLES. True, indeed!

PAPHNUTIUS. To whom may the knowledge of the arts be more worthily and rightly referred than to Him who made things which are knowable and gave us the capacity to understand them?

DISCIPLES. To none other.

PAPHNUTIUS. The more man sees by what marvelous law God has arranged all things by number, by measure, and by weight, the more intensely he will love Him.   80

DISCIPLES. And rightly so!

PAPHNUTIUS. But why do I dwell upon these things which afford so little pleasure?

DISCIPLES. Tell us the cause of your grief, that we may no longer be burdened by the weight of our curiosity.

PAPHNUTIUS. If ever you do find it out, you will not be happy in that knowledge.

DISCIPLES. A man is often sadder when he has satisfied his curiosity, yet he is unable to overcome this fault because it is a part of our weak nature.   90

PAPHNUTIUS. A certain infamous woman lives in this neighborhood.

DISCIPLES. This is dangerous to the people.

---

[2] Here follows a lengthy theological discussion which does not contribute to the dramatic development and is therefore omitted.

PAPHNUTIUS. Her beauty is unsurpassed, her wickedness is unspeakable.

DISCIPLES. Horrible! What is her name?

PAPHNUTIUS. Thais.

DISCIPLES. That harlot!

PAPHNUTIUS. Yes, that one.

DISCIPLES. Her wickedness is known to everyone.   100

PAPHNUTIUS. And no wonder, because she is not satisfied to go to destruction with a few, but she is ready to ensnare all men by the enticements of her beauty and to drag them to ruin with her.

DISCIPLES. How tragic!

PAPHNUTIUS. Not only do wastrels squander their substance by wooing her, but even respectable citizens lay their wealth at her feet, enriching her to their own undoing.

DISCIPLES. Terrible to hear!   110

PAPHNUTIUS. Crowds of lovers flock to her.

DISCIPLES. They destroy themselves.

PAPHNUTIUS. These lovers, in blindness of heart, quarrel and fight for access to her.

DISCIPLES. One vice begets another.

PAPHNUTIUS. When the struggle begins, sometimes fist fights result in broken noses and jaws; other times they attack with weapons so shamelessly that the threshold of the vile house is drenched with blood.

DISCIPLES. O detestable sin!   120

PAPHNUTIUS. This is the insult to the Creator which I mourn; this is the cause of my grief.

DISCIPLES. We do not doubt that you rightly grieve aloud about this; and that the heavenly citizens mourn with you.

PAPHNUTIUS. What if I were to approach her in the disguise of a lover; might she by chance turn from her wayward life?

DISCIPLES. He Who has inspired you with this idea is able to bring about its fulfillment.   130

PAPHNUTIUS. Support me, meanwhile, with your fervent prayers that I may not be overcome by the wiles of the wicked serpent.

DISCIPLES. May He Who laid low the king of darkness give you victory against the enemy!

SCENE 2

PAPHNUTIUS. Look at the young men in the market-place. I shall go to them first and inquire where I may find the woman for whom I am looking.

YOUTHS. Look, a stranger is coming toward us. Let us find out what he wants.   140

PAPHNUTIUS. Hello! Young men, who are you?

YOUTHS. We are citizens of this city.

PAPHNUTIUS. Greetings!

YOUNG MEN. And the same to you; whether a native of this country or a stranger.

PAPHNUTIUS. A stranger, for I have just now arrived.

YOUNG MEN. Why do you come? What do you seek?

PAPHNUTIUS. I cannot say.

YOUNG MEN. Why not?

PAPHNUTIUS. Because I cannot reveal it.   150

YOUNG MEN. It is better that you reveal it, because if you are a stranger, it will be difficult to transact any business with us citizens.

PAPHNUTIUS. What if I did tell you and in the telling I should raise some obstacle for myself?

YOUNG MEN. Not from us.

PAPHNUTIUS. I take you at your word, trusting your loyalty; I'll tell you my secret.

YOUNG MEN. There will be no disloyalty on our part, no harm shall come to you.   160

PAPHNUTIUS. I have learned from reports of certain persons that a woman, sweet and gracious to all, and loved by all, lives among you.

YOUNG MEN. Do you know her name?

PAPHNUTIUS. Yes, I do know it.

YOUNG MEN. Won't you tell us?

PAPHNUTIUS. Thais.

YOUNG MEN. Thais! She is the harlot.

PAPHNUTIUS. They say she is the most beautiful and most exquisite of all women.   170

YOUNG MEN. Those who told you this have not deceived you.

PAPHNUTIUS. For her sake, I undertook the difficulty of a long journey; I came to see her.

YOUNG MEN. There is nothing to keep you from seeing her.

PAPHNUTIUS. Where does she stay?

YOUNG MEN. In that house near by.
PAPHNUTIUS. That one to which you are pointing?
YOUNG MEN. Yes, that one.   180
PAPHNUTIUS. I shall go there.
YOUNG MEN. If you wish, we shall go with you.
PAPHNUTIUS. I prefer to go alone.
YOUNG MEN. As you prefer.

SCENE 3

PAPHNUTIUS. Thais, are you there? I am looking for you.
THAIS. Who is this stranger who calls on me?
PAPHNUTIUS. Your lover.
THAIS. Whoever woos me in love receives from me an equal return of love.   190
PAPHNUTIUS. Oh Thais, Thais! How many miles have I traveled that I might be able to speak with you and that I might be able to see your face.
THAIS. I shall not withdraw nor refuse my company.
PAPHNUTIUS. The secrecy of our conversation demands the protection of a more secluded spot.
THAIS. Here is a well-furnished room, a pleasant place.
PAPHNUTIUS. Is there not some place more secluded than this, where we can converse more secretly?
THAIS. There is another place so hidden, so secret that   200
it is known to no one but me and God.
PAPHNUTIUS. What God?
THAIS. The true God.
PAPHNUTIUS. Do you believe that He knows everything?
THAIS. I know nothing is hidden from Him.
PAPHNUTIUS. Do you believe that He is unmindful of the deeds of the wicked or that He does not guard His justice?
THAIS. I believe that He weighs the merits of every man in the balance of His justice and that every man   210
will be rewarded or punished according to his deeds.
PAPHNUTIUS. O Christ! How wonderful is the goodness of Your patience toward us, for You see men wilfully sinning and yet You delay to punish them.
THAIS. Why do you turn pale? Why do you weep?
PAPHNUTIUS. I tremble at your presumption. I weep over your sinfulness because, knowing such things, you have dragged so many souls to ruin.

THAIS. Alas, alas! I am unhappy.

PAPHNUTIUS. All the more justly you shall be damned,   220
the more presumptuously you have knowingly offended
the majesty of the Divinity.

THAIS. Oh, no! What are you doing? Why do you
threaten wretched me?

PAPHNUTIUS. The punishment of hellfire hangs over
you if you persist in sin.

THAIS. The severity of your correction has shaken me
to the very depths of my heart.

PAPHNUTIUS. Oh, would that you might be shaken to
the depths of your heart by fear, that you might no   230
longer consent to dangerous passion.

THAIS. What place can be left in my heart for sinful
pleasure where only the bitterness of inward grief and
the new dread of an awakened conscience prevail?

PAPHNUTIUS. This is my desire: when the thorns of sin
have been rooted from your heart, the tears of repentance
may flow.

THAIS. Oh, if you could believe, oh, if you could hope
that I, stained with thousands and thousands of defile-
ments, could ever be purified, or by any act of contrition   240
merit pardon!

PAPHNUTIUS. There is no sin so grievous, no fault so
great that cannot be atoned for by the tears of repentance, if followed by good deeds.

THAIS. My Father, I beg you to show me by the performance of what good deeds I can merit the gift of
reconciliation.

PAPHNUTIUS. Despise the world. Flee the companion-
ship of your dissolute lovers.

THAIS. And then what will I do?   250

PAPHNUTIUS. Retire to some secluded place where, ex-
amining yourself, you will mourn the enormity of your
sinfulness.

THAIS. If you know this will be effective, I will go
without a moment's delay.

PAPHNUTIUS. I am certain that it will be effective.

THAIS. Give me a moment's time, that I may collect
the wealth which I have gained by evil means and have
hoarded for a long time.

PAPHNUTIUS. Do not worry about that. There will be   260
plenty of men who will find it and use it.

THAIS. I am not concerned to keep it for myself, nor

do I wish to give it to my friends. Furthermore, I will not try to give it to the poor, because I do not think the price of sin to be suitable for good works.

PAPHNUTIUS. You think rightly, but what do you plan to do with your possessions?

THAIS. I would cast them to the flames and reduce them to ashes.

PAPHNUTIUS. Why?   270

THAIS. That those things which I have acquired by evil deeds may not remain in the world as an insult to the Creator of the world.

PAPHNUTIUS. How changed you are from what you were when you burned with sinful passion and desired only riches!

THAIS. Perhaps I shall change still more, God willing.

PAPHNUTIUS. It is not difficult for His unchangeable substance to change things as He wills.

THAIS. I shall go and carry out what I have planned.   280

PAPHNUTIUS. Go in peace, and return to me quickly.

SCENE 4

THAIS. Come together, hasten, my wicked lovers.

LOVERS. The voice of Thais is calling us; let us hasten to go to her lest we offend her by being late.

THAIS. Hurry, come to me that I may speak with you.

LOVERS. O Thais, Thais! Why do you wish a funeral pyre for yourself? What are you building? Why do you heap your many and precious treasures near the flames?

THAIS. You ask?

LOVERS. We wonder greatly.   290

THAIS. I shall explain quickly.

LOVERS. Please do.

THAIS. Behold!

LOVERS. Stop, stop Thais. What are you doing? Are you insane?

THAIS. I am not insane; I am in my right mind.

LOVERS. But why waste four hundred pounds of gold and many other riches?

THAIS. All which I unjustly extorted from you, I would burn that you may have no spark of hope that I may   300 yield any more to your love.

LOVERS. Stop! Delay a little and tell us the cause of your worry.

THAIS. I will not delay and I will not speak with you.

LOVERS. Why do you scorn us by your disdain? Do you accuse us of any unfaithfulness? Have we not always satisfied your wishes? But you, without cause, treat us with unjust hatred.

THAIS. Go away. Do not clutch and tear my garments. It is enough that, in the past, I have yielded to you in   310 sinning. The end of sinning is at hand. It is time for my departure.

LOVERS. Where is she going?

THAIS. Where none of you will ever see me.

LOVERS. Indeed! What marvel is this that Thais, our delight, who always strove for wealth, who never withdrew her heart from pleasure, who gave herself completely to desire, has now destroyed so much gold and gems and has spurned us, her lovers, with insults and suddenly disappears?   320

SCENE 5

THAIS. Father Paphnutius, I am here, ready to follow you.

PAPHNUTIUS. Because you delayed in coming, I was very worried, thinking you were again involved in worldly affairs.

THAIS. Do not fear, because I would not change my mind. Now, I have taken care of my affairs as I wished, and I have publicly renounced my lovers.

PAPHNUTIUS. Because you have renounced them, you may now be united to your heavenly Spouse.   330

THAIS. Then you ought to point out to me, as with your rod, what I should do.

PAPHNUTIUS. Follow me.

THAIS. I shall follow in your footsteps, oh, would that I might also follow in your way of life.

SCENE 6

PAPHNUTIUS. Here is a convent where lives a community of holy virgins. Here I wish you to remain during the time of your penance.

THAIS. That I will do. I have no objections.

PAPHNUTIUS. I will go inside and persuade the abbess,   340 the superior of the nuns, to receive you.

THAIS. What do you wish me to do in the meantime?

PAPHNUTIUS. Come in with me.

THAIS. As you direct.

PAPHNUTIUS. Look, the abbess is coming. I wonder who told her so quickly that we were here.

THAIS. Rumor, which spreads very quickly.

SCENE 7

PAPHNUTIUS. You come opportunely, Venerable Abbess, I was just coming to see you.

ABBESS. You are welcome, Reverend Father Paph-   350
nutius; beloved of God, may your coming be blessed!

PAPHNUTIUS. May the grace of the Father of all shed upon you the peace of His eternal blessing!

ABBESS. What brings Your Holiness to visit my humble lodging?

PAPHNUTIUS. I need your help in an urgent crisis.

ABBESS. Only tell me what you desire and I shall do all in my power to comply with your wishes.

PAPHNUTIUS. I have brought a half-dead kid, recently snatched from the fangs of the wolves, whom I wish to   360
be cherished in your pity and healed by your care until she has cast aside the rough goatskin and put on the soft fleece of the lamb.

ABBESS. Explain what you mean more clearly.

PAPHNUTIUS. This woman whom you see led the life of a harlot.

ABBESS. What a pity!

PAPHNUTIUS. She gave herself entirely to lust.

ABBESS. She has brought ruin upon herself.

PAPHNUTIUS. And now, with my encouragement and   370
with the help of Christ, the vanities which she followed she now rejects in hatred, and she embraces chastity.

ABBESS. Thanks be to the Author of this change.

PAPHNUTIUS. Because illness of the soul, like illness of the body, must be cured by contrary remedies, it follows that she must be withdrawn from the common cares of the world and be cloistered in a narrow cell where she can more freely meditate on her own sins.

ABBESS. Indeed, this is very necessary.

PAPHNUTIUS. Command that a cell be prepared as soon   380
as possible.

ABBESS. It will be done immediately.

PAPHNUTIUS. Let there be no entrance, no access but

a small window through which she may receive a portion of food which you must give her sparingly on certain days at specified hours.

ABBESS. I am afraid that the weakness of her delicate constitution can hardly endure the difficulty of so great a trial.

PAPHNUTIUS. There is no need to fear, for a grievous 390 fault demands a severe remedy.

ABBESS. Yes, indeed!

PAPHNUTIUS. Further delay concerns me because she may be corrupted by the visit of her former lovers.

ABBESS. There is no need for delay. You can enclose her at once. The cell which you wish is ready.

PAPHNUTIUS. Good! Enter, Thais, a dwelling well-suited for atonement of your sins.

THAIS. How narrow, how dark, and how uncomfortable a dwelling for a weak woman!   400

PAPHNUTIUS. Why do you dislike the dwelling? Why do you shrink from entering? It is fitting that one who was wayward and undisciplined should now suffer the confinements of a narrow cell.

THAIS. A heart accustomed to lust or passion rarely welcomes a more rigid life.

PAPHNUTIUS. Therefore, such a heart should be bound by the reins of strict discipline until it no longer struggles against it.

THAIS. Whatever your fatherly goodness orders, my 410 weakness shall not refuse to undergo, but there is a certain inconvenience in this dwelling which my frailty finds it difficult to accept.

PAPHNUTIUS. What is this inconvenience?

THAIS. I blush to mention it.

PAPHNUTIUS. Do not blush, be honest about it.

ABBESS. What could be more inconvenient, what more difficult than to be forced to take care of all the needs of the body in one place? Without a doubt the cell will soon become uninhabitable.   420

PAPHNUTIUS. Fear the bitterness of hellfire and do not be afraid of transitory things.

THAIS. My weakness compels me to fear.

PAPHNUTIUS. It is fitting that the sweetness of falsely flattering delight should be atoned for by bitterness.

THAIS. I do not refuse, I do not deny that I, who am stained by sin, deserve to live in a foul and loathsome place, but what grieves me more intensely is that there is no place where I may fittingly and religiously call upon the name of the Divine Majesty. 430

PAPHNUTIUS. But are you confident that with your defiled lips you can invoke the name of the Divine Purity?

THAIS. But from whom can I hope for pardon? Or by whose Mercy can I be saved if I am forbidden to invoke Him against Whom I have sinned, and to Whom alone the offering of our prayers must be made?

PAPHNUTIUS. You ought to pray, not only in words, but in tears; not only in the sound of your musical voice, but in the moaning of a contrite heart.

THAIS. But if I am forbidden to pray to God in words, 440 how can I hope for pardon?

PAPHNUTIUS. The more perfectly you humble yourself, the sooner will you merit pardon. Say only this: "You Who have created me, have mercy on me!"

THAIS. I need His mercy lest I be overcome in the doubtful struggle.

PAPHNUTIUS. Struggle bravely that you may be able to win the victory joyfully.

THAIS. You must pray for me that I may merit the palm of victory. 450

PAPHNUTIUS. There is no need to tell me that. It is now time for me to return to my beloved solitude and to see my dear disciples. Therefore to your care, to your goodness, Venerable Abbess, I entrust this captive, that you may nourish her weak body with the necessities of life and generously refresh her soul with wise counsel.

ABBESS. Do not be concerned about her. I will cherish her with motherly affection.

PAPHNUTIUS. Then I shall go.

ABBESS. May you go in peace! 460

SCENE 8

DISCIPLES. Who knocks at our door?

PAPHNUTIUS. It is I.

DISCIPLES. It is the voice of our Father Paphnutius.

PAPHNUTIUS. Unbolt the door.

DISCIPLES. Greetings, good Father!

PAPHNUTIUS. Greetings to you!

DISCIPLES. We missed you greatly in your long absence.

PAPHNUTIUS. I am glad I went away.

DISCIPLES. What has become of Thais?   470

PAPHNUTIUS. That which I desired.

DISCIPLES. Where is she staying?

PAPHNUTIUS. In a narrow cell where she mourns her sins.

DISCIPLES. Praise to the Exalted Trinity!

PAPHNUTIUS. And blessed be His awful Name now and forever!

DISCIPLES. Amen.

SCENE 9

PAPHNUTIUS. Behold, three years of Thais' penance have passed, and I do not know whether or not atone-   480
ment has been acceptable to God. I will arise and go to my Brother Anthony, that by his help I may learn the truth about her.

SCENE 10

ANTHONY. What unexpected pleasure is mine? What new happiness comes my way? Is this not my brother and fellow hermit, Paphnutius? Indeed, it is he.

PAPHNUTIUS. Yes, indeed it is I.

ANTHONY. It is well, Brother, you have come. You have delighted me with this coming.

PAPHNUTIUS. I am as delighted to see you as you are   490
to see me.

ANTHONY. What is this happy occasion, so pleasing to us both, which brings you to our hermitage?

PAPHNUTIUS. I will explain.

ANTHONY. Yes, do.

PAPHNUTIUS. Three years ago, there lived some dis-
tance away a harlot by the name of Thais, who not only gave herself over to destruction, but even was wont to draw many with her to ruin.

ANTHONY. Alas! A pitiable way for a woman to live.   500

PAPHNUTIUS. I went to her disguised as a lover. At first I soothed her passionate heart with gentle exhortations; later I put fear into this same heart with sharper re-
proofs.

ANTHONY. Such remedies were necessary for her passionate temperament.

PAPHNUTIUS. Finally she yielded, and despising her evil

ways, she chose chastity and consented to be confined in
a very narrow cell.

ANTHONY. I am so relieved to hear this that my whole   510
being rejoices.

PAPHNUTIUS. This is in keeping with your sanctity, and
I indeed greatly rejoice at her conversion; yet, nevertheless, I am somewhat concerned, because I fear that her
wickedness can hardly bear the long trial.

ANTHONY. Where there is true love, there is holy compassion.

PAPHNUTIUS. Therefore, I beg your love that you and
your disciples will wish to continue with me in fervent
prayer until a sign from heaven will be given to us   520
whether the mercy of Divine Providence has pardoned
her because of her repentant tears.

ANTHONY. We gladly grant your request.

PAPHNUTIUS. I do not doubt but that God will very
soon hear your prayers.

SCENE 11

ANTHONY. Behold! The gospel's promise is fulfilled in
us.

PAPHNUTIUS. What is this promise?

ANTHONY. Truly this, that they who pray together are
able to gain all things.   530

PAPHNUTIUS. What do you mean?

ANTHONY. A certain vision has been revealed to Paul,
my disciple.

PAPHNUTIUS. Summon him.

ANTHONY. Come here, Paul, and tell Paphnutius what
you have seen.

PAUL. In a vision, I saw a magnificent couch in heaven
spread with a snow-white coverlet; near it stood four
shining virgins as if guarding it, and as I was gazing at
the wondrous brightness, I said to myself, "This glory is 540
fit for my father and Lord Anthony."

ANTHONY. I am not worthy of such honor.

PAUL. When I was thus speaking, a Divine Voice said,
"This glory is not for Anthony as you hope, but it must
be kept for Thais, the harlot."

PAPHNUTIUS. Praise to the sweetness of Your mercy, O
Christ, the only begotten Son of God, because You have
been so graciously pleased to comfort my sorrow.

ANTHONY. Christ deserves such praise.

PAPHNUTIUS. I shall go at once and visit my captive.   550

ANTHONY. It is time that you promise her the hope of pardon and the solace of eternal beatitude.

SCENE 12

PAPHNUTIUS. Thais, my daughter, open the window and let me see you.

THAIS. Who speaks?

PAPHNUTIUS. Paphnutius, your father.

THAIS. How it is that I merit such happiness, that you deign to visit me, a sinner?

PAPHNUTIUS. Although absent from you in body for three years, nevertheless I was greatly concerned for your   560
welfare.

THAIS. I do not doubt that.

PAPHNUTIUS. Tell me the story of your conversion, the manner of your repentance.

THAIS. I am able to tell you this, that I know I have done nothing acceptable to God.

PAPHNUTIUS. If God counts iniquities, which one of us would be saved?

THAIS. If you wish to know what I did: I gathered the multitude of my sins before my conscience as if they   570
were a great bundle, and I kept them before my mind so that, even as I was always aware of the offensiveness of this place, so also the fear of hellfire was always in my heart.

PAPHNUTIUS. You have atoned for your sins by penance, therefore you have merited pardon.

THAIS. Oh, would that it were true!

PAPHNUTIUS. Give me your hand that I may lead you away.

THAIS. Do not, Reverend Father, do not take me away   580
from this wretched cell, but let me stay in this place suited to my deserts.

PAPHNUTIUS. It is time, your fears allayed, that you begin to hope for life because your penance is acceptable to God.

THAIS. May all the angels praise His mercy because He has not despised the humility of a contrite heart.

PAPHNUTIUS. Be steadfast in the fear of the Lord and abide in His love, for after fifteen days, by the grace of heavenly fervor, you will be in Paradise.
          590

THAIS. Oh, would that I deserved to escape punishment or at least to be burned in a less intense fire, for not by my own merits do I deserve everlasting happiness.

PAPHNUTIUS. God's free gift does not take into consideration man's merit, because were it given for merit, it would not be called grace.

THAIS. Therefore let all the heavenly company, and all the universe, and also all species of animals, and all surging waters praise Him who not only endures sinners, but ever freely bestows rewards upon penitents. 600

PAPHNUTIUS. From the beginning this was His wont, to have mercy rather than to destroy.

SCENE 13[3]

THAIS. Venerable Father, do not leave me, but stay with me and console me in this hour of my death.

PAPHNUTIUS. I will not leave you, I will not go away until your soul enters heaven, and I shall lay your body in the grave.

THAIS. Lo! Death is approaching.

PAPHNUTIUS. Now is the time to pray.

THAIS. You who created me, have mercy upon me! 610 Grant that the soul which you created return to You.

PAPHNUTIUS. Oh, uncreated Being, truly form without matter, Who created man: man who is not that which is, but consists of diverse elements, grant that the various parts of this mortal may happily be united with the source of its origin by which the soul, endowed with immortality, may share in the celestial joys, and the body peacefully rest in the gentle embrace of its native earth until the dust of her ashes be gathered again and the breath of life return to her reawakened body. This 620 same Thais may rise again in a perfect body as she was, and be at home among the snow-white lambs and be led into the joys of Eternity. Grant this, Thou above Who art what Thou art, Who in the Unity of the Trinity lives and reigns world without end.

---

[3] Fifteen days later, as suggested in the fifth speech from the end of the preceding scene. Thais is obviously in her cell, probably lying on a cot with Paphnutius standing or kneeling beside it.

Pagan Remains

It is impossible to tell how early in European history we would be likely to encounter pagan Celtic and Teutonic drama—in a form, of course, not less rudimentary than anywhere else in the world—if any of it had been written down and preserved. We are safe in assuming, nevertheless, that some primitive form of theater, intimately related to seasonal rites dealing chiefly with winter and spring, was already well established by the time Celtic and Germanic Europe was converted to Christianity. They were not completely eradicated by Christianity but assimilated by the medieval Christian world in the form of dimly understood folk performances, to some extent paralleling Christmas and Easter, respectively the great winter and spring festivals of Christianity. In essence, the pagan pieces that have come down to us re-enact death and resurrection rites concerned with the dying of the vegetation in the winter and the return of the vegetation in the spring. But they have been reduced to the status of games, mummings, and other forms of play, such as maypole dancing. As such they have survived into modern times. In medieval England, they constituted a secondary source of dramatic entertainment and semi-literary as well as completely nonliterary folk theater; and as such they are of greater interest to folklorists than to students of dramatic literature. Nevertheless, this area of medieval theater deserves some representation, and the *Christmas Play of St. George* will do at least as well as other remains of folk drama.

A number of Robin Hood plays have survived, and we have the text of the dialogue that accompanied the sword dances which constituted another form of folk entertainment closely related to death-and-resurrection magic. (See the "Shetland Sword Dance" in John Quincy Adams' *Chief Pre-Shakespearean Dramas*, Boston, Houghton Mifflin Company, pp. 350–351.) The Revesby Sword Play (see *ibid.*, pp. 357–64) is known to have been "acted by a set of Plow Boys or Morris Dancers, in riband dresses, with swords, on October 20, 1779, at Revesby Abbey, in Lincolnshire. . . ." The dancing with swords dimly reflects some form of sacrifice of an animal, or perhaps (in primitive times) of a human being, to the vegetation spirit. In addition, there were preserved a number of St. George Plays, dealing with the exploits of England's patron saint, St. George, who slays a dragon and a "Turkish Knight." St. George is himself slain, and a Doctor provides a medicine that brings the combatants back to life. These plays, which must have started long before 1,000 A.D., lost their ritualistic significance to such a degree that the resurrection-of-the-vegetation," "return-of-spring," idea embodied in the Doctor, was forgotten; as a result, the plays were performed during Christmas rather than Easter and "Father Christmas" appears as the master of ceremonies. The Turkish Knight entered these plays during the Crusades to perform the familiar role of the opponent to a Christian knight. He slays St. George, who in dying and being brought back to life recalls the old Vegetation Spirit of many an ancient rite under such names as Attis and Thammuz. St. George is also called in various versions *Prince* George or even *King* George.

Thomas Hardy incorporated a description of a country performance of this type of folk play, as he remembered it from his youth, in his famous novel *The Return of the Native*. (See also: *The Play of St. George,* based on the version in *The Return of the Native* and completed from other versions and local tradition by Thomas Hardy, privately printed by Mrs. Hardy in 1921 and published by Samuel French in 1928.) The tradition was continued, for long, by word of mouth. Thus the text of the Oxfordshire St. George Play, printed in 1874, was taken down "from the lips of one of the performers in 1853" who had performed it in 1803. Max Beerbohm saw a performance as late as 1907. The following version presents the representative features of these folk pieces, which were also to be found in other parts of England. We can imagine the "mummers" bursting in, as Kenneth Grahame recalled in his *Golden Age*, "powdering the red brick floor with snow from their barbaric bedizenments; and stamping and crossing and declaiming till all was whirl and riot and shout"—breaking in on a country household "with song and ordered masque and a terrible clashing of wooden swords."[1]

---

[1] For additional material, see E. O. James, *Christian Myth and Ritual*, London, 1933, and A. Brown, "Folklore Elements in Medieval Drama," *Folk Lore*, lxiii, 65-78, 1952.

A Christmas Mumming: The Play of Saint [Prince] George

(In the midst of much singing, dancing and feasting, enter some mummers or performers, led by FATHER CHRISTMAS, *who is swinging a mighty club.)*

FATHER CHRISTMAS. Here come I, old Father Christmas,
Welcome, or welcome not.
I hope Old Father Christmas
Will never be forgot.

I have not come here to laugh or to jeer,
But for a pocketful of money and a skinful of beer
To show some sport or pastime,
Gentlemen and Ladies, in the Christmas-time.

If you will not believe what I now say,
Come in the Turkish Knight! Clear the way.   10
(Enter the TURKISH KNIGHT.)
TURKISH KNIGHT. Open the doors and let me in!
I hope your favors now to win;
Whether I rise, or whether I fall,
I'll do my best to please you all.

Prince George is here, and swears he will come in;
And if he does, I know he'll pierce my skin.
If you do not believe what I now say,
Come in the King of Egypt!—Clear the way!
(Enter the KING OF EGYPT.)
KING OF EGYPT. Here I, the King of Egypt, boldly do
   appear.
Prince George, Prince George, walk in, my son and heir!   20
Walk in, my son, Prince George, and boldly play thy part
That all the people here may see thy wondrous art.
(Enter PRINCE GEORGE.)
PRINCE GEORGE. Here come I, Saint George; from
   Britain I have sprung.
I'll fight the Dragon bold, for my wonders have begun:
I'll clip his wings, he shall not fly;
I'll cut him down, or else I'll die.
(Enter THE DRAGON.)

THE DRAGON. Who's he that seeks the Dragon's blood
And calls so angry and so loud?
That English dog, will he before me stand?
I'll cut him down with my courageous hand.   30
With my long teeth and my scurvy jaw
Of such as he I break up half a score.
  (PRINCE GEORGE *and* THE DRAGON *fight;* THE DRAGON
  is killed.)
FATHER CHRISTMAS. Is there a Doctor to be found
All ready, near at hand,
To cure a deep and deadly wound
And make the champion stand!
  (*Enter a* DOCTOR, *holding a bottle of medicine under
  his arm.*)
All ready, near at hand,
To cure a deep and deadly wound
And make the champion stand!   40
  FATHER CHRISTMAS. What can you cure?

  DOCTOR. All sorts of diseases,
Whatever you pleases,
The phthisic, the palsy, and the gout.
Whatever the disorder, I soon draw it out.
  FATHER CHRISTMAS. What is your fee?
  DOCTOR. Fifteen pounds is all my fee,
The money you lay down.
But since 'tis such a rogue as he,
I'll cure him for ten pound.   50
I have a little bottle of Elucumpane:
  (*to the actor who impersonates* THE DRAGON.)
Here Jack, take a little of this flip-flop,
Pour it down thy tip-top,
Then rise up and fight again.
  (*The* DOCTOR *gives him the medicine.* THE DRAGON
  comes to life again, and fights with ST. [PRINCE] GEORGE,
  and is killed again.)
  PRINCE GEORGE. Here I am, St. George, a worthy
    champion bold,
And with my sword and spear I've won three crowns of
    gold.
I've found the fiery Dragon and brought him to the
    slaughter;
And with that I've won fair Sabra, the King of Egypt's
    daughter.

(*The* TURKISH KNIGHT *advances.*)

TURKISH KNIGHT. Here come I, the Turkish Knight,
Come from the Turkish land to fight,   60
I'll fight St. George, who is my foe,
And make him yield before I go:
He brags to such a high degree
He thinks that none can do the like of he.

    PRINCE GEORGE. Where is that Turk that will before
      me stand?
I'll cut him down with my courageous hand.

    (*They fight: the* TURKISH KNIGHT *is defeated and falls
on one knee.*)

    TURKISH KNIGHT. Oh! Pardon me, Prince George,
      pardon of thee I crave.
Oh! Pardon me this night and I will be thy slave.

    PRINCE GEORGE. I'll never pardon a Turkish Knight,
So rise thou up again and try thy might.   70

    (*They fight again, and the* TURKISH KNIGHT *is killed.*
FATHER CHRISTMAS *calls once more for a* DOCTOR,
who appears quickly and cures the KNIGHT.

    Then the DOCTOR *is given a basin of "girdy grout,"*[1]
*following which he is given a kick and driven out by
the actors.*

    Then FAIR SABRA, *the King of Egypt's daughter,
appears and goes [or dances] toward* PRINCE GEORGE
to become his wife.)

FATHER CHRISTMAS. So, ladies and gentlemen, your
    sport has now ended.
Therefore, behold this box, which is highly commended!
The box it would speak, if it had but a tongue,
Come throw in your money and think it no wrong.

    (FATHER CHRISTMAS *starts collecting money in his box.*)

---

[1] Coarse meal; a symbol of vegetation, suggesting the recurrence of spring.

The Christian Ritual Beginnings

It was inevitable, one supposes, that the Church, which was for many centuries hostile to the theater of decadent Rome and the itinerant players, or mimes, who continued its comic tradition should have become the seedbed of a new European drama. Born within the Church and a direct development from its ritual, it is properly designated as ecclesiastical or liturgical drama.

The celebration of the Mass was itself a highly dramatic event, and antiphonal singing had in it the germs of dramatic dialogue. Supplying words to the wordless sequences of the Mass—that is, to the melodies sung to vowel sounds (or *neumes*) only—particularly at the Christmas and Easter services, was the first step toward creating the new plays. The texts, known as *tropes*, were at first few and rudimentary (we offer here the earliest of these, the tenth-century *Quem quaeritis*, from the Benedictine Abbey of St. Gall in Switzerland), but they multiplied and expanded from the eleventh to the thirteenth centuries. The Introit trope was a chanted dialogue between an "Angel" and the women (the Marys) who come for Christ's body at the beginning of the Easter service. Soon detached from this position, the trope became a separate little scene performed at matins on Easter morning. The important element of impersonation entered into the performances, which had the characteristics of a tiny opera, with four persons impersonating the three women and the angel, at an improvised sepulcher. Before long, lines were added to the original text, and a truly dramatic little play in Latin was the result.

A similar trope was elaborated for Christmas, with a manger substituted for the sepulcher, and with the dialogue of the three Marys looking for the crucified Christ adapted for the three shepherds greeting the infant Savior and his Mother; and the angel or angels could be replaced by a midwife or midwives (*obstetrices*) as interlocutors. The result was a Christmas version known as the Office of the Shepherds, the *Officium Pastorum*. Combined with pantomimes associated with the Easter and Christmas rites, these performances set the precedent for other theatrical "productions." Thus the "Twelfth

Day" celebration brought the Magi, the three wise kings, bearing gifts and wearing splendid oriental robes; since they were led by a star (no doubt suspended from the roof of the church or cathedral), this trope constituted the "office" of the star, the *Officium Stellae*. The addition of the Massacre of the Innocents, ordered by Herod, king of Judea, because it was foretold that a child born at Christmas would become king of the Jews, introduced another little performance. It was the *Ordo Rachelis*, consisting chiefly of a lament by Rachel, the representative of the grieving mothers of the slain children (the author of this "play" must have taken his cue from the Old Testament phrase of "Rachel weeping for her children") as well as efforts by other characters to comfort her. And another episode, an *Ordo Prophetarum*, brought the prophets of Israel to testify to the coming of Christ.

Before long, other episodes from sacred history were added, until numerous high points from the Creation to the Crucifixion, and past this event right up to the Last Judgment, became the subject of separate little plays in medieval Latin. The biblical source was also elaborated and given supporting details of local color; thus, Mary Magdalene before her conversion was shown entertaining a lover, singing a song, and purchasing cosmetics. In time, the Latin of these liturgical dramas became mixed with vernacular dialogue; and the performances moved from choir to nave to the exterior of the church.

Elaborated further, as a rule, and written entirely in the vernacular, the plays became the possession of the trade guilds of medieval towns, and when presented in chronological succession from the Creation to Doomsday, they constituted the cycles or Passion plays which constitute the major achievement of the medieval theater. These plays and their often spectacular productions naturally overshadowed the liturgical drama. But there can be no doubt that it proved effective within the church, that it could develop into lengthier intermediate drama as impressive as the twelfth-century Anglo-Norman *Adam*, and that many a chanted passage in even the simplest liturgical drama written entirely in Latin (as the *Adam* is not) had lyrical beauty and power. An example is the following stanza from the *Pastores*, in which the shepherds adoring the Mother and Child chant: "Hail Virgin without equal./ Remaining a virgin, the bride of God./ Before the ages he was generated/ In the heart of the Father./ Let us

worship him now embodied/ In the flesh of the Mother." In
the original Latin this reads:

> *Salve, virgo singularis,*
> *Virgo manens, Deus paris!*
> *Ante sæcla generatum*
> *Corde patris,*
> *Adoremus nunc creatum*
> *Carne matris.*

The high standards of Latin hymnology were naturally not
foreign to the clerical authors of ecclesiastical drama.

The *Quem Quaeritis* Trope

From the Introit of the Mass at Easter found in a tenth-
century manuscript in the monastery of Saint Gall.

INTERROGATIO. *Quem quæritis in sepulchro, o Christicolæ?*
RESPONSIO. *Jesum Nazarenum crucifixum, o cælicolæ.*
ANGELI. *Non est hic; surrexit, sicut prædixerat. Ite, nuntiate
quia surrexit de sepulchro.*

Question [by the ANGELS]. Whom do ye seek in the sepul-
cher, O followers of Christ?
Answer [by the MARYS]. Jesus of Nazareth, who was cruci-
fied, just as he foretold.
The ANGELS. He is not here: he is risen, just as he foretold.
Go, announce that he is risen from the sepulcher.

NOTE. The women, the Marys, and the Angels are not actually
impersonated, so that this trope consists merely of ques-
tions and answers in the form of sung dialogue during the
Mass, sung by the two halves of the choir.
Ultimately, the tropes were shifted from their position in the
Mass to the service of the hours in the monasteries—to the
matins, the prayers which precede daybreak. The trope was
now free to develop into a little play or opera.
The tropes appear to have first been composed in France, and
they constituted a dramatic development of liturgical music.

A Pantomime for Easter Day

Modernized from *A Description . . . of the Ancient Monuments, Rites and Customs. . . .* of the Monastical Church of Durham (England).

There was in the Abbey Church of Durham a very solemn service on Easter Day, between three and four o'clock in the morning, in honor of the Resurrection. Two of the oldest monks of the Choir came to the Sepulcher, which had been set up on Good Friday, after the Passion, all covered with red velvet and embroidered with gold, and censed it, each monk sitting on his knees before the Sepulcher.

Then, both rising, they came to the Sepulcher, out of which, with great devotion and reverence, they took a marvelous, beautiful Image of the Savior, representing the Resurrection, with a cross in his hand, in the breast whereof was enclosed, in bright crystal, the Holy Sacrament of the altar, through which crystal the Blessed Host was conspicuous to the beholders.

Then, after the elevation of the said picture, carried by the said two monks upon a fair, velvet cushion, all embroidered, singing the anthem of *Christus resurgens,* they brought it to the High Altar, placing it upright in the center, the two monks kneeling before the Altar and censing it all the time while the rest of the choir was singing the aforementioned anthem of *Christus resurgens.*

This anthem being ended, the two monks took up the cushions and the picture from the Altar, supporting it between them. Then they proceeded in progression, from the High Altar to the south Choir door, where four elderly Gentlemen, belonging to the Prior, had been appointed to await their coming. They held up a most rich Canopy of purple velvet, attached with red silk and gold fringe. And at every corner did stand one of these Gentlemen to bear the Canopy over the image with the Holy Sacrament, carried by two monks round about the Church, the entire Choir attending it with goodly torches and a great store of other lights, all singing, rejoicing, and praising God most devoutly, till they came to the High Altar again, on which they placed the Image, where it was to remain until Ascension Day.

An Easter Resurrection Play

An early "liturgical play" showing how the trope became a real little drama involving impersonation and action, as well as an extension of the sung dialogue. From the *Regularis Concordia* of St. Ethelwold, *circa* 965–975. Translated from the Latin.

While the third lesson of the matins is being chanted, let four brethren [monks] dress themselves; of whom let one, wearing an alb, enter as if to take part in the service; and let him without being observed approach the place of the sepulcher, where, holding a palm in his hand, let him sit down quietly. While the third responsory is being sung, let the remaining three brethren follow, all of them wearing copes and carrying censers filled with incense. Then slowly, in the manner of seeking something, let them move toward the place of the sepulcher.

These things are to be performed in imitation of the Angel seated in the tomb, and of the women coming with spices to anoint the body of Jesus. When therefore the seated Angel shall see the three women, as if straying about and looking for something, approach him, let him begin to sing in a dulcet voice of medium pitch:

Whom seek ye in the sepulcher, O followers of Christ?

When he has sung this to the end, let the three ["women"] respond in unison:

Jesus of Nazareth, who was crucified, O celestial one.

To whom
that one:

He is not here; he is risen, just as he foretold.
Go, announce that he is risen from the dead.

At the word of this command, let the three [women] turn to the Choir, and say:

Alleluia! The Lord is risen today,
The strong lion, the Christ, the Son of God.
Give thanks to God, eia!*   hurrah!

This said, let the Angel, again seating himself, as if recalling them, sing the anthem

Venite, et Videte locum—

Come, and see the place where the Lord was laid. Alleluia!
   Alleluia!
And saying this, let him rise, and let him lift the veil and
   show them the place bare of the cross, but only the cloths
   lying there with which the cross was wrapped. Seeing this,
   let the women set down the censers they carried into the
   sepulcher, and let them pick up the cloth and spread it
   out before the eyes of the clergy; and, as if making known
   that the Lord had risen and was not now wrapped in this
   linen, let them sing this anthem
Surrexit Dominus de sepulchro—
The Lord is risen from the sepulcher,
Who for us hung upon the cross.
And let them place the cloth upon the altar. The anthem
   being ended, let the Prior, rejoicing with them at the triumph of our King, in that, having conquered death, he
   arose, begin the hymn:
Te, Deum, laudamus—
We praise thee, O God.

The Orléans Sepulcher

Translated from the Thirteenth-Century Manuscript from
Orléans, France.

To make the representation of the Lord's sepulcher, first let
   three monks, prepared and clothed in the likeness of the
   three Marys, advance slowly and as if sorrowful, alternately
   singing. The First of these shall say:
THE FIRST. Alas! the good shepherd is killed,
Whom no guilt stained.
   O lamentable event!
THE SECOND. Alas! the true Shepherd is dead
Who gave life to the upright!
   O lamentable death!
THE THIRD. Alas! sinful race of Judaica
Whom a dire madness makes frenzied!
   Detestable people!
THE FIRST. Why condemned ye to an impious death   10

The Holy One with savage hate?
 O dreadful rage!
THE SECOND. How has this righteous man deserved
To be crucified?
 O race accursed!
THE THIRD. Alas! what are we wretched ones to do,
Bereft of our sweet Master?
 Alas! lamentable fate!
THE FIRST. Let us therefore go expeditiously,
To do the only thing we can do,   20
 With mind devout.
THE SECOND. With preservative of spices
Let us anoint the most holy body,
 With the most costly ones possible.
THE THIRD. Let a mixture of spikenard be brought
Lest in the tomb putrefy
 The blessed flesh.

When they have entered the choir area, let them go towards the sepulcher as if seeking something, singing
 together this verse:
But we cannot open this without assistance.
Who shall roll away the stone from the door of the
 sepulcher?
To whom let the Angel respond, seated at the head of
 the tomb, clothed in an alb gilded over, his head
 covered with a coif, yet unadorned with the *infula*,[1]
 holding in his left hand a palm and in his right hand
 a candelabrum full of candles. And let him say in a
 modulated and grave voice:
Whom seek ye in the sepulcher, O followers of Christ?   30
 THE WOMEN. Jesus of Nazareth, who was crucified, O
 celestial one.
To them let the Angel respond:
Why, O followers of Christ, seek ye the living among the
 dead?
He is not here, he is risen, as he foretold to his disciples.
Remember now what he said to you in Galilea,
That it was proper for Christ to suffer, and on the
 third day
To rise with glory.

[1] Flaps hanging from the back of the miter.

Let the women, turning toward the people [that is, the
congregation], sing:
To the sepulcher of the Lord we have come
Lamenting. We have seen the angel of God seated
And heard him saying that He is risen from the dead.

After this let Mary Magdalene, having left the other two
women, go to the sepulcher; into which looking many
times, let her say:
Alas the grief! alas! how dire the anguish of grief   40
That I am bereft of the presence of my beloved Master!
Alas! who bore away the body, so dear, from the tomb?

Then let her go swiftly to those brethren [monks] who
in the likeness of Peter and John should present them-
selves with heads erect; and standing before them as if
overcome with grief, let her say:
They have taken away my Lord,
And I know not where they have laid him;
And the tomb has been found empty,
And the sudarium[2] with the muslin cloth lying within.

Then let these, upon hearing her, proceed swiftly to the
sepulcher, as if running. But let the younger, Saint
John, upon arriving, stand outside the sepulcher, while
the elder, Saint Peter, following him, immediately
enters in; after which John also enters. Then when
they have come out, let John, as if wondering, say:
Marvelous are the things we have seen!
Hath the Lord been taken away by stealth?
To whom Peter:
Nay, as he predicted while alive,
The Lord, I believe, is risen.
    JOHN. But why did he leave in the sepulcher   50
The sudarium with the linen cloth?
    PETER. Because to one rising from the dead
These things were not necessary.
Nay, they remain here
As tokens of His resurrection.

Then, as they are going out, let Mary approach the
sepulcher, and let her first say:
Alas the grief! alas! how dire the anguish of grief,

---

[2] The handkerchief the legendary St. Veronica gave Jesus on His way to
the cross, to wipe the sweat from His face; as He did so, He impressed His
portrait on the cloth.

That I am bereft of the presence of my beloved Master!
Alas! who bore away the body, so dear, from the tomb?

To whom let two Angels sitting inside the sepulcher
    speak, saying:
Woman, why weepest thou?   60
    MARY. Because they have taken away my Lord,
And I know not where they have laid him.
    ANGEL. Weep not, Mary; the Lord is risen.
        Alleluia!
    MARY. My heart is burning with desire
To see my Lord.
I seek, and I do not find
Where they have laid him.
        Alleluia!

In the meanwhile let one monk come, made up in the
    likeness of a Gardener, and standing at the head of
    the sepulcher, let him say:
Woman, why weepest thou? Whom seekest thou?   70
    MARY. Sir, if thou hast borne him away, tell me where
        thou hast laid him, and I will take him away.
And He [Christ in the likeness of the Gardener]:
Mary!
And falling prostrate at his feet, let Mary say:
Rabboni!
Thereupon let him draw himself back; and as if avoid-
    ing her touch, let him say:
Noli me tangere. . . .
Touch me not, for I am not yet ascended to my Father
    and your Father, to my Lord and your Lord.

Thus let the Gardener go out. But let Mary, having
    turned toward the people, say:
Rejoice with me, all ye who love the Lord, for He whom
    I sought has appeared to me, and while I was
    weeping at the tomb I saw the Lord. Alleluia!
Then let the two Angels come to the door of the sepul-
    cher in such a way that they are visible outside, and
    let them say:
Come and see the place where the Lord was laid.
        Alleluia!
Nolite timere vos—
Be not affrighted: 80
Change now your sorrowful countenance

And proclaim the living Jesus!
Go now into Galilea.
If it please you to see, hasten,
Go quickly, and tell His disciples that
The Lord is risen from the dead.
     Alleluia!

Then let the women, going away from the sepulcher,
    say to the people:
The Lord is risen from the sepulcher,
Who for us hung upon the cross!
     Alleluia!   90
Having done this, let them unfold the muslin cloth,
    saying to the people:
Look you, friends, these are the cloths of the blessed body
Which lay abandoned in the empty tomb.

Then let them place the cloth upon the altar; and turn-
    ing themselves about, let them sing alternately these
    verses:
    THE FIRST. The God of Gods has arisen today!
    THE SECOND. In vain do ye seal the stone, O men of
      Judea!
    THE THIRD. Join now with the people of Christ!

Likewise let THE FIRST say:
The King of the angels has arisen today!
    THE SECOND. The throng of the righteous is led out of
      hell!
    THE THIRD. The door of the kingdom of heaven has
      been opened.

In the meantime let him who had previously appeared
    as the Gardener come in the likeness of the Lord,
    clothed in a dazzling white robe, adorned with a white
    infula[3] with a precious *phylacterium*[4] on his head,
    holding in his right hand a cross with the *labarum*,[5]
    in his left hand a *paratorium*[6] woven of gold, and let
    him say to the women:
Be not affrighted: go, tell my brothers that they shall go
    into Galilea: there they shall see me, just as I
    foretold to them.

[3] Here probably a fillet of wool.
[4] A small, square, leather box containing a piece of parchment on which
passages of Scripture have been inscribed in Hebrew.
[5] The imperial standard of the Roman emperors.
[6] The pall that covers the chalice used in celebrating Mass.

THE CHOIR: Alleluia! The Lord is risen today!   100
Then let all say in unison:
The strong Lion, the Christ, the Son of God!
And let the choir say:
Te Deum laudamus. . . .
We praise thee, O God! [etc.]

The English Passion Play

This section consists of individual plays dealing as a rule with individual biblical episodes. They are taken from the various surviving mystery or miracle play cycles, except for the *Brome Abraham and Isaac,* which was recovered from a manuscript in a commonplace-book (a collection of passages for reference) preserved at Brome Manor, Suffolk, England. This fourteenth-century masterpiece may never have been part of any cycle, although we cannot be sure of this. Taken together, the plays comprise a cycle of sorts, consisting of some of the best plays to be found in the surviving texts, although they did not all appear together in any single cycle.

As a good deal has been said about the mystery or miracle plays and their cycles, each of which constitutes a sort of Passion play such as those that survived in Central Europe (at Oberammergau, for example), they are not discussed here. But I list below the titles of a complete cycle, in order to give the reader an idea of size and character of a cycle made up of individual plays such as those included here. It is to be noted, however, that not all the separate plays of this or any other cycle are fully developed or have equal merit.

The plays of the complete York Cycle, containing the titles of the pageants, and the names of the craft or trade guilds known to have produced or to have been responsible for the productions of the individual pageants are given below. The York Passion Play is the most extensive of the extant English cycles.

YORK CYCLE

1. The Creation, and the Fall of Lucifer (The Barkers', or Tanners', Pageant).
2. The Creation—up to the Fifth Day (Plasterers).
3. Creation of Adam and Eve (Cardmakers).
4. Adam and Eve in Eden (Fullers).
5. Fall of Man (Coopers).
6. Expulsion from Eden (Armourers).
7. Sacrifice of Cain and Abel (Glovers).
8. Building of the Ark (Shipwrights).
9. Noah and his Wife; Flood (Fishers and Mariners).
10. Abraham and Isaac (Parchmenters and Bookbinders).

11. Departure of the Israelites from Egypt; Ten Plagues; Crossing of the Red Sea (Hosiers).
12. Annunciation and Visitation (Spicers).
13. Joseph's Trouble about Mary (Pewterers and Founders).
14. Journey to Bethlehem; Birth of Jesus (Tile-thatchers).
15. Shepherds (Chandlers[1]).
16. Coming of the Three Kings to Herod (Masons).
17. Coming of the Kings; Adoration (Goldsmiths).
18. Flight into Egypt (Marshals[2]).
19. Slaughter of the Innocents (Girdlers and Nailers).
20. Christ with the Doctors (Spurriers and Lorimers[3]).
21. Baptism of Jesus (Barbers).
22. Temptation (Smiths).
23. Transfiguration (Curriers[4]).
24. Woman Taken in Adultery; Lazarus (Capmakers).
25. Christ's Entry into Jerusalem (Skinners).
26. Conspiracy (Cutlers).
27. Last Supper (Bakers).
28. Agony and Betrayal (Cordwainers).
29. Peter's Denial; Jesus before Caiaphas (Bowyers and Fletchers).
30. Dream of Pilate's Wife; Jesus before Pilate (Tapiters[5] and Couchers).
31. Trial before Herod (Litsters[6]).
32. Second Accusation before Pilate; Remorse of Judas; Purchase of the Field of Blood (Cooks and Water-leaders).
33. Second Trial before Pilate (Tilemakers).
34. Christ Led to Calvary (Shearmen).
35. Crucifixion (Pinners and Painters).
36. Mortification of Christ; Burial (Butchers).
37. Harrowing of Hell (Saddlers).
38. Resurrection (Carpenters).
39. Christ's Appearance to Mary Magdalene (Winedrawers).
40. Travellers to Emmaus (Sledmen).
41. Purification of Mary; Simeon and Anna (Hatmakers, Masons, Labourers).
42. Incredulity of Thomas (Scriveners).
43. Ascension (Tailors).
44. Descent of the Holy Spirit (Potters).

[1] Candlemakers.
[2] Grooms, men who take care of horses.
[3] Spurmakers and makers of bits, etc.
[4] Men who dress leather.
[5] Makers of tapestry and carpets.
[6] Dyers.

45. The Death of Mary (Drapers[7]).
46. The Appearance of Mary to Thomas (Weavers).
47. Assumption and Coronation of the Virgin (Ostlers[8]).
48. Judgment Day (Mercers[9]).

In addition to the York cycle, we have extant a Chester cycle of twenty-five pieces; a so-called Towneley Cycle, probably performed at Wakefield in Yorkshire, of thirty-two plays (Towneley is merely the name of the family that possessed the manuscript for a long time); and the N Town Cycle, wrongly designated as the Coventry Cycle (*Ludus Coventriae*), with forty-two plays extant. The last-mentioned is sometimes designated the "Hegge Plays," after the name of the owner of the fifteenth-century manuscript. The "N" may stand for Nomen, so that the name of the town or towns where the performances were given could be filled in.

[7] Dealers in cloth and dry goods.
[8] Stablemen, hostlers.
[9] Dealers in textiles.

The Creation and the Fall of Lucifer[1]
The York Pageant of Barkers (Tanners)

A MODERNIZED VERSION BY JOHN GASSNER

Characters
GOD
ANGEL SERAPHIM
ANGEL CHERUBIM
LUCIFER (FIRST ANGEL LUCIFER)
SECOND ANGEL (later, SECOND DEVIL)

SCENE 1

Heaven.

(GOD *addresses himself to the* ANGELS.)
GOD. I am Alpha and Omega, the Life,
The Way, the Truth, the first and the last.

[1] The stanzas consist of eight lines of alliterative verse each with a more or less fixed rhyme scene (*ababcddc*, or *ababcccc*).

I am gracious and great, and without beginning:
I am maker unmade, and all might is in me,
I am life and the way to all well-being,
I am foremost and first—as I bid so shall it be.
My blessing upon all my bliss shall be spending;
And descending, shall all from harm be defending,
My body in bliss forever abiding
Unending withouten* any ending.   without/10

Since I am maker unmade and most so of might
And ever shall be endless and nought is but I,
Unto my dignity dear shall be dight*   made
A place full of plenty to my pleasure to ply*   mold
And therewith also will I have wrought
Many divers doings amain,
Which work shall metely* contain;   meekly, or.
And all shall be made even of nought.

But only the worthy work of my will
In my spirit shall inspire the might of me;   20
And truly at first my thoughts to fulfill
At once in my blessing I bid that here be
A bliss all-sheltering about me;
In which bliss I bid that there be here
Nine orders of angels full clear
In loving to forever laud me.

   (*Here the* ANGELS *sing the "Te deum."*)
Underneath me now an island I neven,*   name
Which island shall be the Earth. There at once shall be
Earth wholly, and Hell, and highest Heaven
And all that wealth shall wield I give ye.   30
This grant I to you, ministers mine,
As long as ye are stable in thought;
While that all creatures that are nought
Shall to my prison be sent to pine.

   (*addressing* LUCIFER.)
Of all that I have made the most next to me
I make thee master and mirror of my might.
I shield thee at once in bliss to be
And I name thee "Lucifer" as bearer of light.
No thing here shall thee be harming
In this bliss shall be thy dwelling   40
And may all wealth in thy wielding
Be while thou art obediently yielding.

(*Then the* ANGELS *sing "Sanctus, Santus, Sanctus, dominus deus sabaoth."*)

THE ANGEL SERAPHIM. Ah merciful Maker, full much is thy might
Who has all this work so worthily wrought.
Ever loved be that lovely Lord for his light
That us mighty has made who were before this nought,
In bliss to abide. In his blessing
Ever lasting, in love, let us laud him
That protects us closely about him
So mirth may nevermore be missing   50

FIRST ANGEL LUCIFER. All the mirth that is made is marked in me!
The beams of my brightness are burning so bright
And so seemly in sight myself I now see,
For like a lord am I left to dwell in this light.
Fairer by far than anyone here,
In me there is no point to impair;
I feel myself so well-formed and fair,
My power surpassing has no peer.   60

CHERUBIM. Lord, with a lasting love we love Thee alone,
Oh mighty Maker that marked us and made us
And wrought us thus worthily to live in this wone,*   dwelling
That never feeling of filth may foul us nor fade us.
All bliss is here abiding about us
As long as we are stable in thought
In the worship of Him that us has wrought,
And of harm we never need fear thus.

LUCIFER. Oh, how I am well-formed and figured full fit!
The form of all fairness upon me is fixed;   70
All wealth is in my power; by my wit!
I know the beams of my brightness are made best.
My showing is shimmering and shining;
So bigly to blessing am I brought
I need annoy myself for nought.
And never any pain shall I be minding

SERAPHIM. With all our wit we worship thy will,
Thou glorious God, the ground of all grace;
Aye with steadfast sound let us stand still,
Fed, Lord, with the food of thy fair face.   80

In life that is truly ever-lasting,
Thy gift, Lord, thou art ever dealing;
And whoever that food may be feeling,
To see thy fair face is never fasting.

(LUCIFER *continues to vaunt his pride, and his companions show that they are equally filled with self-admiration and pride while accepting him as their leader.*)

LUCIFER. How worthily wrought with worship this
My being, my glittering joyously gleams.
I'm so mightily made that my grace I may not miss
And ever keep in brightness my beams.
I need have no fear of losing bliss,
All wealth in my hands am I wielding,   90
And never shall be yielding
On the heights of the highest heaven.

There shall I set myself, full seemly to sight,
To receive due reverence through right of renown
And I shall be like unto Him that is highest on height.
Oh, how noble and wise am I!
—But—what is this?—all goes down!
(*He and the other bad angels start falling down.*)
My might and my main* from me fly!   strength
Help, my fellows! In faith, I am falling
SECOND FALLEN ANGEL. From heaven are we cast
down on all hand   100

To woe are we going, a fallen band.[2]

SCENE 2

A region of Hell.

LUCIFER. Out! Out! Helpless am I, the heat so great
here,
This is a dungeon of dole in which we alight!
What have I become that was so comely and clear?
Now am I most loathsome that once was so bright,
My brightness is blackest and blue now.
My bale is ever beating and burning.
It makes me go howling and groaning.
Alas, oh welaway! I boil enough in woe now.

[2] "A fallen band" is a slight addition by the translator.

SECOND DEVIL. Out! Out! I am mad with woe, my
    wit is all spent now,   110
All our food is filth that we find before us;
We, sheltered in bliss, in bale are we burnt now!
Out Lucifer, lurdan,* our light hast thou lost,   worthless one
Thy deeds to this dole have so brought us,
To dire destruction didst thou lead us,
Thou that wast our light and our leader,
Who to the highest of heavens did call us.

    LUCIFER. Welaway!
Woe is me now! Now it is worse than it was.
Unthriving you chide—I uttered but a thought!
    SECOND DEVIL. Oh, lurdan! You have lost us—   120
    LUCIFER. Ye lie, ye lie—alas!
I wist* not this woe should be wrought.   knew
On, on, you, lurdans, who smother me in smoke!
    SECOND DEVIL. This woe hast *thou* wrought.
    LUCIFER.   Ye lie, ye lie!

    SECOND DEVIL. *Thou* liest, and for that thou shalt
    pay.
Oh, lurdan, have at you I may!
    (*He strikes* LUCIFER.)

SCENE 3

Heaven.

    CHERUBIM. Ah, Lord!
Beloved be thy name that us this light lent!
Since Lucifer our leader is lighted so low
For his disobedience in bale to be brent,*   burnt/130
Thy righteousness in thy rewards do show—
Each work even as it is wrought
Through grace of thy merciful might;
The cause I see it in sight,
Wherefore to bale* he is brought.   suffering
    GOD. Those fools from their fairness into fantasies
    fell
And made moan of the might that marked them and
    made them.
Therefore according to their works in woe, shall they
    dwell,
For some are fallen into filth that evermore shall
    foul them

And never shall have grace to gain peace;   140
So surpassing of power they thought themselves
They would not worship him that made them;
For this my wrath shall ever go with them.

And all that worship me shall live here, iwis!*   surely
Wherefore in my work go forth now I will.
Since their might is now marred that meant all amiss,
In my image to fill this place of bliss
Mankind of mold* will I make   earth, clay
All things that shall his wishes fill
To which his desires shall him take.   150

And in my first making to muster my might,
Since Earth is vain and void and murkiness as well,
I bid with my blessing that the angels give light
To the earth which faded when the fiends fell—
In hell alone shall never murkiness be missing.
The darkness thus I name "the night,"
While "the day" call I this light!

And now in my blessing I twin them in two,
The night from the day, so meet they never
But either to their separate gates they go,   160
Both the night and the day their duties leasing.
For the good of all I shall this be without ceasing!—
Now this day's work is surely pleasing
For all this here has been to do;
And straightway now I give it my blessing.

Man's Disobedience and the Fall of Man[1]

The York Pageant of the Coopers

A MODERNIZED VERSION BY JOHN GASSNER

Characters

GOD   EVE
SATAN   ADAM
        ANGEL

[1] Note here the use of the eleven-line stanza.

SCENE 1

A region of Hell.

SATAN. For woe my wits are in a whirl here!
This moves me greatly in my mind:
That Godhead whom I saw so clear
I perceived that He would take his nature
    From a being of a kind
That he had wrought, and I was angered
That these not angels were to be!
For we were fair and bright
And therefore thought that He
Our nature take he might   10
Yet He disdained me.[2]

The nature of *man* He thought to take
And thereat had I great envy.
But He has made to man a mate,
So fast to her I will haste
That ready way,
With purpose fixed to put by*   to set aside
And try to steal from God that prey.
My labor were well set
Might I him so betray,   20
And from him this mankind get,
And this soon I shall essay.*   attempt

SCENE 2

*In Paradise, Satan appears in the shape of a "worm"
—that is, a serpent.*
    SATAN. In a worm's* likeness I will wend*   serpent's/go
And attempt to feign a rousing lie:
Eve! Eve!
    EVE.   Who is there?
    SATAN.   I! A Friend!
And for thy good is the journey
I hither sought.
Of all the fruit that you see high
In Paradise, why eat you nought?
    EVE. We may of them take   30
All that good is in our thought

---

[2] Observe the introduction of a motive for Lucifer's rebellion against God.

Save one tree, lest we mistake
And to harm be brought.

    SATAN. And why *that tree*—that would I wit*—   know
Any more than any other nigh?
    EVE. For our Lord God forbids to try
The fruit thereof. Adam and I
May not come near,
For if we did both should die,
He said, and lose our solace here.   40
    SATAN. Yea, Eve, attend to my intent
Take heed and you shall hear
What all this matter meant
That he moved you to fear.

To eat thereof he did forbid,
I know it well. This is his will
Because he would that none should know
The great virtues that are hid
Therein. For thou wilt see
That who eats this fruit of good and ill   50
Shall be as knowing as is He.
    EVE. Why, what thing art thou
That tells this tale to me?
    SATAN. A worm that knoweth well how
Ye both may worshipped be.

    EVE. What worship should we win thereby?
To eat thereof it needs us nought—
We have lordship to make mastery
Of all things that in earth are wrought.
    SATAN. Woman, away!   60
To a *greater* state ye may be brought
If ye will do as I shall say.
    EVE. To do this we are loath
For this would our God dismay.*   displease
    SATAN. Nay, certain, it will bring no hurt,
Eat it safely ye may.

For peril none therein lies
But advantage and a great winning.
For right as God ye shall be wise,
And peer to Him in everything.   70
Ay, gods shall ye be,
Of ill and good you will have knowing,

And be as wise as is he.

    EVE. Is this truth that thou says?

    SATAN. Yea, why believest thou not me?
I would by no kind of ways
Tell nought but truth to thee.

    EVE. Then will I to thy teaching trust,
And take this fruit unto our food.

    (*And then she must take the apple.*[3]).

    SATAN. Bite on boldly, be not abashed.   80
And make Adam too amend* his mood   improve
And enlarge his bliss

    (*Then* SATAN *retires.*[4])

    EVE. Adam, have here of fruit full good!

    ADAM. Alas, woman, why took'st thou this?
Our Lord commanded us both
To beware this tree of his.
Thy work will make him wroth:
Alas, thou hast done amiss!

    EVE. Nay, Adam, grieve thee not at it,
And I shall tell the reason why: 90
A worm has given me to wit
We shall be as gods, thou and I,
If that we eat
Here of this tree. Adam, thereby,
Fail not this worship so to get,
For we shall be as wise
As God that is so great,
And also of the same great price.
Therefore, eat of this meat.

    ADAM. To eat it I would not eschew   100
Might I be sure of thy sayings.

    EVE. Bite on boldly, for it is true:
We shall be gods and know all things.

    ADAM. To win that name,
I shall taste it at thy teaching.

    (*He takes and eats.*[5] *Instantly, he is seized with
remorse.*)

Alas, what have I done? For shame!
I'll counsel, woe worth thee!

---

[3] "*Et tunc debet accipere pomum*" reads the manuscript direction.
[4] *Tunc Satanas recedet.*
[5] *Accipit et comedit.*

Ah, Eve, thou art to blame,
To this hast thou enticed me.—
And my body now fills me with shame,   110

   (looking at himself)

For I am naked, as I think—
   Eve. Alas, Adam, right so am I!
   Adam. And for sorrow sere why might we not sink?
For we have grieved God Almighty
      That made me man,
Broken His bidding bitterly,
      Alas, that ever we began!
This work, Eve, hast thou wrought,
And made this bad bargain.
   Eve. Nay, Adam, blame me nought.   120
   Adam. Away, dear Eve, whom then?

   Eve. The worm to blame well worthy were:
With tales untrue we were betrayed.
   Adam. Alas that I listened to thy lore,
Or trusted the trifles thou to me said,
So may I bid,*   pray
For I may curse that bitter braid*   trick
And dreary thing that I did.
And our shape, with shame it grieves—
Wherewith shall our bodies be hid?   130
   (Eve *picks up some leaves, twines them together
and starts to cover herself, and gives* Adam *some
leaves too.*)
   Eve. Let us take this fig-leaf
Since now befalls us this grief.

   Adam. Right as thou say'st so shall it be,
For we are naked and all bare.
Full wondrous fain would I hide me
From the Lord's sight, if I wist* where;   knew
      Where, I would care nought!
   God *(calling)*. Adam! Adam!
   Adam.   Lord?
   God.   Where art thou? Yare!
   Adam. I hear thee, Lord, and see thee not.
   God. Say, whereto does it belong,[6]   140
This work why hast thou wrought?

---

[6] "What is the reason for this?"

ADAM. Lord, Eve made me do this wrong,
And to that breach me brought.

GOD. Say, Eve, why hast thou made thy mate
Eat fruit I bade thee to let hang alway
And commanded none of it to take?
EVE (*weeping*). A worm, Lord, enticed me thereto:
So, welaway!
That ever I this deed did do!
GOD. Ah wicked worm, woe work thee aye*!   forever/150
For thou in this manner
Hast made them such affray,
My curse I give thee here
With all the might I may.

And on thy womb* then shalt thou glide,   belly
And be ever full of enmity
To all mankind on every side;
And earth shall all thy substance be
To eat and drink.
Adam and Eve, also, ye   160
In earth then shall ye sweat and swink*   toil
And labor for your food.
ADAM. Alas, why may we not sink?
We that had the whole world's good,
We shall have much grief to think.

(GOD *turns to an* ANGEL.)
GOD. Now cherubim, my angel bright
To Middle-Earth be swift to drive these two.
ANGEL. All ready, Lord, as it is right,
Since Thy will is that it be so,
And thy liking.—   170
Adam and Eve, do you two go,
For here may ye make no dwelling.
Go ye fast to fare
And of sorrow may ye sing.
ADAM. Alas, for sorrow and care
Our hands may we wring!
(*The* ANGEL *drives* ADAM *and* EVE *out of Paradise.*)

THE FIRST MURDER
The Murder of Abel
(Mactatio Abel)
The Wakefield Glovers' Pageant

A MODERNIZED VERSION BY JOHN GASSNER

Characters

GARCIO* (Cain's boy servant named   boy
 Pikeharnes*)   thief
CAIN
ABEL
GOD

SCENE 1[1]

(*A boy enters cockily and playfully.* CAIN *is heard
calling in the distance.*)

GARCIO. All hail! all hail! both blithe and glad
For here come I, a merry lad.
Silence your din, my master bad,
  Else may the devil you speed.
Know you not I have come before?
But to work now and whoever chatters any more,
He must blow my black hole
Both behind and before
  Till his teeth bleed.
 (*Addressing the audience humorously.*)
  Fellows here! I forbid   10
To make either noise or cry.
  Whoso is so hardy to do that deed
The devil hang him up on the gallows to dry.

Fellows, I am a full great man.
As a good farmer is my master known,
  Full well ye all him ken.*   know
Begin he with you to strive

[1] There are no scene divisions in the original text.

Be sure that you'll never thrive!
But I think, by God in life,
       Some of you are his men.*   workers/20
    (*Making a sign to the audience to be silent.*)
But let your lips cover your teeth,
Rascals everyone!
       And if my master come, welcome him then.
Farewell, I must be gone.
    (*He goes out quickly as* CAIN *appears, ploughing
    and shouting to his ploughteam of oxen and
    horses.*)
    CAIN. Gee up, Gray-horn![2] Gray-horn! and Grime,
       look out!
Pull on! God give you an evil bout.[3]
Ye stand so still like a dizzy lout!
       What! will you no further, mare?
Whoa! Let me see how Down will fare.
All the same, you rogue, pull on a while, 'ware!   30
What! it seems you have no fear of me?
    (*He strikes the mare.*)
       I say, Donnyng, go yare!
       Aha! God give thee sorrow and care!
    (*The mare bestirs herself.*)
Lo! now heard she what I said.
But for all that, you are the worst mare
That ever in plow I have had.

    (*Shouting.*)
How! Pikeharnes, how! come hither fast.
    (*The boy returns, muttering grumpily.*)
    GARCIO. I hope, God forbid it, that thou ever thrive.
    CAIN. What, boy, must I both hold and drive?
Hearest thou not when I cry?   40
    (*The boy now drives the team.*)
    GARCIO. Say Mall and Stolt, will ye not go?
Lemyng, Morell, White-horns, go!
Now, will ye see how fast they hie![4]

    CAIN (*reprovingly*). God give thee sorrow! These
       beasts—it's your not feeding them that mars!

---

    [2] Cain has a plough-team of four oxen and four horses. Gray-horn is
obviously an ox.
    [3] literally, "God give you ill to befall."
    [4] The boy means that the horses won't budge. He is saying sarcastically,
"Now will you not see how they hurry!"

GARCIO (*sarcastically*). Their provender, sir, I lay
    behind their arse,
And tie them fast, I do, by their necks,
And, to be sure, I put many stones in their racks.
    CAIN (*striking him*). Let this pay thee for all thy
    cheek.
    GARCIO (*striking him in return*). And have it back
    again! Right?
    CAIN (*retreating in surprise*). I am thy master! Wilt
    thou fight?   50
    GARCIO. Yea, with the same measure and weight!
What I borrow I will requite.
    CAIN. Enough! Call on the team to speed
That we may plow this land.
    GARCIO. Harrow, Morell, go in haste—
    (*Aside, under his breath.*)
And let the plough stand . . .

    (ABEL, CAIN's *brother, enters.*)
    ABEL. God, as he both may and can,
Speed thee, brother, and thy man.
    CAIN. Come kiss mine arse, I don't want to rail,
But *away from here* thou art welcome—   60
Thou shouldst have waited till I called out "Hail!"
Come nearer and either drive the team or hold the
    plow
And kiss the devil's bum,
For that is thee most lief.*   dear
    ABEL. Brother, there is none hereabout now
That would thee grieve.

But dear brother, hear my saw:*   speech
It is the custom of our law
All that work as the wise
Shall worship God with sacrifice.   70
Our father bade us, our father taught
That our tenth[5] to God should be brought.
Come forth, brother, and let us go
To worship God. We tarry too long:
Give we Him a part of our fee,
Whether corn or cattle it be.

    [5] "tenth" refers to tithes—the tenth of the crop reserved for God as a
burnt offering.

And therefore, brother, let us leave;
But first cleanse us from the fiend
     Before we make sacrifice,
So bliss without an end   80
     Shall we get with our service

Of him that is our salvation's leech*   physician
   CAIN. Ho! Let forth your geese, the fox will preach![6]
How long wilt thou me impeach
     With thy sermonizing?
Hold thy tongue still, I say,
Where the good wife rubbed the hay!
Or sit down in the devil's way
     With thy vain carping.

Should I leave my plow and everything   90
And go with thee to make offering?
Nay! thou findest me not so mad!
Go to the devil, and say I so bade.
What does God give thee to praise him so?
Me gives He nought but sorrow and woe.

   ABEL. Cain, leave this vain carping,
For God gives thee all thy living.
   CAIN. Yet borrowed I never a farthing
Of him here in my hand!
   ABEL. Brother, as our elders gave command,   100
First should we tend* with our hand   tithe
Then to his glory bring the brand.[7]

   CAIN. My farthing is in the priest's hand
Since the last time I offered.
   ABEL. Dear brother, let us cross the land:
I would that our tithes were already proferred.

   CAIN. Whee! Whereof should I tithe, dear brother?
For I am each year worse off than the other.
     My winnings are but mean,
     No wonder that I be lean.   110
Full long to him I may complain!,

[6] When the fox starts preaching, you might as well give up your geese. The old proverb is: "When the fox preacheth, keep an eye on your geese [if you don't want them to be stolen]."
[7] And the "tenth" should be "brend"—that is, burned.

For, by Him that us dearly bought,[8]
I think that he will lend me nought.

ABEL. Certain, all the good that has to thee grown[9]
Of God's good grace is but a loan.

CAIN. Lends He *me?* May such thrift come to thee!
For He has ever yet been my foe.
For had He my friend been,
Otherwise it would have been seen.
When all men's corn was fair in the field   120
Then was my own not worth a needle.
When I wanted to sow and lacked seed,
And of corn had full great need,
Then gave he me none of his;
(*Pointing to his harvest.*)
No more will I give him of this!
Hardly hold me to blame
If I serve him of the same.

audience may find themselves pitying Cain.
he didn't do anything for me, so I won't for him—

ABEL. Dear brother, say not so,
But let us forth together go.
Good brother, let us soon,   130
No longer should we here abide.

CAIN (*sarcastically*). Yea, yea! the words you waste!
The devil speed me if *I* have haste
As long as I may live
To divide my goods and give
Either to God or to a man
Of anything I ever won;
For had I given away my good
Then might I go with a ripped hood,
And it is better to hold what I own   140
Than to go from door to door and beg.

ABEL. Brother, come forth in God's good name,
I am afraid we shall get blame,
Hie* we fast that we get there.   hasten
CAIN. You may run on ahead and in the devil's
     name fare!
Welaway, man, I hold thee mad!
Thinkest thou now that I gad
About to give away goods!—

[8] Note the anachronism of Cain's swearing by Christ, who appears much
later in the course of biblical history.
[9] literally, "all the good [goods] thou has *in wone*"—that is, "customarily."

What need have I my labor to lose
To tear my hose and wear out my shoes?   150

    ABEL. Dear brother it were great wonder
That thou and I should go asunder;
Then would our father have great wonder—
Are we not brothers, you and I?
    CAIN. No: But cry on, while you think it good
Hear my words: I think thee wood*:   mad
Whether God be blithe or wroth[10]
To divide my goods I am full loath.

I have gone oft in softer guise
Where I thought some profit would arise,   160
    (He pauses for a moment and reflects gloomily.)
But well I see that to go I need.
Now go before, ill may you speed!,
Since go we must in any wise.
    ABEL. Dear brother, why says thou so?
But go we forth together—
Blessed be God, we have fair weather.
    (They cross together to the place of sacrifice.)

SCENE 2

At the place of sacrifice.

    (CAIN and ABEL appear.)
    CAIN. Lay down thy bundle upon the hill.
    ABEL. Forsooth brother, so I will,
God of heaven! take it for good.
    CAIN. Thou shalt tithe first, even if thou be wood*   furious/170
    ABEL (kneeling down on the ground). God that
        made both earth and sky,
I pray to thee thou hear my cry;
And take with thanks, if Thy will be,
The tithe that I offer here to Thee;
For I give it with good intent
To Thee, my Lord, that all has sent.
I burn it now, with steadfast thought,
In worship of Him that all has wrought.
    (ABEL sets fire to his offerings of tithes on the crude
    altar of stone, and they burn with a proper blaze.)
    CAIN. Rise up! Let me, since thou art done.—
    (He kneels.)

[10] "Whether He be pleased or angry."

Lord of Heaven, hear thou my plea,   180
And God forbid you showed me
Gratitude or courtesy![11]
For, as I enjoy these two legs
It is full sore, against my will,
That the tenth of my crops I give here—
Of corn or anything that grows for me.
And now will I begin then
Since I must needs my tithe bren*—   burn
One sheaf, *one,* and this makes *two.*
　　(*He holds them, as if weighing them, and they seem
　　to him too good to give away.*)
But neither of these may I forego.   190
　　(*Hesitating.*)
Two, two, now this is *three*—

Yea, this also shall remain with me!
For I will choose and for myself the best sheaves shall
　　have.
This hold I for profit—this sheaf
Oh! Oh! four! lo, here!
　　(*Grudgingly he adds another thin sheaf to the small
　　pile on the one side, having reserved the largest
　　sheaves for himself.*)
Better grew not for me this year!
At the proper season I sowed fair corn,
Yet was it mostly, when it was shorn,
Thistles and briars in great plenty
And all kinds of weeds that might be.   200
Four sheaves, four,
　　(*Adding another grudgingly.*)
　　　　　　　　lo, this maketh *five!*
Devil I fast thus long before I thrive!
　　(*Adding a few more grumpily, and then withhold-
　　ing them.*)
Five and six, now this is seven,—
　　(*Taking a full sheaf back hastily.*)
But this gets never God of heavens.
Nor none of *these* four, by my might,
Shall ever come in Godis* sight.   God's
Seven . . . seven . . . now this is—*eight.*

11 That is, "to show me favor."—"God forbid" is said by Cain to God
Himself.

ABEL. Cain, brother, thou are not betaught.[12]

CAIN. Whee! therefore is it as I say,
For I will not deal my goods away.   210
But had I given him this to tend*   tithe
Then wouldst thou say he were my friend,
But I think not, by my hood,*   head
To depart so lightly from my good.
    (*Forcing himself again to be generous . . . but
    holding back the best sheaves, nevertheless.*)
Whee! eight . . . eight . . . and nine . . . and ten is this.
    (*Noticing the tiniest sheaf happily.*)
Whee! This is one we can miss!
    (*Seeing another sheaf.*)
Give him that which lies thore?*   there
It goes against my heart full sore.

ABEL. Pay the tithe right through.

CAIN (*reluctantly*). Whee! Lo, twelve, fifteen, six-
    teen—   220
    (*He counts with deliberate rapidity and carelessness.*)

ABEL. Cain, thou tithest wrong and of the worst.

CAIN. Whee! Come near and hide my een.*   eyes
In the waning of the moon[13] will you be quiet at last,
Or else wilt thou that I wink?[14]
Then shall I do no wrong, I think.
    (*He continues to count with his eyes shut.*)
Let me see now how it is.
        Lo, yet I hold me paid.
    (*He opens his eyes and observes how he has divided
    the sheaves he laid down in favor of himself. He
    approves.*)
I tithed wonderfully well, I guess,
        And *so even* I laid!

ABEL (*disapproving of the division*). Cain, of God
    methinks thou hast no dread.   230

CAIN (*stubbornly*). Now, if He get more, the devil
    me speed!,
As much as one sheaf:
For that came to him light cheap.
Not as much, neither great nor small,
As one might wipe his arse withall.

---

[12] Not devoted to God.
[13] "In an unlucky time"; or, "Confound you!"
[14] "That I shut my eyes."

For that and this that lies here
Have cost me full dear:
Ere it was shorn and brought in stack*   stacked
Had I many a weary back![15]
Therefore ask me no more of this,   240
For I have all that my will is.

  ABEL. Cain, I counsel thee to tithe right
For dread of Him that sits on the height.
    CAIN. How that *I* tithe care thou not a peep,
But tend thy scabbéd sheep,
For if thou to my tithe attend
It will go worse for thee in the end.
    (*Dangling two rich sheaves in front of* ABEL, *scorn-
fully.*)
Woulds't thou I gave Him this sheaf; or this sheaf?
Naw, neither of these two will I leave.
    (*Giving* ABEL *two scrawny sheaves instead.*)
But take this; now has He two.   250
And, now for my soul, this will do.
Though it goes sore against my will
And He shall like this full ill.

  ABEL. Cain, I counsel thee to tithe
So God of heaven be blithe
And be thy friend!
    CAIN.   My friend? Naw, not unless he will—
I have never done him any ill.
If he be never so my foe
I am yet determined to give him no mo.*   more
—But change thy mind, as I did mine.   260
Thou hast not yet tithed thy leprous swine.
    ABEL. If thou hast tithed right thou soon shalt find.
    CAIN. Yea, kiss the devil's arse behind?
The devil hang thee by the neck!
How I have tithed is not for you to reck.
Wilt thou not yet hold thy place?
This jangling I advise you to cease.
And tithe I well or tithe I ill
Bear thee quiet and speak but skill.[16]
—But since thou hast already tithed thine,   270
Now will I set fire on mine.

[15] Cain means he strained his back getting the grain stacked after it was
harvested.
[16] "Speak only what is right."

(*He sets fire to his paltry tithe of sheaves; but it
smoulders; it won't light even when Cain blows
hard on the fire.*)

CAIN. Whee! out! haro! Help me to blow!
It will not burn for me, I trow.*   believe
    (*Choking as he puffs at the fire.*)
Puff! this smoke does me much shame.—
    (*He becomes furious, and bellows.*)
Now burn! In the devil's name.
    (*Retreating from the smoke to a safe distance.*)
Ah! What devil of hell is it—
Almost has my breath been quit!
Had I but blown one blast the more
I had been choked right sore—
It stank like the devil in hell,   280
That longer there I could not dwell.

    ABEL (*disquieted*). Cain, this is not worth one leek!
Thy tithe should burn without this smoke.

    CAIN (*furiously*). Come kiss the devil right on the
        arse,
Because of thee it burns but the worse!
I would that 'twere in thy throat,
The fire, the sheaf, and every sprote.*   sprout
    (*Now GOD is heard from above.*)
GOD.[17] Cain, why art thou such rebel
Against thy brother Abel?
There is no need to quarrel or chide.   290
If thou do well then wilt thou well abide[18]
And be thou sure if thou tithe falsely
    (*Sarcastically.*)
Thou wilt be praised accordingly.

    CAIN (*grumpily*). Why, who is that hob[19] over the
        wall?
Whee! Who was that that piped so small?
Come, go we hence, for perils all!
God is out of his wit.
Come forth, Abel, and let us wend*—   go
Methink that God is *not* my friend;
Far away then will I flit.*   flee/300

[17] Here and in other manuscripts of the medieval plays, God is given by
his Latin designation, *Deus.*
[18] Literally, "thou will get thy mede"—that is, **reward.**
[19] A prankster in Yorkshire folklore.

ABEL. Cain, brother, that is ill done.

CAIN. No, but go we hence soon;
And if I may, I shall be
Where God himself shall not see.

ABEL (*trying to get away from* CAIN). Dear brother,
    I will fare
On the field where our beasts are,
To look out if they be empty or full.

CAIN. Na, na, abide! We have a bone to pick.[20]
Hark! Speak with me before thou go.
What, dost thou think to 'scape so?   310
No, stay! I owe thee a foul play,
And now is the time that I repay.

ABEL. Brother, why are you so in ire?*   anger

CAIN (*gloomily*). Why burned thy tithe in so clear
    a fire
While mine, it but smoked,
Right as it would us both have choked?

ABEL. God's will, I believe, it were
That mine did burn so clear,
If thine smoked, am I to blame?

CAIN. Yea! And thou shalt repay my shame:[21]   320
With cheek-bone straightway
Shall I thee and thy life divide.

(CAIN *strikes* ABEL *down with the jaw-bone of an
animal he has picked up from the ground.*)
So, lie down there and take thy rest—
Thus shall rogues be chastised best.

ABEL (*dying*). Vengeance, vengeance, Lord, I cry!
For I am slain and not guiltily.
(*He dies.*)

CAIN. Yea, lie there, villain, lie there, lie!
(CAIN *addresses the audience arrogantly.*)
And if any of you think I did amiss,
I shall *amend* it *worse* than it is!
That all men may it see   330
Well worse than it is;
Right so shall it be.
But now, since he* is brought to sleep,   Abel
Into some hole fain would I creep;
For fear I quake and am without a thought,

[20] Literally, "we have a crow to pull."
[21] Literally, "thou shalt it sore abite"—that is, "pay."

For I am a dead man if I be caught.
  (Finding a hiding place.)
Here will I lie* these forty days,   hide
And a curse on him who will me raise.[22]
  (GOD *speaks from above.*)
  GOD. Cain! Cain!
  CAIN (*fearfully*). Who is it that calls me?
I am yonder, canst thou not see?   340
  GOD. Cain, where is thy brother Abel?
  CAIN. Why ask me? I do believe in hell,
In hell I think he be—
Whoso were *there* then might he see—
Or somewhere may be sleeping.
  (*Brazening it out . . . curtly.*)
When was he in my keeping?

  GOD. Cain, Cain, thou was wood!
The voice of thy brother's blood
That thou hast slain in false wise
From earth to heaven vengeance cries!   350
And because thou hast cast thy brother down
Here I give thee my malison.*   curse

  CAIN. Yea, deal it about thyself, for I will none,
Or take it to thee when I am gone!
Since I have done so very much sin
That I may not thy mercy win,
And thou has thrust me from thy grace,
I shall hide me from thy face.
And whereso any man may find me,
Let him slay me hardily,   360
And wherever any man I meet
Either in lane or street.
And certainly when I am dead
Bury me in Gudeboure[23] at the quarry-head.
But should I pass this place in good part,[24]
For all men I would not give a fart!

  GOD. Nay, Cain, it shall not be so:
I order that no man another slay,
And he that slays thee, young or old,
He shall be punished sevenfold.

[22] "Who will drive me out of hiding."
[23] A place in the Wakefield area, where a quarry is located.
[24] That is, safely.

CAIN. No matter! I know whither I shall:
In hell I know must be my stall.   370
It is no use mercy to crave;
For even if I pray, I must none have.

But this corpse, I would it were hid,
For some man might come upon it amain.
"Flee, false villain," would he bid,
And suspect I had my brother slain.

But were Pikeharnes, my servant, here,
We should bury him together near.
    (*He calls out.*)
How! Pikeharnes! Scapethrift! How! Pikeharnes, how!
    (*In response to* CAIN's *call,* GARCIO *appears, and*
    CAIN *gives him a blow.*)
    GARCIO (*recoiling*). Master, master!   380
    CAIN. Do you hear, boy? There is a pudding in the
        pot.[25]
        Take thee that, boy, take thee that!
    GARCIO. A curse on thy head under thy hood,
Even though thou were my sire of flesh and blood!
All the day to run and trot
And evermore to be struck is my lot
And buffetings to stand.
    CAIN (*trying to placate him*). Peace, man! I did it
        but to use* my hand!   practice

But hark, boy, I have something to thee to say—
I slew my brother this same day;   390
I pray thee, good boy, if thou may,
To take away the body.
    GARCIO. Whee! Out upon thy villainy!
So thou didst thy brother slay?
    CAIN. Peace, man, for Godis pain!

I said it for a jest.
    GARCIO (*skeptically*). Yea! But for fear of grievance
Here I thee forsake,
We shall have mighty mischance
And the bailiffs will us take.[26]   400

    CAIN. Ah, sir, I cry you mercy. Cease,
And I shall give you a release![27]

[25] "There is business to attend."
[26] Note the anachronistic references to bailiffs in the time of Cain and Abel.
[27] Release for the boy from indenture to Cain, one may assume.

GARCIO (*scornfully*). What, wilt thou cry my peace[28]
Throughout the land?

CAIN. Yea! And I give God at once my vow.
GARCIO. How will you do that, may you never
    prosper?
CAIN. Come stand up my good boy now
And order silence to both man and wife;
And whoso will do after me
Then smooth of fortune shall he be.   410
But thou must be my good boy
And cry "Oyez, Oyez, Oy."[29]

GARCIO (*mocking him*). Browes,* browes, to thy   broth
    boy.

(CAIN *proclaims the king's protection, as was cus-*
tomary in the Middle Ages—while the boy mocks
him with asides to the audience.)

CAIN. I command you in the King's name——
GARCIO. And in my master's, false Cain!
CAIN. That no man them[30] may fault nor blame——
GARCIO. Yea! Cold roast is at my master's hame.*   home
CAIN. Neither with him nor his knave*——   servant
GARCIO. What, I think my master does rave!
CAIN. For they are true, full manifold——   420
GARCIO. My master sups but cabbage cold!
CAIN. The King writes this to you of his will——
GARCIO. Yet ate I never half my fill.
CAIN. The King wills that they be safe——
GARCIO. Yea! A draft of drink fain would I have.
CAIN. On their own let them fare and not
    grieve——
GARCIO. My stomach is ready to receive.
CAIN. Make sure that no man say to them, one or
    the other——
GARCIO. The same is he that slew his brother!
CAIN. Bid every man them love and lout*——   revere/430
GARCIO. Yea, ill-spun weft always foul comes out.
CAIN (*angrily to the boy*). Ill may you prosper if
    thus you go about!

(*He continues to proclaim "the king's protection."*)
Bid that every man them please and pay——

---

[28] "Proclaim that I am under the king's protection."
[29] A call for silence in court, as Cain proclaims the "King's protection"
for the boy, as he promised him.
[30] Meaning Garcio and himself.

GARCIO (*sarcastically*). Yea! give Don, thy horse, a
   wisp of hay!
(*He climbs up a tree out of reach as* CAIN *tries to
strike him.*)
   CAIN. Boy! Come down in twenty devil's way!
May the devil thee take!
For but for Abel, my brother,
Yet knew I never thy mate.
   (*At this* GARCIO, *the boy, addresses the audience.*)
   GARCIO. Now old and young, who here attend,
The same blessing without an end   440
That God of heaven my master has given
Altogether ye may have it.

   CAIN (*to the boy*). Come down yet, in the devil's
   way,
And anger me no more!
And take yonder plow, I say,
And go thou forth fast before.
And then I shall, if I may,
Teach thee another lore.*   lesson
I warn thee, lad, for aye,*   once and for all/450
From now forth evermore
That thou grieve me nought;
For by God's sides, if thou do,
I shall hang thee upon this plow,
By Him that me dear bought![31]
   (GARCIO *goes out, leaving* CAIN *to address the audi-
   ence.*)
Now farewell, fellows all, for I must needs wend
And to the devil be thrall,* world without end;   slave
Ordered is my stall with Satan, the fiend.
Ever ill might them befall that thither me commend,
Beside!
Fare well less and fare well more,   460
For now and evermore
I will go to hide!

---

[31] Another anachronism, of course, since this phrase refers to Jesus Christ.

THE DELUGE

Noah and His Sons
The Wakefield Pageant

A MODERNIZED VERSION BY JOHN GASSNER

Characters
GOD

NOAH	FIRST SON	FIRST SON'S WIFE
NOAH'S WIFE	SECOND SON	SECOND SON'S WIFE
	THIRD SON	THIRD SON'S WIFE

NOAH. Almighty God so true, maker of all this,
Three persons without a doubt, *one* God in endless
    bliss,
Thou hast made both night and day, beast, fowl, and
    fish;
All creature that can live hast Thou wrought at thy
    wish,
As thou well might.
The sun, the moon, verament,*   *truly*
Thou hast made; the firmament,
The stars also full fervent,*   *glowing*
To shine full bright.

Angels hast thou made, all orders, that is,   10
In heaven to have bliss
Full marvellous to name. Yet was there unkindness
More by seven fold that I can well express.
Forwhy?* Because   *why?*
Of all angels in brightness
God gave Lucifer the most lightness,*   *brightness*
Yet proudly he moved his dais[1]
To where he set himself equal with His ways.[2]
He thought himself as worthy as God that him made
In brightness, in beauty. Therefore to degrade   20

---

[1] "Des"—throne or seat; Old French, "deis"; therefore "dais."
[2] Literally, "set himself on a level with Him."

God put him in a low degree soon after, in a brade,*   moment
Him and his company where he should be unglad
For ever.
They shall never get away
From there until Doomsday,
But burn in bale* for aye.*   misery/forever
They shall depart never.

Of the Trinity by agreement, Adam and Eve that
      woman
To multiply without discord in Paradise put He them
And then to both   30
Gave in commandment
On that tree of life to lay no hand.
But yet the false fiend
Made Him with man wroth.*   angry

Enticed man to gluttony, stirred him to sin in pride.
But in Paradise might no sin abide,
And therefore man was put out in that tide*   time
In woe and wandering to be and pains full hard
To know
First on earth, and then in hell—   40
There with fiends to dwell;
But God still mercy cried[3]
To those that to him are true.[4]
Oil of mercy He has promised, I have heard read,[5]
To every living person that would love him and
      dread,
But now before His sight every living man
Most part of day and night sins in word or deed
Full bold:
Some in pride, ire, and envy,
Some in covetousness and gluttony,   50
Some in sloth and lechery,
And other ways manifold.
      (Here there may be a procession of the Seven
      Deadly Sins across the stage.—J.G.)
Therefore I fear lest God take vengeance,
For sin is approved by us without repentance.
Six hundred years and odd have I, without distance,*   doubt
On earth, as any sod, lived with great aggrievance

      [3] Literally, "declared."
      [4] Literally, "that believe in Him" ("trawe").
      [5] Literally, "I have heard tell."

Alway.*   continually
And now I wax old,
Sick, sorry, and cold;—
As muck upon mold*   earth/60
I wither away.

But yet will I cry mercy and call:—
Noah, thy servant, am I, Lord over all!
Lest that I and my children shall fall,
Save us from Villainy and bring us to thy hall
In heaven;
And keep me from sin
With this world in![6]
Comely King of men,
I pray thou hear my stevyn.*   voice/70

(GOD *speaks from above.*)
GOD. Since I have made each thing that is bred,
Duke, emperor, and king, with mine own hand,
To live to their liking by sea and by strand,
Every man to my bidding should bow his head
        Full fervent;
I made man such a creature,
Fairest of favor,
Who must love for ever
        With reason, and repent.

Methought I showed man love when I made him to be   80
All angels above, like to the Trinity.
And now in great reproof full low lies he.
In earth himself to glut with sins that displease me
        Most of all.
Vengeance will I take
In earth, for sin's sake;
My anger will I wake
        Both 'gainst great and small.

I repent full sore that ever made 1 man.
By me he sets no store who am his sovereign;   90
I will destroy therefore beast, man, and woman,
        That evil do.
In earth I see right nought
But sin, all unatoned;

---

[6] Literally, "This world [warld] within."

Of those that well have wrought*   done
    Find I but few.

Therefore shall I undo all this earth and more
With waters that shall flow and rain with hideous
    roar.
I have good cause thereto, since for me no man hath
    awe.
As I say, so shall I do; of vengeance draw my sword   100
    And make end
Of all that beareth life,
Save Noah and his wife;
For they would never strive
    With me nor to offend.

To him to his great gain, hastily will I go—
To Noah at once, at once, to warn him of his woe.
On earth I see but sin reigning to and fro
Among both great men and low
On evil intent.   110
All shall I undo*   "fordo," destroy
With floods that shall flow;
I shall work them woe
That will not repent.

    (GOD, *appearing in human shape, now addresses*
    NOAH, *who has not previously observed His pres-*
    ence.)
Noah, my friend, I thee command thy sorrows to
    dispel:
Do thou but make a ship of nail and board full well.
Thou wast e'er a trusty workman, to me as true as
    steel;
For thy lasting faithful friendship shalt thou feel
    Reward.
Of length thy ship let be   120
Three hundred cubits, I tell thee,
Of height even thirty,
    And fifty also broad.*   wide

Anoint thy ship with pitch and tar, without and
    within;
To keep the water out you must win.[7]

    [7] Literally, "is a clever trick, (*gin*)."

Let no man thee hinder: and three chief* rooms   cabin
    begin.
Thou must use many a beam ere thy present work
       Shall end fully.
Make in thy ship also
Parlors, one or two,   130
And other houses, too,
       For beasts therein must be.

One cubit on height a window shalt thou make,
On the side a door, with skill, shalt thou take,
While with thee shall no man fight, nor do thee any
    hate.
When all is done thus right, thy wife, that is thy
    mate,
       Take in to thee;
Thy three sons of good fame,
Japhet, Sehm and Hame;
       Their wives also, all three.   140

For all shall be fordone that live on earth but ye,
With floods that from above shall fall and that
     plentily;
It shall begin full soon to rain incessantly
After seven days more, and lasting full forty,
       Without fail.
Take into thy ship also
Beasts of each kind, but two,
Male and female, and no mo,
       Ere thou put up thy sail.

That it may thee avail, when all this is wrought,   150
Stuff thy ship with victual, for hunger that ye perish
    not.
The beasts, fowl, and cattle have thou them in
    thought;
For them, it is my counsel, that succour be sought
       In haste;
Thou must have corn and hay,
And other meat alway.
Do now as I say
       In the name of the Holy Ghost.

    NOAH. Ah! benedicite*! What art thou that thus   God's blessing
Thou tells before what shall be? Thou art full
     marvelous!   160

Tell me, for Charity, thy name so gracious.

God. My name is of dignity, and also full glorious
To know.
I am God most mighty,
One God in trinity,
Who made thee and each man to be:
To love me well you owe.

Noah. I thank thee, Lord so dear, that would
    vouchsave
Thus below to appear to a simple knave;*   person
Bless us, Lord, here; this for charity I crave,   170
The better that we may steer the ship that we shall
    have
        Certain.

God. Noah, to thee and to thy fry
My blessing grant I;
Ye shall wax and multiply,
    And fill the earth again,

When all these floods are past and fully gone away.
                  (God *exits.*)
Noah. Lord, homeward will I haste as fast as I may.
My wife will I see and hear what she say.
I am afraid there will be some fray   180
    Between us both;
For she is full testy,
For little oft angry;
If any thing wrong be
    Soon is she wroth.

(Noah's Wife *enters.*)
God-speed, dear wife, how fare ye?
    Wife. Now, as ever might I thrive, the worst is that
    I see thee;
And tell me now at once where hast thou thus long
    been?
To death may we drive, or live for thee
    In want indeed;   190
When we sweat or swink,*   toil
Thou dost what thou think,
Yet of meat or of drink
    Have we much need.

Noah. Wife, we are hard placed with tidings new.

WIFE. Better that thou wert clad in Stafford blue,
For thou art always afraid, be it false or true;
But God knows, I am led, and that may I rue,
    Full ill.
For I dare be thy pledge,   200
From evening unto morrow
Thou speakest ever of sorrow;
    God send thee for once thy fill.

    (*To the women in the audience.*)
We women may curse all ill husbands;
I have one, by Mary, that should loose me of my
    bands;
If he be vexed, I must tarry, wringing both my hands
    For dread.
But some other while,
Yet with game and with guile,
I shall smite and smile   210
    And give him his meed.*   deserts, due
    NOAH. Hold thy tongue, ram-skit, or I shall
    make thee still.
    WIFE. By my thrift, if thou smite, I shall set on
    thee too.
    NOAH. I will try quickly. Have at thee, Jill,
    (*He strikes her.*)
Upon the bone shall it bite.
    WIFE.   Ah, so, marry, thou smitest ill,
    But I suppose
I shall not owe thee more
Ere I quit this floor.
    (*She strikes back with a strap, or thong.*)
Take thee here this thong
To tie up thy hose.   220

    NOAH. Ah, wilt thou so?
    WIFE. Thou shalt have three for two, I promise
    thee well!
    NOAH. And I shall pay *thee* back, though it be a
    sin.
    WIFE. Out upon thee, ho!
    NOAH.   Thou canst both bite and whine
With great noise.
    (*To the men in the audience.*)
For if she wants to strike
She'll be *fast* to strike.

In faith, I hold none the like
In the world.

But I will keep charity, for much must I do.   230
   WIFE. Here shall no man delay thee; I pray thee
     go to.
Full well may we do without thee, as is true!—
To spin will I go now.
   NOAH.   Fare thee well, go.
      But, wife,
Pray for me busily
Ere I come back to thee.
   WIFE. For all that thou prayest for me,
Well might I thrive!
                      (*Exit* WIFE.)
   NOAH. I tarry full long from my work, I trow;*   believe
Now my gear will I fetch and thitherward draw;
I may go full wrong, the truth I know,   240
But if God help not now, I may sit in sorrow, I see.
Now will I try
How I can do carpentry,
In nomine patris, et filii,
     Et spiritus sancti, Amen.[8]
  (*He starts pulling down a tree.*)
To begin with this tree, my bones will I bend.
I trust that the Trinity succor will send—
It fares full fair, as my hand I lend.
Now blessed be He that this can amend*!   set right
  (*Measuring the timber.*)
Lo! here the length,   250
Three hundred cubits evenly;
Of breadth, lo, is it fifty.
The height is an even thirty
Cubits' full strength.
  (*He starts removing his overcoat, or "gown" as he
  grows warm from his work, wearing only his jacket,
  or "coat."*)
My gown will I cast, and work in my coat.
The mast will I make, ere I stir a foot.
My back, I fear, will burst, and this is a sorry note.
It is a wonder that I last, such an old dote,*   dotard
     All dulled.

---

  [8] "In the name of the Father, and of the Son, and of the Holy Ghost.
Amen."

To begin such a work   260
My bones are so stiff,
No wonder if they ache,
    For I am full old.

The top and the sail both will I make,
The helm and the castle also will I take.
This work will never fail that I undertake
    Anon.
This is a noble gin*;   trick
.These nails so they run
Through great and small,
    These boards each one.   270

Window and door, even as he said,
Three chief chambers that are well made,
Pitch and tar full sure thereupon laid,
This will ever endure; I am satisfied.
    And why?
It is better wrought
Than I could have thought.
Him that made all of nought
    I thank only.   280
Now will I hie me, that nothing miscarry,
My wife and my household to bring now hither.
  (*Enter* WIFE, SONS, *and* SONS' WIVES.)
Take heed in good time, wife, and consider;
Hence must we flee one with another
    In haste.
  WIFE. Why, sir, what ails you?
What is that which assails you?
To flee will not avail you
If you be aghast.*   frightened
  NOAH (*seeing his* WIFE *still busy spinning*). There
    is other yarn on the reel⁹   290
  WIFE. Every bit of it! Or you'll get blame.
  NOAH. He that cares for us, blessed be his name!
Has for our safety, to shield us from shame,
    Foresaid*   promised
That all this world about
With waters so stout
That shall run in a rout
    Shall be overlaid.

  ⁹ "There is other business to be done."

He said all shall be slain, save us alone,
Our bairns so obedient, and their wives all three.   300
A ship he bade me fashion, to save us and our goods;
Therefore with all our house thank we his grace,
    The healer of bale.*   *suffering, sorrow*
Hie us fast; go we hither.
    WIFE. I know not whither;
I am dazed and I dither
    For fear at thy tale.

    NOAH. Be not afraid; have done; pack up our gear.
That we be there ere noon, without more fear.
    FIRST SON. It shall full soon be done. Brother, help   310
      me to bear.
    SECOND SON. I shall not long tarry, but take my
      share.
      Brother Shem.
    THIRD SON. Without any boast now
With my might shall I help you.
    WIFE. Yet for fear that she beat you
      Help well thy dame.*   *mother*
    (*They go to the Ark: all except* WIFE *go on board.*)
    NOAH. Now we are there, as we should be,
Get in our gear, our goods, and cattle, ye,
In this vessel here, my children free.*   *admirable*
    WIFE (*hesitating to step on board*).
      I was never barred in before—
    (*Sarcastically.*)
In such an hostelry as this.   320
In faith, I cannot find
Which is before and which is behind!
Shall we be in this thing penned?
Tell me, as you hope to have bliss.

    NOAH (*speaking to her from the deck of the Ark*).
    Dame, as it is right, here must us abide grace;
Therefore, Wife, with good will come into this place.
    WIFE. Sir, nor for Jack nor for Jill, will I turn my
    face
Till I have on this distaff spun a space
    On this rock.[10]
Now down will I set me,   330

---

[10] Literally, "hill."

Yet counsel I no man to stop me,
    For fear of a knock.
  NOAH (*pleading with her*). Behold in the heaven
    the cataracts all
That are open open even now, great and small.
And the planets seven have left their place;
  (*It has started to rain.*)
These thunders and lightning will cause the downfall
    Full stout
On all halls and bowers,
Castles and towers.
Full sharp are these showers   340
    That are pouring all about.

Therefore, wife, have done, come into ship fast
  WIFE (*jeering*). Yea, Noah, go clout your shoes[11];
    the better will they last!
  FIRST DAUGHTER-IN-LAW. Good mother, come in
    soon, for all is overcast,
  SECOND DAUGHTER-IN-LAW. And many a wind blast
Full sharp!
These floods so they run,
Therefore, mother come in!
  WIFE. In faith, yet will I spin:
All in vain ye carp.

  THIRD DAUGHTER-IN-LAW. If you like you may spin,
    mother, in the ship.   350
  NOAH. Now come thee in, dame, on my friendship.
  WIFE. Whether I lose or I win now thy fellowship
I care not a pin; this spindle I shall slip
    Upon this hill
Ere I stir one foot.
  NOAH. Peter! I trow we dote.*   talk foolishly
Without another note
    Come in if ye will.

  WIFE (*giving in somewhat*). Yea, the water comes so
    near, that I sit not dry—
Into the ship quickly therefore will I hie,   360
For dread that I drown here.
  NOAH.   Dame, surely
It hath cost full dear, ye abode so long by
    Out of the ship.

---

[11] "Go mind your business."

WIFE (*defiantly*). I will not do thy bidding.
To go, when you call, skipping.[12]
    NOAH. In faith, for your long tarrying
        You shall taste of the whip.
    WIFE. Spare me not, I pray thee, do even as you
      think;
Thy great words shall not flay me.
    (NOAH *beats her*.)
    NOAH.   Abide, then, dame, and drink;
For beaten thou shalt be with this staff till thou stink.   370
Are my strokes good? Tell me!
    WIFE.   What say you, Wat Wynk[13]?
    NOAH. Speak,
Cry me mercy, I say.
    WIFE. Thereto say I "Nay!"
    NOAH. If thou dost not, by this day,
        Thy head shall I break.

    (*At this the* WIFE *addresses the audience*.)
    WIFE. Lord, would I be easy, and full of good
      cheer,
Might I have but one meal of true widow's fare;
For thy soul I would be pleased to pay for a prayer.
So would others, no doubt, that I see in this place   380
        Of wives that are here,
For the life that they are led
Wish their husbands were dead;
For, as ever I eat bread,
        I would so *my* master were!
    (NOAH *addresses the audience in his turn*.)
    NOAH. Ye men that have wives; whilst they are
      young,
If you love but your lives, chastise their tongue.
Methink my heart rises, liver too, and lung,
To see so much strife among
Wedded men.—But I,   390
As I hope to have bliss,
Shall chastise this.
    WIFE (*defiantly*). Yet you may miss,
Nicoll Neddy![14]

---

[12] Literally, "to go at once"—"from door to midden."
[13] Wat Wynk is a comic nickname.
[14] Derogatory nickname.

NOAH (*threatening her further*). I shall make thee
 still as a stone, thou beginner of blunder![15]
I shall beat thy back and bone, and break all in
 sunder.
(*He beats her. They fight fiercely until both have
had enough.*)
WIFE. Out, alas, I am gone! Out upon thee, man's
 wonder!
NOAH. See how she can groan, and *I* lie under!
 But wife,
Let us this quarrel stop!
For my back is near in two.   400
WIFE (*agreeing*). I am beaten so blue
 That I am all asunder.
FIRST SON. Ah, why fare ye thus? father and mother
 both!
SECOND SON. Ye should not be so spiteful, standing
 all in wroth—
THIRD SON. These weathers are so hideous, with
 many a cough.
NOAH. We will do as ye bid us, we will no more be
 wroth,
 Dear children.
But now to the helm will I bend
And my ship tend.   410
WIFE. I see in the firmament,
 Methink, the seven stars.
(*A time lapse is indicated here.*)
NOAH. This is a great flood, wife, take heed.
WIFE. So methought, as I stood; we are in great
 dread,
 The waves are so wild.
NOAH.   Help, God, in this need
As thou art steersman good, and best to lead
 Of all;
Rule us now in this sea,
As thou didst promise me.
WIFE. This is a parlous case;   420
 Help, God, when we call!

NOAH. Wife, take the steer-tree, and I will assay
The depth of the sea to test if I may.

[15] Reference, probably, to the fall of Adam, encompassed by Eve in the
Garden of Eden. Womankind was often blamed in the Middle Ages for man's
fallen state.

WIFE. That shall I do full wiseıy; now go thy way,
For upon this flood have we sailed many a day
    With sorrow.
  NOAH. Now the water will I sound.
  (*He lowers a plummet to measure the depth of the
water.*)
Ah! It is far to the ground.
This labor to expound
    I have no zeal!   430

Above all this at once, the water is risen late
Cubits fifteen, but in a lower state
It may not be, I ween, for this well I know,
That forty days has rain been; it will therefore abate
    Full lele.*   sure
This water in haste,
Again will I try;
Now am I aghast
  (*He lowers the plummet again.*)
    It has waned a great deal.

Now are the waters ceased and the cataracts stayed,   440
Both the most and the least.
  WIFE. Methinks, by my wit,
The sun shines in the east; is not yonder it?
We should have a good feast did these floods flit,
    And leave us!
  NOAH. We have been here, all we,
Three hundred days and fifty.
  WIFE. Yea, now wanes the sea,
Lord, it is well with us!
  (*He starts to lower the plummet once more.*)
  NOAH. The third time will I probe what deepness
    we bear.   450
  WIFE. How long shall thou delay? Lay in thy line
    there!
  NOAH. I may touch with my hand the ground even
    here.
  WIFE. Then begins to grow with us merry cheer;
    But, husband,
What ground may this be?
  NOAH. The hills of Armenye.*   Armenia
  WIFE. Now blessed be he
    That this for us hath ordained.

NOAH. I see tops of hills here, many at a sight,
Nothing to delay me, the weather is so bright.   460
    WIFE. There are of God's mercy tokens full right.
    NOAH. Dame, thy counsel; what fowl best might,
        And could
With flight of wing
Bring, without tarrying,
Of mercy some tokening
        Either by north or south?

For this is the first day of the tenth month, I would
    wager.
    WIFE. The raven will come again soon
As fast as thou canst cast him forth; have done!   470
He may come back today before noon
        With favor.
    (NOAH *sends out the raven.*)
    NOAH. I will cast out also
Doves, one or two:
    (NOAH *sends out the doves, too.*)
Go your way, go!
        God send you some prey.

Now these fowl are flown into far country,
Pray we fast, each one, kneeling on our knee,
To him that is alone worthiest of degree
That he will send anon our fowls something   480
        To gladden us.
    WIFE. They may not fail of land,
The water so is waning.
    NOAH. Thank we God Almighty,
        The Lord that made us.
    (*A time lapse here.*)
It is a wondrous thing, methink soothly,*   truly
They are so long tarrying, the fowls, that we
Cast out in the morning.
    WIFE.   Sir, it may be
They tarry till they find something to bring.
    NOAH.   The raven is a hungry beast   490
        Alway;
He is without any reason:
If he find no carrion,

As peradventure may befall,
  He will not away.[16]
The dove is more gentle, her I trust myself to;
Like unto the turtle,* she is ever true.   turtle-dove
 WIFE. Here but a little distance she comes—
   (calling to it) Lew! lew!
She brings, in her bill, some tidings new.
  Behold!   500
It is of an olive tree
A branch it seems to me.
 NOAH. It is so, surely,
  Right so is it called.

Dove, bird full blest, fairness thee befall!
Thou art as true for trust as stone in the wall;
Full well it I wist,* thou would come to thy hall.   knew
 WIFE. A true token it is, we shall be saved all.
  For why?
The water since she came   510
Is fallen a fathom
  And more, think I!

 FIRST SON. These floods are gone—father, behold.
 SECOND SON. There is left right none, and so let us
  be bold.
 THIRD SON. As still as a stone our ship is set.
 NOAH. Upon land here anon, fain I would get
  My children dear,
Shem, Japhet, and Hame,
With glee and with game,
Come we together;   520
  We will no longer need to abide here.

 WIFE. Here have we been nigh long enough now,
With sorrow and grief, dread and much woe.
 NOAH. Behold on this green neither cart nor plow
Is left, as I ween, neither tree nor bough,
  Nor other thing.
But all is away.
Many castles, I say,
Great towns of array*   splendor
  Destroyed has this flowing.   530

 [16] "If he finds no carrion, he will persist in looking for it and fail to
return to us."

WIFE. The flood undeterred this world wide
Has swept away everything.
   NOAH. To death they were doomed, proudest of
     pride
Every creature that ever was spied
     With sin.
All are slain
And put into pain.
   WIFE. From thence again
     They may never win.
   NOAH. Win? No, in faith; unless He that might has   540
Would remember their sorrow and admit them to
     grace.
As He in affliction is comfort, I pray him in this
     space,
In heaven high with his own to give us a place;
     That we
With his saints in sight,
And his angels bright,
May come to his light.
     Amen, for charity.

THE BROME

Abraham and Isaac

A MODERNIZED VERSION BY JOHN GASSNER

Characters

ABRAHAM	AN ANGEL
ISAAC	DOCTOR, or teacher

(*A hilly landscape.* ABRAHAM *and* ISAAC *are kneeling on a level piece of ground.*)[1]
   ABRAHAM. Father of Heaven, omnipotent
     With all my heart to thee I call.

[1] Stage directions have been interpolated by the editor, except as noted
below.

Thou has given me both land and rent.
And my livelihood thou hast me sent.
    I thank thee highly evermore for all.

First of the earth thou madest Adam,
    And Eve also to be his wife;
All other creatures from these two came.
And now thou hast granted to me, Abraham,
    Here in this land to lead my life.   10

In my age thou has granted me this
    That this young child with me shall dwell.
I love nothing so much in this,
Except thine own self, dear Father of Bliss,
    As Isaac here, my own sweet son.

I who have many children mo'
    Love them not as half so well.
This fair sweet child he cheers me so
In every place wherever I do go,
    That of no affliction may I tell.   20

And therefore, Father of Heaven, I thee pray
    For his health and also for his grace.
Now, Lord, keep him both night and day
That never discomfort nor dismay
    Come to my child in any place.
  (Rising.)
Now come on, Isaac, my own sweet child,
    Go we home and take our rest.

  ISAAC. Abraham, mine own father so mild,
To follow you I am full pleased,
    Both early and late.   30

  ABRAHAM. Come on, sweet child. I love thee best
    Of all the children that ever I begot.
*(ABRAHAM and ISAAC start on their homeward journey.
GOD and an ANGEL appear.)*
  GOD. Mine angel, fast hie thee thy way,
    And unto middle-earth anon thou go—
Abram's heart now will I assay,
    Whether that he be steadfast or no.

Say I commanded him for to take
    Isaac, his young son that he loves so well,

And with his blood sacrifice he make,
    If any of my friendship he would feel.   40

Show him the way unto the hill
    Where that his sacrifice shall be.
I shall assay now his good will,
    Whether he loveth better his child or me.
All men shall take example by him
    My commandments how to keep.
    (*As the* ANGEL *descends,* ABRAHAM, *moved in spirit,
kneels again.*)
    ABRAHAM. Now, Father of Heaven, that formed
    everything,
    My prayers I make to thee again,
For this day a tender offering
    Here must I give to thee certain.   50
Ah, Lord God, almighty King,
    What manner of beast would'st thou fain?
If I had thereof true knowing,
    It should be done with all my main
        Full soon by me.
To do thy pleasure on a hill,
Verily, it is my will,
    Dear Father, God in Trinity!
    (*The* ANGEL *reaches* ABRAHAM, *while* ISAAC *has wan-
dered off.*)
    ANGEL. Abraham, Abraham, be at rest!
    Our Lord commandeth thee to take   60
Isaac, thy young son whom thou lovest best,
    And with his blood that sacrifice thou make.

Into the Land of Vision do thou go,
    And offer thy child unto thy Lord;
I shall thee lead and also show.
    To God's behest, Abraham, accord,

And follow me upon this green!

    ABRAHAM. Welcome to me be my Lord's command!
    And his word I will not withstand.
    Yet Isaac, my young son in hand,   70
A full dear child to me has been.

I had rather, if God had been pleased,
    To have forborne all the goods that I have,

Than Isaac, my son, should be deceased,—
 So God in heaven my soul may save!

I have loved never a thing so much on earth,
 And now I must the child go kill!
Ah, Lord God, my conscience lacketh mirth!
And yet, my dear Lord, I am sore afeared
 To grudge anything against thy will.   80

I love my child as my life,
 But yet I love my God much more
For though my heart should make any strife
Yet will I not spare for child or wife,
 But do after my dread Lord's lore.

Though I love my son never so well,
 Yet smite off his head soon I shall.
Ah, Father of Heaven! to thee I kneel—
A hard death my son shall feel,
 To honor thee, Lord, withal!   90

 ANGEL. Abraham, Abraham, this is well said,
  And all these commandments look that thou keep,—
But in thy heart be nothing dismayed.

 ABRAHAM. Nay, nay, forsooth, I hold me well repaid
  To please my God to the best that I may.
For though my heart be heavily set
  To see the blood of my own dear son,
Yet for all that I will not let,
But Isaac, my son, I will go get,
  And come as fast as ever we can.   100
 (*The* ANGEL *departs and* ABRAHAM *looks for his son.*)
 ABRAHAM. Now, Isaac, my own son dear,
  Where art thou, child? Speak to me.

 ISAAC. My father, sweet father, I am here,
  And make my prayers to the Trinity.

 ABRAHAM. Rise up, my child, and fast come hither,
  My gentle bairn that art so wise,
For we, too, child, must go together,
  And unto my Lord make sacrifice.
 (ISAAC *rises and goes to him.*)
 ISAAC. I am full ready, my father, lo!
  Given to your hands, I stand right here;   110

And whatsoever ye bid me do, even so
    It shall be done with glad cheer,
      Full well and fine.

  ABRAHAM. Ah, Isaac, my own son so dear,
    God's blessing I give thee, and mine.

Hold this faggot upon thy back,
    And I myself fire shall bring.

  ISAAC. Father, all this here will I pack;
    I am full fain to do your bidding.
  ABRAHAM. Ah, Lord of Heaven!   120
  (ABRAHAM *looks up to heaven, and wrings his hands.*)
This child's words all do wound my heart!
  (*Controlling himself and turning to* ISAAC.)
Now, Isaac, son, go we on our way
    Unto yon mount with all our main.

  ISAAC. Go we, my dear father, as fast as I may;
    To follow you I am full fain,
      Although I be slender.
  (ABRAHAM *stops as they arrive at the mountain, his
eyes fixed on heaven.*)
  ABRAHAM. Ah, Lord, my heart breaketh in twain
    This child's words, they be so tender!
  (*Again controlling himself.*)
Ah, Isaac son, anon lay it down,
    No longer upon thy back it hold,   130
For I must make ready prayer soon
    To honor my Lord God as I was told.
  (ISAAC *drops the faggots.*)
  ISAAC. Lo, my dear father, here it is.
  (*Moving close to him tenderly.*)
    To cheer you always I draw me near.
But, father, I marvel sore at this,
    Why ye make this heavy cheer,

And also, father, even more dread I—
    Where is quick* beast that ye should kill?   living
Both fire and wood we have ready nigh,
    But quick beast have we none on this hill.   140
  (*Anxiously.*)
A quick beast, I wot well, must be slain,
    Your sacrifice to make.

ABRAHAM. Dread thee nought, my child, I would
fain;
Our Lord will send me unto this place
Some manner of beast for to take
Through his command.

ISAAC. Yea, father, but my heart beginneth to quake
To see that sharp sword in your hand.

Why bear ye your sword drawn so?
Of your countenance I have much wonder.   150

ABRAHAM (aside). Ah, Father of Heaven! such is my
woe,
This child here breaks my heart in sunder.

ISAAC. Tell me, my dear father, so that ye cease—
Bear ye your sword drawn for me?

ABRAHAM. Ah, Isaac! sweet son, peace, peace!
For in truth thou break'st my heart in three!

ISAAC. Now truly, on something, father, ye think,
That ye mourn thus more and more.

ABRAHAM. Ah, Lord of Heaven, let thy grace sink,
For my heart was never half so sore!   160

ISAAC. I pray ye, father, that ye will let me know
Whether I shall have any harm or no.

ABRAHAM. Alas, sweet son, I may not tell thee yet,
My heart is now so full of woe.

ISAAC. Dear father, I pray you, hide it not from me,
But some of your thought, I pray tell me.

ABRAHAM. Ah, Isaac, Isaac, I must kill thee!

ISAAC. Kill me, father? Alas, what have I done?

If I have trespassed against you aught,
With a rod ye may make me full mild;   170
And with your sharp sword kill me naught,
For in truth, father, I am but a child.

ABRAHAM. I am full sorry, son, thy blood for to spill,
But truly, child, I may not as I please.

ISAAC. Now I would to God my mother were here on
this hill.

She would kneel for me on both her knees
          To save my life.
And since that my mother is not here,
I pray you, father, change your cheer,
          And kill me not with your knife.   180

    ABRAHAM. Forsooth, my son, save I thee kill,
          I should grieve God right sore, I dread,
It is his commandment and also his will
          That I should do this same deed.

He commanded me, son, for certain,
          To make my sacrifice with thy blood.

    ISAAC. And is it God's will that I should be slain?

    ABRAHAM. Yea, truly, Isaac, my son so good;
          And therefore my hands I wring!

    ISAAC. Now father, against my Lord's will,   190
          I will never grouch, loud or still.
He might a-sent me a better destiny,
          If it had been his pleasure.

    ABRAHAM. Forsooth, son, but that this deed I did,
          Grievously displeased our Lord would be.

    ISAAC. Nay, nay, father, God forbid
          That ever ye should grieve him for me!

Ye have other children, one or two,
          Which ye should love well in natural kind.
I pray you, father, make you no woe;   200
For, be I once dead and from you go,
          I shall be soon out of your mind.

Therefore do our Lord's bidding,
          And when I am dead, then pray for me.
But, good father, tell ye my mother nothing,
Say that I am in another country dwelling.

    ABRAHAM. Ah, Isaac, Isaac, blessed mayest thou be!

My heart beginneth wildly to rise
          To see the blood of thy blessed body!

    ISAAC. Father, since it may be no other wise,   210
          Let it pass over as well as I.

But, father, ere I go unto my death,
>I pray you bless me with your hand.
(ISAAC *kneels;* ABRAHAM *places his hand on the lad's head.*)
ABRAHAM. Now Isaac, with all my breath
>My blessing I give thee upon this land,
>And may God also thereto add his.
Isaac, Isaac, son, up thou stand,
>Thy fair sweet mouth that I may kiss.

ISAAC. Now farewell, my own father so fine,
>And greet well my mother on earth,   220
But I pray you, father, to hide my eyne
>That I see not the stroke of your sharp sword
>That my flesh shall defile.

ABRAHAM. Son, thy words make me to weep full sore;
Now, my dear son Isaac, speak no more.

ISAAC. Ah, my own dear father! wherefore?
>We shall speak together here but a while.

And since that I must needs be dead,
>Yet, my dear father, to you I pray,
Smite but few strokes at my head   230
>And make an end as soon as ye may,
>And tarry not too long.

ABRAHAM. Thy meek words, child, bring me dismay;
>So "wellaway" must be my song,

Except alone for God's good will.
>Ah! Isaac's, my own sweet child,
Kiss me yet again upon this hill;
>In all the world in none so mild!

ISAAC. Now, truly, father, all this tarrying,
>It doth my heart but harm—   240
I pray you, father, make an ending.

ABRAHAM. Come up, sweet son, unto my arm.
(*He binds him.*)
I must bind thy hands too
>Although thou be never so mild.

ISAAC. Ah, mercy, father! Why should ye so do?

ABRAHAM. That thou should'st not stay me, my child.

ISAAC. Indeed nay, father, I will not stay you.
    Do on, for me, your will;
And on the purpose that ye have set you,
    For God's love, keep it steadfast still.   250

I am full sorry this day to die,
    But yet I will not cause my God to grieve.
Do your desire for me hardily;
    My fair sweet father, I do give you leave.

But, father, I pray you ever more,
    Nothing to my mother tell,
If she wist it, she would weep full sore,
    Indeed she loves me, father well,
       God's good bessing may she have!

Now farewell, my mother so sweet,   260
We two are like no more to meet.
  ABRAHAM. Ah! Isaac, Isaac, son, thou makest me
    grieve,
    And with thy words thou so distemperest me.

ISAAC. Indeed, sweet father, I am sorry to grieve you;
    I cry you mercy for what I have done,
And for all trespass ever I did so.
Now, dear father, forgive all I have done.—
    God of Heaven be with me!

  ABRAHAM. Ah! dear child, leave off thy moans!   270
In all thy life thou grieved men ever once.
Now blessed be thou, body and bones,
    That ever thou were bred and born;
Thou hast been to me child full good.
    But in truth, child, though I mourn never so fast,
    Yet must I needs here at the last
In this place shed all thy blood;

Therefore, my dear son, here shalt thou lie,—
    (*He places him on the altar.*)
    Unto my work I must proceed.
In truth, I had as lief myself to die   280
    If God were pleased with the deed
    That I my own body should offer.

ISAAC. Ah, mercy, father, mourn ye no more;
Your weeping maketh my heart sore
    That mine own death I am to suffer.

Your kerchief, father, about my eyes wind.

ABRAHAM. So I shall, my sweetest child on earth.

ISAAC. Now yet, good father, have this in mind,
  And smite me not often with your sharp sword,
    But hastily that it be sped.   290
("*Here* ABRAHAM *laid a cloth on* ISAAC'S *face, thus
saying:*")[2]
ABRAHAM. Now farewell, my child so full of grace.

ISAAC. Ah, father, turn downward my face,
  For of your sharp sword I am ever adread!
(ABRAHAM *looks up to heaven resignedly.*)
ABRAHAM. To do this deed I am full sorry,
  But, Lord, thine behest I will not withstand.

ISAAC. Ah! Father of Heaven, to thee I cry;
  Lord, receive me thou into thy hand!
(ABRAHAM *falters and pleads again.*)
ABRAHAM. Lo, now is the time come for certain,
  That my sword in his neck shall bite.
Ah, Lord! my heart riseth there again,   300
  I may not find it in my heart to smite.
    My heart will not now thereto!
Ah, fain I would work my Lord's will,
But this young innocent lies so still,
I may not find it in my heart him to kill.
    Oh, Father of Heaven! what shall I do?

ISAAC. Ah, mercy, father, why tarry ye so,
  And let me lie there so long on this heath?
Now I would God the stroke were done also;
Father, heartily I pray you, shorten my woe,   310
  And let me not wait thus for my death.

ABRAHAM. Now, heart, why would'st thou not break
  in three?
    Yet shalt thou not make me to my God unmild.
I will no longer stay for thee,
For that my God aggrieved would be.
    Now have thy stroke, my own dear child.
("*Here* ABRAHAM *drew his stroke, and the* ANGEL *took
the sword in his hand suddenly*")[3]
ANGEL. I am an angel, thou mayest see blithe,
  That from heaven to thee is sent.

---

[2] This stage direction appears in the original.
[3] This stage direction appears in the original.

Our Lord thanketh thee a hundred time
    For the keeping of his commandment.   320

He knoweth thy will, and also thy heart,
    That thou dreadst him above all thing;
And some of thy heaviness for to depart
    A fair ram yonder I did bring;

He standeth, lo, among the briars tied.
    Now, Abraham, amend thy mood,
For Isaac, thy young son, here by thy side
    This day shall not shed his blood.

Go, make thy sacrifice with yon ram.
Now farewell, blessed Abraham,   330
For unto heaven I go now home,—
    The way is full straight. . . .
    Take up thy son now free!

                        (*Exit.*)
ABRAHAM. Ah, Lord! I thank thee for thy great grace,
    Now am I eased in diverse wise.
    Arise up, Isaac, my dear son, arise,
Arise up, sweet child, and come to me!

    ISAAC. Ah, mercy, father, why smite ye naught?
        Ah, smite on, father, once with your knife.

    ABRAHAM. Peace, my sweet son, and take no thought,   340
        For our Lord of Heaven hath granted life
        By his angel now,
That thou shalt not die this day, son, truly.

    ISAAC. Ah, father, full glad then were I;
        In truth, father— I say, I—wis,*   know
        That this tale were true!

    ABRAHAM. A hundred times, my son fair of hue,
        For joy thy mouth now will I kiss.

    ISAAC. Ah, my dear father Abraham,
        Will not God be wroth that we do thus?   350

    ABRAHAM. No, no! hardly, my sweet son!
        For yon same ram he hath now sent
        Hither down to us.
Yon beast shall die here in thy stead,
    In the worship of our Lord, alone.
Go fetch him hither, my child, indeed.

Isaac. Father I will go seize him by the head,
    And bring yon beast with me anon.
  (Isaacs *gets the ram.*)
Ah, sheep, sheep, blessed may thou be,
    That ever thou wert sent down hither!   360
Thou shalt this day die for me,
In worship of the Holy Trinity.
      Now come fast and go we together,
        To my father of Heaven.
Though thou be never so gentle and good,
Yet I had liefer thou shed thy blood
      In truth, sheep, than I!
  (*He leads it to* Abraham.)
Lo, father, I have brought here, full smart,
    This gentle sheep, and him to you I give.
  (*With a sigh of relief.*)
But, Lord God, I thank thee with all my heart!   370
    For I am glad that I shall live,
      And kiss once more my dear mother!

Abraham. Now be right merry, my sweet child,
For this quick beast, that is so mild,
    Here I shall offer before all other.

Isaac. And I will fast begin to blow;
    This fire shall burn a full good speed.
  (*Hesitating, however.*)
But, father, if I stoop down low,
Ye will not kill me with your sword, I trow?

Abraham. No, hardly, sweet son; have no dread.   380
    My mourning is past!

Isaac. Yea, but would that sword were sped—
    For, father, it doth make me yet full ill aghast.
(*"Here* Abraham *made his offering, kneeling and say-
ing thus:"*)[4]
Abraham. Now, Lord God of Heaven in Trinity,
    Almighty God omnipotent,
My offering I make in the worship of thee,
    And with this quick beast I thee present.
      Lord, receive thou mine intent,
As thou art God and ground of our grace.

---

[4] This stage direction appears in the original.

GOD. Abraham, Abraham, well mayest thou speed,   390
    And Isaac, thy young son, thee by!
Truly, Abraham, for this deed,
    I shall multiply both your seed   *Spreading of seed*
      As thick as stars be in the sky,
        Both of bigger and less.
And as thick as gravel in the sea,
So thick multiplied your seed shall be;
      This grant I you for your goodness.

Of you shall come fruit unknown,
    And ever be in bliss without end,   400
For ye dread me as God alone
And keep my commandments, every one.
      My blessing I give wheresoever ye wend!

ABRAHAM. Lo, Isaac my son, how think ye
    Of this work that we have wrought?
Full glad and blithe may we be
      That 'gainst the will of God we muttered nought
      On this fair heath.

ISAAC. Ah, father, I thank our Lord every deal
That my wit served me so weel   410
      For God to fear more than my death.

ABRAHAM. Why, dear-worthy son, wert thou afraid?
    Boldly, child, tell me thy lore.

ISAAC. Yea! by my faith, father, be it said,
    I was never so afraid before,
    As I have been on yon hill!
Ah, by my faith, father, I swear
I will nevermore come there,
    Except it be against my will!

ABRAHAM. Yea, come on with me, my own sweet son,   420
    And homeward fast let us be gone.

ISAAC. By my faith, father, thereto I agree!
I had never such good will to go home,
And to speak with my dear mother!

ABRAHAM. Ah, Lord of Heaven, I thank thee,
    For now I may lead home with me
    Isaac, my young son so free,

The gentlest child above all other,—
    This may avowed be.
Now, go we forth, my blessed son.   430

  ISAAC. I grant, father, let us be gone,
For, by my troth, were I home then,
I would never go out as thus again.
I pray God give us grace evermore true,
And all those that we be beholden to!
    (ABRAHAM and ISAAC go out. The DOCTOR enters.)
    DOCTOR. Lo, now sovereigns and sirs, thus did we show
      This solemn story to great and small.
It is a good lesson for both learned and low,
      And even for the wisest of us all,
        Without any barring.   440
For this story showeth you deep
How to our best power we should keep
      God's commandments without doubting.

Think ye, sirs, if God sent an angel,
      And commanded you your child to slay,
By your truth, is there any of you
      That would balk or gainsay?
How think ye now, sirs, thereby?

There be three or four or more, I trow,
And those women that weep so sorrowfully   450
      When that their children from them die
        As nature takes of our kind,
It is folly, as I may well avow,
Against God to grudge or to grieve so low;
For ye shall never see them mischiefed, well I know,
      By land or water,—have this in mind!

And grudge not against our Lord God,
      In wealth or woe whatever he you send,
Though ye be never so hard bestead;
      For when he willeth, he may it amend,   460
His commandments truly if ye keep with good soul,
      As this story hath now showed you before,
And faithfully serve him, while ye be whole,
      That ye may please God both even and morn.
Now Jesu, that wore the crown of thorn,
      Bring us all to heaven's bliss![5]

  [5] The reference to Jesus could remind the audience that Christ's sacrificial death was prefigured in the sacrifice of the ram in place of Isaac.

The Second Shepherds' Play

A MODERNIZED VERSION BY JOHN GASSNER

Characters

FIRST SHEPHERD: COLL   MAK   THE VIRGIN MARY
SECOND SHEPHERD: GIB   MAK'S WIFE: GILL   THE INFANT CHRIST
THIRD SHEPHERD: DAW   AN ANGEL

One unchanged setting, consisting of two huts—one repre-
senting MAK's cottage and the other the manger or stable of
the Nativity. The space between the two huts represents the
moors or fields. The action occurs in Palestine, but only in
name; actually the local color of the play is drawn from the
countryside of Wakefield, England.

On a double-decker pageant wagon in use in medieval Eng-
land, MAK's hut and the Nativity manger could have been set
on different levels, the manger on the topmost level. Any
neutral area would do for the fields of "Palestine."

The action is continuous; although scene divisions have
been added to the original text, there is no need to drop cur-
tains to indicate a lapse of time.—J. G.

SCENE 1.

The moors.

FIRST SHEPHERD. Lord, but these weathers are cold,
    and I am ill-wrapped!
Nearly numb of hand, so long have I napped;
My legs, they fold; my fingers are chapped.
It is not as I would, for I am all lapped
      In sorrow.
In storms and tempest,
Now in the east, now in the west,
Woe is him who has never rest,
      Mid-day or morrow!

But we poor shepherds that walk on the moor,   10
In faith, we are near-hands out of the door.
No wonder, as it stands, if we be poor,

For the tilth of our lands lies as fallow as a floor,
     As ye ken.*   know
We are so lamed,
Overtaxed and blamed,[1]
We are made hand-tamed
     By these gentlery-men.

Thus they rob us of our rest, Our Lady them harry!
These men that are tied fast, their plow must tarry.   20
What men say is for the best, we find it contrary!
Thus are farming-men oppressed, in point to miscarry
     Alive:
Thus the lords hold us under,
Thus they bring us in blunder—
It were great wonder,
     If ever we should thrive.

Let man but get a painted sleeve or brooch nowadays,
Woe to him that grieves him or once gainsays;
No man dare reprove him though he mastery* has,   force/30
     Not a letter!
He can make purveyance
With boast and braggance,
And all is through maintenance
     By men that are better.

There shall come a [lord's] servant proud as a po,*   peacock
And he must borrow my wagon, my plow also:
And I am glad to grant it so that he shall go!
Thus live we in pain, anger, and woe,   40
     By night and day.
He must have if he wants it,
Though I must do without it;
I were better off hangèd
     Than once say him Nay!

It does me good, as I walk thus by my own,
Of this world for to talk in manner of moan.
To my sheep I will stalk and listen anon,
There abide on a ridge or sit on a stone
     Full soon.   50
For I think, pardie!
True men if we be,

[1] Literally, "crushed."

We shall get more company
      Ere it be noon.

(A SECOND SHEPHERD *appears on the moor, without at
first noticing the* FIRST SHEPHERD, *so absorbed is he in
his own thoughts.*)
SECOND SHEPHERD. *Benedicite*[2] and *Dominus!* what
    may this mean?
Why fares this world thus? Oft have we this seen:
Lord, these weathers are spiteful, and the winds are keen,
And the frosts so hideous they water my een:*   eyes
      No lie it be!
Now in dry, now in wet,   60
Now in snow, now in sleet,
When my shoes freeze to my feet,
      It is not at all easy.

But as far as I know, or yet as I go,
We poor wed men suffer much, we do;
We have sorrow then and then, it falls often so.
Poor Cappel, our hen, both to and fro
      She cackles,
But begin she to rock,
To groan or to cluck,   70
Woe is to him, our cock,
      For he is then in shackles!

These men that are wed have not all their will;
When they are set upon, they sigh full still.
God knows they are led full hard and full ill,
In bower or in bed they have their fill
      Beside.
My part have I found,
Know my lesson sound:
Woe is him that is bound,   80
      For he must abide.

But now late in our lives—marvel to me!
That I think my heart breaks such wonder to see:
That, as destiny drives, it should so be
That some men will have two wives, and some have three
      In store.
To some is woe that have any,

---

[2] He pronounces this, by contraction of the Latin for "Bless you," as
"Bencite" or "Bensté."

But so far as I see, I tell ye,
Woe is him that has many,
       For he feels sore.   90

(Addressing the audience.)
But young men awooing, by God that you bought,
Beware of a wedding and mind in your thought
"Had I known" is a thing that serves you nought.
So much still mourning has wedding home brought
       And grief,
With many a sharp shower;
For ye may catch in an hour
What shall savor full sour
       As long as you live.

For, as ever read I scripture, I have *her* I keep near: 100
As sharp as a thistle, as rough as a briar;
She is browed like a bristle with sour-looking cheer.
Had she once wet her whistle, she could sing full clear
       Her Pater-Noster.
She is as great as a whale,
She has a gallon of gall;
By Him that died for us all,
       I would I had run till I lost her!

(By now he has been observed by the FIRST SHEPHERD, *who rouses him from his meditations roughly.)*

FIRST SHEPHERD. God look over the row, you there, that deafly stand!

SECOND SHEPHERD *(startled)*. Yea, the devil in thy maw!
   —In tarrying, friend,   110
Saw you Daw about?

FIRST SHEPHERD.   Yes, on fallow land
I heard him blow. He should be at hand
       Not far.
Stand still!

SECOND SHEPHERD.   Why?

FIRST SHEPHERD. For he comes on, I spy.

SECOND SHEPHERD. He will din us both a lie
       Unless we beware.

(A THIRD SHEPHERD, *a boy called* DAW, *employed by the* SECOND SHEPHERD, *appears. The weather has put him out of humor.)*

THIRD SHEPHERD. Christ's cross me speed, and Saint Nicholas!

Thereof had I need: it is worse than it was!
Whoso can, take heed; and let the world pass;   120
It is ever in dread and brittle as glass,
      And slides.
This world fared never so,
With marvels more and more,
Now in weal, now in woe;
      And everything rides!

Was never since Noah's flood such flood seen,
Winds and rains so rude, and storms so keen;
Some stammered, some stood in doubt, as I ween.
Now God turn all to good! I say as I mean   130
      And ponder.
These floods, so they drown
Both fields and town
And bear all down—
      That it is a wonder.

We that walk in the nights our cattle to keep,
We see sudden sights when other men sleep—
   (*Noticing that he is being observed by the other*
   SHEPHERDS.)
But methinks my heart lightens, I see them peep.
Yea, you tall fellows!—I think I'll give my sheep
      A turn.   140
   (*He is about to turn away, but changes his mind.*)
But this is ill intent,
For as I walk on this bent
I may lightly repent
      And stub my toes.

   (*Pretending to have just seen them.*)
Ah, sir, God you save, and you, master mine!
   (*Coming up to them.*)
A drink fain would I have and somewhat to dine.
   FIRST SHEPHERD. Christ's curse, my knave, thou art a
     lazy swine!
   SECOND SHEPHERD. What, the boy pleases to rave?
     You'll wait on line
      When we have made it.
I'll drum on thy pate!   150
Though the knave comes late,
Yet is he in state
      To dine, if he had it.

THIRD SHEPHERD (*grumbling*). Such servants as I, that
   sweats and swinks,[3]
Eats our bread dry, and that is ill, I thinks!
We are oft wet and weary when master-men winks,
Yet come full lately the dinners and the drinks.
     But neatly,
Both our dame and our sire,
When we have run in the mire,   160
They can nip us of our hire
     And pay us full lately.

But hear my oath: For the food that you serve, I say,
I shall do hereafter—work as you pay:
I shall work a little and a little play,
For yet my supper never on my stomach lay
     In the fields.
I won't complain, but a heap
With my staff I shall leap;
For a thing bought too cheap   170
     Nothing yields.

  FIRST SHEPHERD. Yea, thou wert a fool, lad, a-wooing
   to ride
With one that has but little for spending by his side.
  SECOND SHEPHERD. Peace, boy! And no more jangling
   I'll bide,
Or I shall make thee full sad, by heaven's King, beside,
    For thy gauds.*   tricks or jests
Where are our sheep? Thy japes we scorn.
  THIRD SHEPHERD. Sir, this same day at morn
I left them in the corn
    When the bells rang Lauds.   180

They have pasture good, they cannot go wrong.
  FIRST SHEPHERD. That is right. By the rood, these
   nights are long!
Yet I would, ere we went, one gave us a song.
  SECOND SHEPHERD. So *I* thought as I stood—to cheer
   us along.
  THIRD SHEPHERD.
    I grant!
  FIRST SHEPHERD. Let me sing the tenory.
  SECOND SHEPHERD. And I the treble so high.

---

[3] Works. His speech is ungrammatical.

THIRD SHEPHERD. Then the mean falls to me.
    Let's start the chant.

(*At this point,* MAK *appears, his cloak thrown over his tunic.*)

MAK (*to himself*). Lord, for Thy names seven, that
    made the moon and stars on high   190
Well more than I reckon: Thy will, Lord, leaves me dry
And lacking, so that of my wits I am shy:
Now would God I were in heaven, for there no children
    cry
        So still.*   continuously

FIRST SHEPHERD (*looking around.*) Who is that pipes so
    poor?

MAK (*still grumbling to himself*). Would God knew
    how I endure:
A man that walks on the moor
        Without his will.

(*The* SHEPHERDS *now recognize him as the thief they know.* MAK *is startled, but pretends he does not know them.*)

SECOND SHEPHERD. Mak, where have you been? Tell
    us tidings.

THIRD SHEPHERD. Is *he* come, then let each one take
    heed to his things.   200
(*He takes* MAK's *cloak from him and shakes it, to see whether* MAK *has stolen anything.*)

MAK (*spluttering*). What! I be a yeoman, I tell ye, of
    the king's.
The self and same, sent from a great lording's
        And such.
Fie on you! Go hence
Out of my presence;
I must have reverence—
        You grieve me much!

FIRST SHEPHERD. Why make ye it so quaint, Mak? You
    do wrong.

SECOND SHEPHERD. Mak, play ye the saint? For this do
    ye long? (*He shows* MAK *his fist.*)

THIRD SHEPHERD. I know the knave can deceive, the
    devil him hang!   210

MAK. I shall make complaint and get ye many a
    thwang

At a word
When I tell my lord how ye do.

FIRST SHEPHERD (*sarcastically*). But, Mak, is that **true?**
Come, that southern tooth unscrew[4]
        And set it in a turd.

SECOND SHEPHERD. Mak, the devil in your eyes, a stroke
    will I lend you.

(*He strikes him.*)

THIRD SHEPHERD. Mak, know ye not me? By God, I
    could beat ye too.

(*As he too is about to strike him,* MAK *draws back and
pretends to have just recognized the* SHEPHERDS.)

MAK. God, look—you all three? Methought I should
    know you!
Ye are a fair company.   220

FIRST SHEPHERD.   So you know us, do you!
SECOND SHEPHERD.
        Blast your jest-dealing!
When a man so lately goes
What will good men suppose?
Ye have an ill name one knows
        For sheep-stealing.

MAK. And true as steel I am, know ye not?
But a sickness I feel that makes me full hot:
My belly fares not well, for it is out of estate.

THIRD SHEPHERD (*unsympathetically*). Seldom lies the
    devil dead by the gate!

MAK (*ignoring the thrust*).
        Therefore,   230
Full sore am I and ill;
I stand stone-still,
I ate not a tittle
        This month and more.

FIRST SHEPHERD. How fares thy wife? By my hood, tell
    us true.

MAK. She lies lolling by the road, by the fire too,
And a house full of brew she drinks well too.
Ill speed other things that she will shift
        To do.
Eats as fast as she can,   240
And each year that comes to man

---

[4] In pretending to be in the king's service, the actor playing Mak may
have affected a Southern—that is, London—accent.

She brings forth a brat—an'
  Some years, two.

But were I yet more gracious, and richer at will,
Eaten out of house and home I would be still.
And she is a foul deer, if ye come at her close;
None there is looks worse, as none knows
  Better than I.
Now will ye see what I proffer:
To give all in my coffer   250
And tomorrow next, to offer
  Mass-pence, should she die.

 (*The* SHEPHERDS *have begun to feel drowsy during this recital.*)
SECOND SHEPHERD. So weary with watching is none in
 this shire:
I would sleep if it cost me a part oɩ ꟺy hire.
 THIRD SHEPHERD. And I am cold and naked, and would
 have a fire.
 FIRST SHEPHERD. I am weary of walking, and I have
 run in the mire.
 (*To the* SECOND SHEPHERD.)
  Keep the watch, you!
SECOND SHEPHERD. Nay, I will lie down by,
For I must sleep or die.
 THIRD SHEPHERD. For sleep as good a man's son am I; 260
  It is my due.

 (*They begin to lie down to sleep. But the* THIRD SHEPHERD *eyes* MAK *suspiciously.*)
 THIRD SHEPHERD. But, Mak, come hither; between us
 you shall lie down.
 MAK (*unhappily*). But I may hinder your sleep and
 make you frown.
 (*The* SHEPHERDS *force him down and compel him to stretch out among them, in order to prevent him from robbing them.*)
  Ah well, no dread I heed:
From my head to my toe,
 (*Crossing himself.*)
Manus tuas commendo,
Pontio Pilato,[5]
  Christ's cross me speed.

  [5] "Into your hands I commend myself, Pontius Pilate." The humor lies, of course, in the misquotation.

(Before long the THREE SHEPHERDS *are in a deep sleep,
and* MAK *disentangles himself and rises.)*

MAK. Now were time for a man that lacks what he
    would   270

To stalk privily then into the fold
And nimbly to work, though not to be too bold,
For he might regret the bargain if it were told
      At the ending.
Now time for to work in the dell,
For he needs good counsel
That fain would fare well
      And has but little spending.

*(He begins to work a spell on the sleepers, drawing a
circle around them.)*

But about you a circle round as the moon,
Till I have done what I will, till that it be noon—   280
That ye lie stone-still, until I am done;
And now I shall say thereto of good words a rune
      Anon:
Over your heads my hand I light;
Out go your eyes, blind be your sight!
And now that it may come out right
      I must shift on.

*(He starts to leave in the direction of the sheep further
down the field while the* SHEPHERDS *snore.)*

Lord, but they sleep hard—that may one hear. . . .
Was I never shepherd, but now I will shear;
Though the flock be scared, yet shall I nip near;   290
I must draw hitherward and mend our cheer
      From sorrow.
(He spies a sheep that attracts him.)
A fat sheep, I daresay,
A good fleece, I dare lay;
Repay when I may—
    (Seizing the animal.)
      But this will I *borrow.*

SCENE 2

MAK'S *cottage: the exterior and the interior.*

At first MAK *stands outside and knocks at the door.
Later he enters and the action transpires inside.*

MAK *(knocking).* How, Gill, art thou in? Get us some
    light.

WIFE. Who makes such din this time of the night?
I am set for to spin: I think not I might
Rise a penny to win—a curse on him alight.   300
      So fares she,
A housewife, I ween,
To be raced thus between.
In house may no work be seen
      Because of such small chores that be.

MAK. Good wife, open the door. Do ye not see what
    I bring?
WIFE. Then let thou draw the latch.
(*As he enters.*)
                Ah! come in, my sweeting!
MAK (*grumpily*). Yea, and no thought for my long
    standing!
WIFE (*observing the sheep*). By the naked neck thou
    art like to get thy hanging.
MAK.
      Get away!   310
I am worthy my meat,
For in a pinch can I get
More than they that swink and sweat
      All day.

Thus it fell to my lot, Gill, I had such grace.
    WIFE. It were a foul blot to be hanged for the case.
    MAK. I have escaped oft from as narrow place.
    WIFE. But so long goes the pot to the water, one says,
      At last
Comes it home broken.   320
    MAK. Well I know the token;
But let it never be spoken!—
      Now, come and help fast.

(GILL *helps to take the sheep in.*)
I would it were slain and I sat down to eat:
This twelvemonth was I not so fain for sheep-meat.
    WIFE. Come they ere it be slain and hear the sheep
    bleat—
    MAK. Then might I be taken; cold's the sweat I am in,
    my sweet—
      Go, make fast
The outer door.

WIFE (*going to the door*). Yes, Mak,
  If they came at thy back—   330
MAK. Then got I from that pack
    The devil's own cast.

  WIFE (*coming back*). A good jest I have spied, since
    thou hast none:
  (*Pointing to the cradle.*)
Here shall we hide it till they be gone;
In the cradle may it abide. Let me alone,
And I shall lie beside in childbed and groan.
  MAK.
      Well said!
And I shall say you are light
Of a man-child this night.
  WIFE. How well it is, day bright,   340
    That ever I bred.

This is a good guise and a far cast:
A woman's advice, it helps at the last.
I shall fear never who spies, so thou go fast!
  MAK (*outside, walking in the fields toward the sleeping*
    SHEPHERDS). If I do not come ere they rise, a cold
    blast
      Will blow; back to sleep
I go. Yet sleeps this company,
And I shall slip in privily
As it had never been me
      That carried their sheep.   350

SCENE 3

The moors.

MAK *slips in among the sleepers. The* SHEPHERDS *begin
to stir.*

  FIRST SHEPHERD (*rising*). *Resurrex a mortruis:* reach
    me a hand!
Judas carnas dominus![6] I may not well stand.
My foot sleeps, by Jesus, and I thirst—and
I thought that we laid us full near England.
  SECOND SHEPHERD (*rising*).
      Ah-ye!
Lord, I have slept well!

---

[6] The unlettered shepherd is babbling Latin words he has picked up imperfectly and makes no particular sense.

I am fresh as an eel,
As light I feel
        As leaf on tree.

THIRD SHEPHERD (*awaking but dazed*). *Ben'cite* be
    herein; so my body quakes,   360
My heart is out of my skin with the noise it makes.
Who makes all this din, so my brow aches?
To the door will I win. Hark, fellows, who wakes?
        We were four:
See ye anywhere Mak now?
    FIRST SHEPHERD. We were up ere thou.
    SECOND SHEPHERD. Man, I give God a vow
        That he went nowhere.

THIRD SHEPHERD (*troubled*). Methought he lay wrapped
    up in a wolf-skin.
FIRST SHEPHERD. Many are thus wrapped now—that is,
    within!   370
THIRD SHEPHERD. When we had long napped,
    methought with a gin*   trick
A fat sheep he trapped without making a din.
    SECOND SHEPHERD (*pointing toward* MAK, *who pretends
    to be asleep*).
        Be still:
This dream makes thee wild,
It is but phantom, by the Holy Child![7]
    FIRST SHEPHERD. Now God turn all things mild,
        If it be His will.

(*The* SHEPHERDS *rouse* MAK.)
SECOND SHEPHERD. Rise, Mak, for shame! Ye lie right
    long.
    MAK (*stirring*). Now Christ's Holy Name, be it among
Us! What's this? By Saint James, I am not strong!   380
I hope I am the same—my neck has lain wrong
        All night!
(*As they help him up.*)
Many thanks! Since yester-even,
I swear by Saint Steven,
I was flayed by a dream, so driven
        That my heart was not right.

[7] An anachronism characteristic of naïve folk literature, since the Holy
Child has not yet been born. In the next few lines there are other anachro-
nisms: "Christ's Holy Name," "By Saint James," and "by Saint Steven"—
or Stephen.

Methought my Gill began to croak, full sad
To labor well nigh at first cock—a lad
To add to our flock; and I never glad
To have more to provide, more than ever I had.   390
    Ah, my head!
A house full of young mouths—banes!
The devil knock out their brains!
Woe him that so many brats gains
    And so little bread.

I must go home, by your leave to Gill, I thought.
But first look in my sleeve that I have stolen naught:
I am loath to grieve you or to take from you aught.
    THIRD SHEPHERD. Go forth, and ill may you thrive!
(MAK *leaves*.)
                      Still I would we sought
    This morn   400
Whether we have all our store.
    FIRST SHEPHERD. Good! I will go before.
Let us meet.
    SECOND SHEPHERD. Where?
    THIRD SHEPHERD.
        At the crooked thorn.

SCENE 4

MAK's *cottage*.

MAK (*at his door*). Undo this door! Who is here? How
    long shall I stand?
WIFE. Who makes such a stir, to walk in the
    moon-waning?
MAK. Ah, Gill, what cheer? It is I, Mak, your husband.
WIFE (*grumpily*). Then see we here the devil himself
    in a band,
    Sir Guile!
Lo, he comes with a noise about   410
As if he were held by the snout,
I may not do my work for that lout
    A hand-long while.

MAK. Will ye hear what noise she makes for an excuse
And does nothing but play about and stroke her toes!
    WIFE. Why, who wanders, who wakes, who comes,
    who goes?

Who brews, who bakes—now who do you suppose?
     And more then
That it is pity to behold—
Now in hot, now in cold.   420
Full woefull is the household
     That lacks women.

But what end have ye made with the shepherds, Mak?
   MAK. The last word that they said when I turned my
     back
They would look that they had of their sheep all the
     pack;
I fear they will not be well pleased when they their
     sheep lack,
     Pardie!
But howso the sport goes
I'm the thief they'll suppose
And come with a full nose   430
     To cry out on me.

But thou must do as thou planned.
   WIFE.   They'll find me able!
I shall swaddle it right in my cradle.
When I sup with the Devil I use the long ladle!
I will lie down straightway. Come wrap me.
   MAK (doing so).   I will.
   WIFE (sharply).
     Behind!—
If Coll and his mate come, to our sorrow,
They will nip us full narrow.
   MAK. But I may run and cry "Harrow"
     If the sheep they find.   440

   WIFE. Listen close when they call—they will come
     anon.
Come and make ready all, and sing thou alone:
Sing "Lullay" you shall, for I must groan
And cry out by the wall on Saint Mary and John
     As if sore.
Sing "Lullay" on fast
When you hear them at last,
And if I play a false cast
     Trust me no more!

SCENE 5

The moors, as the SHEPHERDS *meet.*

SECOND SHEPHERD. Ah, Coll, good morn: why sleep ye
    not?   450
  FIRST SHEPHERD. Alas, that ever was I born! We have
    a foul blot—
A fat wether have we lost.
  THIRD SHEPHERD.   God forbid; say it not!
  SECOND SHEPHERD. Who should have done that harm?
    That were a foul spot.
  FIRST SHEPHERD.
        Some knave—beshrew!
I have sought with my dogs
All Horbury shrogs,[8]
And of fifteen hogs*   young sheep
    I lack one ewe.

  THIRD SHEPHERD. Now trust me if ye will—by Saint
    Thomas of Kent!,
Either Mak or Gill a hand to it lent.   460
  FIRST SHEPHERD. Peace, man, be still: I watched when
    he went;
You slander him ill, you ought to repent
    With speed.
  SECOND SHEPHERD. Yet as ever I thrive or be,
Though the good Lord slay me,
I would say it were he
    That did the same deed.

  THIRD SHEPHERD. Go we thither then, I say, and let
    us run fleet;
Till I know the truth, may I never bread eat.
  FIRST SHEPHERD. Nor take drink in my head till with
    him I meet.   470
  SECOND SHEPHERD. I will take to no bed until I him
    greet,
  (*Sarcastically.*)
        My brother!
One promise I will plight:
Till I get him in sight
I will never sleep one night
    Where I sleep another.

   [8] By this is meant the thickets of Horbury, about four miles from Wakefield, where the play was given.

SCENE 6

MAK's *cottage.*

MAK *is heard singing within, while Gill is heard
groaning as though she were delivering a child.*

> THIRD SHEPHERD. Will you hear how they hack away;
>> our sir likes to croon.
> FIRST SHEPHERD. Heard I never none crack so clear out
>> of tune.
Call on him!
> SECOND SHEPHERD. Mak, undo your door—soon!
> MAK. Who is that spoke, as if it were noon   480
>> Aloft?
Who is that, I say?
> (*He opens the door.*)
> THIRD SHEPHERD. Good fellows you'd see, were it day.
> MAK. As far as ye may,
>> Friends, speak soft

Over a sick woman's head that is at malease;
I had sooner be dead than cause her dis-ease.
> WIFE. Go to another place—I cannot breathe; please!
Each foot ye tread goes through my nose with a squeeze,
>> Woe is me.   490
> FIRST SHEPHERD. Tell us, Mak, if ye may:
How fare ye, I say?
> MAK. But are ye in this town today?—
>> How fare *ye?*

Ye have run in the mire and are wet a bit;
I shall make you a fire, if ye will sit.
> (*Pointing at his* WIFE.)
A nurse I would hire; think ye on it.
Well paid is my hire—my dream this is it,
>> In season.
I have brats if ye knew   500
Many more than will do;
> (*With resignation.*)
But, then, we must drink as we brew,
>> And that is but reason!

I would ye dined ere you go; methinks that ye sweat.
> SECOND SHEPHERD. Nay, neither drink nor meat will
>> mend us yet.

MAK (*innocently*). Why, sirs, what ails ye?

THIRD SHEPHERD.   Our sheep we must get

That was stolen. It is great loss that we met.

(MAK *offers a drink*.)

MAK.

        Sirs, drink!

Had I been near,

Someone should have bought it full dear.   510

    FIRST SHEPHERD. Marry, some men think that ye were.

        And that makes us think!

    SECOND SHEPHERD. Mak, some men think that it should
        be ye.

    THIRD SHEPHERD. Either you or your spouse, so say we.

    MAK. Now if ye have suspicion against my Gill or me,

Come and search our house, and then may ye see

        Who had her,

Or if any sheep I got,

Either cow or stot.*   bullock

And Gill, my wife, rose not   520

        Here since she laid her.

If I am not true and loyal, to God I pray

    (*Pointing to the cradle, where the sheep—the alleged
    child—is hidden*.)

That *this* be the first meal I shall eat this day.

    FIRST SHEPHERD. Mak, as I may fare well, take heed,
        I say!

"He learned early to steal that could not say nay."

    (*The* SHEPHERDS *start to search the room, but* GILL
    *waves them away when they approach the cradle near
    her*.)

    WIFE.

        I faint!

Out, thieves, from my dwelling!

Ye come to rob while I am swelling—

    MAK. Your hearts should melt now she's yelling

        In plaint.   530

    WIFE. Away, thieves, from my child; over him don't
        pore.

    MAK. Knew ye how much she has borne, your hearts
        would be sore.

Ye do wrong, I warn you, thus to rummage before

A woman that has suffered—but I say no more!

WIFE (*yelling*).
        Ah, my middle!
I pray to God so mild,
If I ever you beguiled,
.That I *eat* this child
        That lies in this cradle.

MAK (*pretending concern for her*). Peace, woman, for
    God's pain, and cry not so: 540
Thou spill'st thy brain and fill'st me with woe.
    SECOND SHEPHERD (*to the other* TWO SHEPHERDS). I
        think our sheep be slain; what find ye two?
    THIRD SHEPHERD. All this is in vain: we may as well go:
    (*Finding only rags of clothing as he searches.*)
            Only tatters!
I can find no flesh,
Hard nor soft,
Salt nor fresh,
        But two bare platters.

(*But as he approaches the cradle and sniffs the air, he
makes a grimace.*)
Yet live cattle, as I may have bliss, nor tame nor wild,
None has smelled so strong as this—this child!   550
    WIFE (*protesting*). Ah no, so God bless and give me
        joy, this child smells mild.
    FIRST SHEPHERD. We have aimed amiss: We were
        elsewhere beguiled
    (*He is about to leave.*)
    SECOND SHEPHERD (*also giving up the search*).
            Sir, we are done!
But sir—Our Lady him save!—
Is your child a lad?
    MAK (*proudly*). Any lord might him have
            This child to his son.

When he wakens he has a grip that is a joy to see.
    THIRD SHEPHERD. Blessings on his hips, much happiness
        may he see.
But who were his godparents, will ye tell me?   560
    MAK (*floundering*). Blessed be their lips!—
    FIRST SHEPHERD (*aside*). Now, what will the lie be?
    MAK.
        So God them thank,—
Parkin and Gibbon Waller, be it said,

And gentle John Horne in good stead—
He that made the great riot spread,
      He with the big shank.

> SECOND SHEPHERD (*preparing to leave*). Mak, friends
> will we be, for we are all one.
> MAK (*pretending to have been hurt by their sus-
> picions*). We? Now I must hold back, for amends
> is there none.

Farewell, all three, and very glad to see you gone!   570
> (*The* SHEPHERDS *leave the house, and we see them
> outside.*)
> THIRD SHEPHERD. "Fair words may there be, but love
> is there none
>   This year."
> FIRST SHEPHERD (*to the* SECOND). Gave ye the child
> anything?
> SECOND SHEPHERD. No, not a farthing.
> THIRD SHEPHERD. Fast back will I fling:
>   Await ye me here.

> (*He goes back to* MAK's *cottage, the others following
> him.*)

Mak, take it to no grief if I come to thy lad.
> MAK. Nay, ye have grieved me much and made me sad.
> THIRD SHEPHERD. The child it will not grieve, thy little
> day-star so glad;

Mak, with your leave, let me give the child you have had   580
>   But sixpence.
> MAK. Nay, go away; he sleeps!
> THIRD SHEPHERD. Methinks, it peeps.*   whimpers
> MAK. When he wakens, he weeps;
>   I pray you go hence.

> (*The other* SHEPHERDS *enter.*)
> THIRD SHEPHERD (*coming closer*). Give me leave him
> to kiss and to lift up the clout.
> (*He lifts the cover a little.*)

What the devil is this? He has a long snout!
> FIRST SHEPHERD. He is birth-marked amiss; let us not
> waste time hereabout.
> SECOND SHEPHERD. "From an ill-spun woof ever comes
> foul out."
> (*As he looks closer.*)
>   Ay—so!   590

He is like our sheep.
   THIRD SHEPHERD. How, Gib? May I peep?
   FIRST SHEPHERD. "Nature will still creep
       Where it may not go."

   SECOND SHEPHERD. This was a quaint trick and a far
   cast;
It was a high fraud!
   THIRD SHEPHERD. Yea, sirs, I am aghast!
Let's burn this bawd and bind her fast;
A false scold hangs at the last—
       So shalt thou.
   (*He has pulled the covers off.*)
Will ye see how they swaddle   600
His four feet in the middle?
Saw I never in a cradle
       A hornèd lad ere now.

   MAK (*who stands behind them and does not see the
     sheep uncovered; still attempting to brazen it out*).
Peace, bid I! And let be your fare;
I am he that him gat and yon woman him bare.*   bore
   FIRST SHEPHERD (*mocking him*). What devil shall he be
   called, Mak? Lo, God! Mak's heir!
   SECOND SHEPHERD. An end to all jesting; now God give
   thee care
       I say!
   (*As she is lying in bed, the* WIFE *does not see that
   they have completely uncovered the sheep.*)
   WIFE. As pretty child is he
As sits on woman's knee;   610
A dilly-down, perdie,
       To make one gay.

   THIRD SHEPHERD. I know my sheep by the ear-mark—
   this good token.
   MAK. I tell you, sirs, hear me: his nose was broken,
Since, as the priest told me, he was by witchcraft
   bespoken.
   FIRST SHEPHERD. This is false work and must be
   avenged; I have spoken:
       Get weapon!
   WIFE. The child was altered by an elf—
I saw it myself.

When the clock struck twelve,   620
     Was he mis-shapen.

  SECOND SHEPHERD. Ye two are right deft, and belong in
    the same bed.
  FIRST SHEPHERD. Since they maintain their theft, let us
    do them dead.
  (*They seize* MAK.)
  MAK (*seeing the game is up*). If I trespass again, strike
    off my head.
I'll let you be the judge!
  THIRD SHEPHERD (*to the others*). Sirs, instead:
      For this trespass
We need neither curse nor spite,
Nor chide nor fight,
But take him forthright
      And toss him in canvas.   630
  (*They drag* MAK *outside and toss him lustily in a sheet
  while he yells with pain.*)

SCENE 7

The fields near Bethlehem in Judea.

We see the three SHEPHERDS *again, weary after their
sport with* MAK *and tired with walking.*

  FIRST SHEPHERD. Lord, how I am sore and like to burst
    in the breast!
In faith, I can stand no more, therefore will I rest.
  SECOND SHEPHERD. As a sheep of seven score Mak
    weighed in my fist;
To sleep anywhere methink I would list.
  THIRD SHEPHERD.
      Then I pray you,
Lie down on this green.
  FIRST SHEPHERD (*hesitating*). On these thefts to think
    I yet mean.
  THIRD SHEPHERD. Whereto should ye be worried lean?
    Do as I tell you.

  (*They lie down to sleep; but they have barely done so
  when an* ANGEL *appears above. He first sings the hymn
  "Gloria in Excelsis," then addresses the* SHEPHERDS.)
  ANGEL. Rise, herdsmen gentle, for now is He born   640
That shall take from the Fiend what Adam
    had lorn;*   lost, forfeited

That fiend to overthrow this night is He born;
God is made your Friend. Now at this morn,
      He commands,
To Bedlem* you go see: Bethlehem
There lies that divine He
In a crib that full poorly
      Betwixt two beasts stands.
(*The* ANGEL *disappears.*)

FIRST SHEPHERD. This was a quaint voice that ever yet
   I heard.
It is a marvel to relate thus to be stirred.   650
   SECOND SHEPHERD. Of God's son of heaven he spoke
   from above,
All the wood was in lightning as he spoke of love;
   I thought it fair.
   THIRD SHEPHERD. Of a child heard I tell
In Bedlem; I heard it well.
   FIRST SHEPHERD (*pointing to a star that has begun to
   blaze*). Yonder star, above the dell:
      Let us follow him there.

   SECOND SHEPHERD. Say, what was his song? Heard ye
   how he sang it?
Three breves⁹ to a long.
   THIRD SHEPHERD.   Yes, marry, he thwacked it;
Was no crotchet wrong, nor nothing lacked it.   660
   FIRST SHEPHERD. For to sing it again right as he trilled
   it,
      I can, if I may.
   SECOND SHEPHERD. Let me see how ye croon,
Or do ye but bark at the moon?
   THIRD SHEPHERD. Hold your tongues! Have done!
   FIRST SHEPHERD.
      Hark after me, I say!
(*They try to sing the hymn as best they can.*)

   SECOND SHEPHERD. To Bedlem he bade that we should
   go;
I am troubled that we tarry too slow.
   THIRD SHEPHERD. Be merry and not sad: of mirth is
   our song, lo!

---

   ⁹ A "breve" is equal to two whole notes; a "long" is equal to six whole
notes; a "crotchet" is a quarter note.

Everlasting glad in the rewards that will flow,   670
    No plaint may we make.
  FIRST SHEPHERD. Hie we thither, gladly,
Though we be wet and weary;
To that Child and that Lady
    Let us our way take.

  SECOND SHEPHERD. We find by the prophecy—let be
    your din!—
Of David and Isaiah, and more therein,
As prophesied by clergy, that on a virgin
Should He light and lie, to redeem our sin
    And slake it.   680
Our kind from woe
To save—Isaiah said so.—
    "Ecce virgo
    Concipiet a child that is naked."[10]

 ' THIRD SHEPHERD. Full glad may we be, and await that
    day
That lovely day that He shall with His might sway.
Lord, well for me for once and for aye!
Might I but kneel on my knee some word for to say
    To that child.
But the angel said   690
In a crib is He laid,
He is poorly arrayed,
    So meek and mild.

  FIRST SHEPHERD. Patriarchs that have been, and
    prophets beforne,
They desired to have seen this Child that is born;
But they are gone full clean, from life forlorn—
It is we shall see him, ere it be morn
    By token.
When I see Him and feel,
Then shall I know full well   700
It is true as steel
    What prophets have spoken:

To so poor as we are that he should appear,
We the first to find and be his messenger!
  SECOND SHEPHERD. Go we now, let us fare: the place
    must be near.

[10] "Behold, a virgin shall conceive." (Isaiah, 7 : 14).

THIRD SHEPHERD. I am ready and eager: go we together
    To that Light!
Lord! if Thy will it be,
Though we are lowly all three,
Grant us of Thy glee,   710
    To comfort Thy wight.*   creature
(They move on, following the star, to Bethlehem.)

SCENE 8

The stable or manger in Bethlehem.

The SHEPHERDS enter and kneel before the VIRGIN and CHILD.

FIRST SHEPHERD. Hail, comely and clean; hail, young
    child!
Hail, Maker, as I mean, born of maiden so mild!
Thou hast banned, I deem, the devil so wild;
The evil beguiler now goes beguiled.
    (Pointing to the CHILD.)
    Lo, merry He is!
Lo, he laughs, my sweeting,
A welcome greeting!
I have had my meeting—
    (Offering the CHILD some cherries.)
    Have a bob of cherries?   720

SECOND SHEPHERD. Hail, sovereign Savior, for Thou
    hast us sought!
Hail, Nursling, leaf and flower, that all things hath
    wrought!
Hail, full of favor, that made all of nought!
    (Offering a bird.)
Hail, I kneel and I cower. —A bird have I brought
    Without mar.
Hail, little, tiny mop,
Of our creed thou art the crop;
I would drink from thy cup,
    Little day-star.

THIRD SHEPHERD. Hail, darling dear, full of godhead!   730
I pray Thee be near when that I have need.
Hail! Sweet is Thy cheer! And my heart must bleed
To see Thee sit here clothed so poor indeed,
    With no pennies.
Hail! Thy hand put forth to us all—

I bring thee but a ball;
Take and play with it withall,
      And go to the tennis.

  THE VIRGIN MARY. The Father of heaven, God
    omnipotent,
That set all aright, His son has He sent.   740
My name He chose forth, and on me His light spent;
And I conceived Him forthwith through His might as
    God meant:
      And now is the Child born.
May He keep you from woe!
I shall pray Him so.
Tell the glad news as ye go,
      And remember this morn.

  FIRST SHEPHERD. Farewell, Lady, so fair to behold
With thy child on thy knee.
  SECOND SHEPHERD.   —But he lies full cold.—
Lord, it is well with me! Now we go, as ye behold.   750
  THIRD SHEPHERD. In truth, already it seems to be told
      Full oft—
  FIRST SHEPHERD. What grace we have found.
  SECOND SHEPHERD. Come forth! Now are we won!
  THIRD SHEPHERD. To sing of it we're bound:
      Let us sing aloft!
(*They leave the stable, singing.*)

The Pageant of the Shearmen and Tailors of Coventry

A MODERNIZED VERSION BY JOHN GASSNER

EDITORIAL NOTE. This play is one of the two extant plays of a lost Coventry cycle and amounts to a telescopic account of several New Testament events. The episodes thus amalgamated into a single play here are "The Prophecy of Isaiah," given as a Prologue; "The Annunciation" ("the tidings brought to Mary"); "The Nativity," along with the visitation of "The Shepherds" and of "The Magi" ("The Three Kings"); "The Massacre of the Innocents"; and "The Flight to Egypt," although this last episode is merely given as a report by King Herod's herald.

Each of these episodes was separately elaborated into a play, or "pageant," in one or more of the other cycles, which in their totality constituted the medieval English "Passion plays." The most famous elaboration is *The Second Shepherds' Play* from the Wakefield Cycle, which precedes this selection. Another interesting example is the Chester cycle *Massacre of the Innocents,* in which medieval knighthood is satirized in the mock-heroic manner of Cervantes' *Don Quixote,* composed several hundred years later.

Characters

ISAIAH (in the Prologue)	THE HERALD
THE VIRGIN MARY	FIRST, SECOND, and THIRD
THE ANGEL GABRIEL	KING
JOSEPH	FIRST and SECOND ANGEL
FIRST, SECOND, and THIRD	FIRST and SECOND KNIGHT
SHEPHERD	FIRST, SECOND, and THIRD
KING HEROD	WOMAN

PROLOGUE

(ISAIAH *appears on the bare stage, and addresses the audience.*)

ISAIAH. The Sovereign that seeth every secret
May He save ye all and make perfect and strong

And give you grace with His mercy to meet,
For now in great misery is mankind bound,
The Serpent having given man so mortal a wound
That no creature can obtain for him release
Till God's old anointment of Judah shall cease.
And the *right* root in Israel spring
That shall bring forth the grain of wholeness;
And out of danger He shall us bring   10
Into that region where He is king,
Which above all other far doth abound;
And that cruel Satan he shall confound.

Wherefore I come here upon this ground,
To comfort every creature of birth;
For I, Isaiah the prophet, have found
Many sweet matters whereof we may make mirth,
In this same wise;
For though that Adam be deemed to death,
With all his children, as Abel and Seth,   20
Lo, where a remedy shall rise:

Behold, a maid shall conceive a child
And get us more grace than ever man had.
His glorious birth shall redeem man again
From bondage and thrall.—
More of this matter fain would I tell,
But longer time I have not here to dwell.
The Lord, that is merciful, his mercy soon in us may
    prove
To save our souls from darkness of hell,
And to his bliss bring, as he is both lord and king,   30
And shall be everlasting *in sæcula sæculorum*,[1] Amen.

Scene 1

(*The* Virgin Mary, *and, to meet her, the* Angel
Gabriel.)
Gabriel. Hail, Mary, full of grace, our Lord God is
    with thee;
Above all women that ever was,
Lady, blessed may you be.

Mary. Almighty father, and king of bliss,
From all distresses save me now,

---

1 "For ever and ever."

For inwardly my spirit troubled is,
I am amazed and know not how.

GABRIEL. Dread nothing, maiden, of this;
From heaven above hither am I sent   40
On embassy from that King of bliss
Unto thee, lady and virgin reverent,
Saluting thee here as most excellent,
Whose virtue above all other abounds.
The Holy Ghost on thee shall light
And shadow thy soul soon with virtue
From the Father that is on height;
These words, fair maid, they are full true:
This child that of thee shall be born
Is the Second Person in Trinity,   50
He shall save that was forlorn,*   lost
And the fiend's power destroy shall he.

MARY. Now that it be that Lord's will
His high pleasure to fulfil,
As his handmaid I submit me.

GABRIEL. Now fare well, Lady, of the mighty most,
Unto the godhead I thee commit.

MARY. That Lord thee guide in every place,
And lowly may he lead me, my savior he.
  (*The* ANGEL *departs, and* JOSEPH *comes in.*)
  JOSEPH. Mary, my wife so dear,   60
How do you do, dame, and what cheer
Is with you this tide*?   time

MARY. Truly, husband, I am here
Our Lord's will to abide.

JOSEPH. Now to Bethlehem must I wend,*   go
And feel myself so full of care
Were I to leave thee thus far alone;
God knows the while, dame, how you should fare.

MARY. Go boldly husband, dread nothing,
For I will walk with you on the way;   70
I trust in God, almighty king,
To speed right well our journey.

JOSEPH. Now I thank you, Mary, of your goodness,
That ye my words will not blame;

And since to Bethlehem we shall us dress,
Go we together in God's holy name.
(*They set out for Bethlehem.*)

Scene 2

JOSEPH. Now to Bethlehem have we leagues three,
The day is nigh spent, it draweth toward night;
Fain at your ease, dame, I would you should be,
For you grow all weary, it seemeth in my sight.   80

MARY. Unto some place, Joseph, kindly lead,
That I might rest me with grace in this tide.

JOSEPH. Lo, blessed Mary, here shall ye stay,
And for help to town will I wend.
Is not this the best, dame? what say ye?

MARY. God have mercy, Joseph, my husband so meek;
And heartily I pray you, go now from me.

JOSEPH. That shall be done in haste, Mary, so sweet.
(JOSEPH *goes out on one side;* MARY *goes out on the
other to await his return*).
(*A* SHEPHERD *appears.*)
FIRST SHEPHERD. Now, God, that art in Trinity,
May Thou save my fellows and me;   90
For I know not where my sheep be
This night; it is so cold.
Now it is nigh the midst of the night;
This weather is dark and dim of light,
That of them can I have no sight,
Standing here on this wold.
But now to make their hearts light
Now will I full right stand upon this hill,
And to them call with all my might,
Full well my voice they know———   100
What ho, fellows, ho, hoo, ho.

(*Two other* SHEPHERDS *appear.*)
SECOND SHEPHERD. Hark, Sim, hark! I hear our brother
     on the hill,
This is his voice; right well I know;
Therefore toward him let us go,
And follow his call if we will.—
See, Sim, see where he stands on ground!

I am right glad to have him found.
Brother, where hast thou been so long,
And this night is so cold.

 FIRST SHEPHERD. Ah! friends, there came a gust of wind
  with a mist suddenly,   110
That straight, off my way, went I,
And had a grievous fright.
Then to go knew I not whither,
But travelled on this hill, hither and thither.
I was so weary of this cold weather
That near passed was my might.

 THIRD SHEPHERD. Brother, now we be past that fright,
And it is far into the night,
Full soon will spring the daylight,
It draweth full near the tide.   120
Here awhile let us rest;
Till the sun rise in the east
Let us all here abide.
 (*The* SHEPHERDS *draw forth their food, and eat and
 drink. As they drink they see the star.*)
 THIRD SHEPHERD. Brother, look up and behold,
What thing is yonder, that shineth so bright?
As long as ever I have watched my fold
Yet never saw I such a sight in any night.
Aha! Now is come the time that our fathers have told,
That in the winter's night so cold
A child of maiden mother would be born   130
In whom all prophecies shall be fulfilled.

 FIRST SHEPHERD. Truth it is without nay,
So saith the prophet Isaye;
That a child should be born of a maid so bright,
In winter, nigh the shortest day,
Or else in the middest of the night.

 SECOND SHEPHERD. Loved be God, most of might,
That our grace is to see that sight!
Pray we to him as it is right,
If that his will it be,   140
That we may have knowledge of this signification,
And why it appeareth in this fashion.
And ever to him let us give laudation,
While on earth we be.

(*Here the* ANGELS *sing, "Gloria in excelsis Deo."*[2])
THIRD SHEPHERD. Hark! They sing above in the
    clouds clear;
Heard I never of so sweet a choir!
Now, gentle brother, let us draw near
To hear their harmony.

FIRST SHEPHERD. Brother, mirth and solace is come
For by the sweetness of their song   150
God's Son is come, whom we have looked for long—
As signifieth this star that we now see.

SECOND SHEPHERD. "Gloria in excelsis," that was their
    song;
What say ye, fellows, sang they not so?

FIRST SHEPHERD. That is well said; now go we hence,
To worship that child of high magnificence,
And that we may sing in his presence, lo!,
"Et in terra pax omnibus."[3]
(*The* ANGELS *appear to the* SHEPHERDS.)
FIRST ANGEL. Shepherds fair, dread ye nothing
      Of this star that ye do see;   160
      For this same morn, God's son is born
      In Bethlehem, of a maiden free.

SECOND ANGEL. Hie you thither in haste;
      It is his will ye shall him see
      Lying in a crib, of poor repast;
      Yet of David's line come is he.
(*The* ANGELS *disappear. The* SHEPHERDS *go out, as if
on their way to Bethlehem, singing.*)
As I out rode this passing night,
Of three jolly shepherds I saw a sight;
And all about their fold, a star shone bright.
      They sang terly, terlow!   170
      So merrily the shepherds their pipes can blow.

SCENE 3

*At the Manger—*MARY *and* JOSEPH *with the* CHILD.
(*Enter the three* SHEPHERDS. *They kneel in adoration
before the* CHILD.)
FIRST SHEPHERD. Hail! Maid, mother, and wife so mild!

[2] "Glory to God in the Highest."
[3] "And on earth peace among men."

As the angel said, so have we found.
I have nothing to present to thy child
But my pipe.
   (*He presses the pipe into the infant's fist.*)
               Hold, hold, take it in thy hand,
This pipe in which much pleasure I have found.
And now to honor Thy glorious birth
Thou shall have it to make thee mirth.

   SECOND SHEPHERD. Now hail to Thee child and to thy
      dame,
For in poor lodgings here art thou laid;   180
So the angel said and told us thy name.
Hold, take thou here my hat on thy head,
And now of one thing thou art well sped;
Of weather thou hast no need to complain,
Of wind, nor sun, hail, snow, and rain.

   THIRD SHEPHERD. Hail be thou, lord over water and
      lands;
For thy coming all we may make mirth;
Have here my mittens to put on thy hands,
Other treasure have I none to present thee with.

   MARY. Now, herdsmen kind, for your coming,   190
To my child shall I pray
As he is heaven's King, to grant you his blessing,
And to his bliss that ye may come at your last day.
   (*The* SHEPHERDS *sing.*)
Down from heaven, from heaven so high,
Of angels there came a great company,
With mirth and joy and great solemnity.
      They sang terly, terlow!
      So merrily the shepherds their pipes can blow.
                          (*The* SHEPHERDS *go out.*)

                         SCENE 4

                 Outside KING HEROD's *Palace.*

   (HEROD *appears, followed by his* HERALD.)
   HEROD (*boasting extravagantly*). I am the mightiest
      conqueror that ever walked on ground,
For I am even he that made both heaven and hell,   200
And with my mighty power I hold up the world around.

Magog and Madroc[4] both did I confound,
And with this bright sword their bones I cut asunder,
That all the wide world at those blows did wonder.
I am the cause of this great light and thunder;
It is through my fury that they such noise do make;
My fearful countenance the clouds so encumber
That oftentimes for dread thereof the earth doth quake.
Look! When I with malice this bright sword do shake,
All the whole world, from the North to the South,   210
I may them destroy with one word of my mouth.
To recount unto you my innumerable substance,
That were too much for any tongue to tell;
For all the whole Orient is under mine obedience,
And prince I am of Purgatory and chief captain of Hell;
And those tyrannous traitors by force may I compel
My enemies to vanquish and even to dust them drive,
And with a wink of mine eye not one to leave alive.
    (*To the* HERALD.)
And therefore my herald here, called Calcas,
Warn thou every port that no ships arrive;   220
Nor also any stranger through my realms pass,
But they for their passage shall pay marks five.
Now speed thee forth hastily,
For all the whole Orient is under mine obedience,
Upon a gallows hanged shall be,
And, by Mahound, of me they get no grace.
    HERALD. Now, lord and master, in all the haste
Thy worthy will it shall be wrought;
And thy royal countries shall be passed
In as short time as can be thought.   230
                        (*Exit the* HERALD.)
    HEROD. Now shall our regions throughout be sought,
In every place both East and West;
If any catiffs to me be brought,
It shall be nothing for their best.
And the while that I do rest,
Trumpets, viols, and other harmony
Shall bless the waking of my majesty.
    (HEROD *goes into the palace.* THE FIRST KING, *or*
    MAGUS, *from a far country, enters.*)
    FIRST KING. Now blessed be God, for his sweet news,
For yonder a fair bright star do I see.

    ⁴ Biblical giants.

Now is he come to us,   240
As the prophet said that it should be.
He said there should a babe be born
Coming out of the root of Jesse,
To save mankind that was forlorn*—   lost
And truly come now is he!
Reverence and worship to him will I do,
As God and man, that all made of nought.
    (*The* SECOND KING *enters.*)
    SECOND KING. Out of my way I think that I am,
For tokens of this country can I none see.
Now God that on earth madest man   250
Send me some knowledge of where I be.
To worship that child is mine intent;
Forth now will I take my way.
I trust some company God hath me sent,
For yonder I see a king labor on the way.—
Toward him now will I ride.
Hark, comely king, I pray,
In what land will ye thus ride,
Or whither lies your journey?

    FIRST KING. To seek a child is mine intent,   260
Whom the prophets have meant;
The time is come; now is he sent—
By yonder star here may you see.

    SECOND KING. I pray you with your licence,
To ride with you unto his presence;
To him will I offer frankincense,
For the head of the whole church shall he be.
    (*The* THIRD KING *enters.*)
    THIRD KING. I ride wandering in ways wide,
Over mountains and dales I know not where I am.
Now, king of all kings, send me such guide,   270
That I might have some knowledge of this country's name.
But two kings yonder I see; to them will I ride,
For to have their company; I trust they will me abide.
Hail, comely kings and noble;
Good sirs, I pray you, whither do ye fare?
    FIRST KING. To seek a child is our intent,
Which is betokened by yonder star you may see.
    SECOND KING (*holding up a chalice that sparkles*). To
      him propose this present.
    THIRD KING. Sirs, I pray you and that right humbly

That I may ride with you in company.   280
   (*They welcome him to join them.*)
To almighty God now pray we
That this precious person we may see.
   (*The* KINGS *go out. Then* HEROD *and the* HERALD
   appear.)
   HERALD. Hail, Lord, most of might.
Thy commandment is right.
Into this land are come tonight
Three kings and with a great company.
   HEROD. What do those kings in this country?

   HERALD. To seek a king and a child, they say.

   HEROD. Of what age should he be?

   HERALD. Scant twelve days old fully.   290

   HEROD. And was he so late born?

   HERALD. Ay, sir, so they told me this same day in the
     morn.
   HEROD. Now, on pain of death, bring them me before.
And therefore, herald, hie thee in haste,
Ere that those kings the country have passed;
Look thou bring them all three before my sight.
And in Jerusalem inquire more of that child;
But I warn thee that thy words be mild,
For there must thou care and craft use.
   HERALD. Lord, I am ready at your bidding,   300
To serve thee as my lord and king.
For joy thereof, lo, how I spring
With light heart and fresh gamboling,
Aloft here on this mold.

   HEROD. Then speed thee forth hastily,
And look thou bear thee modestly.
   (*Enter the* KINGS *at one side; the* HERALD *approaches.*)
   HERALD. Hail, sir kings, in your degree;
Herod, king of these countries wide,
Desireth to speak with you all three,
And for your coming doth abide.*   wait/310

   FIRST KING. Sir, at his will we are prepared,
Hie us, brother, unto that lord's place
To speak with him we would be fain;
That child that we seek, may he grant us of his grace.

(*The* HERALD *leads them to* HEROD.)
HERALD. Hail, lord without peer,
These three kings here have we brought.

HEROD. Now welcome, sir kings, in company;
But my brightness, sirs, fear ye not.
Sir kings, as I understand,
A star hath guided you into my land,   320
Wherein great trouble you have found
By reason of its beams bright.
Wherefore, I pray you heartily,
The very truth that ye would certify
How long it is surely
Since of that star ye had first sight?

FIRST KING. Sir king, the very truth to say
And for to show you, as it is best,
This same is even the twelfth day
Since it appeared to us in the West.   330
HEROD (*slyly*). Brother king, then is there no more to
    say,
But with heart and will keep ye your journey,
And come back to me this same way,
Of your news that I might know.—
You shall triumph in this country,
And with great concord banquet with me.
And that child myself then will I see
And honor him also.

SECOND KING. Sir, your commandment we will fulfil,
And humbly address ourselves thereto;   340
God that wieldeth all things at will
The right way us teach,
Sir king, that we may pass your land in peace.

HEROD. Yes, and walk softly, even at your own ease.
Your passport for a hundred days
Here shall you have of clear command;
Our realm to travel any ways
Here shall ye have by special grant.

THIRD KING. Now farewell, king of high degree!
Humbly of you our leave we take.   350

HEROD. Then adieu, Sir kings all three,
And while I live, be bold of me;

There is nothing in this country
But for your own ye shall it take.
(The three KINGS depart.)
Now these three kings are gone on their way;
Unwisely and unwittingly have they all wrought.
When they come again they shall die the same day,
And thus these vile wretches to death shall be brought:
Such is my liking.
He that against my laws will hold,   360
Be he king, or Cæsar, never so bold,
I shall cast them into care all cold
And to death I shall them bring.
(HEROD goes his way.)

SCENE 5

The Manger

(<i>The three</i> KINGS <i>come in to</i> MARY <i>and the</i> CHILD.)
FIRST KING. Hail, lord, that all this world hath wrought,
Hail, God and man, together both;
For thou hast made all things of nought
Albeit thou liest poorly here.
A cup full of gold here I have thee brought,
In tokening thou art without peer.

SECOND KING. Hail be thou, Lord of high magnificence,   370
In tokening of priesthood and dignity of office,
To thee I offer a cup full of incense,
For it behoveth thee to have such sacrifice.

THIRD KING. Hail be thou, lord so long looked for.
I have brought thee myrrh for mortality,
In tokening thou shalt mankind restore
To live by thy death upon a tree.

MARY. God have mercy, kings, of your goodness;
By the guiding of the godhead hither are ye sent;
The provision of my sweet son your ways may redress   380
And heaven reward you for your present.
(<i>The</i> KINGS <i>depart; on their way they say:</i>)
FIRST KING. Sir kings, after our promise
Home by Herod I must needs go.

SECOND KING. Now truly, brother, we can no less;
But I am so far weary, I know not what to do.

THIRD KING. Right so am I, wherefore I pray
Let us all rest us awhile upon this ground.

FIRST KING. Brother, your saying is right to my mind—
The grace of that sweet child save us all sound.
(*The* KINGS *lie down to sleep. An* ANGEL *appears to
them.*)
ANGEL. King of Taurus, Sir Jasper;   390
King of Araby, Sir Balthasar;
Melchior, King of Aginare;
To you now am I sent.
For dread of Herod, go westward home,
Into those parts whence ye came down.
Ye shall be buried there with great renown;
The Holy Ghost this knowledge hath sent.
(*The* ANGEL *disappears. The* KINGS *awake.*)
FIRST KING. Awake, sir kings, I pray,
For the voice of an angel I heard in my dream.

SECOND KING. That is full true what ye say,   400
For he rehearsed our names so plain.

THIRD KING. He bade that we should go down by west,
For dread of Herod's false betray.

FIRST KING. So to do it is the best;
The Child that we have sought guide us the way!
Now farewell, the fairest of men so sweet,
And thanked be Jesus for his message
That we three together so suddenly should meet
That dwell so wide and in strange lands.
And here to make our presentation   410
Unto this king's Son cleansed so clean,
And to his Mother for our salvation,
Of much mirth now may we be
That we so well have made this oblation.

SECOND KING. Now farewell, Sir Jasper, brother to you,
King of Taurus, the most worthy;
Sir Balthasar, also to you I bow,
And thank you both of your good company,
That we together have had.
He that made us to meet on hill,   420
I thank him now, and ever I will,
For now we may go without ill
And of our offering be full glad.

THIRD KING. Now since we must go,
For dread of Herod, that is so wroth,
Now farewell, brother, and brother also;
I take my leave here of you both,
This day on foot.
Now he that made us to meet on plain
And offer to Mary and to her Child,   430
May he give us grace in heaven again
All together to meet.

> (*The three* KINGS *go their ways.* HEROD *and the* HERALD,
> *with* KNIGHTS *in attendance, appear.*)

HERALD. Hail king, most worthiest in might!
Hail, maintainer of courtesy through all this world wide!
Hail, the most mightiest that ever bestrode a steed!
Hail, in thine honor!
These three kings that forth were sent,
And should have come again before thee here present,
Another way, lord, home they went
Contrary to thine honor.   440

HEROD. Another way! Out, out, out!
Have those false traitors done me this deed?
I stamp! I stare! I look all about!
Might I them take, I should burn them.
I rant! I rage! And now run I mad!
Ah! that these villain traitors should mar my plan;
They shall be hanged if I find them.

> (*Here* HEROD *rages on the pageant wagon stage and in
> the street where it stands.*)

Ay! And that brat of Bethlehem he shall be dead.
How say you, sir knights, is not this good counsel,
That all young children for this should be killed,   450
With sword to be slain?
Then shall I, Herod, live in fame,
And all folk fear me and dread,
Thereto will they be full fain.

FIRST KNIGHT. My lord, king Herod by name,
Thy words against my will shall be:
To see so many young children die is shame,
Therefore counsel getst thou none of me!

SECOND KNIGHT. Well said, fellow, my troth I plight;
Sir king, perceive right well you may: 460
So great a murder to see of young folk
Will make a rising in thine own country!

HEROD. A rising! Out, out, out!
(*Here* HEROD *rages again.*)
Out villain wretches, plague upon you I cry;
My will utterly look that it be wrought,
Or upon a gallows both ye shall die,
By Mahound, most mightiest, that me dear hath bought!

FIRST KNIGHT. Now, cruel Herod, since we shall do this
      deed,
All the children of that age die they must need,   470
Your will perforce in this realm must be wrought:
Now with all my might they shall be sought.

SECOND KNIGHT. And I will swear here, upon your bright
      sword,
All the children that I find slain shall be:
That shall make many a mother to weep
And be full sore afeard
In our armor bright when they us see.

HEROD. Now ye have sworn forth to go
See that my will ye work both by day and night,
And then will I for joy trip like a doe.
But when they be dead I warn you bring them before   480
      my sight.
(HEROD *and his retinue go out.* WOMEN *come in with
their children.*)
FIRST WOMAN. I lull my child wondrously sweet,
And in mine arms I do it keep,
Because I would not that it should not cry.

SECOND WOMAN. The babe that is born in Bethlehem
      so meek,
May He save my child and me from villainy.

THIRD WOMAN. Be still, be still, my little child,
The Lord of Lords save both thee and me,
For Herod hath sworn, with words wild,
That all young children slain shall be.
(*The* MOTHERS *then sing their children to sleep:*)
Lulla, lullay, ye little tiny child;   490
By-by, lulla, lullay, ye little tiny child,
      By-by, lulla, lullay.

Oh sisters two, how may we do,
For to preserve this day

This poor youngling for whom we do sing
By-by, lulla, lullay?

Herod the king, in his raging,
Charged he hath this day
His men of might, in his own sight,
All young children to slay.   500

Then woe is me, poor child, for thee
And ever mourn I may;
For thy parting, neither say nor sing
By-by, lulla, lullay.
  (HEROD'S KNIGHTS *appear, fully armed.*)
  FIRST KNIGHT. See here, ye wives, whither are ye away?
What ye bear in your arms needs must we see.
If they be men children, die they must this day,
For at Herod's will all things must be.

  SECOND KNIGHT. And once I them seize,
To slay nought will I spare.   510
We must fulfil Herod's commandments,
Else we be as traitors and cast into care.

  FIRST WOMAN. Sir knights, of your courtesy,
This day shame not your chivalry,
But on my child have pity,
For my sake in this place.

  SECOND WOMAN (*threatening*). He that slays my child
    in sight,
If my strokes on him light,
Be he squire or knight,
I hold him but lost!   520

  THIRD WOMAN. Sit he never so high in saddle
But I shall make his brains addle,
And here with my pot ladle
With him will I fight!
  (*She flourishes a utensil.*)
I shall lay on him here,
With this same womanly gear,
Whether he be king or knight.
  (*The* KNIGHTS *overpower the* WOMEN *and slay the chil-
  dren.*)
  FIRST KNIGHT (*as they go toward* HEROD'S *palace*). Who
    heard ever such a cry

Of women that their children have lost,
And greatly rebuking chivalry,   530
Throughout this realm in every home,
Which many a man's life is like to cost.
For this great wrong that here is done
I fear much vengeance thereof will come.

SECOND KNIGHT. Ay, brother, such tales may we not tell,
Wherefore to the king let us go;
For he is like to bear the peril,
Which was the cause that we did so.
Yet must they all be brought to him,
With wains and wagons full height;   540
I trow there will be a sorry sight.
(*They approach* HEROD.)

FIRST KNIGHT. Lo, Herod king thou mayst now see
How many thousands we have slain.

SECOND KNIGHT. And needs thy will fulfilled be,
But may no man attempt this again!
(*He departs with bowed head. The* HERALD *approaches*
HEROD.)
HERALD. Herod king, I must thee tell,
All thy deeds are come to nought:
This child is gone in Egypt to dwell!
Lo, sire, in thine own land what wonders be wrought.

HEROD. Into Egypt! alas for woe!
Longer in land here I cannot abide: 550
Saddle my palfrey, for in haste must I go;
After yon traitors now will I ride
To slay them!
Now all men I send fast
Into Egypt in haste;
All that country will I go to
So I may come to them!

The Death of Herod

A Variant Version of The Massacre of Innocents from the
Chester Cycle

The SECOND WOMAN defends the child she has been carrying
in her arms, but the SECOND KNIGHT succeeds in killing it.

SECOND WOMAN. Out, out, out, out!
Ye shall be hanged, the whole rout,
Though be ye never so stout!
Full foul ye have done.
This child was brought to me
To look to, thieves; who be ye?
He was not mine, as you may see,
He was the king's son.
I shall tell, while I drye,*   suffer
His child was slain before my eye.   10
Thieves, you shall be hanged high,
When I come to his hall.
But, ere I go, have thou one!
  (*She strikes this knight and another one.*)
And thou another, Sir John!
For to the king I will anon,
To plaint upon you all.
  (*They go to* HEROD, *who is feasting and carousing.*)
  SECOND WOMAN. Lo, lord, look and see
The child that thou sent to me,
Men of thine own maynee*   household
Have slain it, here they be.   20

  HEROD. Fie, woman, fie! God give thee pain,
Why did thou not say that child was mine?
But it is vengeance on me, as drink I wine,
And that is now well seen.

  SECOND WOMAN. Yes, lord, they see well aright
Thy son was like to have been a knight,
For in good harness he was dight,
Painted wondrous gay;
Yet was I never so sore with fright,
When the spears were through him thrust,   30

Lord, so little was my might,
When they began this fray.

HEROD. He was right surely in silk array,
In gold and pearl that was so gay,
They might well know by his array,
He was a king's son;
   (Grieving.)
What the devil is this to say!
Why were thy wits so away?
Could thou not speak, could thou not pray,
And say it was my son?
Alas! what the devil is this to moan?   40
Alas! my days be now done;
I know I must die soon:
Bootless is it to make moan,
Though damnèd I must be;
My legs rot and my arms,
And now I see of fiends swarms—
I have done so many harms—
From Hell coming after me,
For I have done so much woe,
And never good. Since I must go,   50
Therefore I see coming my foe,
To fetch me to hell.
I bequeath here in this place
My soul to be with Sathanas.
I die now, alas! alas!
I may no longer dwell.
   (As HEROD gives signs of dying, a DEMON appears to
   fetch him away. The DEMON first addresses the audi-
   ence.)
   DEMON. 'Ware, 'ware, for now unwarily wakes your woe
And I am swifter than is the doe
To fetch this lord from you   60
In woe evermore to dwell.
   (He shakes a stick at the public.)
And with this crooked cudgel your backs I'll claw
And all false believers burn and blow,
That from the crown of the head to the toe
I leave no right whole fell.*   skin
From Lucifer, my lord, hither I am sent,
To fetch this king's soul here present,
Into hell to bring him there to be spent,

And ever to live in woe.
There fire burns, blow, and brent,*   burns/70
In there shall be this lord verament,*   truly
His place therein evermore is meant,
His body never to go from me.

No more shall you trespass, by my loyalty,
That fill your measures falsely,[1]
Shall bear this lord company—
They get no other grace!
I will bring you thus to woe
And come again and fetch mo*   more
As fast as I may go.   80
     (*Brusquely as* HEROD *dies.*)
Farewell, and have a good day!
     (*He drags* HEROD'S *body away.*)

[1] "That give false measure," as some tapsters apparently did.

The Betrayal of Christ

The Chester Bakers' Play

A MODERNIZED VERSION BY JOHN GASSNER

Characters

JESUS	MASTER OF THE HOUSE
PETER	JUDAS
JOHN	MALCHUS

SCENE 1

On the outskirts of Jerusalem.

(JESUS *appears with his disciples.*)
    JESUS. Brethren all, to me right dear,
Come hither and you shall hear:
The feast of Easter, as you know, draws near
It almost is at hand.
That feast to keep must we
With all great solemnity;

The paschal lamb must eaten be,
As the Law doth command.
Therefore, Peter, look that thou go
And John with thee shall also   10
Preparing all things belonging thereto.
According to the Law.
    PETER. Lord, thy bidding do will we,
But tell us first where the feast shall be,
And we shall do it speedily
And thither will we draw.

    JESUS. Go into the city which ye see,
And there a man meet shall ye
With a waterpot; that beareth he.
So you may him know.   20
Into what house that he shall go
Into the same house enter ye also
And say the master sent ye, too,
His message for to show;
Say, "The master to thee us sent,
To have a place convenient;
The paschal lamb there to eat is my intent,
With my disciples all."
A fair parlor he will show,
Prepare there all things due   30
Where I with my retinue
Fulfil the Law we shall.

SCENE 2

A street in Jerusalem.

(PETER and JOHN *go to speak with a man bearing
a waterpot, and he shows them the house of his
master.*)
    PETER. All hail, good fellow, heartily!
To thy master's house I pray thee hie,
And we must keep thee company,
Our message to him to say.
    THE MAN. Come on your way and follow me,
My master's house soon shall you see,
Lo, here it is verily,
Say now what you will.   40
    (*They go into the house.*)

SCENE 3

Inside the house.

PETER. Sir, the master saluteth thee,
And as messengers sent we be.
Therefore we pray thee heartily
Give heed to us,
The master hath sent us to thee.
A place prepare for him must we;
The paschal lamb to eat will he
With his disciples here.

MASTER OF THE HOUSE. Lo, here a parlor all ready
  dight,*   prepared
With paved floors and windows bright.   50
Make all things ready as you think it right
And have no care or fear.

JOHN. Now, brother Peter, let us hie*   go
The paschal lamb to make ready,
Then to our master go you and I
As fast as we may.
  (*They make the table ready. Then* JESUS *enters
  and seats himself at it.*)
PETER. Thy commandment, Lord, done have we,
The paschal lamb is made ready.

JESUS. Now, brethren, go to your seat,
The paschal lamb now let us eat,
And then shall we of other thing entreat   60
That be of great effect.
For now you know the time has come
That signs and shadows declared to be done;
Therefore make haste that we may soon
All old ways clean reject.

For now a new law will I begin,
To help man out of his sin,
So that he may heaven win,
That which for sin he lost.
And here in presence of you all,   70
Another sacrifice begin I shall,
To bring mankind out of his thrall*   slavery to sin
For help him I must.

Brethren, I tell you who are nigh,
With great desire desired have I
This Passover to eat with you truly
Before my trial.
For I say to you surely,
My father's will almighty
I must fulfil meekly,   80
And ever to it be bound.

(JESUS *takes bread, breaks it, blesses it and gives it
to his disciples.*)
This bread I give here my blessing,
Take ye and eat, brethren, at my bidding.
Believe this bread, without lying,
It is my body,
Which shall die for all mankind
In remission of men's sin:
This I give you to bear in mind.
(*He takes a cup, or chalice, in his hand and raises
it up.*)
Brethren, take this with heart free,
For this is my blood   90
That shall be shed on a tree.
For no longer together drink shall we
Till in heavenly bliss we be
To taste ghostly* food.   spiritual
Brethren, forsooth, I say
One of you shall me betray
That eateth here today
In this company.
    JAMES. Sorrowful for these words are we!
Who it is I cannot see: 100
Perhaps this lot may fall to me—
Lord, tell if it be I.
    (*At this point,* JUDAS *dips his hand in the cup.*)
    JESUS. Through his deceit I am all but dead
That in my cup now wets his bread:
Much woe must fall upon his head;
This wretch must suffer, i-wis.*   certainly, surely
Well were it had he not been born,
For his body and soul are both forlorn—
And yet willed by the Lord is this!
    JUDAS. Dear master, is it I,   110
That shall do this villainy?

JESUS. Thou hast said, Judas, verily,
For surely thou art he:
What thou shalt do, do hastily.
  JUDAS. Farewell, all this company,
For on an errand I must flee—
Undone it may not be.
  (JUDAS *hurries out.*)
  JESUS. Brethren, take up this meat anon,
To another work we must be gone:
Your feet shall washen* be, each one,   washed/120
To show dear charity:
And first myself I will begin
And wash you all that are herein,—
And on this deed shall you put your mind
And the meeker for it be.
  (JESUS *puts on a linen cloth and gets ready to wash*
  PETER's *feet.*)
  PETER. Ah, Lord, shalt thou wash my feet?
  JESUS. That do I, Peter, do not fear,
As thou shalt do to me afterward.
  PETER. Nay, Lord, in no manner I swear
My feet shalt thou wash here.
  JESUS. Unless I wash thee, without a doubt
Of heavenly joy getst thou no part.

  PETER. Nay, Lord, my feet may well be left:
Wash only my hands and my head.
  JESUS (*persistently*). All clean, I have said,
Thy feet shall washen be.
  (*He washes the feet of each of the disciples in turn,
  and wipes them with a cloth.*)
  JESUS. Dear brethren, well may it be
That Lord and Master ye call me.
And right you say that this should be
Since "*I am,*" and I have been of yore.   140

As I have washed your feet,
Lord and Master, as is meet
Do meekly unto each other
As I have done to you before.
  (*After a pause.*)
My little children and my brethren free,
But a little while I may with you be,
And whither I go shall you not go with me;
And now I am on the way!

But this truly is my bidding,
That you love each other in everything.   150
    THOMAS. Lord, we know not, in good faith,
What manner of road thou wilt essay;
Tell us that know we may
That road, so we may go with Thee.
    JESUS. I say to you on this to make no strife:
In me the Way, the Truth, the Life;
And to my Father no man or wife
May come without me;
And if ye know me verily,
You also know my Father on high.   160
And I tell ye hence truly
Know Him you shall—all of ye.
    PHILIP. Lord, let me see thy Father soon,
And that would suffice everyone.
    JESUS. Thou hast gone with me a long time,—
Therefore Philip why do you speak so?
For truly he who sees me
Sees my Father clearly.

And though I go now to my distress,
I do not leave you comfortless,   170
For soon I will come again;
And then your heart, forgetting this woe,
Will gladly learn my bliss to know;
This joy no man can take from you.
Though he were full fain.*   eager

We must rise up now and start anon;
But to my prayers I must first be gone;
So sit you still every one
While to my Father I will call.
    (He starts to leave them.)
Remain awake and have benison*   blessing/180
To keep from falling into temptation:
For the spirit ever to bale* is born   pain
And the flesh is ever ready to fall.
    *(JESUS goes to pray by himself, and his disciples
promptly fall asleep.)*

SCENE 4

    JESUS *(alone)*. Father of Heaven in Majesty,
Glorify, if Thy will it be

Thy son that he may glorify thee,
Now ere hence I wend.
In earth thou has given me power,
And I have done with heart free
The work that thou hast charged me,   190
And brought it to an end.

Thy name have I made men to know,
And spared not thy will to show
To my disciples and bestow,
What thou hast given me;
And now they know verily,
That from the Father sent am I,
Therefore I pray thee especially
To save them through thy mercy.
  (*Then he comes back to his disciples and finds them
  asleep.*)

What, sleep you, brethren, all here?   200
Rise up and make your prayer,
Lest temptation have power
To make you fall;
The flesh is, as I said before,
Inclining to sin of yore,
And spirit busied evermore,
Therefore wake ye all.
  (*They continue to sleep, and he returns to his
  prayers and, raising his voice, he cries:*)
My heart is in great misliking,
For death to me is coming:
Father, if I dare ask one thing   210
Put this away from me;
Every thing to thee possible is,
Nevertheless yet in this
At thy will I am, i-wis.
As thou wilt, let it be.
  (*He returns to his disciples again.*)
You sleep, brethren, still—I see:
Sleep on now all ye;
My time has come taken to be;
From you I must away.
He that hath betrayed me,   220
This night from him will I not flee;
In sorry time born was he,
And so he may well say.

(*Then* JUDAS *comes thither, with soldiers carrying
lanterns, torches, and arms.*)
JESUS. You men, I ask, whom seek ye?

MALCHUS. Jesus of Nazareth, him seek we.

JESUS. Here, all ready, I am he;
What have you to say?

JUDAS. Ah, sweet master, kiss thou me,
For it is long time since I thee see,
And together we will flee,   230
And steal from them away.

JESUS. Whom seek you, men, with such a breath?
FIRST MAN. We seek Jesus of Nazareth.
JESUS. I said before, and still I say,
I am he, in good fay;
Suffer these men to go their way,
And I am at your will.
MALCHUS. False thief, thou shalt go
To Bishop Caiaphas, and that anon,
Or I shall break thee body and bone,   240
If thou be late.
PETER. Thief, if thou be so bold,
My master so to scold,
Thou shalt be quit an hundredfold,
And onward* take thou this!   as an advance
Be thou so bold, as thrive I,
To hold my master here and him tie,
Full dear thou shalt him buy!
Be thou the heathen cold,
Thy ear shall off by God's grace   250
Ere thou pass from this place.
   (PETER *draws his sword, and with it slashes* MAL-
   CHUS's *ear.*)
Go now to Caiaphas,
And bid him make thee right.
MALCHUS. Out! Alas, alas, alas!
By the Lord's bones, mine ear he has!
It is a hard case,
That ever I came out!
JESUS. Peter, put thy sword up on high!
Whosoever with the sword smitheth gladly
With sword shall perish sadly,   260
I tell thee, without doubt.

(JESUS *touches* MALCHUS's *ear, and cures it.*)
   MALCHUS. Ah! well is me! well is me!
My ear is healed well, I see!
So merciful a man as he
Knew I never none.
   FIRST MAN. Yea, but though he have healed thee,
Free of us he shall not be,
But to Sir Caiaphas, as must be,
With us shall he be gone.

   JESUS. As to a thief you come here,   270
With staves and swords and armor,
To take me in foul manner,
And wreak your wicked will?
In our temple I was with you aye
Yet no hand on me would you lay;
But now is come the time and day
Your desire to fulfil.
   FIRST MAN. Come on, caitiff,* to Sir Caiaphas,   villain
Or thou shalt have hard grace!
   (*Hurrying him on.*)
Trot upon a swifter pace,   280
Thou vile hypocrite!
Though Beelzebub[1] and Sathanas*   Satan
Come to help thee in this case,
   (*Binding His hands.*)
Both thy hands that thou hast
Shall be bound tight.
   (*They take* JESUS *away with them.*)

* illiterate ~~society~~ - difficult to create & give parts - rhyming and rhythm helps in learning the different roles.

---

[1] An important demon and associate of Lucifer, or Satan.

The (Wakefield) Crucifixion

A MODERNIZED VERSION BY JOHN GASSNER

Characters

PILATE	LONGEUS
FIRST, SECOND, THIRD,	JESUS
and FOURTH TORTURERS	JOHN
MARY (THE VIRGIN MARY)	NICODEMUS

(PILATE *appears on the stage as a Prologue and addresses the audience.*)

PILATE. Peace, I bid every wight!*   person
Stand as still as stone in wall
While ye are present in my sight
That none of you clatter nor call:
For if you do, your death is hight.*   called
I warn both great and small
With this brand* burnished so bright,   sword
Therefore in peace look ye be all.
    (*There is a commotion among the people.*)
      What? Peace, in the devil's name!
Harlot* and dastards all between   villains/10
On gallows ye'll be made full tame.
Thieves and muckers keen,
Will ye not hold peace when I bid you?
By Mahoun's blood!¹ If ye me teen,*   trouble annoy
I shall ordain for you
Pains that never yet were seen,
     And that anon.
Be ye so bold beggars, I warn you,
Full boldly shall I beat you,
To hell the devil shall draw you,   20
     Body, back, and bond.

     I am a lord that mickle* is of might,   much
Prince of all Jewry, Sir Pilate I hight.*   am called

¹ Refers to a supposedly pagan diety or idol. The word is derived from Mahomet.

Bow to my bidding, both great and small,
    Or else be ye shent.*   destroyed
Therefore keep your tongues, I warn you all,
    And unto us take tent.*   pay attention
  (PILATE *leaves the stage as* JESUS *and the* TORTURERS
  come on.)
  FIRST TORTURER [*dragging* JESUS, *who bears the*
    Cross on his bent shoulders]. All peace, all peace,
    among you all!
And hearken now what shall befall
    To this false chuffer* here   churl, worthless fellow/30
That with his false auguries
Has made himself so God-wise
    Among us many a year.
He calls himself a prophet,
And says that he can bales* beat   miseries, illnesses
    And make all things amend,
But e'er long know we shall
Whether he can overcome his own bale,
    Or 'scape out of our hand.

    Was not this a wonder thing   40
That he durst call himself a king
    And make so great a lie?
    But, by Mahoun! while I may live,
Those proud words shall I never forgive,
    Till he be hanged on high.
  SECOND TORTURER. His pride, fie, we set at nought,
But each man reckon in his thought
    And look that we nought want;
For I shall seek, if that I may,
By the order of knighthood, today,   50
    To make his heart pant.
  THIRD TORTURER. And so shall I, with all my might,
Abate his pride this very night,
    And reckon him a creed.
Lo! he lets on he could no ill,
But he can, ay, when he will,
    Do a full foul deed.
  FIRST TORTURER. That was a noble rede.*   piece of advice
Lo, here I have a band.*   rope/60
If need be, to bind his hand.
    This thong, I trow,* will last.   believe
  SECOND TORTURER. And one to the other side,

That shall abate his pride,
    If it be but drawn fast.
  THIRD TORTURER (*holding up a hammer*). Lo, here
    a hammer and nails also
For to fasten fast our foe
    To this tree full soon.
  FIRST TORTURER. Now dare I say hardly,
He shall with all his idolatry   70
No longer us swell.
  SECOND TORTURER. Since Pilate has him to us given
Have done, quickly, let it be seen,
How we can with him mell.*   deal
    THIRD TORTURER. Now we are at the Mount of
    Calvary,
Have done, fellows, and let now see
    How we can with him play.
  FIRST TORTURER (*pushing* JESUS). In faith, sir, since
    ye called yourself king,
You must prove a worthy thing
    That well must fare.   80
You must joust in tournament,
But sit you fast, lest ye be spent,
    Else down I shall you bear.
  SECOND TORTURER (*buffeting* JESUS). If thou be
    God's son, as thou tells,
Thou canst save thyself—how shouldst thou else?
    Else were it marvel great;
And canst thou not, we will not trow
What thou has said, but make thee mow*   bow to you
    When thou sitt'st in the seat.[2]
  THIRD TORTURER (*throwing him down on the cross*).
    Stand near, fellows, and let us see   90
How we can unhorse our king so free
    By any craft;
Stand thou yonder on yon side,
And we shall see how he can ride.
    And how to wield a shaft.
  FIRST TORTURER (*fitting Him on the cross*). Sir, come
    ye hither, and have done,
And get upon your palfrey soon,
For you are ready now.

  [2] They mockingly relate Christ hanging on the cross to a knight riding a
horse ("palfry").

SECOND TORTURER (*to the* THIRD TORTURER). Knit
   thou a knot, with all thy strength
For to draw this arm at length   100
     Till it come to the bore.
THIRD TORTURER. Thou art mad, man, by this light!
It wants, in each man's sight,
Another half span, and more.
   FIRST TORTURER. Yet draw out this arm, and make it
   fast,
With this rope, that well will last,
     And each man lay hand to.
   SECOND TORTURER. Next drive a nail there through,
And then we shall nothing doubt,
     For it will not burst.   110
   THIRD TORTURER. That shall I do, so might I stand!
   FIRST TORTURER. Hold down his knees.
   SECOND TORTURER. That shall I—
His nurse did never better do.
     Lay on with each hand.
   FIRST TORTURER. Hold it now fast there
One of you the bore shall bear,
     And then it may not fail.
   SECOND TORTURER. Yea, and bring it to the mark.
   THIRD TORTURER. Pull, pull!   120
(*They begin to raise the cross, straining and grunt-
ing.*)
   FIRST TORTURER. Have now!
   SECOND TORTURER. Let see!
   THIRD TORTURER. Aha!
   FIRST TORTURER. Thereto with all my might.
   SECOND TORTURER. Aha, hold still there.
   THIRD TORTURER. So, fellows, look now alive.
(*Calling to some of the spectators, who come to
their assistance.*)
   FIRST TORTURER. Come hither, fellows, and have
   done,
And help that this tree soon
     Be lift with all your sleight.*   skill
   SECOND TORTURER. Fellows, lay on all your hend,* hand/130
For to raise this tree on end
     And let see who is wise.
   THIRD TORTURER. I rede* we do as he says,   advise

Set we the tree on the mortise[3]
    And there will it stand fast.
  FIRST TORTURER. Up with the timber.
  SECOND TORTURER. Hold even amongst us all.
  THIRD TORTURER. Yea, and let it into the mortise
    fall,
For then will it stand best.
  SECOND TORTURER (*He flings a crown of thorns on His*
    head.) Ah, fellow, wear thy crown!   140
  The THIRD TORTURER (*who is a conscientious*
    worker). Trowest thou this timber will come
    down?
  FIRST TORTURER. Ah, it stands up like a mast.
  JESUS. I pray you, people, that pass me by,
That lead your life so pleasantly
    Raise up your heart on high.
Behold if ever ye saw body
Bruised and beaten thus bloody
    Or undone thus dolefully.
In this world was never any wight*   person
    That suffered half so sair.*   sore, sorely/150
My mind, my mien, my might
Is naught but sorrow to sight.
    And comfort? None but care!

My folk, what have I done to thee
That thou all thus dost torment me?
    Thy sin bear I full soon.
How have I grieved* thee? Answer me.   injured
That thou thus nailest me to a tree,
    And all for thine error.
Where shalt thou seek succor?   160
This fault how shalt thou amend
When that thou thy Savior
Driyest to this dishonor
    And nail'st through feet and hend.

All creatures whose kinds may be least,
Beasts and birds, they all have rest
    When they are woebegone.
But God's own son, that should be best,
Has not thereon his head to rest,
    But on his shoulder bone!   170

[3] The upright wood is set into the horizontal.

What kindness more have I not turned to?
Have I not done what I ought to do,
        Made thee in my likeness?
Guiltless thus am I put to pine,
Not for my sin, man, but for thine.
        Thus am I rent on rood!*   the cross
I have shown thee kindness, unkindly thou me
    requitest,
See thus thy wickedness, look how thou me despitest.

My brother, that I came for to buy,*   save
Has hanged me here, thus hideously,   180
        Friends find I few or none.
But, Father, that sittest on throne,
        Forgive thou them this guilt.
I pray to thee for this boon—
They know not what they doon,*   do
        Nor whom they thus have spoilt!
    FIRST TORTURER. (*laughing*). Yes, what we do full
        well we know.
    SECOND TORTURER. Yes, that shall he find within a
        throw.
    MARY (*clasping his feet*). Alas, the dole I dree!* I   suffer
        droop, I go in dread.
Why hang'st thou, son, so high? My woe begins to
        breed.   190
All blemished is thy brow, I see thy body bleed;
In the world, my son, we never had such woe as now
        in our need.
My flesh that I have fed,
In life lovingly I thee led!
Full hard art thou bestead
        Among these foemen fell:*   cruel
Such sorrow for to see,
My dearest child, on thee,
Is more mourning to me
        Than any tongue may tell.   200
Alas! thy holy head
Has not whereon to hold.

Thy face with blood is red,
Once fair as flower in wold.*   field
Glad should I stand in stead!
        Alas, my child, for care!

For all rent is thy hide,
I see on either side
Tears of blood down glide
    Over all thy body bare.   210
Alas that ever I should bide,
To see my son thus fare!
  JOHN (*who has followed her*). Alas, for dule,* my   dole, sorrow
    lady dear!
All for changed is thy cheer,
To see this prince without a peer,
    Thus lapped in woe;
He was thy food, thy fairest one,
Thy love, thy like, thy lovesome son,
That high on tree thus hangs alone
    With body black and blue, alas!   220
To me and many more,
A good master he was.

But, lady, since it is His will
The prophecy to fulfil—
Mankind to redeem of ill
    For which he suffers pain,
He his death as ransom make,
For so the prophets spake—
I counsel thee thy grief to slake,
    Thy weeping may nothing gain   230
Nor thy sorrow:
Our good he buys full fain,*   gladly
Us all from bale* to borrow.   suffering
  MARY (*refusing to be comforted*). Alas, thine eyes as
    crystal clear,
That shone as sun in sight,
That lovely were and dear
Lost they have their light
And are all faded in fear;
All dim then are they dight*—   made
In pain thou hast no peer.   240
Sweet son, tell me thy thought;
What wonders hast thou wrought
To be in pain thus brought
    Thy blessed blood to blend?
Ah, son, think on my woe,
Why will thou from me go?

On earth is no man mo*   more
     That may my mirth⁴ amend.
  JOHN. Comely lady, good and fair,
Fain would I comfort thee;   250
My master told unto us many
That he should suffer every pain,
And die upon a tree,
And to the life rise up again;
Upon the third day should it be
     Full right.
Therefore weeping is not meet
For thee, our Lady sweet:
Our woe he will defeat
     In risen might.   260
  MARY. My sorrow it is so sad,
No solace may me save:
Mourning makes me mad,
No hope of help I have.
I am redeless* and afraid   without advice
For fear that I should rave,
Nought may make me glad,
Till I be in my grave.
Alas! my lamb so mild,
Why wilt thou from me go   270
Among these wolves wild
That work on thee this woe?
For shame, who may thee shield?
For friends now hast thou foe.
Alas, my comely child,
Why will thou from me go?
Maidens, make your moan,
And weep, ye wives, every one,
With me, most sad alone,
     The child that born was best.   280
The heart is stiff as stone
     That for no bale will brest.*   break
  JOHN. Dear lady, well for me
If that I might comfort thee,
For the sorrow that I see
     Shears my heart in sunder.
And when I see my Master hung
In pain so bitter and great

---

⁴ Obviously, "mirth" is not intended to mean "joy" or "merriment" here, but its opposite is meant.

My sorrow has no mate
And cannot find a tongue.   290
    MARY. Alas, death, thou dwellest too long,
Why art thou hid from me?
Sore sighing is my song.
       Ah, death, what has thou done?
With thee will I fare soon,
Since I had children none but one,
Best under sun or moon.
Gabriel! that art so good
One time thou did me greet,
And then I understood.   300
Counsel me now of this,
My life how shall I lead
When from me gone is
He that was my head
      On high?
My death, now, come it is:
My dear son, have mercy!
  JESUS (*opening his eyes and reviving*). My mother
    mild, change thou thy cheer,
Cease from thy sorrow and sighing sere,*   arid, futile
It sits upon my heart full sore.   310
The sorrow is sharp, I suffer here;
But the dole thou drees,* my mother dear,   suffers
Me martyrs mickle* more.   much
Thus wills my father I fare
    To loose mankind from bands;
His son will he not spare.
Therefore, mother make no mourning
Since mankind, through my dying,
    May thus to bliss be brought.
Woman, weep thou right nought,   320
    Take there, John, unto thy child;
John, lo, there, thy mother mild!
  (*Suddenly he groans.*)
Now thirst I wonder sore.
  FIRST TORTURER (*thrusting himself forward and
    offering* JESUS *a sop of vinegar*). Nought but hold
    thy peace,
Thou shalt have drink within a trice,
    Myself shall be thy slave.
Have here the draught that I thee get,

And I shall warrant it is *not sweet*
  By all the good I have.
 SECOND TORTURER (*mocking* JESUS). So, sir, say how
  all your will,   330
For if ye could have holden you still
  Ye had not had this bed.
 THIRD TORTURER. Thou would'st all costs be King
  of Jews,
But by this I trow thou rues
  All that thou has said.
 FOURTH TORTURER. He has him loosed of great
  prophecies
That he should make us tempylles*   temples
  And make it clean fall down;
And then he said he should it raise
As well as it was within three days.   340
  He lied, that know we all;
And for his lies in great despite
We will divide his clothing right
  Unless he knows more of art.
 FIRST TORTURER. Yes, as ever might I thrive,
Soon will we this mantle rive,
  And each man take his part.
 SECOND TORTURER. How, wouldst thou we share this
  cloth?
 THIRD TORTURER. Nay, forsooth, that were I loth,
For then it were all ways spoilt.   350
But assent thou to my law,
And let us all lots draw
  And then is no one beguiled.* deceived, deprived
 (*They sit down to play dice for* JESUS' *garments.*)[5]
 THIRD TORTURER (*looking up at the figure on the
  cross*). If thou be Christ, as men thee call
Come down now among us all
  And bear not thy dismay!
 FIRST TORTURER. Yea, and help myself that we may
  see
And we shall all believe in thee,
  Whatsoever thou say.
 SECOND TORTURER. He calls himself God of might, 360

---

[5] A section is omitted here: The torturers notice the writing on the cross,
one of them reads it, and he protests to Pilate because the writing calls
Christ King of the Jews.

But I would see him display the might
  To do such a deed.
He raised Lazare out of his sleep
But he cannot help himself
  Now in his great need.

JESUS. Eli, Eli, lama sabachthani!
My God, my God! wherefor and why
  Has thou forsaken me?

SECOND TORTURER. Now, hear ye not as well as I
How he can upon Eli cry   370
  Upon this wise?

THIRD TORTURER. Yea, there is no Eli in this country
Shall deliver him from this misery
  No, in no wise.

FIRST TORTURER. I warrant you now at the last
That he shall soon yield the ghost,
  For bursten is his gall.

JESUS. Now is my passion* brought to end,   suffering
Father of heaven, into thy hand
  I do commend my soul.   380

FIRST TORTURER. Let one prick him with a spear,
And if it should do him no wear
  Then is his life near past.

SECOND TORTURER. This blind knight may best do
  that. (*He pushes* LONGEUS, *a blind knight forward.*)

LONGEUS. Make me not do, save I know what.

THIRD TORTURER (*forcing his hand upward*). Naught,
  but strike up fast.

LONGEUS (*having thrust his spear into* JESUS' *side.*)
  Ah! Lord, what may this be?
Once I was blind, now I can see;
God's son, hear me, Jesu!
For this trespass of mine thou rue*   pity/390
For, Lord, other men me made
That I thee struck unto the heart,
I see thou hangest here on high,
And diest to fulfill the prophecy.

FIRST TORTURER. Go we hence, and leave him here
For I shall be his bail this year
  He feels now no more pain . . .
  Nor gets his life again.

(THE TORTURERS *depart. Christ's followers are left
alone.*)

JOSEPH OF ARIMATHEA.[6] Alas, alas, and well-a-way!
That ever I should abide this day.   400
Nicodeme, I would we went indeed
To Sir Pilate, if we might with speed
     His body crave;
I will strive with all my might
For my service to ask that knight
     To grant His body a grave.
  NICODEMUS. Joseph, I will go with thee
To do what is in me,
     For that body to pray.
Our good will and our labor   410
I hope will bring us harbor
     Hereafter one day!
  (*They walk to* PILATE's *throne and kneel.*)
  JOSEPH OF ARIMATHEA. Sir Pilate, God thee save!
Grant me what I crave
     If that it be thy will.
  PILATE. Welcome, Joseph, might thou be,
What so thou askest, I grant it thee
     So that it be not ill.
  JOSEPH OF ARIMATHEA. For my long service, I thee
    pray,
Grant me the body, say me not nay,   420
     Of Jesus, dead on the rood.*   cross
  PILATE. I grant it well, if he dead be;
Good leave shalt thou have of me.
     Do with him what you think good.
  JOSEPH OF ARIMATHEA. Grammercy, sir, for your
    good grace
That you did grant me in this place;
     Go we our way:
Nicodeme, come forthwith,
For I myself shall be the smith
     The nails out for to dray.*   draw/430
  NICODEMUS. Joseph, I am ready still
To go with thee in all good will
To help with all I might.—
  (*They come to the cross, which has been lowered.*)
Pull forth the nails on either side
And I shall hold him up thus right—

  [6] Joseph of Arimathea is supposedly a "Knight" in the Roman army; he
became one of Christ's followers.

(*He is overcome with grief on beholding the limp
body.*)
   Ah, Lord, how art thou in plight!
   JOSEPH OF ARIMATHEA. Help now, fellow, with all
      thy might,
That he be swathed and well dight,*   dressed, covered
   And lay him on this bier:
Bear we him forth into the kirk*   church/440
To the tomb on which I did work
      Full many a year.
   NICODEMUS (*as they bear* JESUS *out*). It shall be so,
      withouten* nay,   without
For Him that died on Good Friday,
   And crowned was with thorn;
   (*Addressing the audience.*)
Save you all that now here be
That Lord that died for ye,
   And rose on Paschal Morn.*   Easter morning

The Resurrection, Harrowing of Hell, and the Last Judgment

A SYNOPTIC VERSION BY JOHN GASSNER[1]

Characters

PILATE	MARY,	PETER
CAIAPHAS	MOTHER OF JAMES	JOHN
ANNAS	MARY SALOME	ADAM
KNIGHTS	MARY MAGDALENE	ISAIAH
MICHAEL	ANGELS	DAVID
GABRIEL	DEVILS	ENOCH
JESUS	SATAN	ELIJAH THE PROPHET
GOD	THE DAMNED SOULS	SETH
MARY,	THE SAVED SOULS	JOHN THE BAPTIST
MOTHER OF JESUS		SIMEON

1 This adaptation is based on the Chester Skinners' Resurrection Play in
the resurrection scenes. The sources of the treatment of the Harrowing of
Hell and The Last Judgment (derived from Chester, Coventry, and Wakefield plays) are indicated later in the text. Except for stage directions and
a few transitional phrases, I have added nothing to the texts of the mystery
plays I have used, but I have omitted a great deal that impressed me as
repetitious and turgid or undramatic in the source.—J.G.

Scene 1

Pilate's Council Hall.

(*Present are* PILATE, *three* KNIGHTS, *and the High
Priests of Jerusalem* CAIAPHAS *and* ANNAS.)

PILATE. Most mighty of estate,
As my name is Sir Pilate.
Honored by rule and by degree,
I gave leave to hang
Jesus on the tree.
Yet dread I lest he will us grieve,
For what I saw I may well believe;
I saw the stones begin to cleave,
And dead men began to heave.
And therefore, Sir Caiaphas, I dread   10
Lest there be peril in that deed.
I saw Him hang on the rood and bleed
Till all his blood was shed,
But just when he would his death take
The weather waxed wondrous black;
Lightning, thunder, and earth began to quake,
Thereof I was adread.
   CAIAPHAS. And this was yesterday about noon.
   PILATE. I let bury him full soon,
In a tomb of stone;   20
And therefore, sirs, among us three
Let us oversee
If there any peril be.
   ANNAS. I saw him and his company
Raise men with sorcery,
That long before were dead.
Lest his body from us reft be,
To guard it well I would speed.
   CAIAPHAS. Yea, Sir Pilate, I tell you right,
Let us order many a hardy knight,   30
Well armed to stand and fight,
That no shame to us fall.
Let us ordain here among us all,
To guard well the corpse.
   PILATE. Now, by Jesus that died on the rood,
I think your counsel is wondrous good,—
   (*He calls to the* KNIGHTS, *who guard his door.*)
So, my knights, who are stout of heart,

Ye who are bold men and smart,
With you I have to do. Come near.

   FIRST KNIGHT. Sir, we be here   40
As bold men, ready bound
To drive all your foemen down
Wherever they may be found.

   PILATE. That I am pleased to understand,
I know ye to be doughty of hand.
But yet something in awe I stand
Of words that he spake.
For I heard him say
That he would rise on the third day.

   SECOND KNIGHT. Let him rise if that he dare!   50
For if I of him should be aware!—
   (*He makes a threatening gesture.*)
I helped to slay him erewhile,
Is he now to defeat us with his guile?

   THIRD KNIGHT. While my fellows here and I
Are awake and stand by,
He 'scapeth not uncaught
Though he must everywhere be sought.

   FIRST KNIGHT. Have good day, sir, we must be gone,
Having given us your charge each one.

   PILATE. Farewell, my best of blood and bone;   60
But give heed to my law lest ye be made to atone!

SCENE 2

   SECOND KNIGHT. Our prince hath sworn that we
      shall die
If the dead Christ from the grave shall fly.
But if we do as the wise,
Though he be bold he shall not rise.

   THIRD KNIGHT. Sir, the most wit here lieth with
      thee
To ordain and to oversee:
The tomb is near at hand,
Set us where we should stand
So that we find him if he rise.   70

   FIRST KNIGHT. I shall now set us so
That if he rise and would go,
One of us or two would have no surprise.
Stand thou here, and (*to the other* KNIGHT) thou here
And I shall stand between you, do not fear.

(Two ANGELS appear at this point and sing "Christ is risen from the dead," whereupon JESUS comes out of the sepulcher, and addresses the "world".)

JESUS. Earthly man that I have wrought,
Awake out of thy sleep!
Earthly man that I have bought,
Of me thou hast no keep!*   care
I am the very prince of peace,   80
And king of all mercy;
Who will of sins have release,
If on me they call and cry,
And if they will of their sins cease.
I am very bread of life,
From heaven I light and am sent.
Who eateth that bread, man or wife,
Shall live with me withouten end.
And that bread that I give
Your wicked life for to amend,   90
Becomes my flesh through your belief.

(The two ANGELS, after JESUS has risen, sit in the tomb, one at the head, and one at the feet.)

FIRST KNIGHT *(amazed)*. Out, alas! where am I?
So bright about it is here by,
That my heart wholly
Out of my breast is shaking:
And I wot* not truly   know
Whether I am asleep or waking.

(He rouses one of his companions.)

SECOND KNIGHT. Where art thou, Sir Bachelor?
About me is wondrous clear,
Yet never was I so hard pressed.   100
My heart in my body here
Is clean heaved out of my breast.

(Then they waken the THIRD KNIGHT.)

FIRST KNIGHT. Yea, we are cursed verily,
For Jesus is risen mightily,
And as dead here did I lie,
Speak could I not, nor spy
Which way He took truly,—
My eyes they were so blind.

THIRD KNIGHT. Alas! what is this great light
Shining here in my sight?   110
Marred am I, main and might,
Power have I none to rise aright.

SECOND KNIGHT. Yea, on my knee I will creep forth,
Till this peril passèd be,
For my way I cannot see,
Neither earth nor stone.
Yea, in wicked time we
Nailed him on the rood,
And, as he said, in days three
Risen he is and gone.   120

I wish we were fast away,
Strive with him we may not.
I will to Caiaphas without stay,
The truth openly to say:
Farewell, sirs, and have good day,
For I will go ahead.
   FIRST KNIGHT. To linger here were no stead
For needs to Sir Pilate we must afoot
And tell him the truth crop and root!
   (*The* KNIGHTS *all go off*.)

SCENE 3

PILATE's *hall*.

SECOND KNIGHT. Hearken, Sir Pilate: 130
Jesu that was on Friday slain,
Through his might is risen again
This third day!
There came no power to fetch him away,
But such a sleep on us he set
That none of us might him let*   stop
To rise and go his way.
   PILATE. Now, by the oath I have to Caesar sworn,
If that you have privily*   secretly
Sold him to his company,   140
Then are you worthy to die.
   THIRD KNIGHT. He rose up in the morning light,
By virtue of his own might:
I know it well
He rose up, as I say now,
And left us lying I know not how,
All bemazed in a swoon,
As though we had been stuck swine.
   PILATE. Fie on thee! thy trust is full bare!
Hie hence fast! I counsel thou fare.   150

FIRST KNIGHT. That time when he his way took,
Durst I neither speak nor look
But lay in soundest dream:
He set his foot upon my back,
That every limb began to crack;
I would not abide such another quake,
For all Jerusalem.

PILATE. Fie on thee, thou tainted dog!
What! lay thou still in that place,   160
And let that flatterer go on, the rogue?
Sir Caiaphas and Sir Annas,
What say you to this trespass?

CAIAPHAS. Now, good sir, I you pray,
Hearken to me what I say,
For much avail us it may;
Pray them now, sir, pardie,
As they love thee,
Here as they stand all three,
To keep well our counsel.   170

ANNAS. Sir Bishop, I say to you verament,*   truly
Unto your counsel I fully assent;
This foolish prophet that we all so rent
Through his witchcraft is stolen away.

PILATE. Now in good faith, full woe is me,
That he is risen thus privily;
Now I pray you, sirs, as you love me,
Keep this counsel till we
Have heard how he escaped.
    (*He gives them money and they go away.*)

SCENE 4

(*At the Sepulcher. Women come in weeping and
seeking* JESUS.)
MARY. For woe I wander and my hands wring;
My heart in sorrow and in sickness   180
Is sadly set and sore.
Him I most loved of all thing,
Alas, is now lying full low,—
Why am I, Lord, still living?
    MARY, MOTHER OF JAMES. Alas! My help, my heal*   healer
        from me is rent;

My Christ, my comfort faded now in clay and spent,
Almighty God omnipotent.

    MARY MAGDALENE. Which of us shall remove this
      great stone—
For move it, alone, I ne may.

    MARY, MOTHER OF JAMES. Sister, miracle is it none?   190
It seems to me as if he were gone,
For on the sepulcher sits someone,
And the stone is rolled away.

    MARY SALOME. Two children here I see sitting,
All of white is their clothing;
Go we near.

    (*They go to look into the sepulcher.*)

    FIRST ANGEL. What seek ye, women, here
With weeping and without cheer?
Jesus, that to you was dear,
Is risen, as ye may see.   200

    SECOND ANGEL. Hold us not in fear;
For he is gone forth into Galilee.

    FIRST ANGEL. Hasten for ought that may befall,
And tell his disciples all.

    MARY MAGDALENE. Ah! hie we fast this word to
      bring,
And tell *Peter* this tiding.

    MARY, MOTHER OF JAMES. Yea, walk thou, sister, by
      one way,
And we another shall essay.*   try

                (*The women hasten away.*)

SCENE 5

The Garden. The women meet PETER *and* JOHN.

    MARY MAGDALENE. Ah! Peter and John, alas! alas!
Some man my Lord stolen has,   210
And put him I wot* not where.   know

    PETER. What, is he removed out of the place?

    MARY MAGDALENE. Yea, surely, all my solace
Is gone and is not there.

    JOHN. Peter, go we thither anon,
To look who hath removed the stone.

    PETER. To *run* I will essay.

                (*They run off together.*)

SCENE 6

At the Sepulcher.

JOHN. Ah, Peter, my brother, in good fay*   faith
The Lord Jesu is away!
   (Stooping, he picks up a linen cloth.)
But his sudary, truth to say,   220
Lying here I find;
By itself, as thou dost mind,
Far from all other clothes it lies;
Mary's words were true!
   PETER. Yea, but as God keep us from woe,
Into the sepulcher let us go
To look if it be *truly* so.
   (They go into the sepulcher—that is, into the en-
   trance—and peer in.)
   (Exclaiming ecstatically.)
Ah, Lord, blessed be thou ever and aye,*   forever
For I find thou hast overcome Death our foe
And risen from the grave today!   230
   (Suddenly overcome with remorse.)
But, Lord, what shall I do for shame
Who forsook thy holy name[2]
If I meet thee on the way.
My sweet lord forsook I thrice,
Worse I was than Judas in vice
My lord so to forsake!
   JOHN. Peter, comfort there be in thy plight,
For thy great repentance our Lord will take.
Go seek we Jesu—one way thou, another I.
   PETER. Ah, well I trust that through his Might   240
My penance shall bring me his Mercy's light.
   (They step out of the tomb and hasten away.)

SCENE 7[3]

The region of Hell. First there is total darkness
except for the glow of sultry fires. But suddenly Hell
is mysteriously filled with a growing light.

---

[2] For having "thrice" denied that he had known Christ and been one of
his followers after Christ was taken.
[3] From the Chester Cooks' and Inkeepers' play of "The Harrowing of
Hell."

ADAM. O sovereign Savior,
Comfort and Counsellor,
Of this great light Thou are the author—
I know this well;
This is a sign that thou wilt succor us
And of the devil be conqueror.
Me thou madest, Lord, of clay,
And gavest Paradise for play;
But through my sin, to say the truth,   250
From thy goodly garden I was put away,
And here have longed, the truth to say,
In thirstiness both day and night.
Now by this light that I can see,
Joy is coming, Lord, through Thee!
Surely it may none other be,
But that thou hast brought me mercy!

ISAIAH. Yea, surely, this same light
I foretold aright:
The people, I did say express,   260
That went about in darkness
Should see a great lightness.

SIMEON. And I too, I Simeon, truth to say;
For when Christ a child was, in good fay,
I already felt without a doubt
Joy to the people of Israel:
Now is it won, that very weal!

JOHN THE BAPTIST. Ah. Lord, I am that prophet
John
That dipped thee in Jordan's flood to baptize thee in,
And preached to everyone of thy coming.   270
With my finger I showed express
Thy mercy concluding righteousness.

SETH. And I, Seth, Adam's son, did pray
That he would grant an angel to me
With the oil of mercy
To anoint my father in his sorrowing
When in old sickness he lay.
To me appeared the angel Michael,
For me to tell
That of this oil I might have none,   280
Made I never so much moan,
Till five thousand years have gone,
And five hundred more.

DAVID. Ah, high God, and king of bliss,
I hope that time now comen* is,   has come
To take out thy folk every one,
For the years all have come and gone.
(*Then* SATAN, *sitting on his throne, speaks to his*
   demons.)
SATAN. Hell-hounds all, all that be here,
Make your bow to this fellowship without fear:
Jesus, that is God's son, dear,   290
Comes he hither with us to dwell?
On him now wreak your hell,
For a *man* he is fully, in fay,
Since greatly death he feared today,
And these words I heard him say,
"My soul is thirsty unto death."
Such as I made halt and blind,
He has healed them to their kind,
Therefore this boaster look that you bind
In bale of hell-breath.   300
SECOND DEMON. Sir Sathanas, what man is he,
That should deprive thee of thy power?
How dare he do against thee.
Greater than thou he seems to be,
And degraded of thy degree
Thou must be soon,—this well I see.
THIRD DEMON. Who is he so bold and strong
That masterly comes us among?
He shall sing a sorry song!
SATAN. Against this shrew* that cometh here   villain/310
I tempted the folk in foulest manner,
To give gall for his dinner
And hang him on a tree;
Now he is dead through me,
And to hell, as you shall see,
He comes anon in fear.
SECOND DEMON. Sir Sathanas, is not this that seer
That raised Lazarus out of here?
SATAN. Yea, this is he that did conspire
Anon to deprive us all.   320
THIRD DEMON. Out, out! alas! by fire
I conjure thee, Sathanas,
Thou suffer him not to come near!

SECOND DEMON. Yea, verily, if he come here,
Vanished is our power,
Over all this fellowship of fear.

(JESUS *enters, and the dead raise a great shout.*)

JESUS. Open up hell gates anon,
You princes of pain every one,
That the son of God may enter in!

SECOND DEMON. Hence, hypocrite, out from this
place,   330
Or thou shalt have but sorry grace!

(JESUS *arrives on the scene.*)

SATAN. Out, alas! what is this?
Saw I never so much bliss,
Since I was warden here!
My masterdom fares amiss.

THIRD DEMON. Yea, Sathanas, thy sovereignty
Fails clean, and therefore must thou flee;
Go forth and fight for thy degree,
Or henceforth our prince thou mayst not be.

(SATAN *rises from his throne.*)

SATAN. My might fails verament,*   truly/340
This prince that is now present
Will soon take from me my prey.
Adam's brood through me were galled,
But now they hence shall all be called
And only I left in hell for aye.

DAVID THE KING. I, David, now may say
My prophecy fulfilled is, in fay.

JESUS. Open ye hell gates, I say,
And let the king of glory enter this way,
That he may fulfil his intent.   350

(*At this the gates of hell burst open, and* JESUS
enters.)

Peace to thee, Adam, my darling,
And all the righteous once on earth living!
To bliss I will you bring,
To live without ending.

MICHAEL. Come, Adam, come forth with me:
Our Lord, upon the tree
Your sins has all forbought;*   paid off
Now shall you have liking and lee,*   salvation
And be restored to degree.

(MICHAEL *leads forth* ADAM *and the saints to paradise, and there they are met by* ENOCH *and* ELIJAH
and the saved THIEF.)

ADAM (*speaks to* ENOCH *and* ELIJAH). Sirs, what
    manner of men be ye,   360
That in body meet us as I see,
That dead came not to hell as we?
When I trespassed,* God told me   sinned
That this place closed should be
To earthly men, to have no entry;
And yet I find you here.
    ENOCH. Sir, I am Enoch, the truth to say,
And here have lived since aye;
And my fellow here
Is Elijah the prophet, as see you may.   370
    ELIJAH. Yea, bodily death, never suffered we
But here ordained we are to be
Till Antichrist arise.
To fight against us shall he,
And slay us in our holy city;
But surely in days three
And a half we shall rise.
    ADAM. And who is that comes here?
    THIEF (*bearing a cross on his shoulder*). I am that
      thief
That hung on the rood tree.   380
Because I had belief
That he was God's son dear,
To him devoutly did I pray
That he would think on me alway;
And he answered and said, "This day
In Paradise thou shalt with me be;"
Then he told me,
This cross upon my back hanging
To the Angel Michael to bring,
That I might have entry.   390
    ADAM. Now go we to bliss both old and young,
To worship God all-willing;
And thitherward let us sing.
    (*They all go out singing,* "Te Deum laudamus, te
    Dominum confitemur."4)

   ⁴ The first lines of the great *Te Deum* hymn: "We praise thee, we ac-
knowledge thee to be the Lord."

Scene 8

The Last Judgment[5]

Time having no reality in this high mystery of salvation and
the fate of the world, Doomsday follows as the last scene to
be played.

(JESUS *descends from Heaven in the company of
the archangels* MICHAEL *and* GABRIEL.)

MICHAEL (*in a mighty voice*). Surgite! All men, arise!
Venite ad judicium! Come ye to Judgment.
For now is set the high justice,
And the day of doom.
Come quickly to this assize,*   trial
Great and small,
And of your answer now take care,   400

What ye shall say when that ye come,
Your answer for to tell.
For when God shall examine, beware!
The truth alone he will hear
And send you to heaven or to hell.
     GABRIEL. Both pope and prince, priest and king,
Quickly come your excuse to bring,
For this it be the day of fear
Neither rags nor riches of great store,
Nor all the devils in hell and fire   410
From this day forth shall hide you more.
     (SOULS *rise from their graves; the earth quakes; and
     the world is consumed by fire.*)
     THE SOULS (*arising*). Ah, ah, ah! cleave asunder, ye
          bodies of clay,
Asunder must ye break to let the soul pass.
     DEMONS (*crying*). What shall we say?
Harrow, we cry, alas and alas!
Is this that day, that day of ire,
When to endless pain we pass?
     THE RISEN SOULS. Ah, Lord,
Let thy mercy spring and spread!
For alas! we hide in mighty dread   420
     GOD (*appears on high*). *Venite, benedicti,* do not fear:
Come, ye blessed ones, ye children dear,
Come hither to me to my hall,

---

[5] From the Coventry Play.

And all the foul worms from you fall.
With my right hand I bless you here.
My blessing burnishes you as beryl bright,
All filth from you cleansing crystal clear,—
And now Peter, to heaven's gate shalt thou go,
The locks to loosen and undo.
  (PETER *proceeds to unlock "heaven's gates."*)
  PETER. The gates of heaven have opened wide;   430
Come, breathren, sit on God's right side,
Where mirth and melody may never miss.
    THE SAVED SOULS. On our knees we creep, we go,
      we glide,
To worship our Lord who so merciful is;
For through his wounds that were so wide
He brings us to his bliss.
    GOD. Welcome, in heaven to sit.
    THE DAMNED SOULS. Mercy, Lord, for our misdeed.
Ah! help us, good lord, in this our need!
    GOD. What have ye wrought your souls to save?   440
To whom have ye done a merciful deed
My mercy to win?
    FIRST DEVIL. And mercy it is that they shall lack;
Their sin is written down in letters black.
    GOD. To the hungry and thirsty asking in my name,
Meat and drink would ye give none;
Of naked men had ye no shame,
Ye had no pity on sick or lame.—
For your love's sake I was rent on the rood,
And for your sake I shed my blood—   450
Why then have ye wrought against my good?
    SECOND DEVIL (*to one sinner*). I have here written
      on thy forehead,
Thou wouldst not give a poor man bread,
But from thy door thou wouldst him chide.
    THIRD DEVIL (*to another sinner*). And in *thy* face
      I here do read,
That if a thirsty man came by thy side
Drink thou wouldst ever hide.
    FOURTH DEVIL (*to still another sinner*).
Nor Mass nor matins wouldst thou hear for shame,
Therefore thou goest to endless flame.
    SATAN (*mockingly*).[6] And ye gatemen of the
      stews,*   brothels/460

[6] From here on the stanzas are derived from the Wakefield and York plays.

Ye adulterers, lechers all
Your bale now brews,
Your pleasures fall.
Every harlot who lures,
Each bawd that procures,
    Welcome to my hall!

Ye liars and lubbers, all who thieve,
All ill-tempered knifers many grieve,
Extortioners and wreckers I gladly receive,
Usurers and jurors who to bribery cleave,   470
    With me you are to dwell.

Also gamesters and dicers
Slanderers and backbiters,
Forgers and all other blighters,
    Welcome to my hell!
  JESUS. Each creature be intent
On the message I now bring:
The wicked world is spent
And I come crowned now as your king.
By my Father in heaven I have been sent   480
To deem* your deeds and make an ending.   judge
Come is the day, the day of judgment,
And of sorrow will each sinner sing.

Here may you see my wounds so wide
The which I suffered for your misdeed
Through heart and head, foot, hand, and hide*   skin
Not for my guilt, but for your need.
Behold my body, back, and side
How dear I bought you, as decreed,
And bitter pains I did abide;   490
To buy you bliss I bled.

Thus hurt your sorrow to abate,
Ye men, thus were ye bought by me.
In all my woe I felt no hate,
I *willed* my fate for love of ye.
Man, with grieving thou shouldst quake
This dreadful day such sight to see:
All this I suffered for thy sake—
Say, man, what suffered thou for *me?*
  (*Addressing the* GOOD SOULS.)

My blessed children on my right hand,   500
Your fate this day ye need not dread,
For now your comfort is near at hand;
Your life in pleasure shall be led.
Come to the kingdom ever lastand*   lasting
For you prepared for your good deed!
Full blithe shall ye be where ye stand,
For great in heaven shall be your meed.*   reward

When I was hungry me ye fed;
To slake my thirst your heart was free;
When I was clotheless me ye clad;   510
Ye would not grieving me see.
When hard to prison I was led
On my pain ye had a loving pity;
Full sick when I was brought to bed,
Kindly ye came to comfort me.

When I was weak and weariest
Ye harbored me so heartfully
Full glad to have me for your guest,
And plained my poverty piteously.
With speed ye brought me of the best   520
And made me lie down peacefully,
Therefore in heaven shall you have your rest
In joy and bliss be near to me.

    FIRST GOOD SOUL (*puzzled*). *When* had we, Lord,
      that all has wrought,
To bring thee meat and drink any need,
Since we on earth had never nought
Except what grace thy Godhead brought?
    SECOND GOOD SOUL. *When* was it that we clothes
      thee brought
Or visited in prison for thy need?
Or help for thee in sickness sought?   530
Lord, *when* did we do this deed?

    JESUS. My blessed children, tell you I may
What time these deeds to me were done:
When any who need had night or day,
Asked for your help and had it soon,
For your free hearts them never said nay
Early or late, midday or noon;
But as often as they would pray
They needed but to ask their boon.

(*Then* JESUS *turns to the* DAMNED SOULS.)
Ye cursed caitiffs* of Cain's kin   villains
That never comforted me in care,   541
You and I apart will fare,
You to dwell forever in bale and sin.
Your bitter dole* shall never spend   suffering
Once ye have entered therein*   [in hell]
Thus to be served for all your sin
Where evils* earned *before* never end.   sufferings

When I had need of drink and meat,
Caitiffs, ye chased me from your gate;
When you sat like lords on easeful seat   550
Weary and wet, I had to wait,
For none of you would think of me
Or pity have on my poor state.
Therefore to Hell you sink, as ye see—
Worthy to go down that way are ye!

When I was sick and sorriest
You visited me not, for I was poor;
In prison when I was oppressed
Not one of you came to me more;
When I could find no place for rest   560
With strokes you drove me from your door,
But ever in your pride full dressed
My flesh, my blood, ye did ignore.

Lacking clothes when I was cold,
In need of you I wandered naked;
House nor harbor, help nor hold*   aid
I had from you none though I quaked,
And none of you my sorrow slaked,
But all forsook me, young and old—
Therefore are ye yourself forsaken.*   forsaken

FIRST DAMNED SOUL. When had thou, Lord, that all
    things has,   571
When was it thou in prison was,
When were you naked and harborless?

SECOND DAMNED SOUL. When was it we saw thee
    sick, alas?
When did we to thee such unkindness
Weary or wet to let thee pass,
When did we thee such wickedness?

JESUS. Caitiffs, as oft as did betide*   happened
That the needy asked for alms in my name;
You heard them not when beggars cried,   580
But hid your ears and were "not at home."
Therefore you must bear this blame:
To the least of men when you this did
In all you did to *me* the same.
    THE DAMNED SOULS (*looking up piteously to* JESUS
       as they descend into the pit with the devils).
    Ah, mercy, good Lord, mighty to tell,
We ask thy pity, and not by any right;
Not after our deeds requite:
We have sinned, we have sinned, we are to blame.
    JESUS (*to the sinners*). Ye cursed caitiffs that from
      Cain came   590
Alas, ye bear a bitter blame—
    (*Then, to the Saved Souls.*)
My chosen children come unto me,
With me in joy and bliss to ever be.
    (*Turning about as if surveying the whole globe.*)
Now is it fulfilled, all my Father's forethought,
And ended is all earthly thing;
All worldly wights* whom I have wrought   persons
After their works have now their dwelling.

PRODUCTION NOTE ON THE ENGLISH MYSTERY PLAYS

There has been more dispute about the staging of the English mystery, as given above, than any general description can
suggest. In staging the plays today more than one method can
be followed without fear of violating indisputably established
standards. Even our acceptance of the tradition of pageant-
wagon staging in England needs to be distinctly qualified; in
some instances, it is necessary to assume recourse to *two*
pageants rather than one for a single play (as in the plays
about Cain, Noah, and the Shepherds), as well as the use of
an *upper stage* (especially for "God") on some pageant wagons,
and also the use of the street or ground level between two
wagons or in front of a pageant wagon. Moreover, the very
practice of staging the plays on different wagons moving from
place to place has been cogently questioned (see Martial Rose's
The Wakefield Mystery Plays, London, 1961, pp. 26-42), and
the use of a fixed multiple stage consisting of an acting place

or *platea* supplied with separate settings, or "mansions," has been predicated for the Wakefield Passion Play cycle that includes the famous Noah play and Second Shepherds' Play; and on this assumption, the last-mentioned work should have used two sets, or "mansions," for Mak's hut and the Christ-child's manger, and a ground level for the fields. It has also been recently surmised that the Wakefield plays could have been staged "in the round" like the Cornish plays and the morality play *The Castle of Perseverence,* for which a ground-plan is extant. Following a town procession on Corpus Christi day, the plays would be acted out in a fixed place on a stage supplied with multiple, simultaneously observable, settings. Both for performance on such a stage and for a "pageant" or wagon-stage type of production, it would sometimes be advisable to draw up a pageant wagon to supplement the action and scenery—a separate "pageant," for example, representing Noah's ark with a large model of a ship would have been a striking detail. The space in front of the pageant wagon should have been large enough to allow the use of real animals, as in the case of Cain's plow, which is supposed to be drawn by eight beasts; and much use was apparently made of gesture and stage movement on the part of the performers, whether in the case of the soldiers and resisting women in the *Massacre of the Innocents* pageant or of devils running rampant during the *Harrowing of Hell* and the Last Judgment pageants. It is also to be noted that some journeying back and forth was required in such pageants as the Noah episode and the shepherds' play.

With abundance of action, scenic effects, costuming, sound effects, and pyrotechnics, the mystery play constituted a true "people's theatre," and its popularity was marked in the first half of the sixteenth century despite the emergence of other types of theatre. There was consequently no sharp division in the sixteenth century between the Middle Ages and the Tudor period. During the Catholic reign of Mary Tudor (1553-1558), indeed, both Wakefield and Lincoln made efforts to revive the medieval religious drama; Wakefield had a passion play festival as late as 1556. Four hundred years later (actually in the year 1961), it was possible for a reviewer to describe the London Mermaid Theatre presentation of eighteen of the thirty-two Wakefield cycle plays in April 1961 as "an inspired vaude show with God in it." (*Variety,* April 19, 1961.)

It would also be erroneous to assume that there was no professionalism in the medieval theatre and that the mystery plays were invariably enacted by members of the trade guilds, although they would partake in the processions preceding the stage production and the individual guilds would provide the subsidy for some particular play suitable for the particular profession—the watercarriers guild, say, for the pageant of Noah and the Flood. Thus it is considered probable that a special religious guild attended to the performances; and the existence of professional acting companies in the Middle Ages has been well authenticated. There are characters and scenes in these plays that need expert acting, in farcical no less than in tragic scenes.

The Cornish Passion Play

In Cornwall, where Passion plays were staged on stationary platforms arranged in a circle rather than on pageant wagons, realism such as we find in the English cycles was not a distinctive feature. In the Cornish plays having their basis in the Bible, Celtic fantasy plays an important part. A fertile imagination or a considerable degree of symbolism informs the writing. Thus as Adam, exiled from Eden after his sin of disobedience, tries to dig the soil for the first time, the earth cries out in protest and resists him; God has to come down from heaven to rebuke the earth before Adam can till it. Thus, too, when Adam is about to die, his son Seth goes to Paradise and brings back from Eden three seeds of the apple Adam bit into before he was expelled. He places the seeds on his father's tongue, and three "rods" or shoots spring from the grave. They have mystical significance, for they ultimately figure in the Crucifixion as the "rood" of the cross on which Christ redeems fallen mankind.

Not all the Cornish plays are remarkable for the fanciful quality of the writing: thus a Noah play is quite ordinary except for providing Noah with a foil and opponent in the person of Tubal Cain, the son of Lamech; and a King David play (*David and Bethsheba*) is noteworthy not for any freely invented episode, but for the direct power of the treatment of David's lust and Bathsheba's ready response to his illicit wooing. But a poet's mystical imagination, no doubt drawing upon folklore, enriches the story of even so historical a character as David. One treatment of David relates him to the Cornish "Legend of the Rood" by making him bring the rods from which the cross will be made to Jerusalem. God sends the angel Gabriel to the king to order him to fetch from "Mount Tabor in arid Arabia" the three mystic shoots planted there by Moses! David locates them and is amazed to find them so *green,* while his Counsellor notes that they are indeed "rods of grace" because they have such a rare fragrance. Brought to Palestine, they instantly prove their mystic power in healing one petitioner of his blindness and another of his lameness. David, finally, is just about to go to plant them in the ground when he learns that they have already mysteriously planted themselves, as it were: a miracle took place in the night while the king was asleep, for the rods are not only rooted in the earth, "but all the three are joined in one," a detail that plainly symbolizes the Trinity. David is, of course, associated with the redemption of man on the Cross because Joseph is of the house of David, who was the son of Jesse. It was, moreover, predicted by Isaiah that the Messiah would come out of the "stem of Jesse" (*Isaiah, 11:1*). "And there shall come forth a rod out of the stem of Jesse/ and a branch shall grow out of his roots," (King James Version); or "There shall come forth a shoot from the stump of Jesse,/ and a branch shall grow out of his roots." (Revised Standard Version, 1952); or "And there shall come forth a rod out of the root of Jesse; and a flower shall rise up out of his root" (Douay Version based on St. Jerome's Latin translation known as The Vulgate, the only translation with which the authors of the Cornish drama would have been familiar).

A dire fate awaits Pontius Pilate after the Crucifixion which he ordered, and his fantastic end is the substance of one of the plays of this Cornish Passion Play or cycle, *The Death of Pilate,* which follows.[1]

The Cornwall Death of Pilate

ADAPTED BY JOHN GASSNER[2]

Characters

TIBERIUS CAESAR	FOUR EXECUTIONERS
COUNSELLOR	JAILER
MESSENGER	SERVANT
PILATE	TRAVELER
VERONICA	DEVILS

---

[1] A two-volume edition of the extant Cornish plays was published in an English translation (*The Ancient Cornish Drama,* edited by A. Norris) in 1859. For other Celtic material, see W. S. Clark, *The Early Irish Stage,* Oxford, 1955.

[2] Adapted from the literal translation by A. Norris in *The Ancient Cornish Drama,* Oxford, 1859.

GENERAL SCENE: *A Playing Circle with a raised platform in the center.*

SCENE 1

TIBERIUS CAESAR (*seated on a throne in the center*):
I am above all people of the world, indeed,
But great is my sadness and need:
A leper I have become!
What is the best to be done?
    COUNSELLOR. Lord, send word to Pilate
That he send forthwith at thy news
Christ, King of the Jews.

He can cure every malady
As He is the very Deity,
The Lord of heaven and earth,   10
Most truly.
    EMPEROR (*to a* MESSENGER).
Light-of-foot, my messenger,
Thou must go
To him immediately!
    MESSENGER (*kneeling*). Lord Tiberius,
What do you want of me?
    EMPEROR. Go to Pilate forthwith;
Pray him that he send me at thy news
Christ, King of the Jews,
God without equal, savior,   20
That he may have favor.
    MESSENGER. Dear Lord, with all fervor,
I will do this errand;
Farewell, I say to thee.
    (*He goes out bowing.*)

SCENE 2

PILATE's "House" in Jerusalem.[3]

MESSENGER. Sir Pilate
Through me thou art greeted by our Emperor,
To send Christ to his palace door,
Christ, the flower of all healers.
    PILATE (*craftily*). Messenger, pray go
Into the country and seek a while;   30

[3] Located at some convenient point in one of the quadrants of the playing circle, in a "theater-in-the-round" production.

If he be in the land, I will go
And seek also myself.
  (*The* MESSENGER *departs.*)

SCENE 3

  (*As the* MESSENGER *walks about "in the country,"*
  VERONICA, *a saintly woman, meets him.*)
  VERONICA. Sweet young man who wanders here,
Whom seekest thou so dear,
Tell me!
  MESSENGER. What is that to thee?
Surely, thou canst not help me!
To seek help the Emperor hath sent me,
For he suffers from leprosy
And finds no doctor to make him well.—   40
Where Jesus is I pray thee tell.
  VERONICA. Jesus who was our Lord, in fay,*   faith
Is dead and gone to clay
Slain by Pilate.
Were he alive yet,
You would have no need to roam.
  MESSENGER (*grieving*). Alas, that I ever came so far
      from home,
Alas that I know not where to go
Or where I shall set foot!
  VERONICA. I am one of his women, lo!   50
And will to the emperor with thee go.
And in His name, by my word,
Shall be made a remedy
To cure his leprosy,
If he believes Christ to be heaven's Lord.
  MESSENGER. Let us then hasten to my Lord,
If he can be healed by thee,
Thou shalt have gold for guerdon:*   reward
And ever shall thy will be done.
  (*They go off together.*)

SCENE 4

The Palace.

  MESSENGER. My lord, be at ease!   60
That same prophet thou didst seek
Has been slain in crucifixion

But a woman is with me, if it please,
Who, through Him, will cure thy affliction.
   EMPEROR. Alas, I will eat no meat,
Because the prophet is dead now.
But woman, what sayest thou?
    VERONICA (*holding out a handkerchief*). Believe in
       Christ, I advise thee.
The print of His face I will show thee,
As He gave it to me on this kerchief of lace: 70
As soon as thou seest His face
He will heal thee, without other salve.
   EMPEROR. What wilt thou have?
Thou wilt find much favor,
Thou shalt be made a lady
Over much land, truly.
   VERONICA. Veronica is my name,
The face of Jesus is with me,
In the likeness made by His sweat;
Whoever sees it yet,   80
And believes in His godhead
He needs must be healed.

In Christ believe, that He is Lord,
And salvation for the people of the world.
Then thou shalt surely be healed
Of thy leprosy.
   EMPEROR (*kneeling*). To Him with a full heart I
    will pray.
As thou art true God and great in grace,
Help me swiftly   90
As thou art Savior.
   (*Pointing to the kerchief.*)
Show it to me, I pray—
That such a thing should be
Is great wonder to me.
Come near as thou lovest me,
For I would speak with thee further
Before parting.
   VERONICA. Look at it, and in the little time now
Shalt thou be cured of thy sorrow
Believe Him to be the God of all   100
And Savior of all soul.
   (*She shows him the kerchief, and he kneels.*)

EMPEROR. Jesus, full of pity,
Thy dear face I will kiss—
   (*He kisses the kerchief.*)
I know that thou will cure me
Of all leprosy;
Lord Christ of heaven and earth, for this
Glory be to thee always!
   (*He is healed of his leprosy.*)
I am healed now.

Blessed be thou,
Who was the Lord of breath   110
And was done to death.
There is no Lord above thee,
God without an equal!
   VERONICA. Since thou art healed now
Know this well
There is no other God than He,
Yet Pilate killed Him.
Vengeance for Him take thou
That was Christ and hath now saved thee.
   EMPEROR. Sweet Veronica, I will do as you tell,   120
For through Him
Cured of malady, I am well.
If Pilate be still in this world,
He shall go to death, most truly,
He and all his company!
   (*Shouting.*)
Executioners, come to me!
   (*Enter the* EXECUTIONERS.)
   FIRST EXECUTIONER. My lord, here we be:
You cried out so mightily
We feared your breath!
   EMPEROR. Go, find Pilate for me
Bring him with might to Rome   130
To be put to death!
   SECOND EXECUTIONER. Let us go to his home,
In Jerusalem is he to be sought.
   THIRD EXECUTIONER (*to the Emperor*). To you he
    shall be brought.
However he be perilous
He shall not withstand us.
   (*They go to seek* PILATE.)

Scene 4

In front of PILATE's Palace.

FOURTH EXECUTIONER. Thou, Pilate, come to my
    Lord!
Thou must certainly go
At thy master's word.
Despite thy mother's son,   140
Or thou wilt be undone.
    PILATE (*following him with suspiciously hearty*
      confidence. . .). I will gladly go to my lord,
Tiberius Caesar, meekly,
For gentle he is to every one,
And in my heart I love him dearly.
    (*They go off together.*)

Scene 5

In Caesar's Palace.

(TIBERIUS *is seated on a high throne as* PILATE *and*
the FIRST EXECUTIONER *enter.*)
FIRST EXECUTIONER. Lord, see the fellow here.
As you have heard it,
He condemned the prophet
To be put upon the rood-tree.
And upon it Jesus died;   150
On His body He suffered dear
To save the race of the sons of men.—
    (*The* EMPEROR *leaps down from his throne angrily;*
    but he seems strangely affected and instead of
    scolding PILATE, *embraces him warmly.*)
EMPEROR. Pilate, thou art most welcome,
As God is my witness, to my home,
For I love thee
As soon as I see thee;
I have no wish to harm thee,
And never shall.
    PILATE (*smoothly*). O Lord, great thanks to you so
      dear!
To you surely I have shown among all lords   160
How much I love thee who on the earth hast no peer.
Gentle art of words,

And art a man without a peer.
   SECOND EXECUTIONER. Is it for this we brought him
     here?
Thou, fellow, thou shalt come out with us below.
   (*The* EXECUTIONERS *seize* PILATE.)
   THIRD EXECUTIONER. Out thou shalt go!
A charm thou must have with thee
Art thou a sorcerer
Whom no man can do injury?
Answer without ado!   170
   (*The* EXECUTIONER *and* PILATE *are now at some
   distance from the* EMPEROR *when the latter is sud-
   denly seized with illness again and cries out, where-
   upon they go no further.* VERONICA *also enters to
   minister to him.*)
   EMPEROR (*becoming remorseful*). Out! harrow,
     harrow!
If Pilate be not slain,
I know not what I shall do;
My heart has so much pain.

When the foul fellow came forward, so trim,
To give way, I was fain.*   glad
And in his answer I found, oh sorrow!,
No cause to punish him.

Tell me, Veronica, dear,
What to do here.   180
   VERONICA. If he comes into your sight,
From injury he will be free
As long as there is wound about him
The garment of Jesus,
It is his undermost garment;
Bring him here again to you
And strip it from him—
There is only this to do!
                     (*She retires.*)
   EMPEROR. My blessings fall on you!
   (*Calling out sternly.*)
Executioners, bring him back   190
That my heart grow light and I prove true.
   (*Three* EXECUTIONERS *approach the* EMPEROR, *who
   is still somewhat distracted.*)
   FIRST EXECUTIONER. Lord, behold us near to you.
To serve your heart's desire.

EMPEROR. Bring Pilate again. Of wit bereaved,
Careless in my dealing with him,
I was deceived.
SECOND EXECUTIONER (*doubtfully*).
I will bring him to you without delay,
Whom we have not dared to slay,
For to look upon him is to love him for aye.
THIRD EXECUTIONER (*whimsically*). However much
    we may love him,   200
I don't mind killing him;
Never shall he sing in choir
One note higher.
    (*He seizes* PILATE *and begins to drag him to the*
    EMPEROR *in the center of the stage.*)
PILATE (*still confident*). I go to him joyfully.
    (*They go up to the* EMPEROR.)
FOURTH EXECUTIONER. Lord, beware the fellow's
    charm.
When you see him before you,
You will not be able to do him harm. . . .
EMPEROR. Now, Pilate, I tell thee, by grace,
I'll have that robe without seam
Which is about thee.   210
PILATE. You are a lord, I deem
The robe I am wearing below
Will not do for you;
It is not clean, but soiled with grime
It has not been washed a long time;
Do not desire it, I pray thee so,
At this time.
EMPEROR. I am not ashamed, Pilate,
Of wearing the garment Jesus wore.
I am anxious to have it,   220
I pray thee take it off; I say no more!
PILATE (*hedging*). Lord, now if I remove it
Before you naked I should be;
It would not be respectful to thee.
EMPEROR. I must have it!
Seek not to parley with me.
PILATE. Alas, since you must have it
Henceforth no peace for me,
I know truly;
    (*He takes the garment off.*)
I do not see now   230

How my life to hold—
Except with much gold.
   EMPEROR. Out on thee,
Thou hast killed Jesus, our Lord
   (*To an* EXECUTIONER.)
Reach me my sword,
That I may slay him as quick as a word.
   VERONICA. Lord, that you shall not, but call
On others to seek out the most cruel death
He may have while he has breath;
For the villain hath caused to die   240
That same Son who made us all,
Sea, and earth, and sky.
   EMPEROR. Into prison he shall go;
A cruel death and trim
I will ordain for him,
And no man shall save him!
Ho, jailer, take him forth
   (*Enter the* JAILER *and a* SERVANT.)
Loiter not now; let no one be afraid—
My commands must be obeyed!
   JAILER. Lord, we are ready,   250
To do whatever it be.
   EMPEROR. Put this fellow into dungeon to rot
And let him have no light at all
He is a sorcerer and see he must not.
And the most cruel death I ordain for him
Who slew Jesus the Savior of all.
   SERVANT. Put him in the lowest pit we shall
Among the vermin unkind;
And a sprightly fellow is "Whip-behind."
   (*He whips* PILATE *away*.)
   JAILER (*following*). Do not spare him, though you
     hear him roar.   260
He shall not for all his cunning stray
Without some harm befalling him!
   SERVANT (*thrusting him toward "prison"*). Now
     until flesh rot
Shalt thou in prison stay
And a hard death thou hast in store.
   PILATE (*stopping—then cannily*). Pray tell me
What death you have decreed for me,
I know well I shall die; great is my anxiety.

JAILER. The cruelest men have ever bore:
In this world trust thou no more!   270
  PILATE. From that preserve myself yet I may.
  (*He stabs himself.*)
Oh! alas and welaway.
  (*He dies.*)

SCENE 6

*At the Court, in the central area where the EM-
PEROR's throne is situated.*
  (*Enter the* JAILER *and the* SERVANT.)
  EMPEROR. In what plight is Pilate
In the place where he is?
Tell me truly.
  JAILER. My lord, that man is dead:
Through pain and sorrow led,
With his knife wondrous suddenly
He smote himself to the heart.
  EMPEROR. A more cruel death on land   280
Than to kill himself with his own hand
No man may find, I think.
Take him by the two feet right smart
And in deep ground his carcass sink,
For I right well believe that here
Men of this body will have fear.

SCENE 7

Outside the City.

  JAILER (*to his* SERVANT). Whip-behind, take his
      head;
By his feet I will drag him dead
Into the grave then.
  SERVANT. I will, by my rear; Amen.
  (*They drop* PILATE *into a grave. But he is at once
  thrown out of the earth with an explosion. They
  leap back.*)
  SERVANT (*who is the first man to come back*). O
      master, by my soul,   290
This is a devil foul,
For out of the earth he has jumped, the slave!
  JAILER. When he leapt from the grave,
I took fright at the noise;

But he surely could not move himself,
Shut in as he was.
   SERVANT. Boldly let us take him at once
And put him into the grave again.
I believe he will in it bide
If he be on Heaven's side—   300
Or else he is a devil.
   (*Looking down at* PILATE's *face, doubtfully.*)
Black indeed is his hue!
   JAILER. If he be not on God's side,
It would take all the parish too
To lay him in the grave.
Let us put him in the earth without more ado!
   (*They put him back in the ground, but the body is
thrown up again.*)
   SERVANT. By my faith, he is a devil hound!
He will not stay a moment under ground!
He is a wicked slave!
   JAILER. Let us go and tell Caesar, knave.   310
                       (*They go off.*)

SCENE 8

At the EMPEROR's *court again.*

   JAILER (*approaching the* EMPEROR). Sir Caesar, lord
     high,
The fellow will never lie
Beneath the ground.
   EMPEROR (*frightened*). Come not nigh!
He was a devil before he died.
And a worse devil now, I fear.
   SERVANT. Sir, Earth parted over him
Threw him out with a sigh
So mighty it was dreadful to hear.
   EMPEROR (*crying out, so that* VERONICA *enters at
his cry*). Oh, what shall I do well-a-way?   320
Against this devil I have found
No defense in any way.
The stench of this corpse will slay
All in my kingdom's bound.
   VERONICA. My lord, in a box of iron
In the river Tiber let him sink.
From there most certainly it is
He will not come up again, I think.

EMPEROR. O Veronica, good counsel this
Thou hast given me.   330
Executioners, come hither quickly!
  (*Impatiently*.)
I almost get my death, I do,
With waiting for you.
  (*Enter the* EXECUTIONERS.)
FIRST EXECUTIONER. Lord, coming from Spain,
I was in the middle of Germany,[4]
When I was called amain:*   quickly
Make known thy will, I pray thee.
  SECOND EXECUTIONER. If there is sorrow in thy
    heart and pain,
Thy will shall be done speedily.
  EMPEROR. Take the body of this freak   340
Which is stinking with a tang
That is accursed, and—
Cast it, in a box of iron, in some creek.
  (FIRST EXECUTIONER *goes out at once*.)
  THIRD EXECUTIONER. At once in a trunk of iron
    shall he be cast
In deepest water.
  FOURTH EXECUTIONER (*doubtfully*). The water will
    not assuredly
Be willing to contain
This bedevilled body.
May fire of the great devil burn it,
So it come no more into this country.   350
  FIRST EXECUTIONER (*returning with assistants*).
    See, I have the iron chest!
And to the water let us run with it.
  SECOND EXECUTIONER. Devil carry him to his place!
Let us go with great speed,
To put him into green water without grace.

SCENE 9

  (*They carry* PILATE's *body in a box to the Tiber*.)
  FOURTH EXECUTIONER. Go, thou cursed Pilate!
To the bottom of it!
Surely thou shalt fall,
And with thee go the curses of all

---

4 The quaint freedom taken with geography by the medieval imagination
is deliberately retained in this adaptation.

For sentencing the Son of God,   360
And Son of Mary.
  (*The body is thrown into the water; the* EXECUTION-
  ERS *go off.*)
  A TRAVELER (*entering*). I shall go and wash my
    hands
Straightway in this water
That they be white and free.
  (*He washes his hands, and is immediately seized
  with mortal sickness.*)
Alas, Death surely is come for me.
The water has done that for me!
  (*He dies.*)

SCENE 10

  MESSENGER. My lord, bring the good wise woman
    hither,
For no man goes over Tiber river
Without Pilate's body slay.
We must put Pilate away,   370
For Jesus' sake, to another place.
  (VERONICA *enters.*)
  EMPEROR (*to her*). Out, out! what shall I do,
I have no one to help me.
That body is accursed surely.
Give me counsel, again.
  VERONICA. Let him be sent to sea
In a boat's hold
Whatever the cost in silver or gold
The boat shall carry him to hell,
My lord, I warrant it, surely.   380
  EMPEROR. Blessings on thee.—
My Executioners, come at once to me!
  (*Enter the* EXECUTIONERS.)
Drag Pilate out of Tiber's stream
And send him in a boat out to sea.
  (*The* EXECUTIONERS *bow and leave.*)

SCENE 11

By the banks of the Tiber.

(*The four* EXECUTIONERS *are seen dragging the
river for the body.*)

FIRST EXECUTIONER. To draw it from this creek
Let drop a grappling iron on the corpse.
　　SECOND EXECUTIONER. I have cast two grappling
　　　irons here,
Out of the water shall the body be won
Though it be heavy as a great stone.
　　(*Straining hard.*)
Now *haul* ye men without a fear,   390
But have a care!
　　THIRD EXECUTIONER. See the hateful carcase rising
　　　fast
Let us drag it onto the grass.
　　(*They drag the body toward the sea.*)

SCENE 12

By the sea.

(*The* EXECUTIONERS *have drawn the body to the
seashore.*)
　　FIRST EXECUTIONER. Without further delay now
Let us put the body into a boat for hell
With the curse of God, His Angels, and saints as well.
　　(*They do so.*)
　　SECOND EXECUTIONER. Go, hoist at once the sail
That he shall go with the wind without fail
And with him the curse of God above.
　　(*They hoist sail.*)
　　THIRD EXECUTIONER. Now let us shove her off!   400
　　(*A terrifying noise is heard as the boat floats out
　　to sea and strikes a rock.*)
Hear the hideous roar
From the rock in the sea.
At his coming the water grows rough;
To my knowledge, certain, many devils
Are carrying him off.
　　FOURTH EXECUTIONER. Let us hasten from devils
　　　coming for their spoil;
I hear them shout so gleefully
I fear their toil!
　　(*The* EXECUTIONERS *run off. Enter* DEVILS *carrying*
　　PILATE's *body.*)
　　LUCIFER. My devils, all together,
I pray you come without fear   410

To fetch, along with his soul so dear,
The body of Pilate,

In roaring fire he is to remain,
And in torment ceaselessly,
So his song shall be "O woe is me,
That I was born into this world of pain!"
    BEELZEBUB. This body accursed falls to us;
Not fit to be in earth, nor in water, nor in brine,
It is surely mine.
Ship never passed around   420
This way that was not drowned;
He deserved no bliss,
But to be overwhelmed with fire.
    LUCIFER. From the water raised he is
Brought ashore again,
To go down with us in the abyss.
    SATAN (boasting, gleefully). Mast and sail made
      ready for him,
Upon a rock he was cast for me plain
And fell into my toils.
    BEELZEBUB. That rock opened with fear: 430
There we received him neat.
His voice horrible to hear,
In fire and smoke and great heat,
In that rock he shall ever remain.
    LUCIFER. Scorching heat, piercing cold, and pain,
Monstrously grimacing devils
He will find, with us pent,
And all kinds of torment.
    BEELZEBUB. Now everyone lend a hand
To float him in this same beer.   440
While thou, devil Tulfric, a plain-chant sing!
    TULFRIC (singing with devilish obscenity). Yah, kiss
      my rear!
Its end is out here
So long behind.
Beelzebub and Satan kind,
You sing the great drone bass
While I sing a fine treble
To please any devil
And bring Pilate to his place.

The Morality Play

Standing between the vital "mystery" plays and the vigorous folk farces, the morality plays represented the conscience, the learning, and the moralizing inclinations of the Middle Ages. Developing out of a medieval matrix of homilies and allegories, this form of drama, involving much invention of plot and characters, had an especially strong vogue in England and played an important part in the transition from medieval to Elizabethan drama. The morality plays reflected the important cultural interests of a period extending from the middle of the fourteenth century to the middle of the sixteenth. These were *moralistic* (but were combined with the medieval penchant for folksy farce), *humanistic* during the period of renaissance infiltration into England, and *politico-religious* when Britain entered upon a period of conflict between Catholicism and Protestantism. To the historian, the morality plays are invaluable, even if they displease students of dramatic literature. Even for the latter, however, the moralities have an interest, for the use of personified abstractions on the stage reflects a widely diffused allegorical tendency also apparent in medieval painting, sculpture, and poetic composition. The most influential poem of the Middle Ages north of Italy, the French *Roman de la Rose,* is an allegory, as is indeed the greatest of all medieval poems, Dante's *Divine Comedy.* The outstanding Elizabethan narrative poem, Edmund Spenser's *The Faëry Queen,* is also an allegory, and the morality-play pattern continued to be followed to some degree even by Elizabethan playwrights. The morality play was well rooted in English life because it possessed popular elements of moral generalization, religious belief, and farcical horseplay.

In a single fully developed morality play (which may have originally comprised such cycles as the mystery plays and was once possibly presented on pageant wagons) the public could encounter a great diversity of material. No cycle, indeed, has come down to us, but a distinct pattern appears in a long single play such as *The Castle of Perseverance,* the earliest and most primitive intact example, produced around 1425 on a stationary stage consisting of separate platforms or scaffolds.

Three themes were dominant in the morality play—a conflict of the Virtues and the Vices for man's soul, a so-called *psychomachia* while man is alive; a coming of Death, or "Summoning" of man to his final hour, and the Judgment to follow; and a Debate of Mercy and Peace against Truth and Justice for the soul of the deceased. All three elements are present in *The Castle of Perseverance,* which runs to 3,600 lines of verse. To the first-mentioned conflict of Vices and Virtues belonged the allegorical presentation of the Seven Deadly Sins, in which each sin was vividly impersonated; Marlowe included this spectacular feature in his *Doctor Faustus,* produced toward the end of the sixteenth century. An especially vivid impersonation was that of the so-called Vice, a mischief-making devil whose pranks enlivened some morality plays. A popular stage figure, the Vice was not easily banished from the theater, and his close relatives appeared in the Elizabethan theater as clowns and pranksters.

The late-fifteenth-century *Everyman* is a complete little play and is the masterpiece of the species. But it is in effect only one of the units of a complete "morality"—the part that consists of the coming of Death—and the play should be properly called *The Summoning of Everyman.* Brevity is one of the virtues of *Everyman,* and another is unity; the play is all of one piece, for it is unified in situation, thought, and tone. It is greatly superior not only to the early *Castle of Perseverance,* which is four times as long, but to morality plays written in its own time or later, such as *Mankind* (in which a comic Devil causes humanity to fall from grace), the poet John Skelton's lengthy *Magnificence* (which deplores extravagance), John Rastell's *The Nature of the Four Elements* (which recommends the study of Nature to its early-sixteenth-century audience), and *Lusty Juventus* (a Protestant propaganda piece written about 1550). If the characters in *Everyman* are abstractions, they nevertheless possess considerable color and individuality, they typify human experience instead of aridly defining it. The one serious defect of the play, written in four-stress couplets with occasional quatrains, is its weak metrification, for as E. K. Chambers puts it (in his *English Literature at the Close of the Middle Ages,* p. 62), "the stressing is very irregular, and rhymes often fail or are imperfect."

Some infrequently noted features of *Everyman* should be set down here. Its essential dramatic form is that of a *journey;* Everyman in his loneliness and fear cries out for company, but only Good-Deeds is willing to accompany him to the grave. For a time, Five Wits, Strength, Discretion, and Beauty follow him, but they all abandon him before the journey takes its final turn. Finally, as Everyman and Good-Deeds descend together into the grave, Knowledge, which has been man's guide up to this point, also departs (as knowledge must), but not before expressing confidence that Good-Deeds will save the man from perdition. It is also noteworthy that, whereas other religious morality plays stress the importance of Mercy or Divine Grace, *Everyman* relies on the efficacy of "Good-Deeds" or "good works." The theological content of the play is thus simplified and made to bear directly on the human drama.

The source of *Everyman* has been traced to an allegorical tale in an eighth-century work, *Barlaam and Josaphat,* ascribed to St. John Damascene, which has been in turn traced to a Buddhist source. The Messenger of Death in the Buddhist text, a collection of parables by the Buddha, summons man on a journey. Three of his four wives refuse to accompany him, but the fourth resolves to follow him through thick and thin. The three wives in this parable are Man's body, his wealth, and his relations and friends, while the fourth wife represents his Intentions or Deeds. These alone follow him into his next life, and whether his next incarnation will raise his status or lower it will be determined by his intentions or deeds in his previous life. Whatever the literary source of *Everyman,* however, the play is in complete accord with Christian belief and hope. It is not doctrinaire in its teachings but, as it were, spontaneously affirmative; and this is what makes it a play for the popular theater, although we actually have no evidence that this eminently stageworthy piece was ever staged in its own time.

Everyman

A MODERNIZED VERSION BY JOHN GASSNER

Characters

EVERYMAN	STRENGTH
GOD: ADONAI*	DISCRETION
DEATH	FIVE-WITS
MESSENGER	BEAUTY
FELLOWSHIP	KNOWLEDGE
COUSIN	CONFESSION
KINDRED	ANGEL
GOODS	DOCTOR
GOOD-DEEDS	

* The Lord.

Here Beginneth a Treatise How the High Father of Heaven Sendeth Death to Summon All Creatures to Come and Give Account of Their Lives in This World and Is in the Manner of a Moral Play.

PROLOGUE

MESSENGER. I pray you all give your audience,
And hear this matter with reverence,
By figure a moral play—
The *Summoning of Everyman* called it is,
That of our lives and ending shows
How transitory we be all our day.
This matter is wondrous precious,
But the intent of it is more gracious,
And sweet to bear away.
The story saith,—Man, in the beginning,   10
Look well, and take good heed to the ending,
Be you never so gay!
Ye think sin in the beginning full sweet,
Which in the end causeth the soul to weep,
When the body lieth in clay.
Here shall you see how Fellowship and Jollity,

And Strength, Pleasure, and Beauty,
Will fade from thee as flower in May.
For ye shall hear how our heaven's king
Calleth Everyman to a general reckoning.   20
Give audience, and hear what he doth say.
   (GOD *appears and speaks.*)
   GOD. I perceive here in my majesty,
How that all creatures be to me unkind,
Living without dread in worldly prosperity.
Of spiritual sight the people be so blind,
Drowned in sin, they know me not for their God;
In worldly riches is all their mind,
They fear not my righteousness, the sharp rod;
My law that I showed, when I for them died,
They clean forget, and shedding of my blood red;   30
I hung between two, it cannot be denied;
To get men life I suffered to be dead;
I healed their feet, with thorns hurt was my head—
I could do no more than I did truly,
And now I see the people do clean forsake me.
They love the seven deadly sins damnable;
And pride, covetize, wrath, and lechery,
Now in the world be made commendable;
And thus they leave of angels the heavenly company;
Every man liveth so after his own pleasure,   40
And yet of their life they be nothing sure.
I see the more that I forbear
The worse they be from year to year;
All that liveth impaireth fast,
Therefore I will with all my haste
Have a reckoning of Everyman's person
For if I leave the people thus alone
In their life and wicked tempests,
Verily they will become much worse than beasts;
For now one would by envy another eat;   50
Charity they all do clean forget.
I hoped well that every man
In my glory should make his mansion,
And thereto I had them all elect;
But now I see, like traitors abject,
They thank me not for pleasure that I them meant,
Nor yet for their being that I to them have lent;
I proffer the people great multitude of mercy,
But few there be that ask it heartily;

They be so cumbered with worldly riches,   60
That needs on them I must do justice,
On Everyman living without fear.
Where art thou, Death, thou mighty messenger?
   (*Enter* DEATH.)
   DEATH. Almighty God, I am here at Thy will,
Thy commandment to fulfil.
   GOD. Go thou to Everyman,
And show him in my name
A pilgrimage he must on him take,
Which he in no wise may escape;
And that he bring with him a sure reckoning   70
Without delay or any tarrying.
   (GOD *withdraws.*)
   DEATH. Lord, I will in the world run over all,
And cruelly search out both great and small;
Every man I will beset that liveth beastly
Out of God's law, and dreadeth not folly.
He that loveth riches will I strike with my dart,
His sight to blind, and from heaven him to part,
Except that Alms be his good friend,
In hell for to dwell, world without end.
Lo, yonder I see Everyman walking;   80
Full little he thinketh on my coming.
His mind is on fleshly lusts and treasure,
And great pain it shall cause him to endure
Before the Lord, heaven's King.
Everyman, stand still! whither art thou going
Thus gaily? Hast thou thy maker forgot?
   (*Enter* EVERYMAN.)
   EVERYMAN. Why askst thou?
Why would you know?
   DEATH. Yea, sir, I will show you.
In great haste I am sent to thee   90
From God out of his majesty.
   EVERYMAN. What, sent to me?
   DEATH. Yea, certainly.
Though thou have forgot him here,
He thinketh on thee in the heavenly sphere,
As, ere we depart, thou shalt know.
   EVERYMAN. What desireth God of me?
   DEATH. That shall I show thee;
A reckoning he will needs have
Without any longer respite.   100

EVERYMAN. To give a reckoning longer leisure I
    crave;
This blind matter troubleth my wit.
    DEATH. On thee thou must take a long journey.
Therefore thy book of accounts with thee thou bring;
For turn again thou canst not by any way,
And look thou be sure of thy reckoning:
For before God thou shalt answer, and show
Thy many bad deeds and good but a few;
How thou hast spent thy life, and in what wise,
Before the Great Lord of Paradise.   110
Make preparation that we be on the way,
For know thou well, thou shalt make none attorney.
    EVERYMAN. Full unready I am such reckoning to
    give,
I know thee not. What messenger art thou?
    DEATH. I am Death, that no man dreadeth.
That every man arrests and no man spareth;
For it is God's commandment
That all to me should be obedient.
    EVERYMAN. O Death, thou comest when I had thee
    least in mind;
In thy power it lieth me to save,   120
Yet of my goods will I give thee, if ye will be kind,
Yea, a thousand pound shalt thou have,
But defer this matter till another day!
    DEATH. Everyman, it may not be by no way;
I set not by gold, silver, nor riches,
Nor by pope, emperor, king, duke, nor princes,
For if I would receive gifts great,
All the world I might get;
But my custom is clean contrary.
I give thee no respite. Come, do not tarry!   130
    EVERYMAN. Alas, shall I have no longer respite?
I may say Death giveth no warning.
To think on thee it maketh my heart sick,
For all unready is my book of reckoning.
But twelve year if I might have abiding,
My counting book I would make so clear
That thy reckoning I should not need to fear.
Wherefore, Death, I pray thee, for God's mercy,
Spare me till I be provided of remedy.
    DEATH. Thee availeth not to cry, weep, and pray,   140
But haste thee lightly that thou go the journey,

And prove thy friends if thou can.
For, know thou well, the tide abideth no man,
And in the world each living creature
For Adam's sin must die by nature.
   EVERYMAN. Death, if I should this pilgrimage take,
And my reckoning surely make,
Show me, for Saint Charity,
Should I not come again shortly?
   DEATH. No, Everyman. If thou be once there   150
Thou mayst nevermore come here,
Trust me verily.
   EVERYMAN. O Gracious God, in the high seat
     celestial,
Have mercy on me in this my need;
Shall I have no company from this vale terrestrial
Of mine acquaintance the way to lead?
   DEATH. Yea, if any be so hardy
That would go with thee and bear thee company.
Hasten to be gone to God's magnificence,
Thy reckoning to give before his presence.   160
What, thinkest thou thy life is given thee,
And thy worldly goods also?
   EVERYMAN. I had thought so, verily.
   DEATH. Nay, nay, it was but lent thee!
For as soon as thou dost go,
Another awhile shall have it and then go therefro
Even as thou hast done.
Everyman, thou art mad. Thou hast thy wits five,
And here on earth will not amend thy life,
For suddenly do I come.   170
   EVERYMAN. O wretched caitiff, whither shall I flee,
That I might escape this endless sorrow!
Now, gentle Death, spare me till to-morrow,
That I may amend me
With good advisement.
   DEATH. Nay, thereto I will not consent,
Nor no man will I respite,
But to the heart suddenly I shall smite
Without any advisement.
And now out of thy sight I will me hie.   180
See thou make thee ready shortly,
For thou mayst say this is the day
That no man living may escape away.
                (DEATH *withdraws.*)

EVERYMAN. Alas, I may well weep with sighs deep.
Now have I no manner of company
To help me in my journey, and me to keep.
And also my writing is full unready!
What shall I do now for to excuse me?
I would to God I had never been begot!
To my soul a full great profit it would be,   190
For now I fear pains huge and hot.
The time passeth. Lord, help me that all wrought!
For though I mourn it availeth nought.
The day passeth, and is almost gone.
I know not well what is to be done.
To whom were I best my complaint to make?
What if I to Fellowship thereof spake,
And showed him of this sudden chance?
For in him is all mine affiance,
We have in the world so many a day   200
Been good friends in sport and play.
I see him yonder, certainly—
I trust that he will bear me company.
Therefore him I will ask to ease my sorrow.
    (FELLOWSHIP *enters*.)
Well met, good Fellowship, and good morrow!
    FELLOWSHIP. Everyman, good morrow by this day.
Sir, why lookest thou so piteously?
If any thing be amiss, I pray thee, say,
That I may help to remedy.
    EVERYMAN. Yea, good Fellowship, yea,   210
I am in great jeopardy.
    FELLOWSHIP. My true friend, show to me your
        mind;
I will not forsake thee, unto my life's end,
In the way of good company.
    EVERYMAN. That was well spoken, and lovingly.
    FELLOWSHIP. Sir, I must needs know your heavi-
        ness—
I have pity to see you in any distress.
If any have wronged you ye shall revenged be,
Though I on the ground be slain for thee,
Though that I knew before that I should die.   220
    EVERYMAN. Verily, Fellowship, gramercy.
    FELLOWSHIP. Tush! by thy thanks I set not a straw.
Show me your grief and say no more.
    EVERYMAN. If I my heart should to you break,

And then you turned your mind from me
And would not comfort me when you hear me speak,
Then should I ten times sorrier be.
   FELLOWSHIP. Sir, I say as I will do indeed.
   EVERYMAN. Then be you good friend in need—
I have found you true here before. 230
   FELLOWSHIP. And so ye shall evermore.
For, in faith, if thou go to Hell,
I will not forsake thee by the way!
   EVERYMAN. Ye speak like a friend, I believe you well.
I shall try deserve thy love, if I may.
   FELLOWSHIP. I speak of no deserving, by this day.
For he that will say and nothing do
Is not worthy with good company to go.
Therefore show me the grief of your mind,
As to your friend most loving and kind. 240
   EVERYMAN. I shall show you how it is:
Commanded I am to go a journey,
A long way, hard and dangerous,
And give a straight count without delay
Before the high judge Adonai.
Wherefore I pray you, bear me company,
As ye have promised, in this journey.
   FELLOWSHIP. This is matter indeed! Promise is duty,
But, if I should take such a voyage on me,
I know it well, it should be to my pain. 250
Also it maketh me afeard, for certain.
But let us take counsel here as well as we can,
For thy words would balk a strong man.
   EVERYMAN. Why, ye said, if I had need,
Ye would me never forsake, quick nor dead,
Though it were to Hell truly.
   FELLOWSHIP. So I said, certainly,
But from such pleasures set me aside, thee sooth to
     say!
And also, if we took such a journey,
When should we come again? 260
   EVERYMAN. Nay, never again till the day of doom.
   FELLOWSHIP. In faith, then I will not come there!
Who hath thee these tidings brought?
   EVERYMAN. Indeed, Death was with me here.
   FELLOWSHIP. Now, by God that all hath bought,
If Death were the messenger,
For no man living here to-day

Would I go that loathsome journey—
Nay, nor for the father that begat me!
   EVERYMAN. Ye promised otherwise, pardie.   270
    FELLOWSHIP. I know well I did say so truly.
And yet if thou wilt eat, and drink, and make good
    cheer,
Or haunt together women's lusty company,
I would not forsake you, while the day is clear,
Trust me verily!
   EVERYMAN. Yea, thereto ye would be ready—
To go to mirth, solace, and play,
Your mind will sooner apply
Than to bear me company in my far journey.
   FELLOWSHIP. Now, in good faith, I will not that
    way.   280
But if thou wilt murder, or any man kill,
In that I will help thee with a good will!
   EVERYMAN. O that is a simple advice indeed!
Gentle fellow, help me in my necessity—
We have loved long, and now I need,
And now, gentle Fellowship, remember me.
   FELLOWSHIP. Whether ye have loved me or no,
By Saint John, I will not with thee go.
   EVERYMAN. Yet I pray thee, take the labor, and do
    so much for me
To bring me forward, for Saint Charity,   290
And comfort me till I come outside the town.
   FELLOWSHIP. Nay, if thou wouldst give me a new
    gown,
I will not a foot with thee go.
But hadst thou tarried I would not leave thee so.
And so now, God speed thee in thy journey,
For from thee I will depart as fast as I may.
   EVERYMAN. Whither away, Fellowship? will you for-
    sake me?
   FELLOWSHIP. Yea, by my fay, to God I bequeath
    thee.
   EVERYMAN. Farewell, good Fellowship, for thee my
    heart is sore.
Adieu for ever, I shall see thee no more.   300
   FELLOWSHIP. In faith, Everyman, farewell now at
    the end;
From you I will remember that parting is mourning.
                   (*Exit* FELLOWSHIP.)

EVERYMAN. Alack! shall we thus depart indeed?
Our Lady, help, without more comfort,
Lo, Fellowship forsaketh me in my most need:
For help in this world whither shall I resort?
Fellowship before with me would merry make,
And now little sorrow for me doth he take.
It is said, in prosperity men friends may find
Which in adversity be full unkind.   310
Now whither for succor shall I flee,
Since that Fellowship hath forsaken me?
To my kinsmen go I will truly,
Praying them to help me in my necessity.
I believe that they will do so,
For "kind will creep where it may not go."
I will go try, for yonder I see them go.
Where be ye now, my friends and kinsmen?
   (KINDRED *and* COUSIN *appear.*)
   KINDRED. Here be we now at your commandment.
Cousin, I pray you show us your intent   320
In any wise, and do not spare.
   COUSIN. Yea, Everyman, and to us declare
If ye be disposed to go any whither,
For know you well we will live and die together.
   KINDRED. In wealth and woe we will with you hold,
For with his kin a man may be bold.
   EVERYMAN. Gramercy, my friends and kinsmen
     kind.
Now shall I show you the grief of my mind.
I was commanded by a messenger,
That is an High King's chief officer.   330
He bade me go a pilgrimage to my pain,
And I know well I shall never come again.
Also I must give a reckoning straight,
For I have a great enemy, that hath me in wait,
And intendeth me to hinder.
   KINDRED. What account is that which ye must
     render?
That would I know.
   EVERYMAN. Of all my works I must show
How I have lived and my days spent.
Also of ill deeds, that I have used   340
In my time, since life was me lent.
And of all virtues that I have refused.
Therefore I pray you go thither with me,

To help to make my account, for Saint Charity.
    COUSIN. What, to go thither? Is that the matter?
Nay, Everyman, I had liefer fast bread and water
All this five year and more.
    EVERYMAN. Alas, that ever I was born!
For now shall I never be merry
If you forsake me.   350
    KINDRED. Ah, sir, what, ye be a merry man!
Take good heart to you, and make no moan.
But one thing I warn you, by Saint Anne,
As for me, ye shall go alone.
    EVERYMAN. My Cousin, will you not with me go?
    COUSIN. No, by our Lady, I have the cramp in my
      toe.
Wait not for me, for, so God me speed,
I will forsake you in your most need.
    KINDRED. It availeth not us to entice.
You shall have my maid with all my heart;   360
She loveth to go to feasts, there to be nice,
And to dance, and abroad to start.
I will give her leave to help you in that journey,
If that you and she will agree.
    EVERYMAN. Now show me the very effect of your
      mind—
Will you go with me, or abide behind?
    KINDRED. Abide behind? yea, that I will if I may!
Therefore farewell until another day.
    EVERYMAN. How should I be merry or glad?
For fair promises men to me make,   370
But when I have most need they me forsake.
I am deceived, alas—that maketh me sad.
    COUSIN. Cousin Everyman, farewell now,
For verily I will not go with you.
Also of mine own an unready reckoning
I have to account; therefore I make tarrying.
Now, God keep thee, for now I go.
                  (*Exit* KINDRED *and* COUSIN.)
    EVERYMAN. Ah, Jesus, is all come hereto?
Lo, fair words make fools fain.
They promise and nothing will do certain.   380
My kinsmen promised me faithfully
For to abide with me steadfastly,
And now fast away do they flee.
Even so Fellowship promised me.

What friend were best for me to provide?
I lose my time here longer to abide.
Yet in my mind a thing there is—
All my life I have loved Riches;
If that my Goods now help me might,
It would make my heart full light.   390
I will speak to him in this distress.—
Where art thou, my Goods and Riches?
  Goods. Who calleth me? Everyman, what haste thou
    hast!
I lie here in corners, trussed and piled so high,
And in chests I am locked so fast,
Also sacked in bags, thou mayst see with thine eye,
I cannot stir; in packs so low I lie.
What would ye have, what do you say?
  Everyman. Come hither, Goods, in all the haste
    thou may,
For of counsel I must desire thee.   400
  Goods. Sir, if ye in the world have trouble or
    adversity,
That can I help you to remedy shortly. *temporary*
  Everyman. It is another disease that grieveth me.
In this world it is not, I tell thee so.
I am sent for another way to go,
To give a straight account general
Before the highest Jupiter of all.
And all my life I have had joy and pleasure in thee.
Therefore I pray thee go with me,
For, peradventure, thou mayst before God Almighty   410
My reckoning help to clean and purify.
For it is said ever us among,
That money maketh all right that is wrong.
  Goods. Nay, Everyman, I sing another song,
I follow no man in such voyages.
For if I went with thee
Thou shouldst fare much the worse for me.
For because on me thou did bend thy mind,   *more = more problems*
Thy reckoning I have made blotted and blind,
That thine account thou canst not make truly—   420
And that hast thou for the love of me.
  Everyman. That would grieve me full sore,
When I should come to that fearful answer.
Up, let us go thither together.

GOODS. Nay, not so, I am too brittle, I may not
    endure.
I will follow no man one foot, be ye sure.
    EVERYMAN. Alas, I have loved thee, and had great
        pleasure
All my life-days on goods and treasure.
    GOODS. That is to thy damnation without ending.
For love of me is contrary to the love everlasting   430
But if thou hadst loved me moderately,
And to the poor hadst given part of me,
Then shouldst thou not in this dolor be,
Nor in this great sorrow and care.
    EVERYMAN. No, now was I deceived ere I was aware,
And all I blame on my misusing of time.
    GOODS. What, thinkest thou that I am thine?
    EVERYMAN. I had thought so.
    GOODS. Nay, Everyman, I say no.
But for a while was I lent thee,   440
A season thou hast had me in prosperity.
My condition it is man's soul to kill—
If I save one, a thousand I do spill.
Thinkest thou that I will follow thee?
Nay, from this world, not verily.
    EVERYMAN. I had thought otherwise.
    GOODS. Therefore to thy soul Goods is a thief;
For when thou art dead, this is my game
Another to deceive in ways the same,
As I have done thee, and all to his soul's grief   450
    EVERYMAN. O false Goods, cursed thou be!
Thou traitor to God, that hast deceived me,
And snatched me in thy snare.
    GOODS. Marry, thou brought thyself in care,
Whereof I am glad—
I must needs laugh; I cannot be sad.
    EVERYMAN. Ah, Goods, thou hast had long my
        heartly love;
I gave thee that which should be the Lord's above.
But wilt thou not go with me indeed?
I pray thee truth to say.   460
    GOODS. No, so God me speed,
Therefore farewell, and have good day.
                                        (*Exit* GOODS.)
    EVERYMAN. O, to whom shall I make my moan
For to go with me in that heavy journey?

First Fellowship said he would with me be gone;
His words were very pleasant and gay,
But afterward he left me alone.
Then spake I to my kinsmen all in despair,
And they also gave me words fair.
They lacked no fair speaking,   470
But they forsook me in the ending.
Then went I to my Goods that I loved best,
In hope to have comfort, but there had I least.
For my Goods sharply did me tell
That he bringeth many into Hell.
Then of myself I was ashamed,
And so I am worthy to be blamed,
Thus may I well myself hate.
Of whom shall I now counsel take?
I think that I shall never speed   480
Till that I go to my Good-Deed,
But, alas, she is so weak,
That she can neither go nor speak.
Yet will I venture on her now.—
My Good-Deeds, where be you?
   (*Enter* Good-Deeds.)
   GOOD-DEEDS. Here I lie cold in the ground.
Thy sins have me sore-bound
That I cannot stir.
   EVERYMAN. O, Good-Deeds, I stand in fear;
I must pray you for counsel,   490
For help now would come right well.
   GOOD-DEEDS. Everyman, I have understanding
That you be summoned account to make
Before Messias, of Jerusalem the King.
If you walk by me that journey I would take.
   EVERYMAN. Therefore I come to you, my moan to
     make—
I pray you, that ye will go with me.
   GOOD-DEEDS. I would full fain, but I cannot stand,
     verily.
   EVERYMAN. Why, is there anything did you befall?
   GOOD-DEEDS. Yea, sir, and I may thank you of all;   500
If ye had perfectly cheered me,
Your book of account now full ready would be.
Look on the books of your works and deeds—
Oh, see how they under your feet lie,
Unto your soul's heaviness.

EVERYMAN. Our Lord Jesus, help me!
For one letter here I cannot see.
    GOOD-DEEDS. There is a blind reckoning in time of
      distress!
    EVERYMAN. Good-Deeds, I pray you, help me in
      this need.
Or else I am for ever damned indeed.   510
Therefore help me to a reckoning
Before the Redeemer of all thing,
That king is, and was, and ever shall.
    GOOD-DEEDS. Everyman, I am sorry for your fall,
And fain would I help you, if I were able.
    EVERYMAN. Good-Deeds, your counsel I pray you
      give me.
    GOOD-DEEDS. That shall I do verily.
Though that on my feet I may not go,
I have a sister that shall with you also,
Called Knowledge, which shall with you abide,   520
To help you to make that dreadful reckoning.
    (*Enter* KNOWLEDGE.)
    KNOWLEDGE. Everyman, I will go with thee, and be
      thy guide,
In utmost need to go by thy side.
    EVERYMAN. In good condition I am now in every
      thing,
And am wholly content with this good thing.
Thanked be God, my Creator!
    GOOD-DEEDS. And when he hath brought thee there
Where thou shalt heal me of my smart,
Then go you with your reckoning and your Good-
      Deeds together
For to make you joyful at heart   530
Before the blessed Trinity.
    EVERYMAN. My Good-Deeds, gramercy;
I am well content, certainly,
With your words sweet.
    KNOWLEDGE. Now go we together lovingly,
To Confession's cleansing river.
    EVERYMAN. For joy I weep. I would we were there!
But, I pray you, give me cognition
Where dwelleth that holy man, Confession.
    KNOWLEDGE. In the house of salvation.   540
We shall find him in that place

That shall comfort us by God's grace.
  (CONFESSION *appears*.)
Lo, this is Confession; kneel down and ask mercy,
For he is in good conceit with God Almighty.
  EVERYMAN. O glorious fountain that all uncleanness
    doth clarify,
Wash from me the spots of vices unclean,
That on me no sin may be seen.
I come with Knowledge for my redemption,
Repent with hearty and full contrition.
For I am commanded a pilgrimage to take,   550
And straight accounts before God to make.
Now, I pray you, Shrift, mother of Salvation,
Help my good deeds to make a piteous exclamation.
  CONFESSION. I know your sorrow well, Everyman.
Because with Knowledge ye come to me,
I will comfort you as well as I can,
And a precious jewel I will give thee,
Called penance, wise voider of adversity.
Therewith shall thy body chastised be,
With abstinence and perseverance in God's service.   560
Here shalt thou receive that scourge of me
Which is penance strong that you must endure,
To remember thy Savior was scourged for thee
With sharp scourges, and suffered it patiently.
So must thou, ere thou escape that painful pilgrimage;
Knowledge, keep him in this voyage,
And by that time Good-Deeds will be with thee.
And in any wise, be sure of mercy,
For your time draweth fast, if you will saved be.
Ask God mercy, and He will grant truly;   570
When with the scourge of penance man bind,
The oil of forgiveness then shall he find.
  EVERYMAN. Thanked be God for his gracious work!
For now I will my penance begin.
This hath rejoiced and lighted my heart,
Though the knots be painful and hard within.
  KNOWLEDGE. Everyman, look that ye your penance
    fulfil,
Whatever pain it to you be,
And Knowledge shall give you counsel at will.
How your accounts ye shall make clearly.   580
  EVERYMAN. O eternal God, O heavenly figure,
O way of righteousness, O goodly vision,

Which descended down in a virgin pure
Because He would Everyman redeem,
Which Adam forfeited by his disobedience.
O blessed Godhead, elect and divine,
Forgive my grievous offence,
Here I cry Thee mercy in this presence.
O soul's treasure, O ransomer and redeemer
Of all the world, hope and leader,   590
Mirror of joy, and founder of mercy,
Which illumineth heaven and earth thereby,
Hear my clamorous complaint, though it late be,
Receive my prayers. Unworthy in this heavy life
Though I be, a sinner most abominable,
Yet let my name be written in Moses' table;
O Mary, pray to the Maker of everything,
To help me at my ending,
And save me from the power of my enemy,
For Death assaileth me strongly.   600
And, Lady, that I may by means of thy prayer
Of your Son's glory be the partaker,
By the pity of his Passion I it crave,
I beseech you, help my soul to save.—
Knowledge, give me the scourge of penance,
My flesh therewith shall give a quittance.
I will now begin, if God give me grace.
        KNOWLEDGE. Everyman, God give you time and
            space.
Thus I bequeath you into the hands of our Savior,
Thus may you make your reckoning sure.   610
        EVERYMAN. In the name of the blessed Trinity,
My body sore punished shall be.
Take this body for the sin of the flesh!
Thou that delightest to go gay and fresh,
And in the way of damnation didst me bring,
Now suffer therefore strokes and punishing.
Now of penance I will wade the water clear,
To save me from Purgatory, that sharp fire.
        (GOOD-DEEDS *joins them as he smites himself.*)
        GOOD-DEEDS. I thank God, now I can walk and go,
And am delivered of my sickness and woe.   620
Therefore with Everyman I will go, and not spare—
His good works I will help him to declare.
        KNOWLEDGE. Now, Everyman, be merry and glad.
Your Good-Deeds cometh now, ye may not be sad.

Now is your Good-Deeds whole and sound,
Going upright upon the ground.
   EVERYMAN. My heart is light, and shall be ever-
      more,
Now I will smite faster than I did before.
   GOOD-DEEDS. Everyman, pilgrim, my special friend,
Blessed be thou without end.   630
For thee is prepared the eternal glory.
Ye have made me whole and sound,
Therefore I will bide by thee in every round.
   EVERYMAN. Welcome, my Good-Deeds! Now I hear
      thy voice,
I weep for very sweetness of love.
   KNOWLEDGE. Be no more sad, but ever rejoice,
God seeth thy being from his throne aloft.
Put on this garment which is so soft—
Wet with your tears it is.
Or else before God you may it miss,   640
When you to your journey's end shall come.
   EVERYMAN. Gentle Knowledge, what is its name?
   KNOWLEDGE. It is a garment of sorrow:
From pain it will divide you;
Contrition it is,
That getteth forgiveness;
It pleaseth God passing well.
   GOOD-DEEDS. Everyman, will you wear it for your
      heal?
   (EVERYMAN *puts on the robe.*)
   EVERYMAN. Now blessed be Jesu, Mary's Son!
For now have I on true contrition.   650
And let us go now without tarrying.
Good-Deeds, have we clear our reckoning?
   GOOD-DEEDS. Yea, indeed I have it here.
   EVERYMAN. Then I trust we need not fear;
Now, friends, let us not part in twain.
   KNOWLEDGE. Nay, Everyman, that will we not, cer-
     tain.
   GOOD-DEEDS. Yet must thou lead with thee
Three persons of great might.
   EVERYMAN. Who should they be?
   GOOD-DEEDS. Discretion and Strength they hight,   660
And thy Beauty may not abide behind.
   KNOWLEDGE. Also you must call to mind
Your Five-Wits as for your counselors.

GOOD-DEEDS. You must have them ready at all
    hours.
EVERYMAN. How shall I get them hither?
KNOWLEDGE. You must call them all together,
And they will hear you incontinent.
EVERYMAN. My friends, come hither and be present,
Discretion, Strength, my Five-Wits, and Beauty.
    (DISCRETION, STRENGTH, FIVE-WITS and BEAUTY enter.)
BEAUTY. Here at your will we be all ready.   670
What will ye that we should do?
GOOD-DEEDS. That ye would with Everyman go,
And help him in his pilgrimage.
Advise me, will ye with him or not in that voyage?
STRENGTH. We will bring him all thither,
To his help and comfort, ye may believe me.
DISCRETION. So will we go with him all together.
EVERYMAN. Almighty God, loved mayest thou be,
I give thee laud that I have hither brought
Strength, Discretion, Beauty, and Five-Wits; I lack
    nought!   680
And my Good-Deeds, with Knowledge clear,
All stay in my company at my will here;
I desire no more to my business.
STRENGTH. And I, Strength, will stand by you in
    distress,
Though thou wouldest in battle fight on the ground.
FIVE-WITS. And though it were through the world
    round,
We will not depart for sweet nor sour.
BEAUTY. No more will I unto death's hour,
Whatsoever thereof befall.
DISCRETION. Everyman, advise you first of all,   680
Go with a good advisement and deliberation.
We all give you virtuous monition
That all shall be well.
EVERYMAN. My friends, hearken what I will tell.
I pray God reward you in his heavenly sphere.
Now hearken, all that be here,
For I will make my testament
Here before every one present.
In alms half my good I will give with my hands twain
In the way of charity, with good intent,   700
And the other half shall remain
In quiet to be returned where it ought to be.

This I do in despite of the fiend of hell,
To go quit of his peril
Ever after and this day.
   KNOWLEDGE. Everyman, hearken what I say.
Go to priesthood, I advise,
And receive of him in any wise
The holy sacrament and ointment together,
Then shortly see ye turn again hither.   710
We will all await you here.
   FIVE-WITS. Yea, Everyman, haste you that ye ready
     be.
There is no emperor, king, duke, nor baron,
That of God hath commission,
As hath the least priest in the world's design.
For of the blessed sacraments pure and benign,
He beareth the keys and thereof hath the cure
For man's redemption, that is ever sure;
Which God for our soul's medicine
Gave us out of his heart with great pine.   720
Here in this transitory life, for thee and me,
The blessed sacraments seven there be,
Baptism, confirmation, with priesthood good,
And the sacrament of God's precious flesh and blood,
Marriage, the holy extreme unction, and penance;
These seven be good to have in remembrance,
Gracious sacraments of high divinity.
   EVERYMAN. Fain would I receive that holy body
And meekly to my spiritual father I will go.
   FIVE-WITS. Everyman, that is the best that ye can
    do.   730
God will you to salvation bring,
For priesthood exceedeth all other thing.
To us Holy Scripture they do teach,
And convert man from his sin heaven to reach;
God hath to them more power given
Than to any angel that is in heaven.
With five words he may consecrate
God's body in flesh and blood to make,
And holdeth his maker between his hands,
The priest bindeth and unbindeth all bands,   740
Both in earth and in heaven,
He ministers all the sacraments seven.—
Though we kissed thy feet thou wert worthy,
Thou art surgeon that cureth sin deadly.

No remedy we find that is good
But only under priesthood.
Everyman, God gave priests that dignity,
And setteth them in his stead among us to be—
Thus be they above angels in degree.

                         (EVERYMAN *departs*.)

   KNOWLEDGE. If priests be good it is so surely!   750
But when Jesus hanged on the cross with great smart
There he *gave*, out of his blessed heart,
The same sacrament in great torment:
He *sold* them not to us, that Lord Omnipotent!
Therefore Saint Peter, the apostle, doth say
That Jesu's curse have all they
Who God their Savior do buy or sell,
Or for any money do take or tell.
Sinful priests have to sinners bad example been.
Their children sit by other men's fires, I have seen;   760
And some priests haunt women's company,
With unclean life, in lusts of lechery:
These be with sin made blind.
   FIVE-WITS. I trust to God no such may we find.
Therefore let us priesthood honor,
And follow their doctrine for our souls' succor.
We be their sheep, and they shepherds be
By whom we all are kept in surety.
Peace, for yonder I see Everyman come,
Who hath made true satisfaction.   770
GOOD-DEEDS. Methinketh it is he indeed.
   (EVERYMAN *returns*.)
   EVERYMAN. Now Jesu all our labor speed,
I have received the sacrament for my redemption,
And then mine extreme unction.
Blessed be all they that counseled me to take it!
And now, friends, let us go without longer respite,
I thank God that ye have tarried so long.
Now set each of you on this rod your hand,
And shortly follow me.
I go before, there I would be, God be our guide!   780
   STRENGTH. Everyman, we will not from you go,
Till ye have gone this voyage long.
   DISCRETION. I, Discretion, will bide by you also.
   KNOWLEDGE. And though this pilgrimage be never
      so strong,
I will never part from you, too.

EVERYMAN. I will be as sure by thee
As ever I stood by Judas Maccabee.
   (*They approach the grave.*)
   EVERYMAN. Alas, I am so faint I may not stand,
My limbs under me do fold.
Friends, let us not turn again to this land,   790
Not for all the world's gold,
For into this cave must I creep
And turn to the earth and there sleep.
   BEAUTY. What, into this grave? Alas!
   EVERYMAN. Yea, there shall you consume more and
      less.
   BEAUTY. And what, should I smother here?
   EVERYMAN. Yea, by my faith, and never more ap-
      pear.
In this world live no more we shall,
But in heaven before the highest lord of all.
   BEAUTY. I cross out all this, adieu by Saint John!   800
I take my cap in my lap and am gone.
   EVERYMAN. What, Beauty, whither will ye?
   BEAUTY. Peace, I am deaf! I look not behind me,
Not if thou would give me all the gold in thy chest.
                              (BEAUTY *departs.*)
   EVERYMAN. Alas, in whom may I trust?
Beauty fast away doth hie—
She promised with me to live and die.
   STRENGTH. Everyman, I will thee also forsake and
      deny.
Thy game liketh me not at all.
   EVERYMAN. Why, then ye will forsake me all.   810
Sweet Strength, tarry a little space.
   STRENGTH. Nay, sir, by the rood of grace
I will hie me from thee first,
Though thou weep till thy heart burst.
   EVERYMAN. Ye would ever bide by me, ye said.
   STRENGTH. Yea, I have you far enough conveyed.
Ye be old enough, I understand,
Your pilgrimage to take on hand;
I repent me that I hither came.
   EVERYMAN. Strength, you to displease I am to blame;   820
Will you break promise that is debt?
   STRENGTH. In faith, I care not.
Thou art but a fool to complain,
You spend your speech and waste your brain—

Go thrust thee into the ground!

EVERYMAN. I had thought surer I should have you
found.

(*Exit* STRENGTH.)

He that trusteth in his Strength
She deceiveth him at the length.
Both Strength and Beauty forsaking me,
Yet they promised me fair and lovingly.   830

DISCRETION. Everyman, I will after Strength be
gone,
As for me I will leave you alone.

EVERYMAN. Why, Discretion, will ye forsake me?

DISCRETION. Yea, in faith, I will go from thee,
For when Strength goeth before
I follow after evermore.

EVERYMAN. Yet, I pray thee, for the love of Trinity,
Look in my grave once piteously.

DISCRETION. Nay, so nigh will I not come.
Farewell, every one!   840

(*Exit* DISCRETION.)

EVERYMAN. O all thing faileth, save God alone;
Beauty, Strength, and Discretion;
For when Death bloweth his blast
They all run from me full fast.

FIVE-WITS. Everyman, my leave now of thee I take;
I will follow the other, for here I thee forsake.

EVERYMAN. Alas! then my I wail and weep,
For I took you for my best friend.

FIVE-WITS. I will not longer thee keep.
Now farewell, and there an end.   850

(*Exit* FIVE-WITS.)

EVERYMAN. O Jesu, help, all have forsaken me!

GOOD-DEEDS. Nay, Everyman, I will bide with thee,
I will not forsake thee indeed,
Thou shalt find me a good friend at need.

EVERYMAN. Gramercy, Good-Deeds, now, may I true
friends see.
They have forsaken me every one.
I loved them better than my Good-Deeds alone.
Knowledge, will ye forsake me also?

KNOWLEDGE. Yea, Everyman, when ye to death do
go,
But not yet for no manner of danger.   860

EVERYMAN. Gramercy, Knowledge, with all my
    heart.
KNOWLEDGE. Nay, yet I will not from hence depart,
Till I be sure where ye shall come.
EVERYMAN. Methinketh, alas, that I must be on,
To make my reckoning and debts to pay,
For I see my time is nigh spent away.
Take example, all ye that this do hear or see,
How they that I loved best do forsake me,
Except my Good-Deeds that bideth truly.
GOOD-DEEDS. All earthly things are but vanity: 870
Beauty, Strength, and Discretion, do man forsake,
Foolish friends and kinsmen, that fair spake,
All flee save Good-Deeds, and he am I.
EVERYMAN. Have mercy on me, God most mighty;
And stand by me, thou Mother and Maid, holy Mary.
GOOD-DEEDS. Fear not, I will speak for thee.
EVERYMAN. Here I cry God mercy.
GOOD-DEEDS. Shorten our end, and diminish our
    pain.
Let us go and never come again.
EVERYMAN. Into Thy hands, Lord, my soul I com-
    mend.   880
Receive it, Lord, that it be not lost!
As thou boughtest me, me so defend,
And rescue from the fiend's boast,
That I may appear with that blessed host
That shall be saved at the day of doom.
In manus tuas—of might's utmost
Forever—*commendo spiritum meum.*
    (EVERYMAN *and* GOOD-DEEDS *enter the grave.*)
    KNOWLEDGE. Now hath he suffered what we all shall
    endure,
But Good-Deeds shall make all sure.
Now hath he made ending—   890
Methinketh I hear angels sing
And make great joy and melody,
Where Everyman's soul received shall be.
    (*An* ANGEL *appears.*)
    ANGEL. Come, excellent elect spouse to Jesu!
Hereabove thou shalt go
Because of thy singular virtue.
Now the soul is taken from the body so,
    Thy reckoning is crystal-clear.

Now shalt thou into the heavenly sphere,
Unto which all ye shall come   900
That live well before the day of doom.

EPILOGUE

DOCTOR. This moral men may have in mind:
Ye hearers, take it of worth, old and young,
And forsake pride, for he deceiveth you in the end,
And remember Beauty, Five-Wits, Strength, and
    Discretion,
They all at the last do Everyman forsake,
Alone his Good-Deeds there doth he take.
But beware, if they be small
Before God, man hath no help at all.
No excuse may there be for Everyman—   910
Alas, what shall he do then?
For after death amends may no man make,
For then mercy and pity him forsake.
If his reckoning be not clear when he come,
God will say—*ite maledicti in ignem æternum*.[1]
And he that hath his account whole and sound,
High in heaven he shall be crowned,
Unto which place God bring us all thither
That we may live body and soul together.
Thereto help blessed Trinity.   920
Amen, say ye, for Saint Charity.
Thus endeth this moral play of Everyman.

[1] Go into the eternal fire, ye cursed ones.

The Interlude

A relatively new form of entertainment arose in England during the early decades of the sixteenth century. It was a type of discursive comedy or farce similar to the medieval *débat*, or debate, and it was intended to amuse as well as, now and then, teach its audience. Short on plot and long on discussion, the interludes did not so much thrive on any public stage as appear as a form of private entertainment in the halls of great houses. They were one-act farces in which the moral was unobtrusive and was secondary to the liveliness of the humorous situation and argument. It is almost impossible to define this new genre more closely.

The "interlude" is associated with one name above any other, that of John Heywood (*circa* 1497–1578), a master of the royal choir school who was employed as a musician at the court until 1528. After the triumph of Protestantism in England, Heywood, who remained a loyal Catholic to the end of his days, led a precarious existence. He narrowly escaped hanging for his apparent participation in a plot in 1544 against the life of Archbishop Cranmer, the Protestant Archbishop of Canterbury. Early in the reign of Queen Elizabeth, he left England forever; befriended by the Jesuits in France, he died sometime after 1578 at Louvain. A cultivated and well connected man, whose son Jasper translated plays by Seneca into English and whose daughter Elizabeth become the mother of the famous poet John Donne, John Heywood brought wide interests and a keen spirit to the writing of these intellectual exercises in farce and comedy.

Among these, *The Play of the Weather* is a clever entertainment in which various people on being given a chance to request the weather that suits them best, make such contradictory demands that Jupiter decides to leave the weather unchanged. *John John, Tib, and Sir John,* a play attributed to Heywood, is an amusing domestic triangle farce which has the merit of possessing a developing dramatic action. But *The Four PP*—a four-way discussion involving familiar figures of medieval life such as a pardoner and a palmer, or pilgrim— is the ideal play with which to represent the genre of the interlude. It is a discussion rather than an intrigue like the

previously mentioned play; and it is enlivened with wit and
shrewd references to daily life.

John Heywood did not have a monopoly on the writing of
interludes. A well-known early example of the interlude is
a debate between rivals for a Roman senator's daughter
(Lucrece), *Fulgens and Lucres,* written about 1497 by Henry
Medwall, who was chaplain to the Archbishop of Canterbury
during the reign of Henry VII. But John Heywood gave the
interlude its keenest edge; and if there was no future for this
essentially medieval form of literature, the reason is that the
English theater was leaving the Middle Ages. After 1550 England favored types of comedy more full-bodied in characterization and decidedly more active than any discussion could be.

The Play Called the Four PP

By John Heywood

An Interlude of

A PALMER	A POTHECARY*
A PARDONER	A PEDLAR

* An apothecary or pharmacist.

(*Enter a* PALMER.)

PALMER. Now God be here! Who keepeth this
　　place?
Now, by my faith, I cry you mercy!
Of reason I must sue for grace,
My rudeness showeth me now so homely.
Whereof your pardon axed* and won,　　　　　　　　　asked
I sue you, as courtesy doth me bind,
To tell this which shall be begun
In order as may come best in mind.
I am a palmer,* as ye see,　　　　　　　　　　　　pilgrim[1]
Which of my life much part hath spent　　　　　　　10

[1] A pilgrim who visited the Holy Land was wont to carry a palm leaf as
a sign that he had been there, and was therefore called a "palmer."

In many a fair and far country,
As pilgrims do of good intent.
At Jerusalem have I been
Before Christ's blessèd sepulture;
The Mount of Calvary have I seen,
A holy place, ye may be sure;
To Josophat and Olivet
On foot, God wot,* I went right bare,   knows
Many a salt tear did I sweat
Before this carcase could come there.   20
Yet have I been at Rome also,
And gone the stations all arow,*   one after another
Saint Peter's shrine, and many mo*   more
Than, If I told, all ye do know,
Except that there be any such
That hath been there and diligently
Hath taken heed and markèd much,
Then can they speak as much as I.
Then at the Rhodes also I was,
And round about to Amias;   30
At Saint Toncomber; and Saint Trunnion;
At Saint Botolph; and Saint Anne of Buxton;
On the hills of Armony,* where I see Noah's ark;   Armenia
With holy Job; and Saint George in Southwark;
At Waltham; and at Walsingham;
And at the good Rood of Dagenham;
At Saint Cornelius; at Saint James in Gales;
And at Saint Winifred's Well in Wales;
At Our Lady of Boston; at Saint Edmundsbury;
And straight to Saint Patrick's Purgatory;   40
At Redburne; and at the Blood of Hales,
Where pilgrims' pains right much avails;
At Saint Davy's; and at Saint Denis;
At Saint Matthew; and Saint Mark in Venice;
At Master John Shorn; at Canterbury;
The great God of Catwade; at King Henry;
At Saint Saviour's; at Our Lady of Southwell;
At Crome; at Willesden; and at Muswell;
At Saint Richard; and at Saint Roke;
And at Our Lady that standeth in the oak.[2]   50
To these, with other many one,
Devoutly have I prayed and gone,

[2] A shrine to the Virgin Mary at the side of a road beside an oak.

Praying to them to pray for me
Unto the Blessed Trinity;
By whose prayers and my daily pain
I trust the sooner to obtain
For my salvation grace and mercy.
For, be ye sure, I think surely
Who seeketh saints for Christ's sake
And namely* such as pain do take   especially/60
On foot to punish their frail body
Shall thereby merit more highly
Than by anything done by man.

   (*Enter a* PARDONER *speaking.*)

   PARDONER. And when ye have gone as far as ye can,
For all your labour and ghostly intent
Yet welcome home as wise as ye went!

    PALMER. Why, sir, despise ye pilgrimage?

   PARDONER. Nay, 'fore God, sir! Then did I rage![3]
I think ye right well occupied
To seek these saints on every side.   70
Also your pain I not dispraise it;
But yet I discommend your wit;
And, ere we go, even so shall ye,
If ye in this will answer me:
I pray you, show what the cause is
Ye went all these pilgrimages.

    PALMER. Forsooth, this life I did begin
To rid the bondage of my sin;
For which these saints, rehearsed ere this,
I have both sought and seen, iwis,*   surely/80
Beseeching them to be record
Of all my pain unto the Lord
That giveth all remission
Upon each man's contrition.
And by their good mediation,
Upon mine humble submission,
I trust to have in very deed
For my soul's health the better speed.

   PARDONER. Now is your own confession likely
To make yourself a fool quickly   90
For I perceive ye would obtain
None other thing for all your pain
But only grace your soul to save.

---

   [3] Then I would be mad.

Now, mark in this what wit ye have
To seek so far, and help so nigh!
Even here at home is remedy,
For at your door myself doth dwell,
Who could have saved your soul as well
As all your wide wandering shall do,
Though ye went thrice to Jericho.   100
Now, since ye might have sped at home,
What have ye won by running at* Rome?   *to
   PALMER. If this be true that ye have moved,*   *maintained
Then is my wit indeed reproved!
But let us hear first what ye are.
   PARDONER. Truly, I am a pardoner.
   PALMER. Truly a pardoner, that may be true,
But a true pardoner doth not ensue!
Right seldom is it seen, or never,
That truth and pardoners dwell together;   110
For, be your pardons never so great,
Yet them to enlarge ye will not let*   *forbear
With such lies that oft-times, Christ wot,
Ye seem to have what ye have not.
Wherefore I went myself to the self thing[4]
In every place, and, without faining,
Had as much pardon there *assuredly*
As ye can promise me here *doubtfully*.
Howbeit, I think ye do but scoff.
But if ye had all the pardon ye speak of,   120
And no whit of pardon graunted
In any place where I have haunted,
Yet of my labour I nothing repent.
God hath respect how each time is spent;
And, as in his knowledge all is regarded,
So by his goodness all is rewarded.
   PARDONER. By the first part of this last tale
It seemeth you come late from the ale!
For reason on your side so far doth fail
That ye leave reasoning and begin to rail;   130
Wherein ye forget your own part clearly,
For ye be as untrue as I;
And in one point ye are beyond me,
For ye may lie by authority,
And all that hath wandered so far

[4] The thing itself.

That no man can be their controller.*   contradictor
And, where ye esteem your labour so much,
I say yet again my pardon be such
That, if there were a thousand souls on a heap,
I would bring them all to heaven as good cheap   140
As ye have brought yourself on pilgrimage
In the last quarter of your voyage,
Which is far a* this side heaven, by God!   on
There your labour and pardon is odd,⁵
With small cost and without any pain,
These pardons bringeth them to heaven plain.
Give me but a penny or two pence,
And as soon as the soul departeth hence,
In half an hour—or three quarters at most—
The soul is in heaven with the Holy Ghost!   150

    (*While he is speaking, enter a* POTHECARY)
    POTHECARY. Send ye any souls to heaven by water?
    PARDONER. If we did, sir, what is the matter?
    POTHECARY. By God, I have a dry soul should
      thither!

I pray you let our souls go to heaven together.*   together
So busy you twain be in souls' health,
May not a pothecary come in by stealth?
Yes, that I will, by Saint Anthony!
And, by the leave of this company,
Prove ye false knaves both, ere we go,
In part of your sayings, as this, lo: 160
    (*To the* PALMER.)
Thou by thy travel thinkest heaven to get;
    (*To the* PARDONER.)
And thou by pardons and relics countest no let*   obstacle
To send thine own soul to heaven sure,
And all other whom thou list* to procure.   want
If I took an action, then were they blank;
For, like thieves, the knaves rob away my thank.
All souls in heaven having relief,
Shall they thank your crafts? Nay, thank mine, chief!
No soul, ye know, entereth heaven-gate
Till from the body he be separate;   170
And whom have ye known die honestly
Without help of the pothecary?
Nay, all that cometh to our handling,

---

⁵ Whereas your labor is disproportionate to the pardon obtained by it.

Except ye hap* to come to hanging—   happen
That way, perchance, ye shall not mister*   need
To go to heaven without a glister!*   enema clyster
But, be ye sure, I would be woe
If ye should chance to beguile me so.
As good to lie with me a-night
As hang abroad in the moonlight!   180
There is no choice to flee my hand
But, as I said, into the band.*   hanging rope
Since of our souls the multitude
I send to heaven, when all is viewed,
Who should but I, then, altogither
Have thank of all their coming thither?
    PARDONER. If ye killed a thousand in an hour's
      space,
When come they to heaven, dying from state of grace?
    POTHECARY. If a thousand pardons about your
      necks were tied,
When come they to heaven if they never died?   190
    PALMER. Long life after good works, indeed,
Doth hinder man's receipt of meed,*   reward
And death before one duty done
May make us think we die too soon.
Yet better tarry [for] a thing, then have it,
Than go too soon and vainly crave it.
    PARDONER. The longer ye dwell in communication,
The less shall you like this imagination;
For ye may perceive, even at the first chop,*   from the start
Your tale is trapped in such a stop   200
That, at the least, ye seem worse than we.
    POTHECARY. By the Mass, I hold us naught, all
      three!
    (*While he is speaking, the* PEDLAR *enters.*)
    PEDLAR. By Our Lady, then have I gone wrong!
And yet to be here I thought long.
    POTHECARY. Brother, ye have gone wrong no whit.*   not at all
I praise your fortune and your wit
That can direct you so discreetly
To plant you in this company:
Thou a palmer, and thou a pardoner,
I a pothecary.
    PEDLAR.   And I a pedlar!   210
    POTHECARY. Now, on my faith, full well matched!
Where the devil were we four hatched?

PEDLAR. That maketh no matter, since we be
    matched.
I could be merry if that I catched*   caught, acquired
Some money for part of the ware in my pack.
    POTHECARY. What the devil hast thou there at thy
    back?
    PEDLAR. Why, dost thou not know that every pedler
In every trifle must be a meddler,
Specially in women's triflings,—
Those use we chief above all things.   220
Which things to see, if ye be disposed,
Behold what ware here is disclosed.
This gear* showeth itself in such beauty   stuff
That each man thinketh it saith: "Come, buy me!"
Look, where yourself can like to be chooser,
Yourself shall make price, though I be loser![6]
Is here nothing for my father Palmer?
Have ye not a wanton* in a corner   mistress
For your walking to holy places?
By Christ, I have heard of as strange cases!   230
Who liveth in love, or love would win,
Even at this pack he must begin,
Where is right many a proper token,
Of which by name part shall be spoken:
Gloves, pins, combs, glasses unspotted,
Pomanders, hooks, and laces knotted,
Brooches, rings, and all manner beads,
Lace, round and flat, for women's heads,
Needles, thread, thimbles, shears, and all such
    knacks*—   knick-knacks
Where lovers be, no such things lacks—   240
Cypress, swathbands, ribands, and sleevelaces,[7]
Girdles, knives, purses, and pincases.
    POTHECARY. Do women buy their pincases of you?
    PEDLAR. Yea, that they do, I make God avow!
    POTHECARY. So mote* I thrive, then, for my part,   might
I beshrew thy knave's naked heart
For making my wife's pincase so wide,
The pins fall out, they cannot abide.
Great pins must she have, one or other;
If she lose one, she will find another!   250
Wherein I find cause to complain,

[6] "I'll let you fix the price yourself . . ."
[7] Fine lawn, swaddling clothes, ribbons, and laces for trimming sleeves.

New pins to her pleasure and my pain!
   PARDONER. Sir, ye seem well seen in women's causes.
I pray you, tell me what causeth this,
That women, after their arising,
Be so long in their apparelling?
   PEDLAR. Forsooth, women have many lets,*   hindrances
And they be masked in many nets,
As frontlets, fillets, partlets* and bracelets;   ruffs
And then their bonnets, and their poignets.*   wristlets/260
By these lets and nets the let is such
That speed is small when haste is much.
   POTHECARY. Another cause why they come not
     forward,
Which maketh them daily to draw backward,
And yet is a thing they cannot forbear—
The trimming and pinning up their gear,
Specially their fiddling with the tail-pin;
And, when they would have it prick in,
If it chance to double in the cloth
Then be they wood* and sweareth an oath,   mad/270
Till it stand right, they will not forsake it.
Thus, though it may not, yet would they make it.
But be ye sure they do but defar it,
For, when they would make it, oft-times mar it.
But prick them and pin them as much as ye will,
And yet will they look for pinnings still!
So that I durst hold* you a joint   wager
Ye shall never have them at a full point.
   PEDLAR. Let women's matters pass, and mark mine!
Whatever their points be, these points be fine.   280
Wherefore, if ye be willing to buy,
Lay down money! Come off quickly!
   PALMER. Nay, by my troth, we be like friars:
We are but beggars, we be no buyers.
   PARDONER. Sir, ye may show your ware for your
     mind,
But I think ye shall no profit find.
   PEDLAR. Well, though this journey acquit no cost,[8]
Yet think I not my labor lost;
For, by the faith of my body,
I like full well this company,   290
Up shall this pack, for it is plain

---

[8] "Though this trip doesn't earn me enough to pay for expenses."

I came not hither all for gain.
Who may not play one day in a week
May think his thrift is far to seek!
Devise what pastime ye think best,
And make ye sure to find me prest.*   ready
   POTHECARY. Why, be ye so universal
That you can do whatsoever ye shall?
   PEDLAR. Sir, if ye list to appose* me,   question
What I can do then shall ye see.   300
   POTHECARY. Then tell me this: be ye perfect in
     drinking?
   PEDLAR. Perfect in drinking as may be wished by
     thinking!
   POTHECARY. Then after your drinking, how? Fall ye
     to winking?
   PEDLAR. Sir, after drinking, while the shot is
     tinking,[9]
Some heads be swinking,* but mine will be sinking,   swimming
And upon drinking mine eyes will be pinking,*   blinking
For winking to drinking is always linking.*   connected
   POTHECARY. Then drink and sleep ye can well do.
But, if ye were desired thereto,
I pray you, tell me, can you sing?   310
   PEDLAR. Sir, I have some sight in singing.
   POTHECARY. But is your breast anything sweet?
   PEDLAR. Whatever my breast be, my voice is meet.
   POTHECARY. That answer showeth you a right
     singing man!
Now what is your will, good father, than?*   then
   PALMER. What helpeth will where is no skill?
   PARDONER. And what helpeth skill where is no will?
   POTHECARY. For will or skill, what helpeth it
Where froward knaves be lacking wit?
Leave of this curiosity;[10]   320
And who that list, sing after me!
   (*Here they sing.*)
   PEDLAR. This liketh me well, so mote I thee![11]
   PARDONER. So help me God, it liketh not me!
Where company is met and well agreed,
Good pastime doth right well indeed;
But who can set in dalliance

---

[9] "While the money is clinking."
[10] "Cease this quibbling."
[11] "So may I thrive."

Men set in such a variance
As we were set ere ye came in?
Which strife this man did first begin,
    (*Pointing to the* PALMER.)
Alleging that such men as use,*   are accustomed/330
For love of God, and not refuse
On foot to go from place to place
A pilgrimage, calling for grace,
Shall in that pain with penitence
Obtain discharge of conscience,*   guilt
Comparing that life for the best
Induction to our endless* rest.   eternal
Upon these words our matter grew;
For, if he could avow them true,
As good to be a gardener   340
As for to be a pardoner.
But, when I heard him so far wide,
I then approached and replied,
Saying this: that this indulgence,
Having the foresaid penitence,
Dischargeth man of all offence
With much more profit than this pretence.
I ask but twopence at the most,
Iwis, this is not very great cost,
And from all pain, without despair,   350
My soul for his—keep even his chair,[12]
And when he dieth he may be sure
To come to heaven, even at pleasure.
And more than heaven he cannot get,
How far soever he list* to jet.*   wishes/venture
Then is his pain more than his wit
To walk to heaven, since he may sit!
Sir, as we were in this contention,
In came this daw* with his invention,   dolt, fool
    (*Pointing to the* POTHECARY.)
Reviling us, himself avaunting*   boasting/360
That all the souls to heaven ascending
Are most bound to the pothecary,
Because he helpeth most men to die;
Before which death he sayeth, indeed,
No soul in heaven can have his meed.
    PEDLAR. Why, do pothecaries kill men?

[12] May even sit in ease.

POTHECARY. By God, men say so now and then!

PEDLAR. And I thought ye would not have mist

To make men live as long as ye list.*   desire

POTHECARY. As long as we list? Nay, long as they
   can!   370

PEDLAR. So might we live without you than.*   then

POTHECARY. Yea, but yet it is necessary

For to have a pothecary;

For when ye feel your conscience ready,

I can send you to heaven quickly.

Wherefore, concerning our matter here,

Above these twain I am best, clear.

And, if ye list to take me so,

I am content you, and no mo,*   more

Shall be our judge as in this case,   380

Which of us three shall take the best place.

   PEDLAR. I neither will judge the best nor worst;

For, be ye blest or be ye curst,

Ye know it is no whit my sleigh*   skill

To be a judge in matters of weight.

It behoveth no pedlars nor proctors

To take on them judgement as doctors.

But if your minds be only set

To work for soul's health, ye be well met,

For each of you somewhat doth show   390

That souls toward heaven by you do grow.

Then, if ye can so well agree

To continue together all three,

And all you three obey one will,

Then all your minds ye may fulfil:

As, if ye came all to one man

Who should go pilgrimage more than he can,

   (*To the* PALMER.)

In that ye, palmer, as debite,*   deputy

May clearly discharge him, perdie;

   (*To the* PARDONER.)

And for all other sins, once had contrition,   400

Your pardons giveth him full remission;

   (*To the* POTHECARY.)

And then ye, master pothecary,

May send him to heaven by-and-by.*   immediately

POTHECARY. If he taste this box nigh about the
   prime,[13]

---

[13] The church service for the first hour of the day.

By the Mass, he is in heaven ere evensong time!
My craft is such that I can right well
Send my friends to heaven and myself to hell.
But, sirs, mark this man, for he is wise
Who could devise such a device;
For if we three may be as one,   410
Then be we Lords every one;
Between us all could not be missed
To save the souls of whom we list.
But, for good order, at a word,
Twain of us must wait on the third;
And unto that I do agree,
For both you twain shall wait on me!
   PARDONER. What chance is this that such an elf*   poor devil
Command two knaves,* beside himself?   servants
Nay, nay, my friend, that will not be;   420
I am too good to wait on thee!
   PALMER. By Our Lady, and I would be loth
To wait on the better of you both!
   PEDLAR. Yet be ye sure, for all this doubt,
This waiting must be brought about.
Men cannot prosper, wilfully led;
All thing decayeth where is no head.
Wherefore, doubtless, mark what I say:
To one of you three twain must obey;
And, since ye cannot agree in voice   430
Who shall be head, there is no choice
But to devise some manner thing
Wherein ye all be like cunning;
And in the same who can do best,
The other twain to make them prest*   ready
In every thing of his intent
Wholly to be at commandment.
And now have I found one mastery*   art
That ye can do indifferently,*   equally
And is neither selling nor buying,   440
But even only very lying!
And all ye three can lie as well
As can the falsest devil in hell.
And, though afore ye heard me grudge
In greater matters to be your judge,
Yet in lying I can* some skill;   have
And, if I shall be judge, I will.
And, be ye sure, without flattery,

Where my conscience findeth the mastery
There shall my judgment strait be found,   450
Though I might win a thousand pound.
    PALMER. Sir, for lying, though I can do it,
Yet am I loth for to go to it.
    PEDLAR (*To the* PALMER). Ye have not cause to fear
        to be bold,
For ye may be here uncontrolled.
    (*To the* PARDONER.)
And ye in this have good advantage,
For lying is your common usage.
    (*To the* POTHECARY.)
And you in lying be well sped,
For all your craft doth stand in falsehead.
    (*To all three.*)
Ye need not care who shall begin,   460
For each of you may hope to win.
Now speak, all three, even as ye find:
Be ye agreed to follow my mind?
    PALMER. Yea, by my troth, I am content.
    PARDONER. Now, in good faith, and I assent.
    POTHECARY. If I denied, I were a noddy,   fool
For all is mine, by God's body!
    (*Here the* POTHECARY *hoppeth.*)
    PALMER. Here were a hopper to hop for the ring!
But, sir, this gear* goeth not by hopping.   business
    POTHECARY. Sir, in this hopping I will hop so well   470
That my tongue shall hop as well as my heel;
Upon which hopping I hope, and not doubt it,
To hope so that ye shall hope without it.
    PALMER. Sir, I will neither boast not brawl,
But take such fortune as may fall;
And, if ye win this mastery,
I will obey you quietly.
And sure I think that quietness
In any man is great riches,
In any manner company,   480
To rule or be ruled indifferently.*   equally, equably
    PARDONER. By that boast thou seemest a
        beggar indeed.
What can thy quietness help us at need?
If we should starve, thou hast not, I think,
One penny to buy us one pot of drink.
Nay, if riches might rule the roast,

Behold what cause I have to boast!
  (*He opens his pack.*)
Lo, here be pardons half a dozen.
For ghostly* riches they have no cozen;*   spiritual/cheating
And, moreover, to me they bring   490
Sufficient succour for my living.
And here be relics of such a kind
As in this world no man can find.
Kneel down, all three, and, when ye leave kissing,
Who list to offer shall have my blissing!*   blessing
Friends, here shall ye see even anone
Of All-Hallows the blessed jaw-bone,
Kiss it hardily,* with good devotion!   confidently
    POTHECARY. This kiss shall bring us much
      promotion.
Fogh! by Saint Saviour, I never kissed a worse!   500
Ye were as good kiss All-Hallows' arse!
For, by All-Hallows, methinketh
That All-Hallows' breath stinketh.
    PALMER. Ye judge All-Hallows' breath unknown;
If any breath stink, it is your own.
    POTHECARY. I know mine own breath from
      All-Hollows',
Or else it were time to kiss the gallows.
    PARDONER. Nay, sirs, behold, here may ye see
The great-toe of the Trinity.
Who to this toe any money vow'th,*   promises (voweth)/510
And once may roll it in his mouth,
All his life after, I undertake,
He shall be rid of the tooth-ache.
    POTHECARY. I pray you, turn that relic about!
Either the Trinity had the gout,
Or else, because it is three toes in one,
God made it much as three toes alone.
    PARDONER. Well, let that pass, and look upon this;
Here is a relic that doth not miss
To help the least as well as the most.   520
This is a buttock-bone of Pentecost!
    POTHECARY. By Christ, and yet, for all your boast,
This relic hath beshitten the roast!
    PARDONER. Mark well this relic—here is a
      whipper!*   a winner
My friends, unfeigned, here is a slipper
Of one of the Seven Sleepers, be sure.

Doubtless this kiss shall do you great pleasure,
For all these two days it shall so ease you
That none other savours shall displease you.
   POTHECARY. All these two days! Nay, all this two
    year!   530
For all the savours that may come here
Can be no worse; for, at a word,
One of the Seven Sleepers trod in a turd.
   PEDLAR. Sir, methinketh your devotion is but small.   faith
   PARDONER. Small? Marry, methinketh he hath none
    at all!
   POTHECARY. What the devil care I what ye think?
Shall I praise relics when they stink?
   PARDONER. Here is an eye-tooth of the Great Turk.
Whose eyes be once set on this piece of work
May haply lose part of his eyesight,   540
But not all till he be blind outright.
   POTHECARY. Whatsoever any other man see'th,
I have no devotion to Turks' teeth;
For, although I never saw a greater,
Yet methinketh I have seen many better.
   PARDONER. Here is a box full of humble-bees
That stung Eve as she sat on her knees
Tasting the fruit to her forbidden.
Who kisseth the bees within this hidden
Shall have as much pardon, of right,   550
As for any relic he kissed this night.
   PALMER. Sir, I will kiss them, with all my heart.
   POTHECARY. Kiss them again, and take my part,
For I am not worthy—nay, let be!
Those bees that stung Eve shall not sting me!
   PARDONER. Good friends, I have yet herein this glass,
Which on the drink at the wedding was
Of Adam and Eve undoubtedly.
If ye honour this relic devoutly,
Although ye thirst no whit the less,   560
Yet shall ye drink the more, doubtless,
After which drinking ye shall be as meet*   fit
To stand on your head as on your feet.
   POTHECARY. Yea, marry, now I can ye thank!
In presence of this the rest be blank.
Would God this relic had come rather!*   sooner
Kiss that relic well, good father!
Such is the pain that ye palmers take

To kiss the pardon-bowl for the drink's sake.
O holy yeast, that looketh full sour and stale,   570
For God's body help me to a cup of ale!
The more I behold thee, the more I thirst;
The oftener I kiss thee, more like to burst!
But since I kiss thee so devoutly,
Hire me, and help me with drink till I die!
What, so much praying and so little speed?
    PARDONER. Yea, for God knoweth when it is need
To send folks drink; but, by Saint Anthony,
I ween* he hath sent you too much already.   believe
    POTHECARY. If I have never the more for thee,   580
Then be the relics no riches to me,
Nor to thyself, except they be
More beneficial than I can see.
Richer is one box of this triacle*   balsam
Than all thy relics that do no miracle.
If thou hadst prayed but half so much to me
As I have prayed to thy relics and thee,
Nothing concerning mine occupation
But straight should have wrought in operation.
And, as in value I pass you an ace,   590
Here lieth much riches in little space—
I have a box of rhubarb here,
Which is as dainty as it is dear.
So help me God and halidom,*   holydom
Of this I would not give a dram
To the best friend I have in England's ground,
Though he would give me twenty pound;
For, though the stomach do it abhor,
It purgeth you clean from the color,*   choler, bile
And maketh your stomach sore to walter,*   rumble/600
That ye shall never come to the halter.
    PEDLAR. Then is that medicine a sovereign thing
To preserve a man from hanging.
    POTHECARY. If ye will taste but this crumb that
      ye see,
If ever ye be hanged, never trust me!
Here have I diapompholicus—
A special ointment, as doctors discuss;
For a fistula or a canker
This ointment is even sheet-anchor,
For this medicine helpeth one and other,   610
Or bringeth them in case* that they need no other.   a state

Here is syrapus de Byzansis—
A little thing is enough of this,
For even the weight of one scruple
Shall make you strong as a cripple.
Here be other: as, diosfialios,
Diagalanga, and sticados,
Blanka manna, diospoliticon,
Mercury sublime, and metridaticon,
Pelitory, and arsefetita,   620
Cassy, and colloquintita.
These be the things that break all strife
Between man's sickness and his life.
From all pain these shall you deliver,
And set you even at rest for ever!
Here is a medicine—no more like the same
Which commonly is called thus by name
Alikakabus or alkakengy—
A goodly thing for dogs that be mangy.
Such be these medicines that I can   630
Help a dog as well as a man.
Not one thing here particularly
But worketh universally,
For it doth me as much good when I sell it
As all the buyers that taste it or smell it.
Now, since my medicines be so special,
And in operation so general,
And ready to work whensoever they shall,
So that in riches I am principal,
If any reward may entreat ye,   640
I beseech your maship* be good to me,   mastership
And ye shall have a box of marmalade
So fine that ye may dig it with a spade.
　　PEDLAR. Sir, I thank you; but your reward
Is not the thing that I regard.
I must, and will, be indifferent:*   impartial
Wherefore proceed in your intent.
　　POTHECARY. Now, if I wish* this wish no sin,   knew
I would to God I might begin!
　　PARDONER. I am content that thou lie first.   650
　　PALMER. Even so am I; and say thy worst!
Now let us hear of all thy lies
The greatest lie thou mayst devise,
And in the fewest words thou can.
　　POTHECARY. Forsooth, ye be an honest man.

PALMER. There said ye much! but yet no lie.

PARDONER. Now lie ye both, by Our Lady!
Thou liest in boast of his honesty,
And he hath lied in affirming thee.

POTHECARY. If we both lie, and ye say true,   660
Then of these lies your part adieu!
And if ye win, make none avaunt;*   boast
For ye are sure of one ill servaunt.

    (*To the* PALMER.)
Ye may perceive by the words he gave
He taketh your maship but for a knave.
But who told true, or lied indeed,
That will I know ere we proceed.
Sir, after that I first began
To praise you for an honest man,
When ye affirmed it for no lie—   670
Now, by our faith, speak even truly—
Thought ye your affirmation true?

PALMER. Yea, marry, aye! for I would ye knew
I think myself an honest man.

POTHECARY. What, thought ye in the contrary than?

PARDONER. In that I said the contrary,
I think from truth I did not vary.

POTHECARY. And what of my words?

PARDONER.   I thought ye lied.

POTHECARY. And so thought I, by God that died!   680
Now have you twain each for himself laid
That none hath lied aught, but both true said;
And of us twain none hath denied,
But both affirmed, that I have lied:
Now since ye both your truth confess,
And that we both my lie so witness
That twain of us three in one agree—
And that the liar the winner must be—
Who could provide such evidence
As I have done in this pretence?

    (*To the* PEDLAR.)
Methinketh this matter sufficient   690
To cause you to give judgement,
And to give me the mastery,
For ye perceive these knaves cannot lie.

PALMER. Though neither of us as yet had lied,
Yet what we can do is untried;

For yet we have devised nothing,
But answered you and given hearing.
    PEDLAR. Therefore I have devised one way
Whereby all three your minds may say:
For each of you one tale shall tell;   700
And which of you telleth most marvel
And most unlike to be true,
Shall most prevail, whatever ensue.
    POTHECARY. If ye be set in marvelling,
Then shall ye hear a marvellous thing;
And though, indeed, all be not true,
Yet sure the most part shall be new.
I did a cure, no longer ago
But *Anno Domini millesimo,*
On a woman, young and so fair   710
That never have I seen a gayer.
God save all women from that likeness!
This wanton had the falling sickness,
Which by descent came lineally,
For her mother had it naturally.
Wherefore, this woman to recure*   recover
It was more hard, ye may be sure.
But, though I boast my craft is such
That in such things I can do much,
How oft she fell were much to report;   720
But her head so giddy and her heels so short
That, with the twinkling of an eye,
Down would she fall even by and by.*   immediately
But, ere she would arise again,
I showed much practice, much to my pain;
For the tallest* man within this town   bravest
Should not with ease have broken her sown.*   swoon
Although for life I did not doubt her
Yet did I take more pain about her
Than I would take with my own sister.   730
Sir, at the last I gave her a glister,*   enema
I thrust a tampion in her tewel[14]
And bade her keep it for a jewel.
But I knew it so heavy to carry
That I was sure it would not tarry;
For where gunpowder is once fired
The tampion* will no longer be hired.*   plug/used

[14] "I thrust a plug in her opening (anus)."

Which was well seen in time of this chance;
For, when I had charged this ordinance,*   cannon
Suddenly, as it had thundered,   740
Even at a clap loosed her bombard.
Now mark, for here beginneth the revel:
This tampion flew ten long mile level,
To a fair castle of lime and stone—
For strength I know not such a one—
Which stood upon an hill full high,
At foot whereof a river ran by,
So deep, till chance had it forbidden,
Well might the Regent there have ridden.[15]
But when this tampion on this castle light,   750
It put the walls so far to flight
That down they came each upon other,
No stone left standing, by God's Mother!
But rolled down so fast the hill
In such a number, and so did fill,
From bottom to brim, from shore to shore,
This foresaid river, so deep before,
That who list* now to walk thereto,   desires
May wade it over and wet no shoe.
So was this castle laid wide open   760
That every man might see the token.
But—in a good hour may these words be spoken!—
After the tampion on the walls was wroken,
And piece by piece in pieces broken,
And she[16] delivered with such violence
Of all her inconvenience,
I left her in good health and lust,
And so she doth continue, I trust!
    PEDLAR. Sir, in your cure I can nothing tell;
But to our purpose ye have said well.   770
    PARDONER. Well, sir, then mark what I can say!
I have been a pardoner many a day,
And done greater cures ghostly*   spiritual
Than ever he did bodily;
Namely,* this one which ye shall hear,   especially
Of one departed within this seven year,
A friend of mine, and likewise I
To her again was as friendly—
Who fell so sick so suddenly

---

[15] A large battleship of Henry VIII's navy.
[16] The Pothecary's woman patient.

That dead she was even by-and-by,*   immediately/780
And never spake with priest nor clark,
Nor had no whit of this holy wark,*   work
For I was thence, it could not be;
Yet heard, I say, she asked for me.
But when I bethought me how this chanced,
And that I have to heaven advanced
So many souls to me but strangers
And could not keep my friend from dangers,
But she to die so dangerously
For her soul's health especially,   790
That was the thing that grieved me so
That nothing could release my woe
Till I had tried even out of hand
In what estate her soul did stand.
For which trial, short tale to make,
I took this journey for her sake.
Give ear, for here beginneth the story!
From hence I went to purgatory,
And took with me this gear in my fist,
Whereby I may do there what I list.*   wish/800
I knocked, and was let in quickly;
But, Lord, how low the souls made curtsy!
And I to every soul again
Did give a beck them to retain,
And axed* them this question than: asked
If that the soul of such a woman
Did late among them there appear.
Whereto they said she came not here.
Then feared I much it was not well.
Alas! thought I, she is in hell!   810
For with her life I was so acquainted
That sure I thought she was not sainted.
With this it chanced me to sneeze;
'Christ help!' quoth a soul that lay for his fees.[17]
"Those words," quoth I, "thou shalt not lees!"*   lose
Then with these pardons of all degrees
I paid his toll, and set him so quite
That straight to heaven he took his flight.
And I from thence to hell that night,
To help this woman, if I might,   820
Not as who saith by authority,

[17] A soul that lay in Purgatory for inability to pay fees to the church
for shortening his term.

But by the way of entreaty.
And first to the devil that kept the gate
I came, and spake after this rate:
"All hail, sir devil!" and made low curtsy.
"Welcome!" quoth he, this smilingly:
He knew me well, and I at last
Remembered him since long time past,
For, as good hap* would have it chance,   luck
This devil and I were of old acquaintance,   830
For oft in the play of Corpus Christi
He hath played the devil at Coventry.
By his acquaintance and my behavior
He showed to me right friendly favor.
And—to make my return the shorter—
I said to this devil: "Good master porter,
For all old love, if it lie in your power,
Help me to speak with my lord and your."
"Be sure," quoth he, "no tongue can tell
What time thou couldest have come so well,   840
For this day Lucifer fell,
Which is our festival in hell.
Nothing unreasonable craved this day
That shall in hell have any nay.[18]
But yet beware thou come not in
Till time thou may thy passport win.
Wherefore stand still, and I will wit
If I can get thy safe-conduct."
He tarried not, but shortly gat* it,   got
Under seal, and the devil's hand at it,   850
In ample wise, as ye shall hear.
Thus it began: "Lucifer,
By the power of God chief devil of hell,
To all the devils that there do dwell,
And every of them, we send greeting,
Under straight charge and commanding,
That they aiding and assistant be
To such a pardoner"—and named me—
"So that he may at liberty
Pass safe without his jeopardy   860
Till that he be from us extinct*   passed away
And clearly out of hell's precinct.
And, his pardons to keep safeguard,

[18] Every reasonable request shall be granted this day which is our festival celebrating the fall of Lucifer from heaven into hell.

We will they lie in the porter's ward.
Given in the furnace of our palace,
In our high court of matters of malice,
Such a day and year of our reign."
"God save the devil!" quoth I, "for plain,
I trust this writing to be sure."
"Then put thy trust," quoth he, "in ure,*   use/870
Since thou art sure to take no harm."
This devil and I walked arm in arm,
So far till he had brought me thither
Where all the devils of hell togither
Stood in array in such apparel
As for that day there meetly fell:
Their horns well gilt, their claws full clean,
Their tails well kempt, and, as I ween,*   think
With sothery* butter their bodies anointed—   sweet
I never saw devils so well appointed.   880
The master devil sat in his jacket,
And all the souls were playing at racket.
None other rackets they had in hand
Save every soul a good firebrand;
Wherewith they played so prettily
That Lucifer laughed merrily,
And all the residue of the fiends
Did laugh full well together like friends.
But of my friend I saw no whit,
Nor durst not axe* for her as yet.   ask/890
Anon all this rout was brought in silence,
And I by an usher brought in presence.
Then to Lucifer low as I could
I knelt. Which he so well allowed
That thus he becked,* and, by saint Anthony,   nodded
He smiled on me well-favoredly,
Bending his brows, as broad as barn-durs,*   doors
Shaking his ears, as rugged as burs,
Rolling his eyes, as round as two bushels,
Flashing the fire out of his nose-thrill,   900
Gnashing his teeth so vaingloriously
That methought time to fall to flattery.
Wherewith I told, as I shall tell:
"O pleasant picture! O prince of hell!
Featured in fashion abominable!
And since that it is inestimable
For me to praise thee worthily,

I leave off praise, unworthy
To give thee praise, beseeching thee
To hear my suit, and then to be   910
So good to grant the thing I crave.
And, to be short, this would I have—
The soul of one which hither is flitted
Delivered hence, and to me remitted.
And in this doing, though all be not quit,*   made even
Yet some part I shall deserve it,
As thus: I am a pardoner,
And over souls, as a controller,
Throughout the earth my power doth stand,
Where many a soul lieth on my hand,   920
That speed in matters as I use them,
As I receive them or refuse them;
Whereby, what time thy pleasure is
Ye shall require any part of this,
The least devil here that can come thither
Shall choose a soul and bring him hither."
"Now," quoth* the devil, "we are well pleased!   said
What is his name thou wouldest have eased?"
"Nay," quoth I, "be it good or evil,
My coming is for a she devil."   930
"What callest her?" quoth he, "thou whoreson!"
"Forsooth," quoth I, "Margery Coorson."
"Now, by our honour," said Lucifer,
"No devil in hell shall withhold her!
And if thou wouldest have twenty mo,*   more women
Were not for justice, they should go.
For all we devils within this den
Have more to do with two women
Than with all the charge* we have beside.   inmates
Wherefore, if thou our friend will be tried,   940
Apply thy pardons to women so
That unto us there come no mo."
To do my best I promised by oath.
Which I have kept; for, as the faith go'th,*   goeth
At these days to heaven I do procure
Ten women to one man, be sure.
Then of Lucifer my leave I took,
And straight unto the master cook.
I was had into the kitchen,
For Margery's office was therein.   950
All things handled there discreetly,

For every soul beareth office meetly,*   properly
Which might be seen to see her sit
So busily turning of the spit;
For many a spit here hath she turned,
And many a good spit hath she burned,
And many a spit full hot hath toasted
Before the meat could be half roasted.
And, ere the meat were half roasted indeed,
I took her then from the spit for speed.   960
But when she saw this brought to pass,
To tell the joy wherein she was,
And of all the devils, for joy how they
Did roar at her delivery,*   release
And how the chains in hell did ring,
And how all the souls therein did sing,
And how we were brought to the gate,
And how we took our leave thereat—
Be sure lack of time suffereth nat*   not
To rehearse* the twentieth part of that!   repeat/970
Wherefore, this tale to conclude briefly,
This woman thanked me chiefly
That she was rid of this endless death;
And so we departed* on Newmarket Heath.   separated
And if that any man do mind her,
Who list* to seek her, there shall he find her!   desires
    PEDLAR. Sir, ye have sought her wondrous well;
And, where ye found her, as ye tell,
To hear the chance ye found in hell,
I find ye were in great parell.*   peril/980
    PALMER. His tale is all much parellous;
But part is much more marvellous.
As where he said the devils complain
That women put them to such pain
By their conditions so crooked and crabbed,
Frowardly fashioned, so wayward and wrabbed,*   perverse
So far in division, and stirring such strife,
That all the devils be weary of their life!
This in effect he told for truth;
Whereby much marvel to me ensu'th,*   ensues/990
That women in hell such shrews can be,
And here so gentle, as far as I see.
Yet have I seen many a mile,
And many a woman in the while—
Not one good city, town, nor borough

In Christendom but I have been thorough,
And this I would ye should understand:
I have seen women five hundred thousand
Wives and widows, maids and married,
And oft with them have long time tarried,   1000
Yet in all places where I have been,
Of all the women that I have seen,
I never saw, nor knew, in my conscience,
Any one woman out of patience.
   POTHECARY. By the Mass, there is a great lie!
   PARDONER. I never heard a greater, by Our Lady!
   PEDLAR. A greater? nay, know ye any so great?
   PALMER. Sir, whether that I lose or get,*   win
For my part, judgement shall be prayed.*   asked for
   PARDONER. And I desire as he hath said.   1010
   POTHECARY. Proceed, and ye shall be obeyed.
   PEDLAR. Then shall not judgement be delayed.
Of all these three, if each man's tale
In Paul's Churchyard[19] were set on sale
In some man's hand that hath the sleight,*   skill
He should sure sell these tales by weight.
For, as they weigh, so be they worth.
But which weigheth best? to that now forth!
   (*To the* POTHECARY.)
Sir, all the tale that ye did tell
I bear in mind; (*to the* PARDONER) and yours as well;   1020
And, as ye saw the matter meetly,
So lied ye both well and discreetly.
Yet were your lies with the least, trust me!
   (*To the* POTHECARY.)
For, if ye had said ye had made flee
Ten tampions, out of ten women's tails,
Ten times ten mile, to ten castles or jails,
And fill ten rivers, ten times so deep
As ten of that which your castle stones did keep—
   (*To the* PARDONER.)
Or if ye ten times had bodily
Fet* ten souls out of purgatory,   fetch, bring/1030
And ten times so many out of hell,
Yet, by these ten bones,* I could right well   fingers
Ten times sooner all that have believed
Than the tenth part of that he [the Palmer] hath
    meved.*   presented

   [19] Booksellers' Row in London.

POTHECARY. Two knaves before one lacketh two
    knaves of five;
Then one, and then one, and both knaves alive;
Then two, and then two, and three at a cast;*   reckoning
Thou knave, and thou knave, and thou knave, at last!
    (*To the* PEDLAR.)
Nay, knave, if ye try me by number,
I will as knavishly you accumber.*   overwhelm/1040
Your mind is all on your privy* tithe,   private
For all in ten methinketh your wit lithe.*   lieth
Now ten times I beseech Him that high sits
Thy wife's ten commandments* may search thy   fingernails(?)
    five wits;
Then ten of my turds in ten of thy teeth,
And ten on thy nose, which every man see'th.
And twenty times ten this wish I wold,*   would
That thou hadest been hanged at ten year old!
For thou goest about to make me a slave.
I will thou know that I am a gentleman, knave!   1050
    (*Pointing to the* PARDONER.)
And here is another shall take my part.
    PARDONER. Nay, first I beshrew your knave's heart
Ere I take part in your knavery!
I will speak fair, by Our Lady!
    (*To the* PEDLAR.)
Sir, I beseech your maship* to be   mastership
As good as ye can be to me.
    PEDLAR. I would be glad to do you good,
And him also, be he never so wood.*   mad
But doubt you not I will now do
The thing my conscience leadeth me to.   1060
Both your tales I take far impossible,
Yet take I his farther incredible.
Not only the thing itself alloweth it,
But also the boldness thereof avoweth it.
    (*To the* POTHECARY.)
I know not where your tale to try,*   test
    (*To the* PARDONER.)
Nor yours, but in hell or purgatory;
But his boldness hath faced a lie
That may be tried even in this company,
As, if ye list, to take this order:
Among the women in this border,   1070
Take three of the youngest and three of the oldest,

Three of the hottest and three of the coldest,
Three of the wisest and three of the shrewdest,
Three of the chastest and three of the lewdest,
Three of the lowest and three of the highest,
Three of the farthest and three of the nighest,
Three of the fairest and three of the maddest,
Three of the foulest and three of the saddest*—   most earnest
And when all these threes be had asunder,
Of each three, two, justly by number,   1080
Shall be found shrews, except this fall,
That ye hap to find them shrews all!
Himself for truth all this doth know,
And oft hath tried some of this row;
And yet he sweareth, by his conscience,
He never saw woman break patience!
Wherefore, considered with true intent,
His lie to be so evident,
And to appear so evidently
That both you affirmed it a lie,   1090
And that my conscience so deeply
So deep hath sought this thing to try,
And tried it with mind indifferent,*   impartial
Thus I award, by way of judgement—
Of all the lies ye all have spent
His lie to be most excellent.
    PALMER. Sir, though ye were bound of equity
To do as ye have done to me,
Yet do I thank you of your pain,
And will requite some part again.   1100
    PARDONER. Marry, sir, ye can no less do
But thank him as much as it cometh to.
And so will I do for my part:
    (*To the* PEDLAR.)
Now a vengeance on thy knave's heart!
I never knew pedlar a judge before,
Nor never will trust peddling-knave more!
    (*The* POTHECARY *begins to curtsy to the* PALMER.)
What dost thou there, thou whoreson noddy?*   fool
    POTHECARY. By the Mass, learn to make curtsy!
Curtsy before, and curtsy behind him,
And then on each side—the devil blind him!   1110
Nay, when I have it perfectly,
Ye shall have the devil and all of curtsy!
But it is not soon learned, brother,

One knave to make curtsy to another.
Yet, when I am angry, that is the worst,
I shall call my master knave at the first.
    PALMER. Then would some master perhaps clout ye!
But, as for me, ye need not doubt ye;
For I had liefer be without ye
Than have such business about ye.   1120
    PARDONER. So help me God, so were ye better!
What, should a beggar be a jetter?*   boaster
It were no whit your honesty
To have us twain jet after ye.
    POTHECARY. Sir, be ye sure he telleth you true.
If we should wait,* this would ensue: attend you
It would be said—trust me at a word—
Two knaves made curtsy to the third.
    PEDLAR (*To the* PALMER.) Now, by my troth, to
      speak my mind,
Since they be so loth to be assigned,[20]   1130
To let them loose I think it best,
And so shall ye live best in rest.
    PALMER. Sir, I am not on them so fond
To compel them to keep their bond.
    (*To the* POTHECARY *and* PARDONER.)
And, since ye list* not to wait on me,   wish
I clearly of waiting* discharge ye.   attending me
    PARDONER. Marry, sir, I heartily thank you!
    POTHECARY. And I likewise, I make God avow!
    PEDLAR. Now be ye all even as ye begun;
No man hath lost, nor no man hath won.   1140
Yet in the debate wherewith ye began,
By way of advice I will speak as I can;
    (*To the* PALMER.)
I do perceive that pilgrimage
Is chief the thing ye have in usage;
Whereto, in effect, for love of Christ
Ye have, or should have, been enticed.
And who so doth, with such intent,
Doth well declare his time well spent.
    (*To the* PARDONER.)
And so do ye in your pretence,
If ye procure thus indulgence   1150
Unto your neighbors charitably
For love of them in God only.

    [20] Given assignments.

All this may be right well applied
To show you both well occupied;
For, though ye walk not both one way,
Yet, walking thus, this dare I say,
That both your walks come to one end.
And so for all that do pretend,
By aid of God's grace, to ensue*   follow
Any manner kind of virtue: 1160
As, some great alms for to give,
Some in wilful poverty to live,
Some to make highways and such other warks,*   works
And some to maintain priests and clarks*   clerics
To sing and pray for soul departed—
These, with all other virtues well marked,
Although they be of sundry kinds,
Yet be they not used with sundry minds;
But, as God only doth those move,
So every man, only for His love,   1170
With love and dread obediently
Worketh in these virtues uniformly.
Thus every virtue, if we list* to scan,   desire
Is pleasant to God and thankful to man;
And who that by grace of the Holy Ghost
To any one virtue is moved most,
That man, by that grace, that one apply,
And therein serve God most plentifully!
Yet not that one so far wide to wrest,*   overstrain
So liking the same to mislike the rest;   1180
For who so wresteth his work is in vain.
And even in that case I perceive you twain,
Liking your virtue in such wise
That each other's virtue you do despise.
Who walketh this way for God would find him,
The farther they seek him, the farther behind him.
One kind of virtue to despise another
Is like as the sister might hang the brother.
    POTHECARY. For fear lest such perils to me might
        fall,
I thank God I use no virtue at all!   1190
    PEDLAR. That is of all the very worst way!
For more hard it is, as I have heard say,
To begin virtue where none is pretended*   intended
Than, where it is begun, the abuse to
    be mended.

Howbeit, ye be not all* to begin,*   altogether/beginners
One sign of virtue ye are entered in,
As this I suppose ye did say true,
In that ye said ye use no virtue;
In the which words, I dare well report,
Ye are well beloved of all this sort,   1200
By your railing here openly
At pardons and relics so lewdly.

    POTHECARY. In that I think my fault not great;
For all that he hath I know counterfeit.

    PEDLAR. For his, and all other that ye know feigned,*   pretended
Ye be neither counselled nor constrained
To any such thing in any such case
To give any reverence in any such place;
But where ye doubt the truth, not knowing,
Believing the best, good may be growing.   1210
In judging the best, no harm at the lest,*   least
In judging the worst, no good at the best.
But best in these things, it seemeth to me,
To take no judgment upon ye;
But, as the Church doth judge or take them,
So do ye receive or forsake them;
And so, be sure, ye cannot err,
But may be a fruitful follower.

    POTHECARY. Go ye before, and, as I am true man,
I will follow as fast as I can.   1220

    PARDONER. And so will I; for he hath said so well,
Reason would we should follow his counsel.

    (To the audience.)

    PALMER. Then to our reason God give us His grace,
That we may follow with faith so firmly
His commandments that we may purchase
His love, and so consequently
To believe his Church fast and faithfully;
So that we may, according to his promise,
Be kept out of error in any wise.
And all that hath 'scaped us here by negligence,   1230
We clearly revoke and forsake it.
To pass the time in this without offence
Was the cause why the maker did make it;
And so we humbly beseech you take it;
Beseeching Our Lord to prosper you all
In the faith of his Church Universal!

Tudor Comedy

Displacing the crude little folk farces that appeared throughout the Middle Ages on traveling actors' platforms and local stages, classical imitations appeared throughout Western Europe with the spread of the Renaissance. Performances of the comedies of Plautus and Terence, as well as of imitations both in Latin and the vernacular, came into fashion in Italy during the first few decades of the sixteenth century. By the fourth decade, English scholars and teachers were drawn to the same enterprise; and since the plays were written for academic performance, they became known as School Plays. Some of these are as slight but lively as *Thersites* (1537), a sort of burlesque about the antics of a cowardly boaster and employing classical names or designations for the characters. This little piece, for example, was based on an imitation of the *Miles Gloriosus* (*The Braggart Soldier*) of Plautus written in Latin by the French humanist Jean Textier, or J. Ravisius Textor as he learnedly called himself, who became rector of the University of Paris in 1520.

Two classic imitations in English cannot be dismissed as academic exercises. They are *Ralph Roister Doister,* written between 1550 and 1553 by the schoolmaster Nicholas Udall (1505–1556), who became headmaster of Westminster School a year before his death, and *Gammer Gurton's Needle,* written between 1552 and 1563 by a "Mr. S., Master of Art," who was probably William Stevenson, a Fellow of Christ's College at Cambridge University, where the play is believed to have been first performed. (Stevenson was ordained a deacon in London in 1552 and was made a prebendary, or honorary canon, at Durham, in 1561; he is known to have died in 1575.)

Ralph Roister Doister is the first fully developed adaptation of Roman comedy that is fundamentally English in spite of its dependence upon classic character types and despite its "regularity"—that is, its five-act structure and unified dramatic action presented in a single setting. Even Ralph Roister Doister, the impudent comic hero of the play, who is plainly descended from the braggart-soldier type introduced into the theater by Roman comedy, is an English character, as is Ralph's amusing hanger-on, Merrygreek, another Roman character type—the parasite who carries on the intrigue of the plot. Englishmen could recognize him as a close relative of the old mischief-making "Vice" of the morality plays. Since the play was to be presented in a school, its author, moreover, made important departures from his classic models in the interests of morality which also happened to serve the interests of local color, English characterization, and realism. The familiar courtesan of Greek and Latin comedy is displaced in *Ralph Roister Doister* by a virtuous English widow (Dame Custance or Constance) who runs an English household with her vivacious English servant women. And she is wooed by a worthy English merchant who takes the precaution of assuring himself that she is an innocent party after she has been maligned. These are not frivolous characters but representatives of the solid British middle class upon which depended the prosperity and power of Elizabethan England.

More important, however, than the domestication of classical comedy by Udall is the fact that he succeeded in producing a lively and gay entertainment, rich in extravagant theatrical details such as the roistering Ralph's siege of Dame Constance's house (he wears a hencoop of sorts on his head for a helmet) and the ingenuity of Merrygreek's reading a letter to her from Ralph in such a way—he merely shifts the punctuation marks —that Ralph's protestations of love sound like deliberate insults. Even Udall's language, which suffers from some stiffness of phrasing, possesses a generous amount of folk flavor. If his audience of schoolboys were expected by their master to derive edification from the spectacle of vanity suffering reproof and folly receiving correction, they were likely to take the instruction because it was blended with so much entertainment. Their instructor was not likely to be put out by this, for like other leaders of Renaissance or "humanist" education, including the great Rabelais, whose laughter may be heard here and there in *Ralph Roister Doister* as well as in *Gammer Gurton's Needle,* schoolmaster Udall believed in combining instruction with pleasure.

Gammer Gurton's Needle is an even livelier farce and even closer to the folk spirit of Elizabethan country life. It is, indeed, a distinctly folksy play wth its village setting, its rustic manners, and its flavorsome dialogue written in fluid rhymed verse. It has a homespun, distinctly "unrefined" yet essentially wholesome, plot. Its author's feeling for common English types is quite remarkable if, as it is certain, his background was scholarly. He may have been a "Master of Arts," but he did not allow scholarship to dampen his spirits, and he did not incur any great obligation to his classic models except in the regular five-act organization and unity of his action.

Above all, it is apparent that the vivacity of the common man has not been crushed by Renaissance scholarship. The drinking song "Back and side go bare" belongs to a species of lyricism that owes nothing to Renaissance refinement and yet is as perfect of its kind as any courtier's song and decidedly more spirited; and if Diccon, the prankster of the play, can find some ancestors in the intriguing slaves of Roman comedy, he is nevertheless an authentic English country figure. Diccon is the "Bedlam" (a former inmate of Bethlehem Hospital) released from what we would now call a mental institution as a harmless lunatic and is licensed to wander about the countryside as a beggar. He sets Gammer Gurton at odds with her neighbor Dame Chat over the alleged theft of a needle and is not above stealing a ham in the midst of the confusion he has produced. A parish curate and a village bailiff, a pair of scolding women, and a heavy-witted bumpkin of a servant round out a country scene that Ben Jonson himself might have enjoyed creating had his literary wanderings brought him in touch with village rather than with city life. *Gammer Gurton's Needle* was intended for the stage rather than for the library; it is "much ado about nothing," but that is the point of the play, and the extravagant action is as good a peg as any on which to hang the author's exhibition of human oddities.

Ralph Roister Doister

A Comedy

By Nicholas Udall

Characters

RALPH ROISTER DOISTER	TOM TRUEPENNY, servant to Dame Custance
MATTHEW MERRYGREEK	
GAWYN GOODLUCK, affianced to Dame Custance	SIM SURESBY, servant to Good-SCRIVENER [luck
TRISTRAM TRUSTY, his friend	DAME CHRISTIAN CUSTANCE, a widow
DOBINET DOUGHTY ⎫ servants to Ralph Roister HARPAX ⎭ Doister	MARGERY MUMBLECRUST, her nurse
	TIBET TALKAPACE ⎫ her ANNOT ALYFACE ⎭ maidens

PROLOGUE

What creature is in health, either young or old,
   But some mirth with modesty will be glad to use—
As we in this interlude* shall now unfold?   comedy
   Wherein all scurrility we utterly refuse,
   Avoiding such mirth wherein is abuse;
Knowing nothing more commendable for a man's rec-
     reation
Than mirth which is used in an honest fashion.

For mirth prolongeth life, and causeth health,
   Mirth recreates our spirits, and voideth* pensiveness,   expels
Mirth increaseth amity, not hindering our wealth;   10
   Mirth is to be used both of more and less,
   Being mixed with virtue in decent comeliness—
As we trust no good nature can gainsay the same.
Which mirth we intend to use, avoiding all blame.

The wise poets long time heretofore,
   Under merry comedies secrets did declare,
Wherein was contained very virtuous lore,
   With mysteries and forewarnings very rare.*   valuable

Such to write neither Plautus nor Terence did
  spare,[1]
Which among the learned at this day bears
  the bell.*   takes the lead/20
These with such other therein did excel.
Our comedy or interlude which we intend to play
  Is named "Roister Doister," indeed,
Which against the vain-glorious doth inveigh,
  Whose humour the roisting* sort continually   roistering
  doth feed.
Thus by your patience, we intend to proceed
In this our interlude by God's leave and grace,
And here I take my leave for a certain space.

ACT I

Scene 1

(Enter "the parasite" MATTHEW MERRYGREEK.)
  MERRYGREEK. As long liveth the merry man, they
    say,
As doth the sorry man, and longer by a day;
Yet the grasshopper, for all his summer piping,
Starveth in winter with hungry griping.
Therefore another said saw* doth men advise   proverb
That they be together both merry and wise.
This lesson must I practise, or else ere long,
With me, Matthew Merrygreek, it will be wrong.
Indeed, men so call me; for, by Him that us bought,
Whatever chance betide, I can take no thought;   10
Yet wisdom would that I did myself bethink
Where to be provided this day of meat and drink;
For know ye, that, for all this merry note of mine,
He might appose* me now that should ask where   embarrass
  I dine.
My living lieth here, and there, of God's grace
Sometime with this good man, sometime in that place,
Sometime Lewis Loiterer biddeth me come near;
Somewhiles Watkin Waster maketh us good cheer;
Sometimes Davy Diceplayer, when he hath well cast,
Keepeth revel-rout as long at it will last;   20
Sometimes Tom Titivile maketh us a feast;

[1] The reference is to the Roman writers of comedy whose example is followed in this play.

Sometime with Sir Hugh Pye I am a bidden guest,
Sometime at Nicol Neverthrive's I get a sop,
Sometime I am feasted with Bryan Blinkinsop,
Sometime I hang on Hankyn Hoddydody's sleeve,
But this day, on Ralph Roister Doister's, by his leave.
For truly of all men he is my chief banker
Both for meat and money, and my chief
    sheet-anchor.
For, sooth* Roister Doister in that* he doth say, flatten/whatever
And require what ye will, ye shall have no nay.   30
But now of Roister Doister somewhat to express,
That ye may esteem him after his worthiness:
In these twenty towns, and seek them throughout,
Is not the like stock whereon to graff a lout.
All the day long is he facing* and craking* swaggering/boasting
Of his great acts in fighting and fraymaking:
But, when Roister Doister is put to his proof,
To keep the Queen's peace is more for his behoof.*   liking
If any woman smile, or cast on him an eye,
Up is he to the hard* ears in love by-and-by!   very/40
And in all the hot haste must she be his wife,
Else farewell his good days and farewell his life!
Master Ralph Roister Doister is but dead and gone
Except she on him take some compassion,
Then chief of counsel must be Matthew Merrygreek:
'What if I for marriage to such an one seek?'
Then must I sooth it,* whatever it is: humor his whim
For what he saith or doth cannot be amiss.
Hold up his yea and nay, be his nown* white   own
    son.*   favorite
Praise and rouse him well, and ye have his heart won, 50
For so well liketh he his own fond fashions
That he taketh pride of false commendations.
But such sport have I with him as I would not lese,*   lose
Though I should be bound to live with bread and
    cheese.
For exalt* him, and have him as ye lust,*   praise/wish
    indeed—
Yea, to hold his finger in a hole for a need.
I can, with a word, make him fain or loth;
I can, with as much, make him pleased or wroth;
I can, when I will, make him merry and glad,
I can, when me lust,* make him sorry and sad;   please/60
I can set him in hope, and eke* in despair;   also

I can make him speak rough, and make him speak
    fair.
But I marvel I see him not all this same day;
I will seek him out—But, lo! he cometh this way.
I have yond espied him sadly coming,
And in love, for twenty pound, by his glumming.*   frowning

Scene 2

(Merrygreek. *Enter* Ralph Roister Doister.)

Roister Doister. Come, death, when thou wilt, I
    am weary of my life!

Merrygreek (*to the audience*). I told you, I, we
    should woo another wife!

Roister Doister. Why did God make me such a
    goodly person?

Merrygreek. He is in by the week.[2] We shall have
    sport anon.

Roister Doister. And where is my trusty friend,
    Matthew Merrygreek?

Merrygreek. I will make as I saw him not. He doth
    me seek.

Roister Doister. I have him espied, methinketh;
    yond is he.
Ho! Matthew Merrygreek, my friend, a word with
    thee!

Merrygreek. I will not* hear him, but make   pretend not to
    as I had haste.
Farewell, all my good friends! The time away doth
    waste,   10
And the tide, they say, tarrieth for no man!

Roister Doister. Thou must with thy good counsel
    help me if thou can.

Merrygreek. God keep thee, worshipful Master
    Roister Doister!
And farewell the lusty Master Roister Doister!

Roister Doister. I must needs speak with thee a
    word or twain.

Merrygreek. Within a month or two I will be here
    again.
Negligence in great affairs, ye know, may mar all.

Roister Doister. Attend upon me now, and well
    reward thee I shall.

[2] "In love, head over heels."

MERRYGREEK. I have take my leave, and the tide is
   well spent.
ROISTER DOISTER. I die except thou help! I pray
   thee, be content.   20
Do thy part well, now, and ask what thou wilt;
For without thy aid my matter is all spilt.*   ruined
   MERRYGREEK. Then, to serve your turn, I will some
      pains take,
And let all mine own affairs alone for your sake.
   ROISTER DOISTER. My whole hope and trust resteth
      only in thee.
   MERRYGREEK. Then can ye not do amiss, whatever
      it be.
   ROISTER DOISTER. Gramercies, Merrygreek! most
      bound to thee I am.
   MERRYGREEK. But up with that heart, and speak out
      like a ram!
Ye speak like a capon* that had the cough now: cock
Be of good cheer! Anon ye shall do well enow.   30
   ROISTER DOISTER. Upon thy comfort I will all things
      well handle.
   MERRYGREEK. So, lo! that is a breast to blow out a
      candle!
But what is this great matter, I would fain know?
We shall find remedy therefore, I trow.*   believe
Do ye lack money? Ye know mine old offers;
Ye have always a key to my purse and coffers.
   ROISTER DOISTER. I thank thee! Had ever man such
      a friend?
   MERRYGREEK. Ye give unto me; I must needs to
      you lend.
   ROISTER DOISTER. Nay, I have money plenty all
      things to discharge.
   MERRYGREEK (aside). That knew I right well when
      I made offer so large.
   ROISTER DOISTER. But it is no such matter.
   MERRYGREEK.   What is
      it than?*   then
Are ye in danger of debt to any man?   41
If ye be, take no thought, nor be not afraid.
Let them hardily* take thought how they shall be   surely
   paid.
   ROISTER DOISTER. Tut! I owe nought!

MERRYGREEK.   What then?
    Fear ye imprisonment?
ROISTER DOISTER. No.
MERRYGREEK. No, I wist,* ye offend not so to be   knew
    shent.*   disgraced
But if ye had, the Tower* could not you so hold   Tower of
But to break out at all times ye would be bold.   London
What is it? Hath any man threatened you to beat?
    ROISTER DOISTER. What is he that durst have put
    me in that heat?   50
He that beateth me—by His arms!—shall well find,
That I will not be far from him, nor run behind.
    MERRYGREEK. That thing know all men ever since
    ye overthrew
The fellow of the lion which Hercules slew.
But what is it, then?
    ROISTER DOISTER.   Of love I make my moan.
    MERRYGREEK. Ah, this foolish love! Wilt ne'er let
    us alone?
But, because ye were refused the last day,*   yesterday
Ye said ye would ne'er more be entangled that way.
I would meddle no more, since I find all so unkind.
    ROISTER DOISTER. Yea, but I cannot so put love out
    of my mind.   60
    MERRYGREEK. But is your love—tell me first, in any
    wise—
In the way of marriage, or of merchandise?
If it may otherwise than lawful be found,
Ye get none of my help for a hundred pound.
    ROISTER DOISTER. No, by my troth; I would have
    her to my wife.
    MERRYGREEK. Then are ye a good man, and God
    save your life!
And what, or who is she, with whom ye are in love?
    ROISTER DOISTER. A woman, whom I know not by
    what means to move.
    MERRYGREEK. Who is it?
    ROISTER DOISTER.   A woman, yond.
    MERRYGREEK.   What is
    her name?
    ROISTER DOISTER.. Her, yonder.
    MERRYGREEK.   Whom?
    ROISTER DOISTER.   Mistress—ah—
    MERRYGREEK.   Fie, fie, for shame!

Love ye, and know not whom but "her, yond," "a
   woman"?
We shall then get you a wife I cannot tell whan.*   71
                                            when
   ROISTER DOISTER. The fair woman that supped
      with us yesternight;
And I heard her name twice or thrice, and had it
   right.
   MERRYGREEK. Yea, ye may see ye ne'er take me to
      good cheer with you;
If ye had, I could have told you her name now.
   ROISTER DOISTER. I was to blame indeed; but the
      next time, perchance—
And she dwelleth in this house.
   MERRYGREEK.   What! Christian
   Custance?*   Constance
   ROISTER DOISTER. Except I have her to my wife, I
      shall run mad.
   MERRYGREEK. Nay, unwise perhaps, but I warrant
      you for mad!   80
   ROISTER DOISTER. I am utterly dead unless I have
      my desire.
   MERRYGREEK. Where be the bellows that blew this
      sudden fire?
   ROISTER DOISTER. I hear she is worth a thousand
      pound and more.
   MERRYGREEK. Yea, but learn this one lesson of me
      afore:
An hundred pound of marriage-money, doubtless,
Is ever thirty pound sterling, or somewhat less,
So that her thousand pound, if she he thrifty,
Is much near about two hundred and fifty,
Howbeit, wooers and windows are never poor!
   ROISTER DOISTER. Is she a widow? I love her better
      therefore.*   for it/90
   MERRYGREEK. But I hear she hath made promise to
      another.
   ROISTER DOISTER. He shall go without her, an* he
      were my brother.   if
   MERRYGREEK. I have heard say—I am right well ad-
      vised—
That she hath to Gawyn Goodluck promised.
   ROISTER DOISTER. What is that Gawyn Goodluck?
   MERRYGREEK.   A merchant man.

ROISTER DOISTER. Shall he speed afore me? Nay,
    sir, by sweet Saint Anne!
Ah, sir, "Backare,"* quoth Mortimer to his sow.   backup!
I will have her mine own self, I make God a vow.
For, I tell thee, she is worth a thousand pound!
    MERRYGREEK. Yet a fitter wife for your maship*   mastership
    might be found.   100
Such a goodly man as you might get one with land,
Besides pounds of gold a thousand, and a thousand,
And a thousand, and a thousand, and a thousand,
And so to the sum of twenty hundred thousand.
Your most goodly personage is worthy of no less.
    ROISTER DOISTER. I am sorry God made me so
    comely, doubtless;
For that maketh me eachwhere so highly favoured,
And all women on me so enamoured.
    MERRYGREEK. "Enamoured," quoth you? Have ye
    spied out that?
Ah, sir, marry, now I see you know what is what.   110
"Enamoured," ka?* Marry, sir, say that again!   quotha (said he)
But I thought not ye had marked it so plain.
    ROISTER DOISTER. Yes, eachwhere they gaze all upon
    me and stare.
    MERRYGREEK. Yea, Malkin,* I warrant you as   slut ("slob")
    much as they dare.
And ye will not believe what they say in the street
When your maship passeth by, all such as I meet,
That sometimes I can scarce find what answer to
    make.
"Who is this?," saith one, "Sir Launcelot du Lake?"
"Who is this? Great Guy of Warwick?," saith another.
"No," say I, "it is the thirteenth Hercules' brother."
"Who is this? Noble Hector of Troy?," saith the
    third.   121
"No, but of the same nest," say I, "it is a
    bird."*   (of the same feather)
"Who is this? Great Goliath, Samson, or Colbrand?"[3]
"No," say I, "but it is a Brute of the Alie Land."[4]
"Who is this? Great Alexander? or Charlemagne?"
"No, it is the tenth Worthy," say I to them again.
I know not if I said well.

[3] The giant in the romance of Guy of Warwick.
[4] Brutus, legendary descendant of Aeneas, the founder of Rome; supposed
to be the ancestor of the British royal line. "Alie Land" is the Holy Land.

ROISTER DOISTER.   Yes; for so I am.

MERRYGREEK. Yea, for there were but nine Worthies
    before ye came.

To some others, the third Cato I do you call.

And so, as well as I can, I answer them all.   130

"Sir, I pray you, what lord, or great gentleman, is
    this?"

"Master Ralph Roister Doister, dame," say I, iwis.*   surely

"O Lord!" saith she then, "What a goodly man it is,

Would Christ I had such a husband as he is!"

"O Lord!" say some, "that the sight of his face we lack!"

"It is enough for you," say I, "to see his back;

His face is for ladies of high and noble parages,*   descent

With whom he hardly 'scapeth great marriages;"

With much more than this—and much otherwise.

ROISTER DOISTER. I can thee thank that thou canst
    such answers devise.   140

But I perceive thou dost me throughly know.

MERRYGREEK. I mark your manners for mine own
    learning, I trow.*   believe

But such is your beauty, and such are your acts,

Such is your personage, and such are your facts,*   achievements

That all women, fair and foul, more and less,

That eye you, they lub* you, they talk of you doubt-   love
    less.

Your pleasant look maketh them all merry;

Ye pass not by, but they laugh till they be weary,

Yea, and money could I have, the truth to tell,

Of many, to bring you that way where they dwell.

ROISTER DOISTER. Merrygreek, for this thy reporting
    well of me—   151

MERRYGREEK. What should I else, sir? it is my duty,
    perdie.*   verily

ROISTER DOISTER. I promise thou shalt not lack,
    while I have a groat.

MERRYGREEK. Faith, sir, and I ne'er had more need
    of a new coat.

ROISTER DOISTER. Thou shalt have one to-morrow,
    and gold for to spend.

MERRYGREEK. Then I trust to bring the day to a
    good end;

For, as for mine own part, having money enow,*   enough

I could live only with the remembrance of you.

But now to your widow, whom you love so hot.

Roister Doister. By Cock, thou sayest truth! I had
    almost forgot.   160
Merrygreek. What if Christian Custance will not
    have you? what?
Roister Doister. Have me? yes, I warrant you,
    never doubt of that,
I know she loveth me, but she dare not speak.
Merrygreek. Indeed, meet* it were somebody   right
    should it break.*   make known
Roister Doister. She looked on me twenty times
    yesternight,
And laughed so—
Merrygreek.   That she could not sit upright?
Roister Doister. No, faith could she not.
Merrygreek.   No, even
    such a thing I cast.*   guessed
Roister Doister. But, for wooing, thou knowest,
    women are shamefast.
But an* she knew my mind, I know she would be   if
    glad,
And think it the best chance that ever she had.   170
Merrygreek. To her,* then, like a man, and be   go to her
    bold forth to start,
Wooers never speed well that have a false* heart.   faint
Roister Doister. What may I best do?
Merrygreek.   Sir, remain
    ye awhile here;
Ere long one or other of her house will appear.
Ye know my mind.
Roister Doister. Yea, now, hardily, let me alone.
Merrygreek. In the meantime, sir, if you please,
    I will home,
And call your musicians; for in this your case
It would set you forth, and all your wooing grace;
Ye may not lack your instruments to play and sing.
Roister Doister. Thou knowest I can do that.
Merrygreek.   As well as anything.   180
Shall I go call your folks, that ye may show a cast?*   sample of ability
Roister Doister. Yea, run, I beseech thee, in all
    possible haste.
Merrygreek. I go.
                         (Exit.)
Roister Doister. Yea, for I love singing out of
    measure,

It comforteth my spirits, and doth me great pleasure.
But who cometh forth yond from my sweetheart
    Custance?
My matter frameth well; this is a lucky chance.

SCENE 3

(*With* ROISTER DOISTER *in the background, enter*
MARGERY MUMBLECRUST, *spinning on the distaff,*
and TIBET TALKAPACE, *sewing.*)

MUMBLECRUST. If this distaff were spun, Margery
    Mumblecrust—

TALKAPACE. Where good stale ale is, will drink no
    water, I trust.

MUMBLECRUST. Dame Custance hath promised us
    good ale and white bread—

TALKAPACE. If she keep not promise I will be-
    shrew her head!

But it will be stark night before I shall have done.

ROISTER DOISTER. I will stand here awhile, and talk
    with them anon.

I hear them speak of Custance, which doth my heart
    good;

To hear her name spoken doth even comfort my
    blood.

MUMBLECRUST. Sit down to your work, Tibet, like a
    good girl.

TALKAPACE. Nurse, meddle you with your spindle
    and your whirl!   10

No haste but good, Madge Mumblecrust; for whip
    and whur,*   hurry

The old proverb doth say, never made good fur.

MUMBLECRUST. Well, ye will sit down to your work
    anon, I trust.

TALKAPACE. Soft fire maketh sweet malt, good Madge
    Mumblecrust.

MUMBLECRUST. And sweet malt maketh jolly good
    ale for the nones.*   afternoon

TALKAPACE. Which will slide down the lane with-
    out any bones.

                                    (*Sings.*)

Old brown bread-crusts must have much good mum-
    bling,

But good ale down your throat hath good easy tum-
    bling.

ROISTER DOISTER. The jolliest wench that ere I
heard! little mouse!

May I not rejoice that she shall dwell in my house?   20

TALKAPACE (*to* MARGERY MUMBLECRUST). So, sirrah,
now this gear* beginneth for to frame.   business

MUMBLECRUST. Thanks to God, though your work
stand still, your tongue is not lame!

TALKAPACE. And, though your teeth be gone, both
so sharp and so fine,

Yet your tongue can run on pattens as well as mine.

MUMBLECRUST. Ye were not nought named Tib
Talkapace.

TALKAPACE. Doth my talk grieve you? Alack, God
save your grace!

MUMBLECRUST. I hold* a groat ye will drink anon   wager
for this gear.

TALKAPACE. And I will pray you the stripes for me
to bear.

MUMBLECRUST. I hold a penny, ye will drink without a cup.

TALKAPACE. Wherein so e'er ye drink, I wot ye
drink all up.   30

(*Enter* ANNOT ALYFACE, *knitting.*)

ALYFACE. By Cock! and well sewed, my good Tibet
Talkapace!

TALKAPACE. And e'en as well knit, my nown*   own
Annot Alyface!

ROISTER DOISTER. See what a sort she keepeth that
must be my wife.

Shall not I, when I have her, lead a merry life?

TALKAPACE. Welcome, my good wench, and sit here
by me just.

ALYFACE. And how doth our old beldame here,
Madge Mumblecrust?

TALKAPACE. Chide, and find faults, and threaten
to complain.

ALYFACE. To make us poor girls shent,* to her is   ashamed
small gain.

MUMBLECRUST. I did neither chide, nor complain,
nor threaten.

ROISTER DOISTER. It would grieve my heart to see
one of them beaten.   40

MUMBLECRUST. I did nothing but bid her work and
hold her peace.

TALKAPACE. So would I, if you could your clatter-
    ing cease;
But the devil cannot make old trot* hold her tongue.   crone
    ALYFACE. Let all these matters pass, and we three
    sing a song!
So shall we pleasantly both the time beguile now
And eke* dispatch all our works ere we can tell how.   also
    TALKAPACE. I shrew* them that say nay, and that   curse
    shall not be I.
    MUMBLECRUST. And I am well content.
    TALKAPACE.   Sing on then, by-and-by.
    ROISTER DOISTER. And I will not away, but listen to
    their song.
Yet Merrygreek and my folks tarry very long.   50
    (TIBET TALKAPACE, ANNOT ALYFACE, *and* MARGERY
    MUMBLECRUST *sing*.)
            Pipe, merry Annot, etc.
Trilla, trilla, trillary.
Work, Tibet; work, Annot; work, Margery!
Sew, Tibet; knit, Annot; spin, Margery!
Let us see who shall win the victory.
    TALKAPACE. This sleeve is not willing to be sewed,
    I trow.
A small thing might make me all in the ground to
    throw!
    (*They sing again.*)
            Pipe, merry Annot, etc.
Trilla, trilla, trillary.
What, Tibet? what, Annot? what, Margery?   60
Ye sleep, but we do not; that shall we try.
Your fingers be numbed, our work will not lie.
    TALKAPACE. If ye do so again, well, I would advise
    you nay.
In good sooth,* one stop* more, and I make holiday.   truth/stitch
    (*They sing a third time.*)
            Pipe, merry Annot, etc.
Trilla, trilla, trillary.
Now, Tibet; Now, Annot; now, Margery;
Now whippet[5] apace for the mastery,
But it will not be, our mouth is so dry.
    TALKAPACE. Ah, each finger is a thumb[6] today
    methink,   70

[5] "Now whip it quickly,"—let's make it fast.
[6] Her fingers, she says, are awkward today.

I care not to let all alone, choose it swim or sink.
  (*They sing a fourth time.*)
          Pipe, merry Annot, etc.
Trilla, trilla, trillary.
When, Tibet? when, Annot? when, Margery?[7]
I will not! I cannot, no more can I!
Then give we all over, and there let it lie.
  (*She casts down her work.*)
  TALKAPACE. There it lieth! The worst is but a
    curried coat,*   a beating
Tut, I am used thereto; I care not a groat!
  ALYFACE. Have we done singing since? Then will I
    in again.   79
Here I found you, and here I leave both twain.
                                        (*She goes out.*)
  MUMBLECRUST. And I will not be long after. Tib
    Talkapace
(*Spying* ROISTER DOISTER.)
  TALKAPACE. What is the matter?
  MUMBLECRUST.   Yond stood a man all this space,
And hath heard all that ever we spake together.
  TALKAPACE. Marry! the more lout he for his
    coming hither!
And the less good he can, to listen maidens' talk!
I care not an I go bid him hence for to walk.
It were well done to know what he maketh here
    away.
  ROISTER DOISTER. Now might I speak to them, if I
    wist* what to say.   knew
  MUMBLECRUST. Nay, we will go both off, and see
    what he is.
  ROISTER DOISTER (*advancing*). One that hath heard
    all your talk and singing, iwis.*   indeed/90
  TALKAPACE. The more to blame you! a good
    thrifty husband*   housekeeper
Would elsewhere have had some better matters
    in hand.
  ROISTER DOISTER. I did it for no harm, but for
    good love I bear
To your dame mistress Custance, I did your talk hear.
And, mistress nurse, I will kiss you for acquaintance.
  MUMBLECRUST (*eagerly*). I come anon, sir.

---

[7] The equivalent of "when," an expression of impatience, would be "now
then," or "let's get going."

TALKAPACE. Faith, I would our dame Custance
Saw this gear!*   business
    MUMBLECRUST. I must first wipe all clean, yea,
    I must.
    TALKAPACE. I'll 'chieve it, doting fool, but it must
    be cust!*   kissed
    MUMBLECRUST. God yield* you, sir! Chad* not   reward/I had
    so much i-chotte* not whan,*   I know/when
Ne'er since chwas bore, chwine, of such a gay
    gentleman!8   100
    ROISTER DOISTER. I will kiss you too, maiden, for
    the good will I bear you.
    TALKAPACE. No, forsooth, by your leave, ye shall
    not kiss me!
    ROISTER DOISTER. Yes; be not afeard; I do not
    disdain you a whit.
    TALKAPACE. Why should I fear you? I have not so
    little wit,
Ye are but a man, I know very well.
    ROISTER DOISTER.   Why, then?
    TALKAPACE. Forsooth, for I will not, I use not to
    kiss men.
    ROISTER DOISTER. I would fain kiss you too, good
    maiden, if I might.
    TALKAPACE. What should that need?
    ROISTER DOISTER. But to honour you, by this light!
I use to kiss all them that I love, to God I vow.
    TALKAPACE. Yea, sir, I pray you, when did ye last
    kiss your cow?   110
    ROISTER DOISTER. Ye might be proud to kiss me, if
    ye were wise.
    TALKAPACE. What promotion were therein?
    ROISTER DOISTER.   Nurse is not so nice,*   coy
    TALKAPACE. Well, I have not been taught to kissing
    and licking.
    ROISTER DOISTER. Yet I thank you, mistress nurse,
    ye made no sticking.*   objection
    MUMBLECRUST. I will not stick for a kiss with such a
    man as you!
    TALKAPACE. They that lust!* I will again to my   like
    sewing now.
(Enter ANNOT ALYFACE.)

---

8 "Not since I was born, I believe, by such a lively gentleman."

ALYFACE. Tidings, ho! tidings! Dame Custance
greeteth you well.

ROISTER DOISTER. Whom? me?

ALYFACE. You, sir? No, sir; I do no such tale tell.

ROISTER DOISTER. But, an she knew me here—

ALYFACE.   Tibet Talkapace,
Your mistress, Custance, and mine, must speak with
your grace.   120

TALKAPACE. With me?

ALYFACE.   Ye must come in to her, out
of all doubts.

TALKAPACE. And my work not half done! A
mischief on all louts!

                                        (*They go out.*)

ROISTER DOISTER. Ah, good sweet nurse!

MUMBLECRUST.   A good sweet gentleman!

ROISTER DOISTER. What?

MUMBLECRUST.   Nay, I cannot tell, sir; but
what thing would you?

ROISTER DOISTER. How doth sweet Custance, my
heart of gold, tell me how?

MUMBLECRUST. She doth very well, sir, and
commends me to you.[9]

ROISTER DOISTER. To me?

MUMBLECRUST.   Yea, to you, sir.

ROISTER DOISTER.   To me?
Nurse, tell me plain, To me?

MUMBLECRUST. Yea.

ROISTER DOISTER.   That word maketh me alive
again!

MUMBLECRUST. She commended me to one last day,
whoe'er it was.

ROISTER DOISTER. That was e'en to me and none
other, by the Mass.   130

MUMBLECRUST. I cannot tell you surely, but one it
was.

ROISTER DOISTER. It was I and none other. This
cometh to good pass.
I promise thee, nurse, I favour her.

MUMBLECRUST.   E'en so, sir.

ROISTER DOISTER. Bid her sue to me for marriage.

MUMBLECRUST.   E'en so, sir.

---

[9] "She sends greetings to you through me."

ROISTER DOISTER. And surely for thy sake, she shall
speed.

MUMBLECRUST. E'en so, sir.

ROISTER DOISTER. I shall be contented to take her.

MUMBLECRUST.   E'en so, sir.

ROISTER DOISTER. But at thy request, and for thy
sake.

MUMBLECRUST. E'en so, sir.

ROISTER DOISTER. And, come, hark in thine ear
what to say.

MUMBLECRUST. (*He tells her a great, long tale in
her ear.*) E'en so, sir.

SCENE 4

(ROISTER DOISTER *and* MARGERY MUMBLECRUST.
Enter MERRYGREEK, DOBINET DOUGHTY, *and* HARPAX)

MERRYGREEK. Come on, sirs, apace; and quit
yourselves like men.

Your pains shall be rewarded.

DOUGHTY.   But I wot* not when.   know

MERRYGREEK. Do your master worship as ye have
done in time past

DOUGHTY. Speak to them; of mine office he shall
have a cast.*   sample

MERRYGREEK. Harpax, look that thou do well, too,
and thy fellow.

HARPAX. I warrant, if he will mine example follow.

MERRYGREEK. Curtsy, whoresons; duck you and
crouch at every word.

DOUGHTY. Yes, whether our master speak earnest or
bord.*   jest

MERRYGREEK. For this lieth upon his preferment
indeed.

DOUGHTY. Oft is he a wooer, but never doth he
speed.   10

MERRYGREEK. But with whom is he now so sadly
rounding* yond?   whispering

DOUGHTY. With *Nobs nicebecetur miserere* fond.[10]

MERRYGREEK (*pretending to believe* ROISTER DOISTER
is in love with the old woman). God be at your
wedding! Be ye sped already?

I did not suppose that your love was so greedy.

[10] "With 'darling have pity on me' foolishly."

I perceive now ye have chose of devotion;
And joy have ye, lady, of your promotion!

    ROISTER DOISTER. Tush, fool, thou art deceived;
       this is not she.

    MERRYGREEK. Well, mock* much of her, and keep   make
       her well, I 'vise ye.

I will take no charge of such a fair piece keeping.

    MUMBLECRUST. What aileth this fellow? He driveth
       me to weeping.   20

    MERRYGREEK. What! weep on the wedding day? Be
       merry, woman!

Though I say it, ye have chose a good gentleman.

    ROISTER DOISTER. Kock's nowns!* what   God's wounds!
       meanest thou man? tut a whistle!*   trifle

    MERRYGREEK (continuing to mock him). Ah, sir,
       be good to her; she is but a gristle!*   a little thing

Ah, sweet lamb and cony!

    ROISTER DOISTER.   Tut, thou art deceived!

    MERRYGREEK. Weep no more, lady; ye shall be well
       received.

Up with some merry noise, sirs, to bring home the
    bride!

    ROISTER DOISTER. Gog's arms, knave! Art thou mad?

I tell thee thou art wide.*   mistaken

    MERRYGREEK. Then ye intend by night to have her
       home brought.

    ROISTER DOISTER. I tell thee, no!

    MERRYGREEK.   How then?

    ROISTER DOISTER. 'Tis neither meant nor thought.   30

    MERRYGREEK. What shall we then do with her?

    ROISTER DOISTER.   Ah, foolish harebrain!

This is not she!

    MERRYGREEK. No is? Why then, unsaid again!

And what young girl is this with your maship so bold?

    ROISTER DOISTER. A girl?

    MERRYGREEK.   Yea; I dare say; scarce yet
       threescore year old.

    ROISTER DOISTER. This same is the fair widow's
       nurse, of whom ye wot.*   know

    MERRYGREEK. Is she but a nurse of a house? Hence
       home, old trot!

Hence at once!

    ROISTER DOISTER. No! no!

MERRYGREEK.   What! an please your maship,
A nurse talk so homely* with one of your worship?   *intimately
ROISTER DOISTER. I will have it so: it is my
  pleasure and will.
MERRYGREEK. Then I am content. Nurse, come
  again; tarry still.   40
ROISTER DOISTER. What! she will help forward this
  my suit for her part.
MERRYGREEK. Then is't mine own pigsny,* and   *darling
  blessing on my heart.
ROISTER DOISTER. This is our best friend, man!
MERRYGREEK.   Then teach her what to say.
MUMBLECRUST. I am taught already.
MERRYGREEK.   Then go, make no delay!
ROISTER DOISTER. Yet hark, one word in thine ear.
MERRYGREEK.   Back, sirs, from his tail!
ROISTER DOISTER. Back villains! Will ye be privy of
  my counsail?*   *counsel
MERRYGREEK. Back, sirs! so! I told you afore
  ye would be shent.*   *put to shame
ROISTER DOISTER. She shall have the first day a
  whole peck of argent.*   *silver
MUMBLECRUST. A peck? *Nomine Patris!*[11] have ye
  so much spare?
ROISTER DOISTER. Yea, and a cart-load thereto, or
  else were it bare,   50
Besides other movables, household stuff, and land.
MUMBLECRUST. Have ye lands too?
ROISTER DOISTER.   An hundred marks.
MERRYGREEK.   Yea, a thousand!
MUMBLECRUST. And have ye cattle too? and sheep
  too?
ROISTER DOISTER. Yea, a few.
MERRYGREEK. He is ashamed the number of them
  to show.
E'en round about him, as many thousand sheep goes,
As he and thou, and I too have fingers and toes.
MUMBLECRUST. And how many years old be you?
ROISTER DOISTER.   Forty at least.
MERRYGREEK. Yea, and thrice forty to them!
ROISTER DOISTER.   Nay, now thou dost jest.
I am not so old; thou misreckonest my years.

---

[11] "In the Name of the Father!"

MERRYGREEK. I know that; but my mind was on
    bullocks and steers.   60
MUMBLECRUST. And what shall I show her your
    mastership's name is?
ROISTER DOISTER. Nay, she shall make suit ere
    she know that, iwis.*   assuredly
MUMBLECRUST. Yet let me somewhat know.
MERRYGREEK.   This is he, understand,
That killed the Blue Spider in Blanchepowder land.
MUMBLECRUST. Yea, Jesus! William! Zee law! Did
    he zo? law!¹²
MERRYGREEK. Yea, and the last elephant that ever
    he saw;
As the beast passed by, he start out of a busk,*   bush
And e'en with pure strength of arms plucked out his
    great tusk.
MUMBLECRUST. Jesus! *Nomine Patris!* what a thing
    was that!
ROISTER DOISTER. Yea, but, Merrygreek, one thing
    thou hast forgot.   70
MERRYGREEK. What?
ROISTER DOISTER.   Of th'other elephant.
MERRYGREEK.   Oh, him that fled away.
ROISTER DOISTER. Yea.
MERRYGREEK.   Yea! he knew that his match
    was in place that day.
Tut, he beat the King of Crickets on Christmas day,
That he crept in a hole, and not a word to say!
MUMBLECRUST. A sore* man, by zembletee!*   fierce/semblance
MERRYGREEK.   Why, he wrung a club
Once, in a fray, out of the hand of Belzebub.
ROISTER DOISTER. And how when Mumfision?
MERRYGREEK.   Oh, your custreling*   young squire
Bore the lantern a-field so before the gosling—
Nay that is too long a matter now to be told:
Never ask his name, nurse, I warrant thee, be bold.   80
He conquererd in one day from Rome to Naples,
And won towns, nurse, as fast as thou canst make
    apples
MUMBLECRUST. O Lord! My heart quaketh for fear!
    He is too sore!
ROISTER DOISTER. Thou makest her too much
    afeard. Merrygreek, no more!
¹² "The lord! Did he so? Lord!"

This tale would 'fear my sweetheart Custance right
    evil.
    MERRYGREEK. Nay, let her take him, nurse, and fear
      not the devil!
But thus is our song dashed. Sirs, ye may home again.
    ROISTER DOISTER. No, shall they not! I charge you
      all here to remain.
The villain slaves! a whole day ere they can be found!
    MERRYGREEK. Couch! On your marrowbones,*   *kneel down*
      whoresons! Down to the ground!   90
Was it meet* he should tarry so long in one place   *right*
Without harmony of music, or some solace?
Whoso hath such bees as your master in his head,
Had need to have his spirits with music to be fed.
By your mastership's licence!
    ROISTER DOISTER.   What is that? a mote?
    MERRYGREEK. No; it was a fowl's feather had light
      on your coat.
    ROISTER DOISTER. I was nigh no feathers since I
      came from my bed.
    MERRYGREEK. No, sir, it was a hair that was fall
      from your head.
    ROISTER DOISTER. My men come when it please
      them—
    MERRYGREEK. By your leave!
    ROISTER DOISTER.   What is that?
    MERRYGREEK. Your gown was foul spotted with the
      foot of a gnat.   100
    ROISTER DOISTER. Their master to offend they are
      nothing afeard.
What now?
    MERRYGREEK. A lousy hair from your mastership's
      beard.
    ALL THE SERVANTS. And sir, for nurse's sake, pardon
      this one offence.
We shall not after this show the like negligence.
    ROISTER DOISTER. I pardon you this once; and come
      sing ne'er the worse!
    MERRYGREEK. How like you the goodness of this
      gentleman, nurse?
    MUMBLECRUST. God save his mastership that so can
      his men forgive!
And I will hear them sing ere I go, by his leave.

ROISTER DOISTER. Marry, and thou shalt, wench!
  Come, we two will dance!
MUMBLECRUST. Nay, I will by mine own self foot
  the song perchance.   110
ROISTER DOISTER. Go to it, sirs, lustily!
MUMBLECRUST.   Pipe up a merry note.
Let me hear it played, I will foot it, for a groat!
  (*They sing.*)

        Whoso to marry a minion* wife   darling
           Hath had good chance and hap,
        Must love her and cherish her all his life,
           And dandle her in his lap.

        If she will fare well, if she will go gay,
           A good husband ever still,
        Whatever she lust* to do or to say,   desires
           Must let her have her own will.   120

        About what affairs soever he go,
           He must show her all his mind;
        None of his counsel she may be kept fro,
           Else is he a man unkind.

ROISTER DOISTER. Now, nurse, take this same letter
  here to thy mistress;
And as my trust is in thee, ply my business.
  MUMBLECRUST. It shall be done.
MERRYGREEK.   Who made it?
ROISTER DOISTER.   I wrote it, each whit.
MERRYGREEK. Then needs it no mending.
ROISTER DOISTER.   No, no!
MERRYGREEK.   No; I know your wit;
I warrant it well.
  MUMBLECRUST. It shall be delivered.
But, if ye speed, shall I be considered?   130
  MERRYGREEK. Whough! dost thou doubt of that?
MUMBLECRUST.   What shall I have?
MERRYGREEK. An hundred times more than thou
  canst devise to crave.
MUMBLECRUST. Shall I have some new gear?* for   clothing
  my old is all spent.
MERRYGREEK. The worst kitchen wench shall go in
  ladies' raiment.
MUMBLECRUST. Yea?
MERRYGREEK. And the worst drudge in the house
  shall go better

Than your mistress doth now.

MUMBLECRUST.   Then I trudge with your letter.

ROISTER DOISTER. Now, may I repose me, Custance
  is mine own.

Let us sing and play homeward, that it may be
    known.

MERRYGREEK. But are you sure that your letter is
    well enough?

ROISTER DOISTER. I wrote it myself!

MERRYGREEK.   Then sing we to dinner!
                    (*They go out singing.*)

SCENE 5

(*Enter* CHRISTIAN CUSTANCE *and* MARGERY MUMBLE-
CRUST)

DAME CUSTANCE. Who took* thee this letter,   gave
    Margery Mumblecrust?

MUMBLECRUST. A lusty gay bachelor took it me of
    trust,13

And if ye seek to him he will 'low* your doing.   approve

DAME CUSTANCE. Yea, but where learned he that
    manner of wooing?

MUMBLECRUST. If to sue to him you will any pains
    take,

He will have you to his wife, he saith, for my sake.

DAME CUSTANCE. Some wise gentleman, belike! I
    am bespoken;

And I thought, verily, this had been some token

From my dear spouse Gawyn Goodluck; whom, when
    him please,

God luckily send home to both our hearts' ease.   10

MUMBLECRUST. A jolly man it is, I wot well by
    report,

And would have you to him for marriage resort.

Best open the writing, and see what it doth speak.

DAME CUSTANCE. At this time, nurse, I will
    neither read nor break.*   open [the letter]

MUMBLECRUST. He promised to give you a
    whole peck of gold.

DAME CUSTANCE. Perchance lack of a pint, when it
    shall be all told!

---

13 "Gave it to me in trust."

MUMBLECRUST. I would take a gay rich husband, an
    I were you.
DAME CUSTANCE. In good sooth, Madge, e'en so
    would I, if I were thou.
But no more of this fond* talk now, let us go in.   foolish
And see thou no more move me folly to begin.   20
Nor bring me no more letters for no man's pleasure,
But* thou know from whom.   except
    MUMBLECRUST.   I warrant ye shall be sure!
                    (*They all go out.*)

ACT II

SCENE 1

(*Enter* DOBINET DOUGHTY.)
DOUGHTY. Where is the house I go to? before or
    behind?
I know not where, nor when, nor how, I shall it find.
If I had ten men's bodies and legs and strength,
This trotting that I have must needs lame me at
    length.
And now that my master is new set on wooing,
I trust there shall none of us find lack of doing.
Two pairs of shoes a day will now be too little
To serve me, I must trot to and fro so mickle.*   much
'Go bear me this token!' 'Carry me this letter!'   9
'Now this is the best way,' 'now that way is better!'
Up before day, sirs, I charge you, an hour or twain!
'Trudge! Do me this message, and bring word quick
    again!'
If one miss but a minute, then: 'His* arms and   Christ's
    wounds,
I would not have slacked for ten thousand pounds!
Nay, see, I beseech you, if my most trusty page
Go not now about to hinder my marriage!'
So fervent hot wooing, and so far from wiving,
I trow never was any creature living.
With every woman is he in some love's pang.
Then up to our lute at midnight, twangledom twang;   20
Then twang with our sonnets, and twang with our
    dumps,*   laments
And heigho from our heart, as heavy as lead lumps;
Then to our recorder* with toodleloodle poop,   flute

As the howlet* out of an ivy bush should whoop;   owl
Anon to our gittern,* thrumpledum, thrumpledum   guitar
    thrum,
Thrumpledum, thrumpledum, thrumpledum,
    thrumpledum, thrum.
Of songs and ballads also he is a maker,
And that can he as finely do as Jack Raker;[14]
Yea, and extempore will he ditties compose—
Foolish Marsyas[15] ne'er made the like, I suppose!   30
Yet must we sing them; as good stuff, I undertake,
As for such a pen-man is well fitting to make.
'Ah, for these long nights! heigho! when will it be
    day?
I fear, ere I come, she will be wooed away.'
Then, when answer is made that it may not be,
'O death, why comest thou not by-and-by?'* saith he.   at once
But then, from his heart to put away sorrow,
He is as far in with some new love next morrow.
But in the mean season we trudge and we trot;
From dayspring to midnight, I sit not, nor rest not.
And now am I sent to Dame Christian Custance;   41
But I fear it will end with a mock for pastance.*   pastime
I bring her a ring, with a token in a clout,*   piece of cloth
And, by all guess, this same is her house out of
    doubt.
I know it now perfect, I am in my right way.
And lo yond the old nurse that was with us last day!*   yesterday

SCENE 2

(DOUGHTY. *Enter* MARGERY MUMBLECRUST.)

MUMBLECRUST. I was ne'er so shook up afore since
    I was born.
That our mistress could not have chid, I would have
    sworn;
And I pray God I die, if I meant any harm,
But for my life-time, this shall be to me a charm!
    DOUGHTY. God you save and see, nurse! And how
        is it with you?
    MUMBLECRUST. Marry, a great deal the worse it is,
        for such as thou!

---

[14] A maker of poor verses.
[15] A legendary flute player who challenged Apollo to a flute-playing contest
and was punished for his presumption.

DOUGHTY. For me? Why so?

MUMBLECRUST. Why, were not thou one of them, say,

That sang and played here with the gentleman last day?

DOUGHTY. Yes; and he would know if you have for him spoken,

And prays you to deliver this ring and token.   10

MUMBLECRUST. Now, by the token* that God   miracle
  tokened, brother,

I will deliver no token, one nor other!

I have once been so shent* for your master's   put to shame
  pleasure,

As I will not be again for all his treasure.

DOUGHTY. He will thank you, woman.

MUMBLECRUST.   I will none of his thank.

                              (*Exit.*)

DOUGHTY. I ween* I am a prophet! this gear*   believe/business
  will prove blank!

But what! should I home again without answer go?

It were better go to Rome on my head than so.

I will tarry here this month, but some of the house

Shall take it of me; and then I care not a louse.   20

But yonder cometh forth a wench—or a lad;

If he have not one Lombard's touch,16 my luck is bad.

SCENE 3

(DOBINET DOUGHTY. *Enter* TOM TRUEPENNY.)

TRUEPENNY. I am clean lost for lack of merry company!

We 'gree not half well within, our wenches and I.

They will command like mistresses; they will forbid,

If they be not served, Truepenny must be chid.

Let them be as merry now as ye can desire,

With turning of a hand our mirth lieth in the mire!

I cannot skill of such changeable mettle,17

There is nothing with them but 'in dock, out nettle!'18

DOUGHTY. Whether is it better that I speak to him first,

Or he first to me? it is good to cast the worst.   10

---

16 The Lombards were bankers in the Middle Ages.
17 "I have no skill to cope with such changeable tempers."
18 The dock-leaf was considered a remedy for nettle stings.

If I begin first, he will smell all my purpose;
Otherwise, I shall not need anything to disclose.
    TRUEPENNY. What boy have we yonder? I will see
      what he is.
    DOUGHTY. He cometh to me. It is hereabout, iwis.*   assuredly
    TRUEPENNY. Wouldest thou aught, friend, that
      thou lookest so about?
    DOUGHTY. Yea; but whether ye can help me or no,
      I doubt.
I seek to one mistress Custance house, here dwelling.
    TRUEPENNY. It is my mistress ye seek to, by your
      telling.
    DOUGHTY. Is there any of that name here but she?
    TRUEPENNY. Not one in all the whole town that I
      know, perdie.   20
    DOUGHTY. A widow she is, I trow?
    TRUEPENNY.   And what an she be?
    DOUGHTY. But ensured* to an husband?   engaged
    TRUEPENNY.   Yea, so think we.
    DOUGHTY. And I dwell with her husband that
      trusteth to be.
    TRUEPENNY. In faith, then must thou needs be
      welcome to me,
Let us for acquaintance shake hands togither;
And whate'er thou be, heartily welcome hither.
    (*Enter* TIBET TALKAPACE *and* ANNOT ALYFACE.)
    TALKAPACE. Well, Truepenny, never but
      flinging!*   rushing around
    ALYFACE.   And frisking!
    TRUEPENNY. Well, Tibet and Annot, still
      swinging and whisking!*   dashing about
    TALKAPACE. But ye roil abroad.*   gad about
    ALYFACE.   In the street, everywhere!
    TRUEPENNY. Where are ye twain, in chambers,
      when ye meet me there?   30
But come hither, fools; I have one now by the hand,
Servant to him that must be our mistress' husband,
Bid him welcome.
    ALYFACE.   To me truly is he welcome!
    TALKAPACE. Forsooth, and as I may say, heartily
      welcome!
    DOUGHTY. I thank you, mistress maids.
    ALYFACE.   I hope we shall better know.
    TALKAPACE. And when will our new master come?

DOUGHTY.   Shortly, I trow.
TALKAPACE. I would it were to-morrow: for till he
    resort,
Our mistress, being a widow, hath small comfort,
And I heard our nurse speak of an husband to-day
Ready for our mistress, a rich man and a gay;   40
And we shall go in our French hoods every day,
In our silk cassocks, I warrant you, fresh and gay,
In our trick ferdegews and biliments[19] of gold;
Brave in our suits of change, seven double fold.
Then shall ye see Tibet, sirs, tread the moss so trim.
Nay, why said I 'tread'? ye shall see her glide and
    swim,
Not lumperdee clumperdee like our spaniel Rig.
    TRUEPENNY. Marry, then, prick-me-dainty,*   my fine lady
    come toast me a fig!
Who shall then know our Tib. Talkapace, trow ye?
    ALYFACE. And why not Annot Alyface as fine as she?
    TRUEPENNY. And what? had Tom Truepenny a
    father, or none?   51
    ALYFACE. Then our pretty newcome man will look
    to be one.
    TRUEPENNY. We four, I trust, shall be a jolly merry
    knot.
Shall we sing a fit to welcome our friend, Annot?
    ALYFACE. Perchance he cannot sing.
    DOUGHTY.   I am at all essays.[20]
    TALKAPACE. By Cock, and the better welcome to us
    always!
(*They sing.*)
               A thing very fit
               For them that have wit,
               And are fellows knit,
       Servants in one house to be,   60
               Is fast for to sit,
               And not oft to flit,
               Nor vary a whit,
       But lovingly to agree.

               No man complaining,
               No other disdaining
               For loss or for gaining,

---

[19] Farthingales and headdresses.
[20] "I am always ready to try anything."

But fellows or friends to be;
   No grudge remaining,
   No work refraining,
   Nor help restraining,   70
But lovingly to agree.

   No man for despite,
   By word or by write*   writing
   His fellow to twite,*   twit
But further in honesty;
   No good turns entwite,*   rebuke
   Nor old sores recite,
   But let all go quite,
And lovingly to agree.   80

   After drudgery,
   When they be weary,
   Then to be merry,
To laugh and sing they be free;
   With chip and cherry
   Heigh derry derry,
   Trill on the berry,
And lovingly to agree.

TALKAPACE. Will you now in with us unto our
   mistress go?
DOUGHTY. I have first for my master an errand or
   two.   90
But I have here from him a token and a ring,
They shall have most thank of her that first doth it
   bring.
TALKAPACE. Marry, that will I!
TRUEPENNY.   See, an Tibet snatch not now!
TALKAPACE. And why may not I, sir, get thanks as
   well as you?
                               (*Exit.*)
ALYFACE. Yet get ye not all; we will go with you
   both,
And have part of your thanks, be ye never so loth!
             (*Exeunt* ANNOT *and* TRUEPENNY.)
DOUGHTY. So* my hands are rid of it; I care for   so long as
   no more.
I may now return home; so durst I not afore.
                               (*Exit.*)

Scene 4

(*Enter* Dame Custance, Tibet Talkapace, Annot
Alyface, *and* Truepenny.)

Dame Custance. Nay, come forth all three! and
    come hither, pretty máid!
Will not so many forewarnings make you afraid?
    Talkapace. Yes, forsooth.
    Dame Custance. But still be a runner up and down?
Still be a bringer of tidings and tokens to town?
    Talkapace. No, forsooth, mistress.
    Dame Custance.   Is all your delight and joy
In whisking and ramping abroad like a tomboy?
    Talkapace. Forsooth, these were there too, Annot
    and Truepenny.
    Truepenny. Yea, but ye alone took it, ye cannot
    deny.
    Alyface. Yea, that ye did.
    Talkapace.   But if I had not, ye train would.
    Dame Custance. You great calf! ye should have
    more wit, so ye should!   10
But why should any of you take such things in hand?
    Talkapace. Because it came from him that must
    be your husband.
    Dame Custance. How do ye know that?
    Talkapace.   Forsooth, the boy did say so.
    Dame Custance. What was his name?
    Alyface.   We asked not.
    Dame Custance.   Did ye? no?
    Alyface. He is not far gone, of likelihood.
    Truepenny.   I will see.
    Dame Custance. If thou canst find him in the
    street, bring him to me.
    Truepenny. Yes.

                          (*He goes out.*)

    Dame Custance. Well, ye naughty girls, if ever I
    perceive
That henceforth you do letters or tokens receive
To bring unto me from any person or place,
Except ye first show me the party face to face,   20
Either thou, or thou, full truly aby* thou shalt.   pay
    Talkapace. Pardon this, and the next time
    powder* me in salt!   preserve

DAME CUSTANCE. I shall make all girls by* you   of
twain to beware.

TALKAPACE. If ever I offend again, do not me spare.
But if ever I see that false boy any more
By your mistress-ship's licence, I tell you afore,
I will rather have my coat twenty times swinged,*   whipped
Than on the naughty wag not to be avenged.

DAME CUSTANCE. Good wenches would not so ramp
abroad idly.
But keep within doors, and ply their work earnestly.
If one would speak with me that is a man likely,   31
Ye shall have right good thank to bring me word
quickly;
But otherwise with messages to come in post
From henceforth, I promise you, shall be to your cost.
Get you in to your work!

TALKAPACE.   Yes, forsooth.

DAME CUSTANCE.   Hence, both
twain;
And let me see you play me such a part again!
(Re-enter TRUEPENNY.)

TRUEPENNY. Mistress, I have run past the far end
of the street,
Yet can I not yonder crafty boy see nor meet.

DAME CUSTANCE. No?

TRUEPENNY.   Yet I looked as far beyond the
people
As one may see out of the top of Paul's steeple.   40

DAME CUSTANCE. Hence in at doors, and let me no
more be vexed!

TRUEPENNY. Forgive me this one fault, and lay on* punish
for the next.
                 (Exit.)

DAME CUSTANCE. Now will I in too; for I think,
so God me mend,
This will prove some foolish matter in the end!
                 (Exit.)

ACT III

SCENE 1

(Enter MATTHEW MERRYGREEK.)
MERRYGREEK. Now say this again:—he hath
somewhat to doing.*   plenty to do

Which* followeth the trace of one that is wooing,   who
Specially that hath no more wit in his head
Than my cousin Roister Doister withal is led.
I am sent in all haste to espy and to mark
How our letters and tokens are likely to wark.
Master Roister Doister must have answer in haste,
For he loveth not to spend much labour in waste.
Now as for Christian Custance, by this light,
Though she had not her troth to Gawyn Goodluck
　　plight,   10
Yet rather than with such a loutish dolt to marry,
I daresay would live a poor life solitary.
But fain would I speak with Custance, if I wist how,
To laugh at the matter. Yond cometh one forth now.

SCENE 2

(MERRYGREEK. *Enter* TIBET TALKAPACE.)
　TALKAPACE. Ah, that I might but once in my life
　　have a sight
Of him that made us all so ill shent: by this light,
He should never escape if I had him by the ear,
But even from his head I would it bite or tear;
Yea, and if one of them were not enow,
I would bite them both off, I make God avow!
　MERRYGREEK. What is he, whom this little mouse
　　doth so threaten?
　TALKAPACE. I would teach him, I trow, to make
　　girls shent or beaten.
　MERRYGREEK. I will call her. Maid, with whom are
　　ye so hasty?
　TALKAPACE. Not with you, sir, but with
　　a little wagpasty,*   mischievous rascal/10
A deceiver of folks by subtle craft and guile.
　MERRYGREEK. I know where she is*: Dobinet   what she means
　　hath wrought some wile.
　TALKAPACE. He brought a ring and token which
　　he said was sent
From our dame's husband; but I wot* well I   knew
　　was shent!*   embarrassed
For it liked her as well,[21] to tell you no lies,
As water in her ship, or salt cast in her eyes.
And yet whence it came neither we nor she can tell.

---

[21] "It displeased her as much."

MERRYGREEK. We shall have sport anon; I like this
    very well!—

And dwell ye here with Mistress Custance, fair maid?

    TALKAPACE. Yea, marry do I, sir. What would ye
    have said?   20

    MERRYGREEK. A little message unto her by word of
    mouth.

    TALKAPACE. No messages, by your leave, nor tokens,
    forsooth!

    MERRYGREEK. Then help me to speak with her.

    TALKAPACE.   With a good will that.

    (*Enter* DAME CUSTANCE.)

Here she cometh forth. Now speak—ye know best
    what.

    DAME CUSTANCE. None other life with you, maid,
    but abroad to skip?

    TALKAPACE. Forsooth, here is one would speak with
    your mistress-ship.

    DAME CUSTANCE. Ah, have ye been learning of more
    messages now?

    TALKAPACE. I would not hear his mind, but bade
    him show it to you.

    DAME CUSTANCE. In at doors!

    TALKAPACE.   I am gone.

    (*She goes indoors.*)

    MERRYGREEK.   Dame
    Custance, God ye save!

    DAME CUSTANCE. Welcome, friend Merrygreek: and
    what thing would ye have?   30

    MERRYGREEK. I am come to you a little matter to
    break.

    DAME CUSTANCE. But see it be honest, else better
    not to speak.

    MERRYGREEK. How feel ye yourself affected here of
    late?

    DAME CUSTANCE. I feel no manner change but after
    the old rate.

But whereby do ye mean?

    MERRYGREEK.   Concerning marriage.

Doth not love lade* you?   wear you down

    DAME CUSTANCE.   I feel no such carriage.* weight

    MERRYGREEK. Do ye feel no pangs of dotage? answer
    me right.

DAME CUSTANCE. I dote so that I make but one
sleep all the night.
But what need all these words?
MERRYGREEK.   Oh Jesus! will ye see
What dissembling creatures these same women be?
The gentleman ye wot* of, whom ye do so love   know of/41
That ye would fain marry him, if ye durst it move,
Among other rich widows, which are of him glad,
Lest ye for losing of him perchance might run mad,
Is now contented that upon your suit making,
Ye be as one in election of taking.
DAME CUSTANCE. What a tale is this! that I wot of?
Whom I love?
MERRYGREEK. Yea, and he is as loving a worm,
again, as a dove.
E'en of very pity he is willing you to take,
Because ye shall not destroy yourself for his sake.   50
DAME CUSTANCE. Marry, God yield his maship!*   mastership
Whatever he be,
It is gentmanly spoken.
MERRYGREEK.   Is it not, trow ye?
If ye have the grace now to offer yourself, ye speed.
DAME CUSTANCE. As much as though I did, this time
it shall not need.
But what gentman is it, I pray you tell me plain,
That wooeth so finely?
MERRYGREEK.   Lo where ye be again,
As though ye knew him not!
DAME CUSTANCE.   Tush, ye speak in jest!
MERRYGREEK. Nay, sure, the party is in good
knacking* earnest;   absolutely
And have you he will, he saith, and have you he must.
DAME CUSTANCE. I am promised during my life;
that is just.   60
MERRYGREEK. Marry, so thinketh he, unto him
alone.
DAME CUSTANCE. No creature hath my faith and
troth but one—
That is Gawyn Goodluck: and if it be not he,
He hath no title this way, whatever he be,
Nor I know none to whom I have such word spoken.
MERRYGREEK. Ye know him not, you, by his letter
and token?

DAME CUSTANCE. Indeed, true it is that a letter I
have;
But I never read it yet, as God me save!
    MERRYGREEK. Ye a woman, and your letter so long
      unread?
    DAME CUSTANCE. Ye may thereby know what haste I
      have to wed.   70
But now who it is for my hand, I know by guess.
    MERRYGREEK. Ah, well I say.
    DAME CUSTANCE.   It is Roister Doister,
      doubtless.
    MERRYGREEK. Will ye never leave this dissimulation?
Ye know him not?
    DAME CUSTANCE. But by imagination;
For no man there is but a very dolt and lout
That to woo a widow would so go about.
He shall never have me his wife while he do live.
    MERRYGREEK. Then will he have you if he may, so
      mote* I thrive!   might
And he biddeth you send him word by me,
That ye humbly beseech him ye may his wife be,   80
And that there shall be no let* in you, nor mistrust,   obstacle
But to be wedded on Sunday next, if he lust;*   desires
And biddeth you to look for him.
    DAME CUSTANCE.   Doth he bid so?
    MERRYGREEK. When he cometh, ask him whether he
      did or no.
    DAME CUSTANCE. Go, say that I bid him keep him
      warm at home!
For, if he come abroad, he shall cough me a mome.[22]
My mind was vexed, I shrew* his head! Sottish dolt!   curse
    MERRYGREEK. He hath in his head—
    DAME CUSTANCE.   As much brain as a bird-
      bolt!*   blunt arrow
    MERRYGREEK. Well, Dame Custance, if he hear you
      thus play choploge*—   chop logic
    DAME CUSTANCE. What will he?
    MERRYGREEK.   Play the devil in
      the horologe.*   clock/90
    DAME CUSTANCE. I defy him, lout!
    MERRYGREEK.   Shall I tell him
      what ye say?

---

[22] "Prove a fool to me."

DAME CUSTANCE. Yea; and add whatsoever thou canst, I thee pray,
And I will avouch it, whatsoever it be.
MERRYGREEK. Then let me alone! we will laugh well, ye shall see.
It will not be long ere he will hither resort.
DAME CUSTANCE. Let him come when him lust,*   desires
I wish no better sport.
Fare ye well. I will in and read my great letter;
I shall to my wooer make answer the better.
(*Exit, leaving* MERRYGREEK *alone on the stage.*)

SCENE 3

MERRYGREEK. Now that the whole answer in my devise doth rest,
I shall paint out our wooer in colours of the best;
And all that I say shall be on Custance's mouth;
She is author of all that I shall speak, forsooth.
But yond cometh Roister Doister now, in a trance.
(*Enter* RALPH ROISTER DOISTER.)
ROISTER DOISTER. Juno[23] send me this day good luck and good chance!
I cannot but come see how Merrygreek doth speed.
MERRYGREEK. I will not see him, but give him a jut,* indeed.   push
I cry your mastership mercy!
ROISTER DOISTER.   And whither now?
MERRYGREEK. As fast as I could run, sir, in post against you.   10
But why speak ye so faintly? or why are ye so sad?
ROISTER DOISTER. Thou knowest the proverb—because I cannot be had.
Hast thou spoken with this woman?
MERRYGREEK.   Yea, that I have!
ROISTER DOISTER. And what, will this gear be?[24]
MERRYGREEK.   No, so God me save!
ROISTER DOISTER. Hast thou a flat answer?
MERRYGREEK   Nay, a sharp answer!
ROISTER DOISTER. What?

[23] Juno (Hera, in the Greek) was the Roman goddess to whom marriages are sacred.
[24] "How will this business turn out?"

MERRYGREEK. Ye shall not, she saith, by her will
    marry her cat!
Ye are such a calf! such an ass! such a block!
Such a lilburn!* such a hoball!* such a lobcock!*   duffer/clown/
                                          bumpkin
And, because ye should come to her at no season,
She despised your maship out of all reason.   20
"Bawawe what ye say," ko* I, "of such a gentman!"   quoth
"Nay, I fear him not," ko she, "do the best he can.
He vaunteth himself for a man of prowess great,
Whereas a good gander, I daresay, may him beat.
And, where he is louted,* and laughed to scorn,   mocked
For the veriest dolt that ever was born,
And veriest lubber, sloven, and beast
Living in this world from the west to the east,
Yet of himself hath he such opinion
That in all the world is not the like minion.*   gallant/30
He thinketh each woman to be brought in dotage*   infatuation
With the only sight of his goodly personage;
Yet none that will have him. We do him lout* and   mock
    flock,*   jeer at
And make him among us our common sportingstock.
And so would I now," ko she, "save only because"—
"Better nay," ko I, "I lust not meddle with daws.
"Ye are happy," ko I, "that ye are a woman!
This would cost you your life in case ye were a man."
    ROISTER DOISTER. Yea, an hundred thousand pound
        should not save her life!
    MERRYGREEK. No, but that ye woo her to have her
        to your wife.   40
But I could not stop her mouth.
    ROISTER DOISTER.   Heigh-ho, alas!
    MERRYGREEK. Be of good cheer, man, and let the
        world pass!
    ROISTER DOISTER. What shall I do, or say now that
        it will not be?
    MERRYGREEK. Ye shall have choice of a thousand as
        good as she.
And ye must pardon her; it is for lack of wit.
    ROISTER DOISTER. Yea, for were not I an husband
        for her fit?
Well, what should I now do?
    MERRYGREEK.   In faith I cannot tell.
    ROISTER DOISTER. I will go home and die!

MERRYGREEK.   Then shall
 I bid toll the bell?
ROISTER DOISTER. No.
MERRYGREEK.   God have mercy on your soul!
 Ah, good gentleman,
That e'er ye should thus die for an unkind woman!   50
Will ye drink once ere ye go?
 ROISTER DOISTER.   No, no, I will none.
 MERRYGREEK. How feel your soul to God?
 ROISTER DOISTER.   I am nigh
 gone.
 MERRYGREEK. And shall we hence straight?
 ROISTER DOISTER.   Yea.
 MERRYGREEK.   *Placebo dilexi*[25]:
Master Roister Doister will straight go home and die,
Our Lord Jesus Christ his soul have mercy upon:
Thus you see today a man, tomorrow John.*   gone, dead
 Yet saving for a woman's extreme cruelty,
He might have lived yet a month or two or three.
 ROISTER DOISTER. Heigh-ho, alas, the pangs of death
 my heart do break!
 MERRYGREEK. Hold your peace! For shame, sir! A 60
 dead man may not speak!
*Ne quando.** What mourners and what torches shall when not
 we have?
 ROISTER DOISTER. None.
 MERRYGREEK. *Dirgie.** He will go darkling to his direct Thou
 grave,
Neque lux, neque crux, neque mourners, *neque*
 clink,[26]
He will steal to heaven, unknowing to God, I think,
*A porta inferi.** Who shall your goods possess? to hell's gate
 ROISTER DOISTER. Thou shalt be my sectour,* executor
 and have all, more and less.
 MERRYGREEK. *Requiem aeternam!** Now, God eternal rest
 reward your mastership!
And I will cry halfpenny-dole for your worship.
Come forth, sirs, hear the doleful news I shall you
 tell!
(*Calls* ROISTER DOISTER'*s servants.*)

---

[25] What follows is a parody of the Roman Catholic service for the dead.
Placebo domino is the beginning of the first antiphon of the Vespers for the
dead.
 [26] "Neither light, nor cross, nor mourners, nor any clinking of the bell."

Our good master here will no longer with us dwell.   70
But in spite of Custance, which hath him wearied,
Let us see his maship solemnly buried;
And while some piece of his soul is yet him within,
Some part of his funerals let us here begin.
Audivi vocem. All men take heed by this one   I heard a voice
    gentleman
How you set your love upon an unkind woman!
For these women be all such mad peevish elves,
They will not be won except it please themselves.
But, in faith, Custance, if ever ye come in hell,
Master Roister Doister shall serve you as well.   80
And will ye needs go from us thus, in very deed?
    ROISTER DOISTER. Yea, in good sadness.
        MERRYGREEK.   Now Jesus
        Christ be your speed!
Good-night, Roger, old knave! Farewell, Roger, old
    knave!
Good-night, Roger, old knave, knave, knap!*   rogue
Nequando. Audivi vocem. Requiem aeternam.
Pray for the late master Roister Doister's soul!
And come forth, parish clerk, let the passing bell toll.
    (*To* ROISTER DOISTER'S *servants.*)
Pray for your master, sirs, and for him ring a peal.
He was your right good master while he was in heal.*   health
    (*The Peal of Bells rung by the Parish Clerk and*
    ROISTER DOISTER'S *four men.*)
    THE FIRST BELL, A TRIPLE. When died he? When
        died he?
    THE SECOND. We have him! we have him!   91
    THE THIRD. Roister Doister! Roister Doister!
    THE FOURTH BELL. He cometh! he cometh!
    THE GREAT BELL. Our own! our own!
Qui Lazarum.   who Lazarus [raised]
    ROISTER DOISTER. Heigh-ho!
    MERRYGREEK.   Dead men go not so fast
In Paradisum.
    ROISTER DOISTER. Heigh-ho!
    MERRYGREEK.   Soft, hear what I have
        cast!
    ROISTER DOISTER. I will hear nothing, I am passed.
    MERRYGREEK.   Whough, wellaway!
Ye may tarry one hour, and hear what I shall say.

Ye were best, sir, for a while to revive again
  And quiet them ere ye go.
  ROISTER DOISTER.   Trowest* thou so?   believest
  MERRYGREEK.   Yea,
    plain.   100
  ROISTER DOISTER. How may I revive, being now so
    far passed?
  MERRYGREEK. I will rub your temples, and fetch
    you again at last.
  ROISTER DOISTER. It will not be possible.
  MERRYGREEK.   Yes, for twenty pound.
  ROISTER DOISTER. Arms!* what dost thou?   God's arms!
  MERRYGREEK.   Fetch you again out of your sound.*   swoon
By this cross, ye were nigh gone indeed! I might feel
Your soul departing within an inch of your heel.
Now follow my counsel.
  ROISTER DOISTER.   What is it?
  MERRYGREEK.   If I were you,
Custance should eft seek to me[27] ere I would bow.
  ROISTER DOISTER. Well, as thou wilt have one, even
    so will I do.
  MERRYGREEK. Then shall ye revive again for an
    hour or two?   110
  ROISTER DOISTER. As thou wilt; I am content, for a
    little space.
  MERRYGREEK. Good hap* is not hasty; yet in   luck
    space* cometh grace.   in time
To speak with Custance yourself should be very well;
What good thereof may come, nor I nor you can tell.
But now the matter standeth upon your marriage,
Ye must now take unto you a lusty courage,
Ye may not speak with a faint heart to Custance,
But with a lusty breast and countenance,
That she may know she hath to answer to a man.
  ROISTER DOISTER. Yes, I can do that as well as any
    can.   120
  MERRYGREEK. Then, because ye must Custance face
    to face woo,
Let us see how to behave yourself ye can do.
Ye must have a portly brag,* after your estate.[28]   dignified bearing
  ROISTER DOISTER. Tush, I can handle that after the
    best rate.

27 "Constance should often plead with me."
28 "As becomes your station in life."

MERRYGREEK. Well done! So lo! Up, man, with your
    head and chin!
Up with that snout, man! So lo! now ye begin!
So! that is somewhat like! But, pranky-coat,* nay,   dandy
    whan?
That is a lusty brute!* Hands under your side, man!   gallant
So lo! Now is it even as it should be!
That is somewhat like, for a man of your degree!   130
Then must ye stately go, jetting* up and down.   strutting
Tut! can ye no better shake the tail of your gown?
There, lo! such a lusty brag it is ye must make!
    ROISTER DOISTER. To come behind and make curtsy,
        thou must some pains take.
    MERRYGREEK. Else were I much to blame, I thank
        your mastership.
The lord one day all to begrime* you with worship!   besmear
Back, sir sauce!* let gentlefolks have elbow room!   saucy fellow
Void, sirs! see ye not Master Roister Doister come?
Make place, my masters!
    ROISTER DOISTER.   Thou jostlest now too nigh.
    MERRYGREEK. Back, all rude louts!
    ROISTER DOISTER.   Tush!
    MERRYGREEK.   I cry your
    maship mercy!   140
Hoighdagh! if fair, fine mistress Custance saw you
    now,
Ralph Roister Doister were her own, I warrant you.
    ROISTER DOISTER. Ne'er an M by your girdle?[29]
    MERRYGREEK.   Your good Mastership's
Mastership were her own Mistress-ship's Mistress-ships,
Ye were take up for hawks,[30] ye were gone, ye were
    gone!
But now one other thing more yet I think upon.
    ROISTER DOISTER. Show what it is.
    MERRYGREEK.   A wooer, be he
    never so poor,
Must play and sing before his best-beloved's door;
How much more, then you?
    ROISTER DOISTER.   Thou speakest well, out of
    doubt.
    MERRYGREEK. And perchance that would make her
        the sooner come out.   150

[29] "Have you no 'M' on you with which to address me as Master?"
[30] "Snapped up as a husband for hawk's meat" (a proverbial phrase).

ROISTER DOISTER. Go call my musicians; bid them
    hie apace.*   come fast
MERRYGREEK. I will be here with them ere ye can
    say *trey ace*.*   a throw at dice
                          (*He goes out.*)
ROISTER DOISTER. This was well said of
    Merrygreek! I 'low* his wit.   approve (allow)
Before my sweetheart's door we will have a fit,*   a bit of music
That, if my love come forth, that I may with her talk,
I doubt not but this gear shall on my side walk.[31]
But lo, how well Merrygreek is returned sence!*   already
    (MERRYGREEK *comes back with the musicians*.)
MERRYGREEK. There hath grown no grass on my
    heel since I went hence!
Lo, here have I brought that* shall make you   what
    pastance.*   pastime
ROISTER DOISTER. Come, sirs, let us sing, to win my
    dear love Custance.   160
(*They sing*.)
        I mun* be married a Sunday;   must
        I mun be married a Sunday;
        Whosoever shall come that way,
           I mun be married a Sunday.

        Roister Doister is my name,
        Roister Doister is my name;
        A lusty brute, I am the same,
           I mun be married a Sunday.

        Christian Custance have I found,
        Christian Custance have I found,   170
        A widow worth a thousand pound.
           I mun be married a Sunday.

        Custance is as sweet as honey,
        Custance is as sweet as honey;
        I her lamb and she my coney,
           I mun be married a Sunday.

        When we shall make our wedding feast,
        When we shall make our wedding feast,
        There shall be cheer for man and beast.
           I mun be married a Sunday.   180
             I mun be married a Sunday, etc.

[31] "I doubt not that this business will turn out in my favor."

MERRYGREEK. Lo, where she cometh! Some countenance to her make,
And ye shall hear me be plain with her for your sake.

SCENE 4

(MERRYGREEK *and* RALPH ROISTER DOISTER. *Enter*
DAME CUSTANCE.)

DAME CUSTANCE. What gauding* and fooling is   sporting
this afore my door?

MERRYGREEK. May not folks be honest, pray you,
though they be poor?

DAME CUSTANCE. As that thing may be true, so rich
folks may be fools.

ROISTER DOISTER. Her talk is as fine as she had
learned in schools.

MERRYGREEK. Look partly toward her, and draw a
little near.

DAME CUSTANCE. Get ye home, idle folks!

MERRYGREEK.   Why, may
not we be here?

Nay, and ye will haze,* haze; otherwise, I tell you   have us
plain,

And* ye will not haze, then give us our gear* again.   if/things

DAME CUSTANCE. Indeed I have of yours much gay
things, God save all.

ROISTER DOISTER. Speak gently to her, and let her
take all.   10

MERRYGREEK. Ye are too tender-hearted; shall she
make us daws?*   fools

Nay, dame, I will be plain with you in my friends'
cause.

ROISTER DOISTER. Let all this pass, sweetheart, and
accept my service!

DAME CUSTANCE. I will not be served with a fool,
in no wise;

When I choose an husband, I hope to take a man.

MERRYGREEK. And where will ye find one which can
do that he can?

Now this man toward you being so kind,

You not to make him an answer somewhat to his
mind!

DAME CUSTANCE. I sent him a full answer by you,
did I not?

MERRYGREEK. And I reported it.

DAME CUSTANCE.   Nay, I must speak it again.   20

ROISTER DOISTER. No, no! he told it all.

MERRYGREEK.   Was I not meetly plain?

ROISTER DOISTER. Yes.

MERRYGREEK. But I would not tell all; for faith,
   if I had,

With you, Dame Custance, ere this hour it had been
   bad,

And not without cause, for this goodly personage

Meant no less than to join with you in marriage.

DAME CUSTANCE. Let him waste no more labour nor
   suit about me.

MERRYGREEK. Ye know not where your preferment*   advantage
   lieth, I see,

He sending you such a token, ring and letter.

DAME CUSTANCE. Marry, here it is; ye never saw a
   better!

(*She holds out a letter.*)

MERRYGREEK. Let us see your letter.

DAME CUSTANCE.   Hold, read it,
   if ye can.   30

And see what letter it is to win a woman!

MERRYGREEK. "To mine own dear coney, bird,
   sweetheart, and pigsny,*   darling

Good Mistress Custance, present these by and by."*   at once

Of this superscription do ye blame the style?

DAME CUSTANCE. With the rest as good stuff as ye
   read a great while!

MERRYGREEK (*reading*). "Sweet mistress, whereas I
   love you nothing at all,

Regarding your substance and riches chief of all,

For your personage, beauty, demeanour and wit

I commend me unto you never a whit.

Sorry to hear report of your good welfare.   40

For (as I hear say) such your conditions are

That ye be worthy favour of no living man;

To be abhorred of every honest man;

To be taken for a woman inclined to vice;

Nothing at all to virtue giving her due price.

Wherefore concerning marriage, ye are thought

Such a fine paragon, as ne'er honest man bought.

And now by these presents I do you advertise

That I am minded to marry you in no wise.

For your goods and substance, I could be content   50
To take you as ye are. If ye mind* to be my wife,   intend, desire
Ye shall be assured for the time of my life
I will keep you right well from good raiment and
    fare;
Ye shall not be kept but in sorrow and care.
Ye shall in no wise live at your own liberty;
Do and say what ye lust, ye shall never please me;
But when ye are merry, I will be all sad,
When ye are sorry, I will be very glad;
When ye seek your heart's ease, I will be unkind;
At no time, in me shall ye much gentleness find.   60
But all things contrary to your will and mind
Shall be done: otherwise I will not be behind
To speak. And as for all them that would do you
    wrong
I will so help and maintain, ye shall not live long.
Nor any foolish dolt shall cumber you but I.
I, whoe'er say nay, will stick by you till I die.
Thus good mistress Custance, the Lord you save and
    keep
From me Roister Doister, whether I wake or sleep.
Who favoureth you no less (ye may be bold)
Than this letter purporteth, which ye have unfold."   70
    DAME CUSTANCE. How by this letter of love? is it
        not fine?
    ROISTER DOISTER. By the arms of Calais, it is none
        of mine!
    MERRYGREEK. Fie, you are foul to blame! this is your
        own hand!
    DAME CUSTANCE (*sarcastically*). Might not a woman
        be proud of such an husband?
    MERRYGREEK. Ah, that ye would in a letter show
        such despite!
    ROISTER DOISTER. Oh, I would I had him here the
        which* did it endite.*   who/write
    MERRYGREEK. Why, ye made it yourself, ye told me
        by this light.
    ROISTER DOISTER. Yea, I meant I wrote it mine own
        self, yesternight.
    DAME CUSTANCE. Iwis,* sir, I would not have sent   assuredly
        you such a mock.
    ROISTER DOISTER. Ye may so take it, but I meant it
        not so, by Cock.   80

MERRYGREEK. Who can blame this woman to fume,
and fret, and rage?
Tut, tut! yourself now have marred your own marriage.
Well, yet, mistress Custance, if ye can this remit,
This gentleman otherwise may your love requit.*   requite
DAME CUSTANCE. No! God be with you both, and
seek no more to me.

> (*She leaves them in a huff.*)

ROISTER DOISTER. Wough! she is gone for ever! I
shall her no more see!
MERRYGREEK. What, weep? fie, for shame! and
blubber? For manhood's sake,
Never let your foe so much pleasure of you take!
Rather play the man's part, and do love refrain.
If she despise you, e'en despise ye her again!32   90
ROISTER DOISTER. By Goss, and for thy sake I defy
her indeed!
MERRYGREEK. Yea, and perchance that way ye shall
much sooner speed;
For one mad property these women have, in fey:*   faith
When ye will, they will not; will not ye, then will
they.
Ah, foolish woman! Ah, most unlucky Custance!
Ah, unfortunate woman! Ah, peevish Custance!
Art thou to thine harms so obstinately bent
That thou canst not see where lieth thine high prefer-
ment?
Canst thou not lub* dis man, which could lub dee*   love/thee
so well?
Art thou so much thine own foe?
ROISTER DOISTER.   Thou dost the truth
tell.   100
MERRYGREEK. Well, I lament.
ROISTER DOISTER.   So do I.
MERRYGREEK.   Wherefore?
ROISTER DOISTER.   For this thing
Because she is gone.
MERRYGREEK.   I mourn for another thing.
ROISTER DOISTER. What is it, Merrygreek, wherefore
thou dost grief take?
MERRYGREEK. That I am not a woman myself for
your sake,

---

32 That is, "despise her back."

I would have you myself, and a straw for yond Gill!*   wench
And mock much of you, though it were against my
    will.
I would not, I warrant you, fall in such a rage
As so to refuse such a goodly personage.
    ROISTER DOISTER. In faith, I heartily thank thee,
    Merrygreek.
    MERRYGREEK. An I were a woman——
    ROISTER DOISTER.   Thou would-
    est to me seek.   110
    MERRYGREEK. For, though I say it a goodly person
    ye be.
    ROISTER DOISTER. No, no.
    MERRYGREEK.   Yes, a goodly man as e'er
    I did see.
    ROISTER DOISTER. No, I am a poor homely man, as
    God made me.
    MERRYGREEK. By the faith that I owe to God, sir,
    but ye be!
Would I might, for your sake, spend a thousand
    pound land.
    ROISTER DOISTER. I dare say thou wouldest have me
    to thy husband.
    MERRYGREEK. Yea; an I were the fairest lady in the
    shire,
And knew you as I know you, and see you now here—
Well, I say no more!
    ROISTER DOISTER. Gramercies,* with all my heart!   thanks
    MERRYGREEK. But since that cannot be, will ye play
    a wise part?   120
    ROISTER DOISTER. How should I?
    MERRYGREEK.   Refrain from Custance awhile now,
And I warrant her soon right glad to seek to you.
Ye shall see her anon come on her knees creeping,
And pray you to be good to her, salt tears weeping.
    ROISTER DOISTER. But what an she come not?
    MERRYGREEK.   In
    faith, then, farewell she!
Or eles if ye be wroth,* ye may avenged be.   angry
    ROISTER DOISTER. By Cock's precious potstick, and
    e'en so I shall!
I will utterly destroy her, and house and all!
But I would be avenged in the mean space,
On that vile scribbler,* that did my wooing disgrace.   scrivener

MERRYGREEK. "Scribbler," ko* you? indeed, he is   quoth
worthy no less.   131
I will call him to you, and ye bid me, doubtless.
ROISTER DOISTER. Yes, for although he had as many
lives,
As a thousand widows, and a thousand wives,
As a thousand lions, and a thousand rats,
A thousand wolves, and a thousand cats,
A thousand bulls, and a thousand calves,
And a thousand legions divided in halves,
He shall never 'scape death on my sword's point—
Though I should be torn therefore joint by joint!   140
MERRYGREEK. Nay, if ye will kill him, I will not
fetch him;
I will not in so much extremity set him.
He may yet amend, sir, and be an honest man.
Therefore pardon him, good soul, as much as ye can.
ROISTER DOISTER. Well, for thy sake, this once with
his life he shall pass.
But I will hew him all to pieces, by the Mass!
MERRYGREEK. Nay, faith, ye shall promise that he
shall no harm have,
Else I will not fetch him.
ROISTER DOISTER.   I shall, so God me save!
But I may chide him a good?*   in earnest
MERRYGREEK.   Yea, that do hardily.
ROISTER DOISTER. Go, then.   150
MERRYGREEK. I return, and bring him to you by-and-by.
        (*Exit, leaving* ROISTER DOISTER *alone on the stage.*)

SCENE 5

ROISTER DOISTER. What is a gentleman but his word
and his promise?
I must now save this villain's life in any wise;
And yet at him already my hands do tickle,
I shall uneth hold them,[33] they will be so fickle.
        (*Enter* MERRYGREEK *and* SCRIVENER.)
But lo an Merrygreek have not brought him sens.*   already
MERRYGREEK. Nay, I would I had of my purse paid
forty pens!
SCRIVENER. So would I, too; but it needed not that
stound.*   at that time

        [33] "I shall find it difficult to keep my hands off him."

MERRYGREEK. But the gentman had rather spent
    five thousand pound;
For it disgraced him at least five times so much.
    SCRIVENER. He disgraced himself, his loutishness is
        such.
    ROISTER DOISTER. How long they stand prating!
        Why comest thou not away?   11
    MERRYGREEK. Come now to himself, and hark what
        he will say.
    SCRIVENER. I am not afraid in his presence to appear.
    ROISTER DOISTER. Art thou come, fellow?
    SCRIVENER.   How think
        you? am I not here?
    ROISTER DOISTER. What hindrance hast thou done
        me, and what villainy?
    SCRIVENER. It hath come of thyself, if thou hast had
        any.
    ROISTER DOISTER. All the stock thou comest of, later
        or rather,*   earlier
From thy first father's grandfather's father's father,
Nor all that shall come of thee, to the world's end,
Though to threescore generations they descend,   20
Can be able to make me a just recompense
For this trespass of thine and this one offence!
    SCRIVENER. Wherein?
    ROISTER DOISTER. Did not you make me a letter,
        brother?
    SCRIVENER. Pay the like hire, I will make you such
        another.
    ROISTER DOISTER. Nay, see and these whoreson
        Pharisees and Scribes
Do not get their living by polling* and bribes!   extortion
If it were not for shame——
    SCRIVENER.   Nay, hold thy hands still!
    MERRYGREEK. Why, did ye not promise that ye
        would not him spill?*   destroy
    SCRIVENER. Let him not spare me.
    ROISTER DOISTER.   Why, wilt thou
        strike me again?
    SCRIVENER. Ye shall have as good as ye bring, of me;
        that is plain.   30
    MERRYGREEK. I cannot blame him, sir, though your
        blows would him grieve.
For he knoweth present death to ensue of all ye give.

ROISTER DOISTER. Well, this man for once hath purchased thy pardon.

SCRIVENER. And what say ye to me? or else I will be
gone.

ROISTER DOISTER. I say the letter thou madest me
was not good.

SCRIVENER. Then did ye wrong copy it, of likelihood.

ROISTER DOISTER. Yes, out of thy copy word for
word I wrote.

SCRIVENER. Then was it as ye prayed to have it, I
wote,*   am certain
But in reading and pointing there was made some
fault.

ROISTER DOISTER. I wot not; but it made all my
matter to halt.   40

SCRIVENER. How say you, is this mine original or no?

ROISTER DOISTER. The self same that I wrote out of,
so mote I go.

SCRIVENER. Look you on your own fist,* and I   handwriting
will look on this,
And let this man be judge whether I read amiss.
"To mine own deal cony, bird, sweetheart, and
pigsny,
Good Mistress Custance, present these by-and-by."
How now? doth not this superscription agree?

ROISTER DOISTER. Read that is within, and there ye
shall the fault see.

SCRIVENER. "Sweet mistress, whereas I love you—
nothing at all
Regarding your riches and substance, chief of all   50
For your personage, beauty, demeanour and wit—
I commend me unto you. Never a whit
Sorry to hear report of your good welfare;
For (as I hear say) such your conditions are
That ye be worthy favour; of no living man
To be abhorred; of every honest man
To be taken for a woman inclined to vice
Nothing at all; to virtue giving her due price.
Wherefore, concerning marriage, ye are thought
Such a fine paragon, as ne'er honest man bought.   60
And now by these presents I do you advertise
That I am minded to marry you—in no wise
For your goods and substance: I can be content

To take you as you are. If ye will be my wife,
Ye shall be assured for the time of my life
I will keep you right well. From good raiment and
  fare,
Ye shall not be kept; but in sorrow and care
Ye shall in no wise live; at your own liberty,
Do and say what ye lust: ye shall never please me
But when ye are merry; I will be all sad   70
When ye are sorry; I will be very glad
When ye seek your heart's ease; I will be unkind
At no time; in me shall ye much gentleness find.
But all things contrary to your will and mind
Shall be done otherwise; I will not be behind
To speak. And as for all they that would do you
  wrong
(I will so help and maintain ye), shall not live long.
Nor any foolish dolt shall cumber you; but I—
I, whoe'er say nay—will stick by you till I die.
Thus, good mistress Custance, the Lord you save and
  keep.   80
From me, Roister Doister, whether I wake or sleep,
Who favoureth you no less (ye may be bold)
Than this letter purporteth, which ye have unfold."
Now, sir, what default can ye find in this letter?
   ROISTER DOISTER. Of truth, in my mind, there can-
    not be a better.
   SCRIVENER. Then was the fault in reading, and not
    in writing—
No, nor I dare say, in the form of enditing.*   writing
But who read this letter, that it sounded so naught?*   bad
   MERRYGREEK. I read it, indeed.
   SCRIVENER.   Ye read it not as ye ought.
   ROISTER DOISTER. Why, thou wretched villain! was
    all this same fault in thee?   90
   MERRYGREEK. I knock your costard* if ye offer to   head
    strike me!
   ROISTER DOISTER. Strikest thou, indeed? and I offer
    but in jest?
   MERRYGREEK. Yea, and rap you again except ye can
    sit in rest.
And I will no longer tarry here, me believe.
   ROISTER DOISTER. What! wilt thou be angry, and I
    do thee forgive?
Fare thou well, scribbler. I cry thee mercy indeed!

SCRIVENER. Fare ye well, bibbler, and worthily may
 ye speed!
ROISTER DOISTER. If it were another but thou, it
 were a knave.
MERRYGREEK. Ye are another yourself, sir, the Lord
 us both save!
Albeit, in this matter I must your pardon crave.   100
Alas! would ye wish in me the wit that ye have?
But, as for my fault, I can quickly amend;
I will show Custance it was I that did offend.
ROISTER DOISTER. By so doing, her anger may be
 reformed.*   appeased
MERRYGREEK. But, if by no entreaty she will be
 turned,
Then set light by her, and be as testy as she,
And do your force upon her with extremity.
ROISTER DOISTER. Come on, therefore, let us go
 home, in sadness.
MERRYGREEK. That, if force shall need, all may be
 in a readiness,
And as for this letter, hardily let all go;   110
We will know where* she refuse you for that or no. whether
       (*They leave the stage.*)

ACT IV

SCENE 1

(*Enter* SIM SURESBY.)
SURESBY. Is there any man but I, Sim Suresby,
 alone,
That would have taken such an enterprise him upon,
In such an outrageous tempest as this was,
Such a dangerous gulf of the sea to pass?
I think verily Neptune's mighty godship
Was angry with some that was in our ship;
And, but for the honesty which in me he found,
I think for the others' sake we had been drowned.
But fie on that servant which for his master's wealth* welfare
Will stick for to hazard both his life and his health! 10
My master, Gawyn Goodluck, after me a day,
Because of the weather, thought best his ship to stay,
And now that I have the rough surges so well past,
God grant I may find all things safe here at last!
Then will I think all my travail well spent.
Now the first point wherefore my master hath me sent

Is to salute Dame Christian Custance, his wife
Espoused, whom he tendereth no less than his life.
I must see how it is with her, well or wrong,
And whether for him she doth not now think long.   20
Then to other friends I have a message or tway;
And then so to return and meet him on the way.
Now will I go knock that I may dispatch with speed—
But lo, forth cometh herself, happily,* indeed!   luckily

SCENE 2

(SIM SURESBY. *Enter* DAME CUSTANCE.)
DAME CUSTANCE. I come to see if any more stirring
   be here.
But what stranger is this which doth to me appear?
   SURESBY. I will speak to her. Dame, the Lord you
   save and see!
   DAME CUSTANCE. What! friend Sim Suresby?
   Forsooth, right welcome ye be!
How doth mine own Gawyn Goodluck? I pray thee
   tell?
   SURESBY. When he knoweth of your health, he will
   be perfect well.
   DAME CUSTANCE. If he have perfect health, I am as
   I would be.
   SURESBY. Such news will please him well; this is as
   it should be.
   DAME CUSTANCE. I think now long for him.
   SURESBY.   And he as long for you.
   DAME CUSTANCE. When will he be at home?
   SURESBY.   His heart is here e'en now;   10
His body cometh after.
   DAME CUSTANCE.   I would see that fain.*   gladly
   SURESBY. As fast as wind and sail can carry it
   amain—
But what two men are yond coming hitherward?
   DAME CUSTANCE. Now, I shrew* their best   curse
   Christmas cheeks, both togetherward!

SCENE 3

(DAME CUSTANCE *and* SURESBY. *Enter* ROISTER
DOISTER *and* MERRYGREEK.)
DAME CUSTANCE. What mean these lewd fellows
   thus to trouble me still?

Sim Suresby here, perchance, shall thereof deem some
    ill,
And shall suspect in me some point of naughtiness,
An they come hitherward.
    Suresby.   What is their business?
    Dame Custance. I have nought to them, nor
      they to me in sadness.*   earnestness
    Suresby. Let us hearken them. Somewhat
      there is,* I fear it.   something is up
    Roister Doister. I will speak out aloud; best that
      she may hear it.
    Merrygreek. Nay, alas, ye may so fear her out of
      her wit!
    Roister Doister. By the cross of my sword, I will
      hurt her no whit!
    Merrygreek. Will ye do no harm indeed? Shall I
      trust your word?   10
    Roister Doister. By Roister Doister's faith, I will
      speak but in bord!*   jest
    Suresby. Let us hearken them. Somewhat there is,
      I fear it.
    Roister Doister. I will speak out aloud, I care not
      who hear it!
Sirs, see that my harness,* my target, and my shield   armor
Be made as bright now as when I was last in field,
As white as I should to war again to-morrow;
For sick shall I be but I work some folk sorrow.
Therefore see that all shine as bright as Saint George
Or as doth a key newly come from the smith's forge
I would have my sword and harness to shine so bright
That I might therewith dim mine enemies' sight,   21
I would have it cast beams as fast, I tell you plain,
As doth the glittering grass after a shower of rain.
And see that, in case I should need to come to arming,
All things may be ready at a minute's warning!
For such chance may chance in an hour, do ye hear?
    Merrygreek. As perchance shall not chance again
      in seven year.
    Roister Doister. Now draw we near to her, and
      hear what shall be said.
    Merrygreek. But I would not have you make her
      too much afraid.
    Roister Doister. Well found, sweet wife, I trust,
      for all this your sour look!   30

DAME CUSTANCE. Wife! why call ye me wife?

SURESBY.   Wife! this gear goeth acrook![34]

MERRYGREEK. Nay, Mistress Custance, I warrant
    you, our letter
Is not as we read e'en now, but much better;
And where ye half stomached* this gentleman afore   resented
For this same letter, ye will love him now therefore.
Nor it is not this letter, though ye were a queen,
That should break marriage between you twain,
    I ween.*   believe, think

DAME CUSTANCE. I did not refuse him for the
    letter's sake.

ROISTER DOISTER. Then ye are content me for your
    husband to take?

DAME CUSTANCE. You for my husband to take?
    nothing less, truly!   40

ROISTER DOISTER. Yea, say so, sweet spouse, afore
    strangers hardily!

MERRYGREEK. And, though I have here his letter of
    love with me,
Yet his ring and tokens he sent keep safe with ye.

DAME CUSTANCE. A mischief take his tokens! and
    him, and thee too.
But what prate I with fools? have I nought else to do?
Come in with me, Sim Suresby, to take some repast.

SURESBY (eager to get away). I must, ere I drink,
    by your leave, go in all haste
To a place or two, with earnest letters of his.

DAME CUSTANCE. Then come drink here with me.

SURESBY.   I thank you.

DAME CUSTANCE.   Do not miss;
You shall have a token to your master with you.   50

SURESBY. No tokens this time, gramercies!* God   thank you
    be with you

                    (He goes away hastily.)

DAME CUSTANCE. Surely this fellow misdeemeth
    some ill in me;
Which thing, but God help, will go near to spill* me.   destroy

ROISTER DOISTER. Yea, farewell, fellow! And tell
    thy master, Goodluck,
That he cometh too late of this blossom to pluck!

---

[34] "This business goes crooked"—this doesn't look right to me.

Let him keep him there still, or at leastwise, make no
    haste;
As for his labour hither, he shall spend in waste:
His betters be in place now!
    MERRYGREEK (*aside*).   As long as it will hold.
    DAME CUSTANCE. I will be even with thee, thou
    beast, thou mayst be bold!*   sure
    ROISTER DOISTER. Will ye have us then?
    DAME CUSTANCE.   I will never have thee!   60
    ROISTER DOISTER. Then will I have you.
    DAME CUSTANCE.   No, the devil shall have thee!
I have gotten this hour more shame and harm by
    thee!
Than all thy life days thou canst do me honesty.
    MERRYGREEK. Why now may ye see what it cometh
    to, in the end,
To make a deadly foe of your most loving friend!
And iwis,* this letter, if ye would hear it now——   certainly
    DAME CUSTANCE. I will hear none of it!
    MERRYGREEK.   In faith, would ravish you.
    DAME CUSTANCE. He hath stained my name for
    ever, this is clear.
    ROISTER DOISTER. I can make all as well in an hour—
    MERRYGREEK.   As ten year.
How say ye? will ye have him?
    DAME CUSTANCE.   No.
    MERRYGREEK.   Will ye take him?   70
    DAME CUSTANCE. I defy him.
    MERRYGREEK.   At my word?
    DAME CUSTANCE.   A shame take him!
Waste no more wind, for it will never be.
    MERRYGREEK. This one fault with twain shall be
    mended, ye shall see.
Gentle Mistress Custance now, sweet Mistress
    Custance,
Honey Mistress Custance now, sweet Mistress
    Custance,
Golden Mistress Custance now, white* Mistress   dear
    Custance,
Silken Mistress Custance now, fair Mistress
    Custance—
    DAME CUSTANCE. Faith, rather than to marry with
    such a doltish lout,
I would match myself with a beggar, out of doubt!

MERRYGREEK. Then I can say no more. To speed
   we are not like,   80
Except ye rap out a rag of your rhetoric.
   DAME CUSTANCE. Speak not of winning me; for it
      shall never be so.
   ROISTER DOISTER. Yes, dame! I will have you,
      whether ye will or no.
I command you to love me! Wherefore should ye not?
Is not my love to you chafing and burning hot?
   MERRYGREEK. To her! that is well said!
   ROISTER DOISTER.   Shall I so break my brain
To dote upon you, and ye not love us again?
   MERRYGREEK. Well said yet!
   DAME CUSTANCE.   Go, to, you goose!
   ROISTER DOISTER.   I say, Kit Custance,
In case ye will not haze,* well, better yes, perchance!   have us
   DAME CUSTANCE. Avaunt, lozel!* Pick thee hence!   lout
   MERRYGREEK.   Well, sir, ye perceive,   90
For all your kind offer, she will not you receive.
   ROISTER DOISTER. Then a straw for her! And a
      straw for her again!
She shall not be my wife, would she never so fain!*   eager
No, and though she would be at ten thousand pound
   cost!*   worth
   MERRYGREEK. Lo, dame, ye may see what an
      husband ye have lost!
   DAME CUSTANCE. Yea, no force;* a jewel much   matter
      better lost than found!
   MERRYGREEK. Ah, ye will not believe how this doth
      my heart wound!
How should a marriage between you be toward,
If both parties draw back and become so froward?*   cantankerous
   ROISTER DOISTER. Nay, dame, I will fire thee out of
      thy house,   100
And destroy thee and all thine, and that by and by.*   soon
   MERRYGREEK. Nay, for the passion of God, sir, do
      not so!
   ROISTER DOISTER. Yes, except she will say yea to
      that* she said no.   what
   DAME CUSTANCE. And what! be there no officers,
      trow we, in town
To check idle loiterers bragging up and down?
Where be they by whom vagabonds should be
   represt,

That poor silly* widows might live in peace and   defenseless
    rest.

Shall I never rid thee out of my company?

I will call for help. What ho! come forth, Truepenny!
    (*Enter* TRUEPENNY.)

    TRUEPENNY. Anon. What is your will, mistress? did
       ye call me?   110

    DAME CUSTANCE. Yea; go run apace, and as fast as
       may be,

Pray Tristram Trusty, my most assured friend,

To be here by and by,* that he may me defend.   at once

    TRUEPENNY. That message so quickly shall be done,
       by God's grace,

That at my return ye shall say, I went apace.
                         (*He runs off.*)

    DAME CUSTANCE. Then shall we see, I trow, whether
       ye shall do me harm!

    ROISTER DOISTER. Yes, in faith, Kit, I shall thee
       and thine so charm,*   overwhelm

That all women incarnate by thee may beware.

    DAME CUSTANCE. Nay, as for charming me, come
       hither if thou dare!

I shall clout thee till thou stink, both thee and thy
    train,   120

And coil* thee mine own hands, and send thee home   beat
    again.

    ROISTER DOISTER. Yea, sayest thou me that, dame?
       Dost thou me threaten?

Go we, I will see whether I shall be beaten.

    MERRYGREEK. Nay, for the pash* of God, let me   Passion
       now treat peace,

For bloodshed will there be, in case this strife
    increase.

Ah, good Dame Custance, take better way with you!

    DAME CUSTANCE. Let him do his worst!

    MERRYGREEK.   Yield in time.

    ROISTER DOISTER.   Come hence, thou!
       (ROISTER DOISTER *and* MERRYGREEK *go off.*)

SCENE 4

(DAME CUSTANCE *left alone.*)

    DAME CUSTANCE. So, sirrah! If I should not with
       him take this way,

I should not be rid of him, I think, till doom's day.
I will call forth my folks, that, without any mocks.
If he comes again, we may give him raps and knocks.
Madge Mumblecrust, come forth! and Tibet Talka-
    pace!
Yea, and come forth, too, Mistress Annot Alyface!
    (*Enter* TIBET TALKAPACE, ANNOT ALYFACE, *and*
    MARGERY MUMBLECRUST.)
    ALYFACE. I come.
    TALKAPACE.   And I am here.
    MUMBLECRUST.   And I am here
    too at length.
    DAME CUSTANCE. Like warriors, if need be, ye must
    show your strength.
The man that this day hath thus beguiled you
Is Ralph Roister Doister, whom ye know well
    enow,*   enough/10
The most lout and dastard that ever on ground trod.
    TALKAPACE. I see all folk mock him when he goeth
    abroad.
    DAME CUSTANCE. What, pretty maid! will ye talk
    when I speak?
    TALKAPACE. No, forsooth, good mistress.
    DAME CUSTANCE.   Will ye my
    tale break?
He threateneth to come hither with all his force to
    fight;
I charge you, if he come, on him with all your might!
    MUMBLECRUST. I with my distaff will reach him one
    rap!
    TALKAPACE. And I with my new broom will sweep
    him one swap,
And then with our great club I will reach him one
    rap!
    ALYFACE. And I with our skimmer will fling him
    one flap!
    TALKAPACE. Then Truepenny's firework will him
    shrewdly fray,
And you with the spit may drive him quite away.
    DAME CUSTANCE. Go, make all ready, that it may be
    e'en so.
    TALKAPACE. For my part, I shrew* them that last   scorn
    about it go!
    (TIBET *and* ANNOT ALYFACE *go to arm themselves.*)

Scene 5

(DAME CUSTANCE, *left alone.*)

DAME CUSTANCE. Truepenny did promise me to run
    a great pace,
My friend Tristram Trusty to fetch into this place.
Indeed he dwelleth hence a good start,* I confess;   distance
But yet a quick messenger might twice since, as I
    guess,
Have gone and come again. Ah, yond I spy him now!
    (*Enter* TRUEPENNY *and* TRISTRAM TRUSTY.)
    TRUEPENNY. Ye are a slow goer, sir, I make God
    avow;
My mistress Custance will in me put all the blame.
Your legs be longer than mine; come apace,* for   fast
    shame!
    DAME CUSTANCE. I can thee thank, Truepenny;
    thou hast done right well.
    TRUEPENNY. Mistress, since I went, no grass hath
    grown on my heel;   10
But Master Tristram Trusty here maketh no speed.
    DAME CUSTANCE. That he came at all, I thank him
    in very deed,
For now have I need of the help of some wise man.
    TRUSTY. Then may I be gone again, for none such
    I am.
    TRUEPENNY. Ye may be by your going; for no alder-
    man
Can go, I dare say, a sadder* pace than ye can.   more solemn
    DAME CUSTANCE. Truepenny, get thee in. Thou
    shalt among them know
How to use thyself, like a proper man, I trow.
    TRUEPENNY. I go.

                                       (*Exit.*)
    DAME CUSTANCE. Now, Tristram Trusty, I thank
    you right much;
For, at my first sending, to come ye never grutch.*   grudge/20
    TRUSTY. Dame Custance, God ye save! and, while
    my life shall last,
For my friend Goodluck's sake ye shall not send in
    wast.*   in vain
    DAME CUSTANCE. He shall give you thanks.
    TRUSTY.   I will do
    much for his sake.

DAME CUSTANCE. But, alack, I fear, great displeasure
   shall be take!
TRUSTY. Wherefore?
DAME CUSTANCE.   For a foolish matter.
TRUSTY.   What is
   your cause?
DAME CUSTANCE. I am ill accombred* with a   encumbered
   couple of daws.*   fools
TRUSTY. Nay, weep not, woman, but tell me what
   your cause is.
As concerning my friend is anything amiss?
   DAME CUSTANCE. No, not on my part; but here was
   Sim Suresby—
   TRUSTY. He was with me and told me so.
DAME CUSTANCE.   And he
   stood by   30
While Ralph Roister Doister, with help of Merry-
   greek,
For promise of marriage did unto me seek.
   TRUSTY. And had ye made any promise before them
   twain?
   DAME CUSTANCE. No; I had rather be torn in pieces
   and slain!
No man hath my faith and troth but Gawyn Good-
   luck,
And that before Suresby did I say, and there stuck,
But of certain letters there were such words spoken—
   TRUSTY. He told me that too.
DAME CUSTANCE.   And of a ring, and
   token,
That Suresby, I spied, did more than half suspect
That I my faith to Gawyn Goodluck did reject.   40
   TRUSTY. But there was no such matter, Dame
   Custance, indeed?
   DAME CUSTANCE. If ever my head thought it, God
   send me ill speed!
Wherefore I beseech you, with me to be a witness
That in all my life I never intended things less,
And what a brainsick fool Ralph Roister Doister is
Yourself know well enough.
   TRUSTY.   Ye say full true, iwis!*   assuredly
   DAME CUSTANCE. Because to be his wife I nor grant
   nor apply,*   consider
Hither will he come, he sweareth, by and by,*   immediately

To kill both me and mine, and beat down my house
flat.
Therefore I pray your aid.

TRUSTY.   I warrant you that.   50

DAME CUSTANCE. Have I so many years lived a sober
life,
And showed myself honest, maid, widow, and wife,
And now to be abused in such a vile sort?
Ye see how poor widows live, all void of comfort!

TRUSTY. I warrant him do you no harm nor wrong
at all.

DAME CUSTANCE. No; but Mathew Merrygreek doth
me most appal,
That he would join himself with such a wretched
lout.

TRUSTY. He doth it for a jest; I know him out of
doubt,
And here cometh Merrygreek.

DAME CUSTANCE.   Then shall we hear his mind.

SCENE 6

(DAME CUSTANCE *and* TRUSTY. *Enter* MERRYGREEK.)

MERRYGREEK. Custance and Trusty both, I do you
here well find.

DAME CUSTANCE. Ah, Matthew Merrygreek, ye have
used me well!

MERRYGREEK. Now for altogether ye must your
answer tell:
Will ye have this man, woman? or else, will ye not?
Else will he come—never boar so brim* nor toast so   furious
hot.

TRUSTY *and* DAME CUSTANCE. But why join ye with
him?

TRUSTY. For mirth?

DAME CUSTANCE.   Or else in sadness?*   seriously

MERRYGREEK. The more fond* of you both!   foolish
hardily* the matter guess.   surely

TRUSTY. Lo, how say ye, dame?

MERRYGREEK.   Why do ye think, Dame Custance,
That in this wooing I have meant aught but pas-
tance?*   pastime

DAME CUSTANCE. Much things ye spake, I wot,* to   know
maintain his dotage.   10

MERRYGREEK. But well might ye judge I spake it all
  in mockage.
For why, is Roister Doister a fit husband for you?
  TRUSTY. I daresay ye never thought it.
  MERRYGREEK.   No; to God
  I vow!
And did not I know afore of the insurance*   engagement
Between Gawyn Goodluck and Christian Custance?
And did not I for the nonce, by my conveyance,*   cunning
Read his letter in a wrong sense for dalliance?
That, if you could have take it up at the first bound,
We should thereat such a sport and pastime have
  found,
That all the whole town should have been the merrier?   20
  DAME CUSTANCE. Ill ache your heads both I was
  never wearier,
Nor never more vexed, since the first day I was born!
  TRUSTY. But very well I wish* he here did all in   knew
  scorn*   fun
  DAME CUSTANCE. But I feared thereof to take dis-
  honesty.*   dishonor
  MERRYGREEK. This should both have made sport
  and showed your honesty;
And Goodluck, I dare swear, your wit therein would
  'low.*   approve
  TRUSTY. Yea, being no worse than we know it to be
  now.
  MERRYGREEK. And nothing yet too late; for, when
  I come to him,
Hither will he repair with a sheep's look full grim,
By plain force and violence to drive you to yield,   30
  DAME CUSTANCE. If ye two bid me, we will with
  him pitch a field,
I and my maids together.
  MERRYGREEK.   Let us see! be bold!
  DAME CUSTANCE. Ye shall see women's war!
  TRUSTY.   That
  fight will I behold.
  MERRYGREEK. If occasion serve, taking his part full
  brim,*   furiously
I will strike at you, but the rap shall light on him,
When we first appear.
  DAME CUSTANCE.   Then will I run away
As though I were afeard.

TRUSTY.   Do you that part well play;
And I will sue for peace.
   MERRYGREEK.   And I will set him on.
Then will he look as fierce as a Cotswold lion.*   sheep
   TRUSTY. But when goest thou for him?
   MERRYGREEK.   That do I
   very now.   40
   DAME CUSTANCE. Ye shall find us here.
   MERRYGREEK.   Well, God have mercy on you!
                              (*He goes off.*)
   TRUSTY. There is no cause of fear. The least boy
   in the street——
   DAME CUSTANCE. Nay, the least girl I have will
   make him take his feet.
But hark! methink they make preparation.
   TRUSTY. No force,* it will be a good recreation.   no matter
   DAME CUSTANCE. I will stand within, and step forth
   speedily,
And so make as though I ran away dreadfully.*   fearfully
                              (*They go off.*)

SCENE 7

(*Enter* ROISTER DOISTER, DOUGHTY, HARPAX,   drummers/
MERRYGREEK *and two drums* with their ensigns.*)   standards
   ROISTER DOISTER. Now, sirs, keep your 'ray;* and   ranks
   see your hearts be stout!
But where be these caitiffs? me think they dare not
   rout!*   stir
How sayest thou, Merrygreek? What doth Kit Cus-
   tance say?
   MERRYGREEK. I am loth to tell you.
   ROISTER DOISTER.   Tush, speak,
   man! yea or nay?
   MERRYGREEK. Forsooth, sir, I have spoken for you
   all that I can.
But, if ye win her, ye must e'en play the man;
E'en to fight it out ye must a man's heart take.
   ROISTER DOISTER. Yes, they shall know, and thou
   knowest, I have a stomacke.*   (am brave)
   MERRYGREEK. "A stomach," quod* you, yea, as good   say
   as e'er man had.
   ROISTER DOISTER. I trow they shall find and feel
   that I am a lad.   10

MERRYGREEK. By this cross, I have seen you eat
  your meat as well[35]
As any that e'er I have seen of or heard tell!
"A stomach," quod you? he that will that deny,
I know was never at dinner in your company!
  ROISTER DOISTER. Nay, the stomach of a man it is
    that I mean!
  MERRYGREEK. Nay, the stomach of a horse, or a dog,
    I ween.
  ROISTER DOISTER. Nay, a man's stomach with a
    weapon, mean I.
  MERRYGREEK. Ten men can scarce match you with a
    spoon in a pie.
  ROISTER DOISTER. Nay, the stomach of a man to try
    in strife.
  MERRYGREEK. I never saw your stomach cloyed yet
    in my life.   20
  ROISTER DOISTER. Tush! I mean in strife or fighting
    to try.
  MERRYGREEK. We shall see how ye will strike now,
    being angry.
  ROISTER DOISTER. Have at thy pate,* then! and save   head
    thy head if thou may!
  MERRYGREEK. Nay, then, have at your pate again,
    by this day!
  ROISTER DOISTER. Nay, thou mayst not strike at me
    again, in no wise.
  MERRYGREEK. I cannot in fight make to you such
    warrantise.
But as for your foes here, let them the bargain 'by.*   abide
  ROISTER DOISTER. Nay, as for they, shall every
    mother's child die.
And in this my fume a little thing might make me
To beat down house and all, and else the devil take
    me!   30
  MERRYGREEK. If I were as ye be, by Gog's dear
    mother,
I would not leave one stone upon another,
Though she would redeem it with twenty thousand
    pounds.
  ROISTER DOISTER. It shall be even so, by His lily*   lovely
    wounds!

---

[35] Merrygreek is playing on the word, taking "stomach" literally, whereas
Ralph Roister used it figuratively as signifying bravery.

MERRYGREEK. Be not at one with her upon any
  amends.
ROISTER DOISTER. No, though she make to me never
  so many friends,
Nor if all the world for her would undertake;
No, not God himself, neither, shall not her peace
  make!
On, therefore! March forward! Soft; stay awhile yet!
MERRYGREEK. On!
ROISTER DOISTER.   Tarry!
MERRYGREEK.   Forth!
ROISTER DOISTER.   Back!
MERRYGREEK.   On!
ROISTER DOISTER.   Soft!
  Now forward set!   40
(*Enter* DAME CUSTANCE.)
DAME CUSTANCE. What business have we here? Out!
  alas, alas!

        (*She pretends fear and runs away.*)
ROISTER DOISTER. Ha, ha, ha, ha, ha!
Didst thou see that, Merrygreek? how afraid she was?
Didst thou see how she fled apace* out of my sight?   quickly
Ah, good sweet Custance! I pity her, by this light!
MERRYGREEK. That tender heart of yours will mar
  altogether.
Thus will ye be turned with wagging of a feather?
ROISTER DOISTER. On, sirs; keep your 'ray!*   ranks
MERRYGREEK.   On! Forth, while this gear* is hot!   affair
ROISTER DOISTER. Soft! The arms of Calais!36 I have
  one thing forgot.
MERRYGREEK. What lack we now?
ROISTER DOISTER.   Retire! or else we be all slain!   50
MERRYGREEK. Back! for the pash of God! back, sirs!
  back again!
What is the great matter?
ROISTER DOISTER.   This hasty forthgoing
Had almost brought us all to utter undoing!
It made me forget a thing most necessary.
MERRYGREEK. Well, remembered of a captain, by
  Saint Mary!
ROISTER DOISTER. It is a thing must be had.
MERRYGREEK.   Let us
  have it, then.

36 A swearing expression.

ROISTER DOISTER. But I wot not where, nor how.

MERRYGREEK.   Then wot not I when.
But what is it?

ROISTER DOISTER. Of a chief thing I am to seek.

MERRYGREEK. Tut! so will ye be, when ye have
    studied a week.
But tell me what it is.

ROISTER DOISTER.   I lack yet an headpiece.*   helmet

MERRYGREEK. The kitchen collocavit*—the best   pail
    hence to Greece,   61
Run, fetch it, Dobinet, and come at once withal,
And bring with thee my potgun,* hanging by the   pistol
    wall!
                        (*Exit* DOUGHTY.)
I have seen your head with it full many a time
Covered as safe as it had been with a skrine;*   screen
And I warrant it save your head from any stroke,
Except perchance to be amazed with the smoke;
I warrant your head therewith—except for the mist—
As safe as if it were fast locked up in a chist,*   chest
And lo, here our Dobinet cometh with it now!   70
    (DOUGHTY *brings the pail.*)

DOUGHTY. It will cover me to the shoulders well
    enow.

MERRYGREEK. Let me see it on.

ROISTER DOISTER.   In faith, it doth
    meetly well.

MERRYGREEK. There can be no fitter thing. Now ye
    must us tell
What to do.

ROISTER DOISTER. Now forth in 'ray,* sirs! and stop   array
    no more!

MERRYGREEK. Now Saint George to borrow![37] Drum,
    dub-a-dub afore!
    (*Enter* TRUSTY.)

TRUSTY. What mean you to do, sir? commit man-
    slaughter?

ROISTER DOISTER. To kill forty such is a matter of
    laughter.

TRUSTY. And who is it, sir, whom ye intend thus to
    spill?*   destroy

ROISTER DOISTER. Foolish Custance, here, forceth
    me against my will.

---

[37] "Now, let Saint George protect us!"

TRUSTY. And is there no mean* your extreme wrath to slake?   *means

She shall some amends unto your good maship make.   80

ROISTER DOISTER. I will none amends.

TRUSTY.   Is her offence so sore?

MERRYGREEK. An he were a lout, she could have done no more.

She hath called him fool, and dressed* him like a fool,   *treated

Mocked him like a fool, used him like a fool.

TRUSTY. Well, yet the sheriff, the justice, or constable,

Her misdemeanour to punish might be able.

ROISTER DOISTER. No, sir! I mine own self will in this present cause

Be sheriff, and justice, and whole judge of the laws,

This matter to amend, all officers be I shall—   90

Constable, bailiff, sergeant—

MERRYGREEK.   And hangman and all.

TRUSTY. Yet a noble courage, and the heart of a man,

Should more honour win by bearing with a woman.

Therefore take the law, and let her answer thereto.

ROISTER DOISTER. Merrygreek, the best way were even so to do.

What honour should it be with a woman to fight?

MERRYGREEK. And what then! will ye thus forgo and lose your right?

ROISTER DOISTER. Nay, I will take the law on her withouten grace.

TRUSTY. Or, if your maship could pardon this one trespace,

I pray you forgive her.

ROISTER DOISTER.   Hoh!

(*Giving the sign to halt the fight.*)

MERRYGREEK.   Tush! tush, sir, do not!   100

Be good, master, to her.

ROISTER DOISTER.   Hoh!

MERRYGREEK (*pretending combativeness*).

                Tush, I say, do not!

And what! shall your people here return straight home?

TRUSTY. Yea; levy the camp, sirs, and hence again, each one!

ROISTER DOISTER. But be still in readiness if I hap to call;

I cannot tell what sudden chance may befall.

MERRYGREEK. Do not off your harness,* sirs, I you   armor
advise,

At the least for this fortnight, in no manner wise:

Perchance in an hour when all ye think least,

Our master's appetite to fight will be best.

But soft; Ere ye go, have one at Custance house!   110

ROISTER DOISTER. Soft, what wilt thou do?

MERRYGREEK.   Once discharge my harque-
bouse;*   arquebus

And, for my heart's ease, have once more with my potgun.

ROISTER DOISTER. Hold thy hands! else is all our purpose fordone.

MERRYGREEK. An* it cost me my life!   if

ROISTER DOISTER.   I say thou shalt not!

MERRYGREEK. By the matte,[38] but I will! Have once more with hail shot!

I will have some pennyworth. I will not lose all.

SCENE 8

(MERRYGREEK, ROISTER DOISTER, DOUGHTY, HARPAX, and drums* before. Enter DAME CUSTANCE.)   drummers

DAME CUSTANCE. What caitiffs are those that so shake my house wall?

MERRYGREEK (pretending anger). Ah, sirrah! now, Custance, if ye had so much wit,

I would see you ask pardon, and yourselves submit.

DAME CUSTANCE. Have I still this ado with a couple of fools?

MERRYGREEK. Hear ye what she saith?

DAME CUSTANCE. Maidens come forth with your tools!

(Enter ANNOT ALYFACE, TIBET TALKAPACE, MARGE MUMBLECRUST, and TRUEPENNY.)

ROISTER DOISTER (calling out warily). In a ray!*   take your ranks

MERRYGREEK.   Dub-
badub, sirrah!

[38] Perhaps "by the Mass."

ROISTER DOISTER. In a ray!

They come suddenly on us.

    MERRYGREEK.   Dubbadub!

    ROISTER DOISTER.   In a ray!

That ever I was born, we are taken tardy!

    MERRYGREEK. Now, sirs, quit* ourselves like tall*   prove/brave
    men and hardy.

    DAME CUSTANCE. On afore, Truepenny! Hold thine
    own, Annot!   10

On toward them, Tibet! for 'scape us they cannot.

Come forth, Madge Mumblecrust! to stand fast
    togither.

    MERRYGREEK. God send us a fair day!

    ROISTER DOISTER.   See, they march
    on hither.

    TALKAPACE. But, mistress!

    DAME CUSTANCE.   What sayest thou?

    TALKAPACE.   Shall
    I go fetch our goose?

    DAME CUSTANCE. What to do?

    TALKAPACE. To yonder captain I will turn her
    loose:

An she gape and hiss at him, as she doth at me,

I durst jeopard my hand she will make him flee.

    DAME CUSTANCE. On Forward!

    ROISTER DOISTER.   They come!

    MERRYGREEK.   Stand!

    ROISTER DOISTER.   Hold!

    MERRYGREEK.   Keep!

    ROISTER DOISTER. There!

    MERRYGREEK.   Strike!

    ROISTER DOISTER.   Take heed.

    DAME CUSTANCE. Well said, Truepenny!

    TRUEPENNY.   Ah,
    whoresons!

    DAME CUSTANCE. Well done, indeed.

    MERRYGREEK. Hold thine own, Harpax! Down with
    them, Dobinet!   20

    DAME CUSTANCE. Now, Madge! Here, Annot! Now,
    stick them, Tibet!

    TALKAPACE. All my chief quarrel is to this same
    little knave

That beguiled me last day. Nothing shall him save.

DOUGHTY. Down with this little quean that hath at
    me such spite!
Save you from her, master; it is a very sprite!
    DAME CUSTANCE. I myself will Mounsire Grand
    Captain undertake!
    ROISTER DOISTER. They win ground.
    MERRYGREEK.   Save yourself,
    sir, for God's sake!
    ROISTER DOISTER. Out alas! I am slain! help!
    MERRYGREEK.   Save
    yourself!
    ROISTER DOISTER. Alas!
    (*He pretends to strike at* CUSTANCE *but hits* ROISTER
    DOISTER *instead.*)
    MERRYGREEK. Nay, then, have at you, mistress!
    ROISTER DOISTER.   Thou
    hittest me, alas!
    MERRYGREEK. I will strike at Custance here.
    ROISTER DOISTER.   Thou
    hittest me!
    MERRYGREEK. So I will!   30
Nay, mistress Custance.
    (*Hits* ROISTER DOISTER *again.*)
    ROISTER DOISTER.   Alas, thou hittest me still!
    MERRYGREEK. Save yourself, sir.
    ROISTER DOISTER.   Help! out! alas, I
    am slain!
    MERRYGREEK. Truce! hold your hands! truce for a
    pissing-while or twain!
Nay, how say you, Custance. For saving of your life,
Will ye yield, and grant to be this gentman's wife?
    DAME CUSTANCE. Ye told me he loved me. Call ye
    this love?
    MERRYGREEK. He loved awhile, even like a turtle-
    dove.
    DAME CUSTANCE. Gay love, God save it, so soon hot,
    so soon cold!
    MERRYGREEK. I am sorry for you. He could love you
    yet, so he could.
    ROISTER DOISTER. Nay, by Cock's precious, she shall
    be none of mine.   40
    MERRYGREEK. Why so?
    ROISTER DOISTER. Come away. By the matte, she is
    mankine!*   like a man

I durst adventure* the loss of my right hand   wager
If she did not slay her other husband:
And see, if she prepare not again to fight!

> MERRYGREEK. What then? Saint George to borrow,*   defend
> our ladies' knight!

> ROISTER DOISTER. Slay else whom she will, by Gog,
> she shall not slay me!

> MERRYGREEK. How then?

> ROISTER DOISTER.   Rather than to be slain, I will flee.

> DAME CUSTANCE. To it again, my knightesses! down
> with them all!

> ROISTER DOISTER. Away, away, away! She will else
> kill us all!

> MERRYGREEK. Nay, stick to it, like an hardy man
> and a tall.   50

> ROISTER DOISTER. Oh, bones! thou hittest me! Away,
> or else die we shall!

> MERRYGREEK. Away, for the pash of our sweet Lord
> Jesus Christ.

> DAME CUSTANCE. Away, lout and lubber! or I shall
> be thy priest.[39]

(MERRYGREEK, ROISTER DOISTER, *and his men run away.*)
So this field is ours, we have driven them all away.

> TALKAPACE. Thanks to God, mistress, ye have had
> a fair day

> DAME CUSTANCE. Well, now go ye in, and make
> yourself some good cheer.

> ALL. We go.

> TRUSTY.   Ah, sir, what a field* we have had   fight
> here!

> DAME CUSTANCE. Friend Tristram, I pray you, be a
> witness with me.

> TRUSTY. Dame Custance, I shall depose* for your   vouch
> honesty,

And now fare ye well, except something else ye
wold.[40]   60

> DAME CUSTANCE. Not now; but when I need to
> send, I will be bold.

I thank you for these pains.

(TRUSTY *leaves.*)

[39] "I shall finish you off,"—"perform the last office for you like a priest."
[40] "Unless you want something else."

                              And now I will get me in.
Now Roister Doister will no more wooing begin!
                                   (She goes off.)

ACT V

SCENE 1

(Enter GAWYN GOODLUCK *and* SIM SURESBY.*)*
GOODLUCK. Sim Suresby, my trusty man, now advise
     thee well,
And see that no false surmises thou me tell:
Was there such ado about Custance, of a truth?
  SURESBY. To report that* I heard and saw, to me   what
     is ruth,*   painful
But both my duty and name and property*   character
Warneth me to you to show fidelity.
It may be well enough, and I wish it so to be;
She may herself discharge,* and try* her honesty,   vindicate/prove
Yet their claim to her, methought, was very large,
For with letters, rings and tokens they did her charge:
Which when I heard and saw, I would none to you
     bring.   11
  GOODLUCK. No, by Saint Marie! I allow* thee in   approve
     that thing!
Ah, sirrah, now I see truth in the proverb old:
All things that shineth is not by and by* pure   immediately
     gold.
If any do live a woman of honesty,
I would have sworn Christian Custance had been she.
  SURESBY. Sir, though I to you be a servant true and
     just,
Yet do not ye therefore your faithful spouse mis-
     trust;
But examine the matter, and if ye shall it find
To be all well, be not ye for my words unkind.   20
  GOODLUCK. I shall do that* is right, and as I see   what
     cause why.
But here cometh Custance forth; we shall know by
     and by.

SCENE 2

*(*GOODLUCK *and* SURESBY. *Enter* DAME CUSTANCE.*)*
DAME CUSTANCE. I come forth to see and hearken
     for news good,

For about this hour is the time, of likelihood,
That Gawyn Goodluck, by the sayings of Suresby,
Would be at home. And lo, yond I see him, I!
What! Gawyn Goodluck, the only hope of my life!
Welcome home! and kiss me, your true espoused wife!

GOODLUCK. Nay, soft, Dame Custance! I must first,
    by your licence,*   permission
See whether all things be clear in your conscience.
I hear of your doings to me very strange.

DAME CUSTANCE. What, fear ye that my faith to-
    wards you should change?   10

GOODLUCK. I must needs mistrust ye be elsewhere
    entangled,
For I hear that certain men with you have wrangled
About the promise of marriage by you to them made.

DAME CUSTANCE. Could any man's report your mind
    therein persuade?

GOODLUCK. Well, ye must therein declare yourself to
    stand clear,
Else I and you, Dame Custance, may not join this
    year.

DAME CUSTANCE. Then would I were dead, and fair
    laid in my grave!
Ah, Suresby! is this the honesty that ye have
To hurt me with your report, not knowing the thing?

SURESBY. If ye be honest, my words can hurt you
    nothing;   20
But what I heard and saw, I might not but report.

DAME CUSTANCE. Ah, Lord, help poor widows, desti-
    tute of comfort!
Truly, most dear spouse, nought was done but for
    pastance.

GOODLUCK. But such kind of sporting is homely*   unbecoming
    dalliance.*   sport

DAME CUSTANCE. If ye knew the truth, ye would
    take all in good part.

GOODLUCK. By your leave, I am not half well skilled
    in that art.

DAME CUSTANCE. It was none but Roister Doister,
    that foolish, mome.*   dolt

GOODLUCK. Yea, Custance, "Better," they say, "a bad
    'scuse than none."

DAME CUSTANCE. Why, Tristram Trusty, sir, your
    true and faithful friend,

Was privy both to the beginning and the end.   30
Let him be the judge, and for me testify.
   GOODLUCK. I will the more credit that he shall verify.
And because I will the truth know e'en as it is,
I will to him myself, and know all without miss.
Come on, Sim Suresby, that before my friend thou
     may
Avouch the same words which thou didst to me say.
                    (GOODLUCK *and* SURESBY *go off*.)

SCENE 3

(DAME CUSTANCE *solo*.)
   DAME CUSTANCE. O Lord! how necessary it is now
     of days,
That each body live uprightly all manner ways;
For let never so little a gap be open,
And be sure of this—the worst shall be spoken!
How innocent stand I in this for deed or thought!
And yet see what mistrust towards me it hath wrought!
But thou, Lord, knowest all folks' thoughts and eke*   also
     intents,
And thou art the deliverer of all innocents.
Thou didst help the advoutress* that she might be   adulteress
     amended;
Much more, then, help, Lord, that* never ill in-   one who
     tended!
Thou didst help Susanna,[41] wrongfully accused,   11
And no less dost thou see, Lord, how I am now abused.
Thou didst help Hester,* when she should have died,   Esther
Help also, good Lord, that my truth may be tried!
Yet if Gawyn Goodluck with Tristram Trusty speak,
I trust of ill report the force shall be but weak.
And lo! yond they come, sadly talking together.
I will abide, and not shrink for their coming hither.

SCENE 4

(DAME CUSTANCE. *Enter* GOODLUCK, TRUSTY, *and*
SURESBY.)
   GOODLUCK. And was it none other than ye to me
     report?
   TRUSTY. No; and here were ye wished to have seen
     the sport.

---

[41] The heroine of the apocryphal book *Susanna and the Elders*.

GOODLUCK. Would I had, rather than half of that in
my purse!

SURESBY. And I do much rejoice the matter was no
worse.

And, like as to open it I was to you faithful,

So of Dame Custance' honest truth I am joyful;

For God forfend that I should hurt her by false report.

GOODLUCK. Well, I will no longer hold her in discomfort

DAME CUSTANCE. Now come they hitherward. I trust
all shall be well.

GOODLUCK. Sweet Custance, neither heart can think
nor tongue tell   10

How much I joy in your constant fidelity.

Come now, kiss me, the pearl of perfect honesty!

DAME CUSTANCE. God let me no longer to continue
in life

Than I shall towards you continue a true wife!

GOODLUCK. Well, now to make you for this some
part of amends,

I shall desire first you, and then such of our friends

As shall to you seem best, to sup at home with me,

Where at your fought field we shall laugh and merry
be.

SURESBY. And mistress, I beseech you, take with me
no grief;*   grudge

I did a true man's part, not wishing you reprief.*   to spare you/20

DAME CUSTANCE. Though hasty reports through surmises growing

May of poor innocents be utter overthrowing,

Yet, because to thy master thou hast a true heart,

And I know mine own truth, I forgive thee for my
part.

GOODLUCK. Go we all to my house, and of this gear
no more!

Go prepare all things, Sim Suresby; hence, run afore!

SURESBY. I go.

(*He leaves.*)

GOODLUCK. But who cometh yond? Matthew Merrygreek.

DAME CUSTANCE. Roister Doister's champion; I
shrew his best cheek!42

---

42 Beshrew his impudence!

TRUSTY. Roister Doister self, your wooer, is with
   him, too.
Surely some thing there is with us they have to do.   30

SCENE 5

(GOODLUCK, TRUSTY, *and* DAME CUSTANCE. *Enter*
MERRYGREEK *and* ROISTER DOISTER.)
MERRYGREEK. Yond I see Gawyn Goodluck, to
   whom lieth my message.
I will first salute him after his long voyage,
And then make all thing well concerning your behalf.
   ROISTER DOISTER. Yea, for the pash of God!
   MERRYGREEK.   Hence out of sight, ye calf,*   fool
Till I have spoke with them, and then I will you fet.
   ROISTER DOISTER. In God's name.
                        (*Exit* ROISTER DOISTER.)
   MERRYGREEK. What, Master Gawyn Goodluck, well
   met!
And from your long voyage I bid you right welcome
   home.
   GOODLUCK. I thank you.
   MERRYGREEK.   I come to you from an
   honest mome.
   GOODLUCK. Who is that?
   MERRYGREEK.   Roister Doister, that doughty
   kite.
   DAME CUSTANCE. Fie! I can scarcely abide ye should
   his name recite.   10
   MERRYGREEK. Ye must take him to favour, and par-
   don all past,
He heareth of your return, and is full ill aghast.
   GOODLUCK. I am right well content he have with us
   some cheer.
   DAME CUSTANCE. Fie upon him, beast! Then will
   not I be there.
   GOODLUCK. Why, Custance! do ye hate him more
   than ye love me?
   DAME CUSTANCE. But for your mind, sir, where he
   were would I not be!
   TRUSTY. He would make us all laugh.
   MERRYGREEK.   Ye ne'er had
   better sport.

GOODLUCK. I pray you, sweet Custance, let him to us
  resort.
DAME CUSTANCE. To your will I assent.
MERRYGREEK.   Why, such
  a fool it is
As no man for good pastime would forgo or miss.   20
GOODLUCK. Fetch him to go with us.
MERRYGREEK.   He will be a
  glad man.
                          (*Goes for* RALPH ROISTER.)
TRUSTY. We must, to make us mirth, maintain him
  all we can.
And lo, yond he cometh, and Merrygreek with him!
  DAME CUSTANCE. At his first entrance ye shall see
  I will him trim!
But first let us hearken the gentleman's wise talk.
  TRUSTY. I pray you, mark, if ever ye saw crane so
  stalk.

                        SCENE 6

(DAME CUSTANCE, GOODLUCK, *and* TRUSTY. *Enter*
  ROISTER DOISTER *and* MERRYGREEK.)
ROISTER DOISTER. May I then be bold?
MERRYGREEK.   I warrant
  you, on my word.
They say they shall be sick but ye be at their board.
ROISTE DOISTER. They were not angry, then?
MERRYGREEK.   Yes,
  at first, and made strange;
But when I said your anger to favour should change,
And therewith had commended you accordingly,
They were all in love with your maship by and by,
And cried you mercy that they had done you wrong.
  ROISTER DOISTER. For why no man, woman, nor
  child can hate me long?
  MERRYGREEK. "We fear," quod they, "he will be
  avenged one day;
Then for a penny give all our lives we may!"   10
  ROISTER DOISTER. Said they so indeed?
MERRYGREEK.   Did they?
  Yea, even with one voice.
"He will forgive all," quod I. Oh, how they did rejoice!
ROISTER DOISTER. Ha, ha, ha!

MERRYGREEK.   "Go fetch him," say
    they, "while he is in good mood,
For, have his anger who lust,* we will not, by the   whoever
    rood!"   desires
    ROISTER DOISTER. I pray God that it be all true that
    thou hast me told
And that she fight no more.
    MERRYGREEK.   I warrant you, be bold.
To them, and salute them!
    ROISTER DOISTER.   Sirs, I greet you all well.
    ALL. Your mastership is welcome!
    DAME CUSTANCE.   Saving my quarrel!
For, sure, I will put you up into the Exchequer—
    MERRYGREEK. Why so? better nay. Wherefore?
    DAME CUSTANCE.   For
    an usurer.   20
    ROISTER DOISTER. I am no usurer, good mistress, by
    His* arms!   God's
    MERRYGREEK. When took he gain of money to any
    man's harms?
    DAME CUSTANCE. Yes, a foul usurer he is, ye shall
    see else—
    ROISTER DOISTER. Didst not thou promise she would
    pick no more quarrels?
    DAME CUSTANCE. He will lend* no blows but he   give
    have in recompense
Fifteen for one: which is too much, of conscience!
    ROISTER DOISTER. Ah, dame, by the ancient law of
    arms, a man
Hath no honour to foil* his hands on a woman.   soil
    DAME CUSTANCE. And, where other usurers take
    their gains yearly,
This man is angry but he have his by and by.   30
    GOODLUCK. Sir, do not for her sake bear me your
    displeasure.
    MERRYGREEK. Well, he shall with you talk thereof
    more at leisure.
Upon your good usage, he will now shake your hand.
    ROISTER DOISTER. And much heartily welcome from
    a strange land.
    MERRYGREEK. Be not afeard, Gawyn, to let him
    shake your fist!
    GOODLUCK. Oh, the most honest gentleman that e'er
    I wist!*   knew

I beseech your maship to take pain to sup with us!
> MERRYGREEK. He shall not say you nay; and I too,
> by Jesus!
Because ye shall be friends, and let all quarrels pass.
> ROISTER DOISTER. I will be as good friends with
> them as ere* I was.   before/40
> MERRYGREEK. Then let me fetch your choir that we
> may have a song.
> ROISTER DOISTER. Go.

(Exit MERRYGREEK.)

> GOODLUCK. I have heard no melody all this year
> long.

(MERRYGREEK *returns with* DOUGHTY *and* HARPAX.)
> MERRYGREEK. Come on, sirs, quickly!
> ROISTER DOISTER.   Sing on, sirs, for my friends' sake.
> DOUGHTY (*surprised*). Call ye these your friends?
> ROISTER DOISTER. Sing on, and no mo words make!
(*They sing.*)
> GOODLUCK. The Lord preserve our most noble
> Queen of renown,
And her virtues reward with the heavenly crown.
> DAME CUSTANCE. The Lord strengthen her most
> excellent Majesty,
Long to reign over us in all prosperity.
> TRUSTY. That her godly proceedings the faith to
> defend
He may 'stablish and maintain through to the end.
> MERRYGREEK. God grant her, as she doth, the
> Gospel to protect,   51
Learning and virtue to advance, and vice to correct.
> ROISTER DOISTER. God grant her loving subjects
> both the mind and grace,
Her most godly proceedings worthily to embrace.
> HARPAX. Her Highness' most worthy counsellors
> God prosper
With honour and love of all men to minister.
> ALL. God grant the nobility her to serve and love,
With all the whoe commonty,* as doth them   commonalty
behove.

AMEN

Gammer Gurton's Needle

By Mr. S., Master of Art

Characters

DICCON, the Bedlam[1]
HODGE, Gammer Gurton's servant
TIB, Gammer Gurton's maid
GAMMER GURTON
COCK, Gammer Gurton's boy
DAME CHAT
DOCTOR RAT, the Curate
DOLL, Dame Chat's maid
SCRAPETHRIFT, Master Bayly's servant
MUTES
MASTER BAYLY, the Bailiff

PROLOGUE

As Gammer Gurton with many a wide stitch
Sat piecing and patching of Hodge her man's brich.*   breeches
By chance or misfortune, as she her gear tost,
In Hodge' leather breeches her needle she lost.
When Diccon the Bedlam had heard by report
That good Gammer Gurton was robbed in this sort,
He quietly persuaded with her in that stound*   crisis
Dame Chat, her dear gossip, this needle had found;
Yet knew she no more of this matter, alas!
Than knoweth Tom, our clerk, what the priest saith
     at mass.   10

Hereof there ensued so fearful a fray,
Mas Doctor was sent for, these gossips to stay,
Because he was curate, and esteemed full wise;
Who found that he sought not, by Diccon's device.
When all things were tumbled and clean out of
     fashion,

---

[1] A "Bedlam" was an inmate of Bethlehem Hospital in London. Discharged patients were licensed to roam about the countryside as beggars in order to support themselves. A "mental case" could, one supposes, be merely eccentric, like Diccon, rather than actually mad.

Whether it were by fortune, or some other
    constellation,
Suddenly the neele* Hodge found by the pricking,   needle
And drew it out of his buttock, where he felt it
    sticking.
Their hearts then at rest with perfect security,   19
With a pot of good ale they struck up their *plaudite.** applause

ACT I

Scene 1

(Diccon *appears on the stage.*)
    Diccon. Many a mile have I walked, divers and
      sundry ways,
And many a good man's house have I been at in my
    days;
Many a gossip's cup in my time have I tasted,
And many a broach and spit have I both turned and
    basted;
Many a piece of bacon have I had out of their balks,[2]
In running over the country, with long and weary
    walks;
Yet came my foot never within those door cheeks,
To seek flesh or fish, garlick, onions, or leeks,
That ever I saw a sort in such a plight
As here within this house appeareth to my sight.   10
There is howling and scowling, all cast in a dump,
With whewling and puling, as though they had lost
    a trump.
Sighing and sobbing, they weep and they wail;
I marvel in my mind what the devil they ail.
The old trot* sits groaning, with alas! and alas!   crone
And Tib wrings her hands, and takes on in worse
    case.
With poor Cock, their boy, they be driven in such fits,
I fear me the folks be not well in their wits.
Ask them what they ail, or who brought them in this
    stay,
They answer not at all, but "alack!" and "welaway!"   20
When I saw it booted not,[3] out at doors I hied me,
And caught a slip of bacon, when I saw that none
    spied me,

---

[2] Beams from which bacon was hung.
[3] "Didn't do any good."

Which I intend not far hence, unless my purpose fail,
Shall serve for a shoeing-horn to draw on two pots
    of ale.

Scene 2

(DICCON *and* HODGE, *touching his trousers.*)

HODGE. See! So cham* arrayed with dabbling in   I am
    the dirt!
She that set me to ditching, ich* would she had the   I
    squirt!
Was never poor soul that such a life had.
Gog's bones! This vilthy glay* has drest me too bad!   filthy day
Gog's soul! See how this stuff tears!
Ich were better to be a bearward* and set to   bear keeper
    keep bears!
By the Mass, here is a gash, a shameful hole indeed!
An one stitch tear further, a man may thrust in his
    head.
    DICCON. By my father's soul, Hodge, if I should
        now be sworn,
I cannot choose but say thy breech is foul betorn,   10
But the next remedy in such a case and hap
Is to planch* on a piece as broad as cap.   clap
    HODGE. Gog's soul, mam, 'tis not yet two days fully
        ended
Since my dame Gurton, cham sure, these breeches
    amended;
But cham made such a drudge to trudge at every need
Chwold* rend it though it were stitched with sturdy   I would
    packthread.
    DICCON. Hodge, let thy breeches go, and speak and
        tell me soon
What devil aileth Gammer Gurton and Tib her maid
    to frown.
    HODGE. Tush, man, th'art deceived: 'tis their daily
        look;
They cower so over the coals, their eyes be bleared
    with smoke.   20
    DICCON. Nay, by the Mass, I perfectly perceived, as
        I came hither,
That either Tib and her dame hath been by the ears
    together,*   quarreled
Or else as great a matter, as thou shalt shortly see.

HODGE. Now, ich beseech our Lord they never
better agree!

DICCON. By Gog's soul, there they sit as still as
stones in the street,

As though they had been taken with fairies, or else
with some ill sprite.*   evil spirit

HODGE. Gog's heart! I durst have laid my cap to a
crown*   wagered

Chwould learn of some prancome* as soon as ich   prank
came to town.

DICCON. Why, Hodge, are thou inspired?* Or didst   mad
thou thereof hear?

HODGE. Nay, but ich saw such a wonder as ich saw
not this seven year.   30

Tom Tankard's cow, by Gog's bones! She set me up
her sail,

And flinging about his half acre, fisking* with   whisking
her tail,

As though there had been in her arse a swarm of
bees;

And chad* not cried "tphrowh, whore," she'd leapt   had I
out of his leas.

DICCON. Why, Hodge, lies the cunning in Tom
Tankard's cow's tail?

HODGE. Well, ich chave* heard some say such   I have
tokens do not fail.

But canst thou not tell, in faith, Diccon, why she
frowns, or whereat?

Hath no* man stolen her ducks or hens, or gelded   any
Gib, her cat?

DICCON. What devil can I tell, man? I could not
have one word!

They gave no more heed to my talk than thou
wouldst to a lord.   40

HODGE. Ich cannot still but muse what marvellous
thing it is.

Chill in⁴ and know myself what matters are amiss.

                                          (*Exit.*)

DICCON. Then farewell, Hodge, awhile, since thou
dost inward haste,

For I will into the good wife Chat's, to feel how the
ale doth taste.

                                          (*Exit.*)

⁴ "I shall go in."

Scene 3

(Hodge *and* Tib.)

Hodge. Cham aghast; by the Mass, ich wot* not
    what to do.   *know*
Chad* need bless me well before ich go them to.*   *I had/to them*
Perchance some felon sprite may haunt our house
    indeed;
And then chwere* but a noddy to venture where   *I were*
    cha* no need.   *I have*
    Tib. Cham worse than mad, by the Mass, to be at
    this stay!
Cham chid, cham blamed, and beaten, all t'hours on
    the day;
Lamed and hunger-starved, pricked up all in jags,*   *tatters*
Having no patch to hide my back save* a few rotten   *except*
    rags!
    Hodge. I say, Tib—if thou be Tib, as I trow* sure   *believe*
    thou be—
What devil make ado is this between our dame and
    thee?   10
    Tib. Gog's bread, Hodge, thou had a good turn
    thou wert not here this while!
It had been better for some of us to have been hence
    a mile;
My gammer* is so out of course and frantic all at   *mistress*
    ones,
That Cock, our boy, and I, poor wench, have felt it
    on our bones.
    Hodge. What is the matter—say on, Tib—whereat
    she taketh so on?
    Tib. She is undone, she saith, alas! Her joy and life
    is gone!
If she hear not of some comfort, she is, faith, but
    dead;
Shall never come within her lips one inch of meat
    nor bread.
    Hodge. By'r Lady, cham not very glad to see her
    in this dump.*   *sullen mood*
Chold* a noble⁵ her stool hath fallen and she hath   *I wager*
    broke her rump.   20
    Tib. Nay, and that were the worst, we would not
    greatly care

⁵ A Tudor coin.

For bursting of her huckle bone or breaking of her
    chair;
But greater, greater, is her grief, as, Hodge, we shall
    all feel!
    HODGE. Gog's wounds, Tib? My grammer has never
      lost her neele?
    TIB. Her neele!
    HODGE.   Her neele!
    TIB. Her neele!
By him that made me, it is true, Hodge,
                        I tell thee.
    HODGE. Gog's sacrament, I would she had lost
      t'heart* out of her belly!   *the heart*
The Devil, or else his dame, they ought* her, sure,   *owed*
    a shame!
How a murrion* came this chance, say, Tib! unto   *plague*
    our dame?
    TIB. My gammer sat her down on her pess,* and   *hassock*
    bade me reach thy breeches,   30
And by and by (a vengeance in it!) or* she had take   *ere*
    two stitches
To clap a clout* upon thine arse, by chance aside she   *patch*
    leers,
And Gib, our cat, in the milk-pan she spied over head
    and ears.
"Ah, whore! Out, thief!" She cried aloud, and swapt*   *threw*
    the breeches down.
Up went her staff, and out leapt Gib at doors into
    the town,
And since that time was never wight* could set their   *person*
    eyes upon it.
Gog's malison* chave, Cock and I, bid twenty times   *curse*
    light on it.
    HODGE. And is not then my breeches sewed up,
      tomorrow that I should wear?
    TIB. No, in faith, Hodge, thy breeches lie for all
      this never the near.*   *readier*
    HODGE. Now a vengeance light on all the sort, that
      better should have kept it,   40
The cat, the house, and Tib, our maid, that better
    should have swept it!
See where she cometh crawling! Come on, in twenty
    devils' way!

Ye have made a fair day's work, have you not? Pray
you, say!

Scene 4

(GAMMER, HODGE, TIB, *and* COCK.)

GAMMER. Alas, Hodge, alas! I may well curse and
ban

This day, that ever I saw it, with Gib and the
milkpan;

For these and ill luck together, as knoweth Cock, my
boy,

Have stuck away my dear neele, and robbed me of
my joy,

My fair long straight neele, that was mine only
treasure;

The first day of my sorrow is, and last end of my
pleasure!

HODGE. Might ha kept it when ye had it! But fools
will be fools still.

Lose that is vast* in your hands ye need not but   fast
ye will.

GAMMER. Go hie thee, Tib, and run thou, whore,*   rascal
to th'end here of the town!

Didst carry out dust in thy lap; seek where thou
pourest it down,   10

And as thou sawest me roking* in the ashes where I   crouching
mourned,

So see in all the heap of dust thou leave no straw
unturned.

TIB. That chall,* Gammer, swith and tite,[6] and   I shall
soon be here again!

GAMMER. Tib, stoop and look down to the ground
to it, and take some pain.

(*Exit* TIB.)

HODGE. Here is a pretty matter, to see this gear how
it goes;

By Gog's soul, I think you would lose your arse an*   if
it were loose!

Your neele lost, it is pity you should lack care and
endless sorrow.

Gog's death! How shall my breeches be sewed? Shall
I go thus tomorrow?

---

[6] Quickly and promptly.

GAMMER. Ah Hodge, Hodge! if that ich could
    find my neele, by the reed,*   rood, cross
Chould* sew thy breeches, ich promise thee, with   I would
    full good double threed,*   thread/20
And set a patch on either knee should last this
    months twain.
Now God and good Saint Sithe I pray to send it home
    again!
    HODGE. Whereto served your hands and eyes but
    this your neele to keep?
What devil had you else to do? Ye kept, ich wot, no
    sheep!
Cham fain* abroad to dig and delve, in water,   disinclined
    mire, and clay,
Sossing and possing[7] in the dirt still from
    day to day.
A hundred things that be abroad cham set* to see   ordered
    them weele,*   well
And four of you sit idle at home, and cannot keep
    a neele!
    GAMMER. My neele! Alas! Ich lost it, Hodge, what
    time ich me up hasted
To save the milk set up for thee, which Gib, our cat,
    hath wasted.   30
    HODGE. The Devil he burst both Gib and Tib, with
    all the rest!
Cham always sure of the worst end, whoever have the
    best!
Where ha you been fidging* abroad since you your   frettting,
    neele lost?   moving
    GAMMER. Within the house, and at the door, sitting
    by this same post,
Where I was looking a long hour before these folks
    came here;
But welaway, all was in vain, my neele is never the
    near!
    HODGE. Set me a candle, let me seek, and grope
    wherever it be.
Gog's heart, ye be so foolish, ich think, you know it
    not when you it see!
    GAMMER. Come hither, Cock; what, Cock, I say!
    COCK.   How, Gammer?

[7] Splashing and tramping.

GAMMER.   Go, hie thee soon,
And grope behind the old brass pan, which thing
   when thou hast done   40
There shalt thou find an old shoe, wherein if thou
   look well,
Thou shalt find lying an inch of a white tallow
   candell.*   candle
Light it, and bring it tite* away.   promptly
    COCK.   That shall be done anon.
    GAMMER. Nay, tarry, Hodge, till thou hast light,
    and then we'll seek each one.
    HODGE. Come away, ye whoreson boy, are ye asleep?
    Ye must have a crier!
    COCK. Ich cannot get the candle light:* here is   lit
    almost no fire.
    HODGE. Chill* hold thee a penny chill* make   I will/that will
    thee come, if that ich may catch thine ears!
Art deaf, thou whoreson boy? Cock, I say; why
   canst not hear 's?
    GAMMER. Beat him not, Hodge, but help the boy,
    and come you two together.
                     (*Exeunt.*)

SCENE 5

(GAMMER, TIB, *and* COCK, *the boy*.)
    GAMMER. How now, Tib? quick, let's hear what
    news thou hast brought hether!
    TIB. Chave* tost and tumbled yonder heap over   I have
    and over again,
And winnowed it through my fingers, as men would
   winnow grain;
Not so much as a hen's turd but in pieces I tare* it,   tore
Or whatsoever clod or clay I found, I did not spare it,
Looking within and eke* without, to find your neele,   also
   alas!
But all in vain and without help! Your neele is where
   it was.*   unfound
    GAMMER. Alas my neele! We shall never meet!
    Adieu, adieu, for aye!
    TIB. Not so, Gammer, we might it find, if we knew
    where it lay.
    COCK. Gog's cross, Gammer, if ye will laugh, look
    in but at the door,   10

And see how Hodge lieth tumbling and tossing amidst
the flour,
Raking there some fire to find among the ashes dead
Where there is not one spark so big as a pin's
head;
At last in a dark corner two sparks he thought he sees
Which were indeed nought else but Gib our cat's two
eyes.
"Puff!" quoth Hodge, thinking thereby to have fire
without doubt;
With that Gib shut her two eyes, and so the fire was
out.
And by and by them opened, even as they were
before;
With that the sparks appeared, even as they had done
of yore;   19
And even as Hodge blew the fire (as he did think),
Gib, as she felt the blast, straightway began to wink;
Till Hodge fell of swearing, as came best to his turn,
The fire was sure bewitched, and therefore would not
burn.
At last Gib up the stairs, among the old posts and
pins,
And Hodge he hied him after, till broke were both
his shins;
Cursing and swearing oaths were never of his making,
That Gib would fire* the house if that she were not   set fire to
taken.

    GAMMER. See, here is all the thought that the
      foolish urchin taketh!
And Tib, methink, at his elbow almost as merry
maketh.
This is all the wit ye have when others make their
moan.   30
Come down, Hodge, where art thou? and let the cat
alone!

    HODGE (*from within the house*). Gog's heart, help
      and come up! Gib in her tail hath fire
And is like to burn all, if she get a little higher!
Come down, quoth you? Nay, then you might count
me a patch.*   fool
The house cometh down on your heads, if it take
once the thatch.[8]

    [8] "If the spark strikes the thatched roof."

GAMMER. It is the cat's eyes, fool, that shineth in
the dark.

HODGE. Hath the cat, do you think, in every eye a
spark?

GAMMER. No, but they shine as like fire as ever
man see.

HODGE. By the Mass, an she burn all, yoush* bear   *you shall
the blame for me!

GAMMER. Come down and help to seek here our
neele, that* it were found.   *so that/40

Down, Tib, on the knees, I say! Down, Cock, to the
ground!

To God I make avow, and so to good Saint Anne,

A candle shall they have apiece, get it where I can,

If I may my neele find in one place or in other.

HODGE (*entering*). Now a vengeance on Gib light,
on Gib and Gib's mother,

And all the generation of cats both far and near!

Look on this ground, whoreson, thinkst thou the
neele is here?

COCK. By my troth, Gammer, methought your neele
here I saw,

But when my fingers touched it I felt it was a straw.

TIB. See, Hodge, what's this? may it not be within
it?

HODGE. Break it, fool, with thy hand, and see an
thou canst find it.   51

TIB. Nay, break it you, Hodge, according to your
word.

HODGE. Gog's sides! fie! it stinks; it is a cat's turd!

It were well done to make thee eat it, by the Mass!

GAMMER. This matter amendeth* not; my neele is   *improves
still where it was.

Our candle is at an end, let us all in quite,

And come another time when we have more light.

(*They leave.*)

ACT II

(*Song.*)

           Back and side go bare, go bare,
           Both foot and hand go cold;
           But belly, God send thee good ale enough,
           Whether it be new or old.
           I cannot eat but little meat,

My stomach is not good;
But sure I think that I can drink
With him that wears a hood.
Though I go bare, take ye no care,
I am nothing a-cold;   10
I stuff my skin so full within
Of jolly good ale and old.
    Back and side go bare, go bare, etc.

I love no roast but a nut brown toast
And a crab* laid in the fire.   crab-apple
A little bread shall do me stead;
Much bread I not desire.
No frost nor snow, no wind, I trow,
Can hurt me if I wold;
I am so wrapped, and throughly lapped   20
Of jolly good ale and old.
    Back and side go bare, etc.

And Tib my wife, that as her life
Loveth well good ale to seek,
Full oft drinks she till ye may see
The tears run down her cheek;
Then doth she troll to me the bowl
Even as a malt-worm* should;   malt-lover
And saith, sweetheart, I took my part
Of this jolly good ale and old.   30
    Back and side go bare, etc.

Now let them drink till they nod and wink,
Even as good fellows should do;
They shall not miss to have the bliss
Good ale doth bring men to;
And all poor souls that have scoured bowls,
Or have them lustly* trolled,   lustily
God save the lives of them and their wives,
Whether they be young or old.
    Back and side go bare, etc.   40

Scene 1

(*Enter* DICCON.)

DICCON. Well done, by Gog's malt! Well sung and
    well said!
Come on, mother Chat, as thou art true maid,
One fresh pot of ale let's see, to make an end

Against this cold weather my naked arms to defend!
This gear it warms the soul! Now, wind, blow on
    the worst!
And let us drink and swill till that our bellies burst!
Now were he a wise man by cunning could define
Which way my journey lieth, or where Diccon will
    dine!
But one good turn I have: be it by night or day,
South, east, north or west, I am never out of my way!
    (*Enter* HODGE.)
    HODGE. Chym* goodly rewarded, cham* I not,   I am/am
    do you think?   11
Chad a goodly dinner for all my sweat and swink!*   toil
Neither butter, cheese, milk, onions, flesh, nor fish,
Save this poor piece of barley bread: 'tis a pleasant
    costly dish!
    DICCON. Hail, fellow Hodge, and well to fare with
    thy meat, if thou have any:
But by thy words, as I them smelled, thy daintrels*   dainties
    be not many.
    HODGE. Daintrels, Diccon? Gog's soul, save this
    piece of dry horsebread,
Cha bit* no bit this livelong day, no crumb come   I have eaten
    in my head:
My guts they yawl-crawl, and all my belly rumbleth;
The puddings* cannot lie still, each one over other   entrails
    tumbleth.   20
By Gog's heart, cham so vexed, and in my belly
    penn'd,*   pained
Chould one piece were at the spitalhouse,* another   hospital
    at the castle end!
    DICCON. Why, Hodge, was there none at home thy
    dinner for to set?
    HODGE. Gog's bread, Diccon, ich came too late, was
    nothing there to get!
Gib (a foul fiend might on her light!) licked the
    milk-pan so clean,
See, Diccon, 'twas not so well washed this seven year,
    as ich ween!*   believe
A pestilence light on all ill luck! Chad thought, yet
    for all this
Of a morsel of bacon behind the door at worst should
    not miss:

By the Mass, thou hast a shameful loss, an it were
    but for thy breeches.

    HODGE. Gog's soul, man, chould give a crown chad*   *if it had*
        it but three stitches.

    DICCON. How sayest thou, Hodge? What should he   50
        have [who] again thy needle got?

    HODGE. By'm vather's* soul, an chad it, chould give   *father's*
        him a new grot.*   *coin*

    DICCON. Canst thou keep counsel in this case?

    HODGE.   Else chwould* my tongue were out.   *I would*

    DICCON. Do thou but then by my advice, and I will
        fetch it without doubt.

    HODGE. Chill* run, chill ride, chill dig, chill delve,   *I will*
        chill toil, chill trudge, shalt see;

Chill hold, chill draw, chill pull, chill pinch, chill
    kneel on my bare knee;

Chill scrape, chill scratch, chill sift, chill seek, chill
    bow, chill bend, chill sweat,

Chill stoop, chill stir, chill cap,[10] chill kneel, chill
    creep on hands and feet;

Chill be thy bondman, Diccon, ich swear by sun and
    moon.

    (Pointing behind to his torn breeches.)

An channot* somewhat to stop this gap, cham   *If I cannot*
    utterly undone!   60

    DICCON. Why, is there any special cause thou takest
        hereat such sorrow?

    HODGE. Kirstian Clack, Tom Simpson's maid, by
        the Mass, comes hither to-morrow,

Cham not able to say, between us what may hap;

She smiled on me the last Sunday when ich put off
    my cap.

    DICCON. Well, Hodge, this is a matter of weight,
        and must be kept close,*   *secret*

It might else turn to both our costs, as the world now
    goes.

Shalt swear to be no blab, Hodge?

    HODGE.   Chill, Diccon.

    DICCON.   Then go to,

Lay thine hand here; say after me as thou shall hear
    me do.

Hast no book?

---

[10] "Take off my cap."

HODGE.   Cha no book, I!

DICCON.   Then needs must force us both

Upon my breech to lay thine hand, and there to take
thine oath.   70

HODGE. I, Hodge, breechless

Swear to Diccon, rechless,

By the cross that I shall kiss,

To keep his counsel close,

And always me to dispose

To work that his pleasure is.

(*Here he kisseth* DICCON's *breech.*)

DICCON. Now, Hodge, see thou take heed,

And do as I thee bid;

For so I judge it meet;

This needle again to win,   80

There is no shift therein

But conjure up a spreet.*   spirit

HODGE. What, the great devil, Diccon, I say?

DICCON. Yea, in good faith, that is the way,

Fetched with some pretty charm.

HODGE. Soft, Diccon, be not too hasty yet,

By the Mass, for ich begin to sweat!

Cham afraid of some harm.

DICCON (*drawing a circle*). Come hither, then, and
stir thee nat*   not

One inch out of this circle plat,*   plot/90

But stand as I thee teach.

HODGE. And shall ich be here safe from their claws?

DICCON. The master devil with his long paws

Here to thee cannot reach.

Now will I settle me to this gear.

HODGE. I say, Diccon, hear me, hear!

Go softly to this matter!

DICCON. What devil, man! Art afraid of nought?*   anything

HODGE. Canst not tarry a little thought

Till ich make a curtsy of water?*   make water/100

DICCON. Stand still to it; why shouldest thou
fear him?

HODGE. Gog's sides, Diccon, methink ich hear him!

And tarry, chal* mar all!   I shall

DICCON. The matter is no worse than I told it.

HODGE. By the Mass, cham able no longer to hold
it!

Too bad! ich must beray* the hall!   befoul

DICCON. Stand to it, Hodge! Stir not, you whoreson!
What devil, be thine arse-strings bursten?
Thyself awhile but stay,
The devil, I smell him, will be here anon.   110
   HODGE. Hold him fast, Diccon, cham gone! Cham
     gone!
Chill not be at that fray!*   affair
   (HODGE, *fearful of the appearance of a devil,
   runs away.*)

SCENE 2

(DICCON *solo.*)
   DICCON. Fie, shitten knave, and out upon thee!
Above all other louts, fie on thee!
Is not here a cleanly prank?
But thy matter was no better,
Nor thy presence here no sweeter,
To fly I can thee thank.

Here is a matter worthy glosing,*   comment
Of Gammer Gurton's needle losing,
And a foul piece of wark!*   work
A man I think might make a play,   10
And need no word to this they say,
Being but half a clark.*   clerk
Soft, let me alone! I will take the charge
This matter further to enlarge
Within a time short.
If ye will mark my toys, and note,
I will give ye leave to cut my throat
If I make not good sport.
   (*Calling out.*)
Dame Chat, I say, where be ye? Within?
   CHAT. (*speaking from inside her house*). Who have
     we there maketh such a din?   20
   DICCON. Here is a good fellow [who] maketh no
     great danger.
   CHAT. What, Diccon? Come near, ye be no stranger.
We be fast set at trump,[11] man, hard by the fire;
Thou shalt set on the king, if thou come a little
     nigher.
   DICCON. Nay, nay, there is no tarrying; I must be
     gone again.

[11] At a game of cards.

But first for you in counsel I have a word or twain.
   CHAT *(to her maid)*. Come hither, Doll! Doll, sit
     down and play this game,
And as thou sawest me do, see thou do even the same.
There is five trumps beside the queen, the hindmost
     thou shalt find her.
Take heed of Sim Glover's wife, she hath an eye
     behind her!   30
   (Comes out of her house.)
Now, Diccon, say your will.
   DICCON.   Nay, soft a little yet;
I would not tell it my sister, the matter is so great.
There I will have you swear by our dear Lady of
     Boulogne,
Saint Dunstan, and Saint Donnyke, with the three
     kings of Cologne,[12]
That ye shall keep it secret.
   CHAT.   Gog's bread! That will I do!
As secret as mine own thought, by God and the devil
     too!
   DICCON. Here is Gammer Gurton, your
     neighbour, a sad and heavy wight:*   sorrowful person
Her goodly fair red cock at home was stole
     this last night.
   CHAT. Gog's soul! Her cock with the yellow legs,
     that nightly crowed so just?*   regularly
   DICCON. That cock is stolen.
   CHAT. What, was he fetched out of the hen's rust?*   roost/40
   DICCON. I cannot tell where the devil he was kept,
     under key or lock;
But Tib hath tickled in Gammers' ear that you should
     steal the cock.
   CHAT. Have I, strong whore?* By bread and salt!—   rogue
   DICCON.   What, soft, I say, be still!
Say not one word for all this gear.
   CHAT.   By the Mass, that I will!
I will have the young whore by the head, and the old
     trot* by the throat.   crone
   DICCON. Not one word, Dame Chat, I say; not one
     word, for my coat!
   CHAT. Shall such a beggar's brawl* as that, thinkest   brat
     thou, make me a thief?

---

[12] The three wise kings, the Magi, who appeared at the Nativity of Christ.

The pox light on her whore's sides, a pestilence and a
   mischief!

Come out, thou hungry needy bitch! O that* my   too bad that
   nails be short!

  DICCON. Gog's bread, woman, hold your peace!
   This gear will else pass sport!   50

I would not for an hundred pound this matter should
   be known,

That I am author of this tale or have abroad it
   blown!

Did ye not swear ye would be ruled before the tale
   I told?

I said ye must all secret keep, and ye said sure ye
   wold.*   would

  CHAT. Would you suffer, yourself, Diccon, such a
   sort to revile you,

With slanderous words to blot your name, and so to
   defile you?

  DICCON. No, Goodwife Chat, I would be loth such
   drabs should blot my name;

But yet ye must so order all that Diccon bear no
   blame.

  CHAT. Go to, then, what is your rede?* Say on your   advice
   mind, ye shall me rule herein.

  DICCON. Godamercy to Dame Chat! In faith thou
   must the gear* begin.   fight/60

It is twenty pound to a goose turd my gammer will
   not tarry

But hitherward she comes as fast as her legs can her
   carry

To brawl with you about her cock; for well I heard
   Tib say

The cock was roasted in your house to breakfast
   yesterday;

And when ye had the carcase eaten, the feathers ye
   out flung,

And Doll, your maid, the legs she hid a foot deep in
   the dung.

  CHAT. Oh, gracious God! My heart it bursts!

  DICCON.   Well, rule yourself a space;

And Gammer Gurton, when she cometh anon into
   this place,

Then to the quean,* let's see, tell her your mind and   common
   spare not.   woman

So shall Diccon blameless be; and then, go to, I care
    not! 70
  CHAT. Then, whore, beware her throat![13] I can
    abide no longer.
In faith, old witch, it shall be seen which of us two
    be stronger!
And, Diccon, but at your request I would not stay*   delay
    one hour.
  DICCON. Well, keep it* till she be here, and then [your anger]
    out let it pour!
In the meanwhile get you in and make no words of
    this.
More of this matter within this hour to hear you shall
    not miss,
Because I knew you are my friend, hide it I could
    not, doubtless.
Ye know your harm, see ye be wise about your own
    business!
So fare ye well.
  CHAT. Nay, soft, Diccon, and drink. What, Doll, I
    say!
Bring here a cup of the best ale; let's see, come
    quickly away! 80
               (*She goes out.*)

SCENE 3

(DICCON *solo, addressing the audience.*)
  DICCON. Ye see, masters, that one end tapped of
    this my short devise!*   plot
Now must we broach th'other, too, before the smoke
    arise;
And by the time they have awhile run, I trust ye
    need not crave it,
But look, what lieth in both their hearts, ye are like,
    sure, to have it.
  (*Enter* HODGE.)
  HODGE. Yea, Gog's soul, art alive yet? What, Diccon,
    dare ich come?
  DICCON. A man is well hied* to trust to thee; I will sped
    say nothing but mum;
But an ye come any nearer, I pray you see all be
    sweet!

[13] "Then let that low woman watch out for her throat."

HODGE. Tush, man, is Gammer's neele found? That
   chould gladly weet.*   know
DICCON. She may thank thee it is not found, for if
   thou had kept thy standing,
The devil he would have fetched it out, even, Hodge,
   at thy commanding.   10
HODGE. Gog's heart, and could he tell nothing
   where the neele might be found?
DICCON. Ye foolish dolt, ye were to seek, ere we had
   got our ground;
Therefore his tale so doubtful was that I could not
   perceive it.
HODGE. Then ich see well something was said,
   chope* one day yet to have it.   I hope
But Diccon, Diccon, did not the devil cry 'ho, ho, ho'?
DICCON. If thou hadst tarried where thou stoodst,
   thou wouldest have said so!
HODGE. Durst swear of a book, chard* him roar,   I heard
   straight after ich was gone.
But tell me, Diccon, what said the knave? Let me
   hear it anon.*   quickly
DICCON. The whoreson talked to me, I know not
   well of what.
One while his tongue it ran and paltered of a cat,   20
Another while he stammered still upon a Rat;
Last of all, there was nothing but every word, Chat,
   Chat;
But this I well perceived before I would him rid,[14]
Between Chat, and the Rat, and the cat, the needle
   is hid.
Now whether Gib, our cat, have eat it in her maw,
Or Doctor Rat, our curate, have found it in the straw,
Or this Dame Chat, your neighbour, have stolen it,
   God he knoweth![15]
But by the morrow at this time, we shall learn how
   the matter goeth.
HODGE. Canst not learn tonight, man? Seest not
   what is here?
(*Pointing behind to his torn breeches.*)
DICCON. 'Tis not possible to make it sooner appear.   30
HODGE. Alas, Diccon, then chave no shift, but—lest
   ich tarry too long—

---

[14] Got rid of him.
[15] Only Gods knows.

Hie me to Sim Glover's shop, there to seek for a
    thong,
Therewith this breech to tache* and tie as ich may.   fasten
    DICCON. To-morrow, Hodge, if we chance to meet,
    shalt see what I will say.

                            (HODGE *leaves him.*)

SCENE 4

(DICCON *solo.*)
    DICCON. Now this gear must forward go, for here
    my gammer cometh.
(*to the audience*) Be still awhile and say nothing;
    make here a little roomth.*   room
(*Enter* GAMMER.)
    GAMMER. Good Lord, shall never be my luck my
    neele again to spie?
Alas, the while! 'tis past my help, where 'tis still it
    must lie!
    DICCON. Now, Jesus! Gammer Gurton, what driveth
    you to this sadness?
I fear me, by my conscience, you will sure fall to
    madness.
    GAMMER. Who is that? What, Diccon? cham lost,
    man! fie, fie!
    DICCON. Marry, fie on them that be worthy! But
    what should be your trouble?
    GAMMER. Alas! The more ich think on it, my sor-
    row it waxeth double.
My goodly tossing* spurrier's neele[16] chave lost ich   fast
    wot not where.   10
    DICCON. Your neele? When?
    GAMMER.   My neele, alas! Ich might full ill it
    spare,
As God himself he knoweth, ne'er one beside chave.
    DICCON. If this be all, good Gammer, I warrant
    you all is save.*   safe
    GAMMER. Why, know you any tidings which way
    my neele is gone?
    DICCON. Yea, that I do doubtless, as ye shall hear
    anon.
A see a thing this matter toucheth, within these twenty
    hours,

---

[16] Spur-maker's needle.

Even at this gate, before my face, by a neighbour of
    yours.

She stooped me down, and up she took a needle or
    a pin.

I durst be sworn it was even yours, by all my mothers'
    kin.

   GAMMER. It was my neele, Diccon, ich wot;* for   I know
    here, even by this post,   20

Ich sat, what time as ich upstart, and so my neele
    it lost.

Who was it, lief* son? Speak, ich pray thee, and   dear
    quickly tell me that!

   DICCON. A subtle quean as any in this town, your
    neighbour here, Dame Chat.

   GAMMER. Dame Chat, Diccon? Let me be gone,
    chill* thither in post haste.   I will go

   DICCON. Take my council yet or* ye go, for fear ye   ere
    walk in waste.

It is a murrain* crafty drab, and froward* to be   plaguy/hard
    pleased;

An ye take not the better way, our needle yet ye
    lese* it: lose

For when she took it up, even before your doors,

"What, soft, Dame Chat," quoth I, 'that same is
    none of yours.'

"Avaunt," quoth she, "Sir knave! What pratest thou
    of that I find?   30

I would thou hast kissed me I wot where"; she meant,
    I know, behind;

And home she went as brag* as it had been a body-   brisk
    louse,

And I after, as bold as it had been the goodman of
    the house.

But there an* ye had heard her, how she began to   if only
    scold!

The tongue it went on pattens, by him that Judas
    sold!

Each other word, I was a knave, and you a whore
    of whores,

Because I spake in your behalf, and said the neele
    was yours.

   GAMMER. Gog's bread, and thinks that calleth thus
    to keep my neele me fro'?*   from me

DICCON. Let her alone, and she minds none other
    but even to dress you so.

GAMMER. By the Mass, chill rather spend the coat
    that is on my back!   40

Thinks the false quean by such a slight that chill my
    neele lack?

DICCON. Sleep not* your gear,[17] I counsel you,   **neglect not**
    but of this take good heed:

Let me be known I told you of it, how well soever
    ye speed.

GAMMER. Chill* in, Diccon, a clean apron to   **I will go**
    take and set before me;

An ich may my neele once see, chill, sure, remember
    thee![18]

                   (*Exit* GAMMER.)

SCENE 5

(DICCON *solo*.)

DICCON. Here will the sport begin; if these two once
    may meet,

Their cheer, durst lay money, will prove scarcely
    sweet.

My gammer, sure, intends to be upon her bones

With staves, or with clubs, or else with cobble stones.

Dame Chat, on the other side, if she be far behind[19]

I am right far deceived; she is given to it of kind.

He that may tarry by it awhile, and that but short,

I warrant him, trust to it, he shall see all the sport.

Into the town will I, my friends to visit there,

And hither straight again to see th'end of this gear.*   **fight**

In the meantime, fellows,[20] pipe up; your fiddles, I
    say, take them,   11

And let your friends hear such mirth as ye can make
    them.

                     (*Exit*.)

ACT III

SCENE 2

(*Enter* HODGE.)

HODGE. Sim Glover, yet gramercy!* Cham meetly   **thanks**
    well sped now,[21]

---

[17] "Don't fail to arm yourself."

[18] "And if I ever see my needle again I will surely remember (reward)
thee."

[19] "If she is less combative."

[20] He is addressing the musicians in the theater.

[21] "Thanks to Sim Glover, I am well equipped now (now that he has
lent me an awl with which to speed the mending of my trousers)."

Th'art even as good a fellow as ever kissed a cow!

Here is a thong indeed, by the Mass, though ich
    speak it;

Tom Tankard's great bald curtal,* I think, could   piebald horse
    not break it!

And when he spied my needle to be so straight and
    hard,

Hays* lent me here his nawl,* to set the gib for-   he has/awl
    ward,22

As for my gammer's neele, the flying fiend go weet!

Chill not now go to the door again with it to meet.

Chould make shift good enough an chad a candle's
    end;

The chief hole in my breech with these two chill
    amend.   10

Scene 2

(*Enter* GAMMER, *who notices* HODGE.)

GAMMER. Now Hodge, mayst now be glad, cha
    news to tell thee;

Ich know who has my neele; ich trust soon shalt it
    see.

HODGE. The devil thou does! Hast heard, Gammer,
    indeed, or dost but jest?

GAMMER. 'Tis as true as steel, Hodge.

HODGE.   Why, know-
    est well where didst lese 't?*   lose it

GAMMER. Ich know who found it, and took it up!
    Shalt see or it be long.

HODGE. God's mother dear! If that be true, farewell
    both nawl and thong!

But who has it, Gammer, say on; chould fain hear
    it disclosed.

GAMMER. That false vixen, that same Dame Chat,
    that counts herself so honest.

HODGE. Who told you so?

GAMMER.   That same did Diccon
    the bedlam, which saw it done.

HODGE. Diccon? It is a vengeable knave, Gammer,
    'tis a bonable* whoreson,   abominable/10

22 "To get things going."

Can do more things than that, else cham deceived
    evil:*   *badly deceived*
By the Mass, ich saw him of late call up a great black
    devil!
O, the knave cried 'Ho, ho!,' he roared and he
    thundered,
And ye'ad* been here, cham sure y'ould murrainly   *if ye had*
    ha wondered.[23]
    GAMMER. Was not thou afraid, Hodge, to see him
      in this place?
    HODGE. No, and chad* come to me, could have   *if he had*
      laid him on the face,
Could have, promised him!
    GAMMER.   But, Hodge, had he no horns to push?
    HODGE. As long as your two arms. Saw ye never
      Friar Rush[24]
Painted on a cloth, with a sidelong cow's tail,
And crooked cloven feet, and many a hooked nail?   20
For all the world, if I should judge, could reckon
    him his brother.
Look, even what face Friar Rush had, the devil had
    such another.
    GAMMER. Now Jesus mercy, Hodge! Did Diccon in
      him bring?
    HODGE. Nay, Gammer, hear me speak, chill tell you
      a greater thing;
The devil (when Diccon had him, ich heard him
    wondrous weel)
Said plainly here before us, that Dame Chat had
    your neele.
    GAMMER. Then let us go, and ask her wherefore she
      minds to keep it;
Seeing we know so much, 'twere a madness now to
    sleep it.
    HODGE. Go to her, Gammer; see ye not where
      she stands in her doors?
Bid her give you the neele, 'tis none of hers but
    yours.   30
            (*They go to* DAME CHAT's *house.*)

[23] "Ye would have plaguily wondered."
[24] An 'evil spirit disguised as a friar; a *Hstory of Friar Rush* was published in 1568.

Scene 3

(Gammer *and* Hodge; Dame Chat, *inside her house.*)

Gammer. Dame Chat, chould pray thee fair, let me
    have that is mine!
Chill not this twenty years take one fart that is thine;
Therefore give me mine own, and let me live[25] beside
    thee.

Chat. Why art thou crept from home hither, to
    mine own doors to chide me?
Hence, doting drab, avaunt, or I shall set thee further!
Intends thou and that knave me in my house to
    murther?

Gammer. Tush, gape not so on me, woman! Shalt
    not yet eat me!
Nor all the friends thou hast in this shall not entreat
    me!
Mine own goods I will have, and ask thee no by-leave,
What woman! Poor folks must have right, though
    the thing you aggrieve.   10

Chat. Give thee thy right, and hang thee up, with
    all thy beggar's brood!
What, wilt thou make me a thief, and say I stole thy
    good?

Gammer. Chill say nothing, ich warrant thee, but
    that ich can prove it well.
Thou fetched my good even from my door, cham
    able this to tell!

Chat. Did I, old witch, steal oft* was thine?   anything
    How should that thing be known?

Gammer. Ich can no tell; but up thou tookst it as
    though it had been thine own,

Chat. Marry, fie on thee, thou old gib, with all my
    very heart!

Gammer. Nay, fie on thee, thou ramp, thou rig,
    with all that take thy part!

Chat. A vengeance on those lips that layeth such
    things to my charge!

Gammer. A vengeance on those callet's* hips,   harlot's
    whose conscience is so large!   20

Chat. Come out, hog!

Gammer.   Come out, hog, and let have me right!

---

[25] That is, live at peace with thee.

CHAT (*coming out*). Thou arrant witch!

GAMMER.   Thou bawdy
   bitch, chill make thee curse this night!

CHAT. A bag and a wallet![26]

GAMMER.   A cart for a callet![27]

CHAT.   Why, weenest* thou thus to   thinkest
   prevail?

I hold* thee a groat I shall patch thy coat!   wager

GAMMER.   Thou wert as good kiss my tail!

Thou slut, thou cut,* thou rakes, thou jakes! Will not   harlot
   shame make thee hide thee?

CHAT. Thou scald, thou bald, thou rotten, thou
   glutton! I will no longer chide thee,

But I will teach thee to keep home.

GAMMER   Wilt thou, drunken beast?

HODGE. Stick to her, Gammer! Take her by the
   head, chill warrant you this feast!

Smite, I say, Gammer! Bite, I say, Gammer! I trow
   ye will be keen!

Where be your nails? Claw her by the jaws, pull me
   out both her eyne*   eyes/30

Gogs' bones, Gammer, hold up your head!

CHAT.   I trow, drab,* I shall dress thee.   harlot

Tarry, thou knave, I hold thee a groat I shall make
   these hands bless* thee!   beat

Take thou this, old whore, for amends, and learn thy
   tongue well to tame,

And say thou met at this bickering, not thy fellow
   but thy dame![28]

HODGE. Where is the strong-stewed whore? Chill
   gear* a whore's mark!   I will
                                                      give her
Stand out one's way,[29] that ich kill none in the dark!

Up, Gammer, an ye be alive! Chill fight now for us
   both.

Come no near me, thou scald callet! To kill thee
   ich were loth.

CHAT. Art here again, thou hoddy peak?* What,   blockhead
   Doll! Bring me out my spite.

HODGE. Chill broach thee with this, by'm father's
   soul, chill conjure that foul sprite!   40

[26] Probably, "a beggar's bag and wallet for thee!"
[27] "A cart for whipping thee for being a harlot!"
[28] "Not thy equal, but thy master (superior)."
[29] "Get out of the way."

(*To* Cock *within the* Gammer's *house.*)

Let door stand, Cock! Why comes, indeed? Keep door,
    thou whoreson boy!

    Chat. Stand to it, thou dastard, for thine ears, ise
      teach thee, a sluttish toy!

    Hodge. Gog's wounds, whore, chill make thee
      avaunt! Take heed, Cock, pull in the latch!

    Chat. I'faith, sir Loose-breech, had ye tarried, ye
      should have found your match!

    Gammer (*knocking her down from behind*). Now
      'ware thy throat, losel,* thouse pay for all!   scoundrel

    Hodge.   Well said, Gammer, by my soul.

House her, souse her, bounce her, trounce her,
    pull out her throat-bowl!*   Adam's apple

    Chat. Comest behind me, thou withered witch? An
      I get once on foot[30]

Thouse pay for all, thou old tarleather!

    (*Picking herself up.*)

                        I'll teach
    thee what 'longs to't!

Take thee this to make up thy mouth, till time thou
    come by more!

    (*She knocks* Gammer Gurton *down and runs away.*)

    Hodge. Up, Gammer, stand on your feet; where is
      the old whore?   50

Faith, would chad her by the face, chould crack
    her callet crown!*   harlot's head

    Gammer (*rising*). Ah, Hodge, Hodge, where was
      thy help, when vixen had me down?

    Hodge. By the Mass, Gammer, but for my staff Chat
      had gone nigh to spill you!

Ich think the harlot had not cared an chad not come,
    to kill you.

But shall we lose our neele thus?

    Gammer.   No, Hodge, chware* loth do so,   I were

Thinkest thou chill take that at her hand? No,
    Hodge, ich tell thee no!

    Hodge. Chould* yet this fray were well take up,   I wish
      and our neele at home.

'Twill be my chance else some to kill, wherever it be
    or whom!

    Gammer. We have a parson, Hodge, thou knows, a
      man esteemèd wise,

    30 "If I get up."

Mast* Doctor Rat; chill for him send, and let me   master
     hear his advise   60
He will her shrive for all this gear, and give her
     penance strait;
Wese* have our neele, else Dame Chat comes ne'er   We shall
     within heaven gate.
     HODGE. Yea, marry, Gammer, that ich think best;
        will you now for him send?
The sooner Doctor Rat be here, the sooner
     wese ha* an end,   we shall have
And hear, Gammer! Diccon's devil, as ich remember
     well,
Of cat, and Chat, and Doctor Rat, a felonous* tale   evil
     did tell.
Chold* you forty pound, that is the way your neele   I wager
     to get again.
     GAMMER. Chill ha him straight! Call out the boy,
        wese make him take the pain.
     HODGE. What, Cock, I say! Come out! What devil!
        Canst not hear?
     (COCK appears.)
     COCK. How now, Hodge? How does Gammer, is yet
        the weather clear?   70
What would chave* me to do?   you have
     GAMMER.   Come hither, Cock,
        anon!
Hence swith to Doctor Rat, hie thee that thou were
     gone,[31]
And pray him come speak with me, cham not well
     at ease.
Shalt have him* at his chamber, or else at Mother   find him
     Bee's;
Else seek him at Hob Filcher's shop, for as chard*   I heard
     it reported.
There is the best ale in all the town, and now is most
     resorted.*   attended
     COCK. An shall ich bring him with me, Gammer?
     GAMMER.   Yea, by and by, good Cock.
     COCK. Shalt see that [he] shall be here anon, else
        let me have on the dock.*   buttock
     HODGE. Now, Gammer, shall we two go in, and
        tarry* for his coming?   wait

    [31] "Run quickly to Doctor Rat and get thee gone."

What devil, woman! Pluck up your heart, and leave
    off all this gluming.*   sulking/80
Though she were stronger at the first, as ich think
    ye did find her,
Yet there ye drest the drunken sow what time ye
    came behind her.
    GAMMER. Nay, nay, cham sure she lost not all, for,
    set th'end to the beginning,
And ich doubt not but she will make small boast of
    her winning.
                        (*Exteunt.*)

SCENE 4

(*Enter* TIB, HODGE, *and* GAMMER.)
    TIB. See, Gammer, Gammer, Gib, our cat, cham
    afraid what* she aileth;   that
She stands me gasping behind the door, as though her
    wind her faileth:
Now let ich doubt what Gib should mean, that now
    she doth so dote.
    HODGE. Hold hither! I chold twenty pound, your
    neele is in her throat.
    (*Thinking the needle is in the cat.*)
Grope her, ich say, methinks ich feel it; does not
    prick your hand?
    GAMMER. Ich can feel nothing.
    HODGE.   No, ich know there's
    not within this land
A murraine* cat than Gib is, betwixt the Thames   more plagury
    and Tyne;
Shase* as much wit in her head almost as chave*   she has/I have
    in mine!
    TIB. Faith, shase eaten something, that will not
    easily down;
Whether she got it at home or abroad in the town   10
Ich cannot tell.
    GAMMER.   Alas, ich fear it be some crooked pin!
And then farewell Gib! She is undone, and lost all
    save the skin!*   fur
    HODGE. 'Tis your neele, woman, I say! Gog's soul!
    gime me a knife,

And chill have it out of her maw or else chall lose
  my life!

  GAMMER. What! Nay, Hodge, fie! Kill not our cat,
    'tis all the cats we ha now.

  HODGE. By the Mass, Dame Chat hays* me so moved   has
    ich care not what I kill, ma* God avow!   I make

Go to, then, Tib, to this gear!* Hold up her tail   business
  and take her!

Chill see what devil is in her guts! Chill take the
  pains to rake her!

  GAMMER. Rake a cat, Hodge! What wouldst thou do?

  HODGE.   What, thinkest that cham not able?

Did not Tom Tankard rake his curtal toore* day   the other
  standing in the stable?

  (*Enter* COCK.)   20

  GAMMER. Soft! Be content, let's hear what news
    Cock bringeth from Mast Rat.

  COCK. Gammer, chave been there as you bade, you
    wot* well about what.   know

'Twill not be long before he come, ich durst swear of*   on
  a book.

He bids you see ye be at home, and there for him to
  look.*   wait

  GAMMER. Where didst thou find him, boy? Was he
    not where I told thee?

  COCK. Yes, yes, even at Hob Filcher's house, by him
    that bought and sold me!

A cup of ale had in his hand, and a crab* lay in   crab-apple
  the fire;

Chad much ado to go and come, all was so full of
  mire.

And, Gammer, one thing I can tell, Hob Filcher's
  nawl was lost,

And Doctor Rat found it again hard beside the door
  post.   30

I chold a penny [he] can say something your neele
  again to set.

  GAMMER. Cham glad to hear so much, Cock, then
    trust he will not let*   fail

To help us herein best he can; therefore till time he
  come

Let us go in; if there be aught to get thou shalt have
  some.

ACT IV

Scene 1

(*Enter* Doctor Rat.)

RAT. A man were better twenty times be a bandog
   and bark,

Than here among such a sort be parish priest or
   clark,*   cleric

Where he shall never be at rest one pissing-while*   short while
   a day,

But he must trudge about the town, this way and
   that way;

Here to a drab, there to a thief, his shoes to tear and
   rent,

And that which is worst of all, at every knave's
   commandment!

I had not sit the space to drink two pots of ale,

But Gammer Gurton's sorry boy was straightway at
   my tail,

And she was sick, and I must come, to do I wot not
   what!

If once her finger's end but ache, trudge! Call for
   Doctor Rat!   10

And when I come not at their call, I only thereby
   lose;

For I am sure to lack* therefore a tithe pig or a goose.   lose

I warrant you, when truth is known, and told they
   have their tale,

The matter whereabout I come is not worth a halfpenny worth of ale;

Yet must I talk so sage and smooth, as though I were
   a gloser*   flatterer

Else, ere the year come at an end, I shall be sure the
   loser.

(*Enter* Gammer.)

What work ye, Gammer Gurton? How? Here is your
   friend Mast Rat.

   GAMMER. Ah, good Mast Doctor! Cha* troubled,   I have
     cha troubled you, chwot* well that!   I know

   RAT. How do ye, woman? Be ye lusty, or be ye not
     well at ease?

   GAMMER. By gis, Master, cham not sick, but yet
     chave a disease.[32]   20

   [32] "But yet I am troubled, uneasy."

Chad* a foul turn now of late, chill tell it you,   I have had
 by gigs!
 RAT. Hath your brown cow cast her calf, or your
 sandy sow her pigs?
 GAMMER. No, but chad been as good they had as
 this,[33] ich wot weel.*   know well
 RAT. What is the matter?
 GAMMER. Alas, alas! Cha lost my good neele!
My neele, I say, and wot ye what,[34] a drab came by
 and spied it,
And when I asked her for the same, the filth flatly
 denied it.
 RAT. What was she that?
 GAMMER. A dame, ich warrant you! She began to
 scold and brawl—
Alas, alas! Come hither, Hodge! This wretch can tell
 you all.

SCENE 2

(DOCTOR RAT *and* GAMMER. *Enter* HODGE.)
HODGE. Good morrow, Gaffer Vicar!
RAT.   Come on, fel-
 low, let us hear!
Thy dame hath said to me thou knowest of all this
 gear;
Let's see what thou canst say.
 HODGE.   By'm fay,* sir, that by my faith
 ye shall.
What matter so ever there was done, ich can tell your
 maship all:
 My Gammer Gurton here, see now,
  sat her down at this door, see now;
 And, as she began to stir her, see now,
  her neele fell to the floor, see now;
 And while her staff she took, see now,
  at Gib her cat to fling, see now,   10
 Her neele was lost in the floor, see now.
  Is not this a wondrous thing, see now?
 Then came the quean Dame Chat, see now,
  to ask for her black cup, see now:
 And even here at this gate, see now,
  she took that neele up, see now:

[33] "But it wouldn't have been worse than this."
[34] "Do you know what."

My Gammer then she yede,* see now,   went
  her neele again to bring, see now,
And was caught by the head, see now.
  Is not this a wondrous thing, see now?   20
She tare my Gammer's coat, see now,
  and scratched her by the face, see now;
Chad thought shad* stopped her throat, see now.   she had
  Is not this a wondrous case, see now?
When ich saw this, ich was wroth,* see now,   angry
  and start between them twain, see now;
Else ich durst* take a book oath, see now,   dare
  my gammer had been slain, see now.

GAMMER. This is even the whole matter, as Hodge
  has plainly told;
And chould fain* be quiet for my part, that chould.   gladly/30
But help us, good Master, beseech ye that ye do:
Else shall we both be beaten and lose our neele too.

RAT. What would ye have me to do? Tell me, that
  I were gone;
I will do the best that I can to set you both at one.[35]
But be ye sure Dame Chat hath this your neele
  found?

(Enter DICCON.)

GAMMER. Here comes the man that see her take it
  up off the ground.
Ask him yourself, Master Rat, if ye believe not me:
And help me to my neele, for God's sake and Saint
  Charity!

RAT. Come near, Diccon, and let us hear what thou
  can express.
Wilt thou be sworn thou seest Dame Chat this woman's
  neele have?   40

DICCON. Nay, by St. Benit, will I not, then might ye
  think me rave!*   mad

GAMMER. Why didst not thou tell me so even here?
  Canst thou for shame deny it?

DICCON. Aye, marry, Gammer; but I said I would
  not abide by it.

RAT. Will you say a thing, and not stick to it to
  try it?

DICCON. "Stick to it," quoth you, Master Rat? Marry
  sir, I defy it!

---

[35] "To make peace between you."

Nay, there is many an honest man, when he such
    blasts hath blown
In his friend's ears, he would be loth the same by him
    were known.
If such a toy be used oft among the honesty,*   *quality folk*
It may beseem a simple man of your and my degree.
    RAT. Then we be never the nearer, for all that you
      can tell!   50
    DICCON. Yea, marry, sir, if ye will do by mine advice
      and counsel.
If Mother Chat see all us here, she knoweth how the
    matter goes;
Therefore I rede* you three go hence, and within   *advise*
    keep close,
And I will into Dame Chat's house, and so the matter
    use,
That ere you could go twice to church I warrant you
    hear news.
She shall look well about her, but, I durst lay a pledge,
Ye shall of Gammer's neele have shortly better knowl-
    edge.
    GAMMER. Now, gentle Diccon, do so, and, good sir,
      let us trudge.
    RAT. By the Mass, I may not tarry so long to be
      your judge.
    DICCON. 'Tis but a little while, man; what! take so
      much pain!   60
If I hear no news of it, I will come sooner again.
    HODGE. Tarry so much, good Master Doctor, of
      your gentleness!
    RAT. Then let us hie us inward, and, Diccon, speed
      thy business.

                      (*They go inside the house.*)

SCENE 3

(DICCON *solo.*)
    DICCON (*to the audience*). Now, sirs, do you no
      more, but keep my counsel just,
And Doctor Rat shall thus catch some good, I trust.
But Mother Chat, my gossip, talk first withal I must:
For she must be chief captain to lay the Rat in the
    dust.
    (DAME CHAT *appears.*)

Good even, Dame Chat, in faith, and well met in this
    place!
    CHAT. Good even, my friend Diccon; whither walk
    ye this pace?
    DICCON. By my truth, even to you, to learn how the
    world goeth.
Heard ye no more of the other matter? Say me, now,
    by your troth!
    CHAT. O yes, Diccon, here the old whore, and
    Hodge, that great knave—
But, in faith, I would thou hadst seen—O Lord, I
    dressed them brave!   10
She bare me two or three souses* behind in the nape   blows
    of the neck,
Till I made her old weasand* to answer again,   windpipe
    "Keck!"
And Hodge, that dirty dastard, that at her elbow
    stands—
If one pair of legs had not been worth two pair of
    hands,
He had had his beard shaven if my nails would have
    served,
And not without a cause, for the knave it well
    deserved.
    DICCON. By the Mass, I can thee thank, wench, thou
    dist so well acquit thee!
    CHAT. An thadst* seen him, Diccon, it would   If thou hadst
    have made thee beshit thee
For laughter. The whoreson dolt at last caught up
    a club,
As though he would have slain the master devil
    Beelzebub.   20
But I set him soon inward.*   drove him inside
    DICCON.   O Lord, there is the
    thing
That Hodge is so offended! That makes him start
    and fling!*   rush about
    CHAT. Why? Makes the knave any moiling,* as ye   fuss
    have seen or heard?
    DICCON. Even now I saw him last, like a madman he
    fared,
And sware by heaven and hell he would awreak*   avenge
    his sorrow,

And leave you never a hen alive by eight of the clock
    to-morrow;
Therefore mark what I say, and my words see that
    ye trust.
Your hens be as good as dead, if ye leave them on
    the rust.*   roost
    CHAT. The knave dare as well go hang himself as
    go upon my ground.
    DICCON. Well, yet take heed I say, I must tell you
    my tale round.*   truly/30
Have you not about your house, behind your furnace
    or lead*   cauldron
A hole where a crafty knave may creep in for need?
    CHAT. Yes, by the Mass, a hole broke down, even
    within these two days.
    DICCON. Hodge he intends this same night to slip in
    there aways.
    CHAT. O Christ! That I were sure of it! In faith
    he should have his meed!*   punishment
    DICCON. Watch well, for the knave will be there as
    sure as is your creed.
I would spend myself a shilling to have him swingèd*   beaten
    well.
    CHAT. I am as glad as a woman can be of this thing
    to hear tell.
By Gog's bones, when he cometh, now that I know
    the matter,
He shall sure at the first skip to leap in scalding
    water,   40
With a worse turn besides; when he will let him come.
    DICCON. I tell you as my sister; you know what
    meaneth 'mum'!

                           (DAME CHAT *leaves*.)

SCENE 4

(DICCON *solo*.)
    DICCON. Now lack I but my doctor to play his part
    again.
And lo where he cometh towards, peradventure, to
    his pain!
    (*Enter* DOCTOR RAT.)
    RAT. What good news, Diccon, fellow? Is Mother
    Chat at home?

DICCON. She is, sir, and she is not, but it please her
    to whom;
Yet did I take her tardy, as subtle as she was.
    RAT. The thing that thou wentst for, hast thou
        brought it to pass?
    DICCON. I have done that* I have done, be it worse,   *what*
        be it better,
And Dame Chat at her wits end I have almost set her.
    RAT. Why, hast thou spied the neele? Quickly, I
        pray thee, tell!
    DICCON. I have spied it, in faith, sir, I handled
        myself so well;   10
And yet the crafty quean had almost take my trump.
But ere all came to an end, I set her in a dump.
    RAT. How so, I pray thee, Diccon?
    DICCON.   Marry, sir, will ye hear?
She was clapped down on the backside, by Cock's
    mother dear,
And there she sat sewing a halter or a band,
With no other thing save Gammer's needle in her
    hand.
As soon as any knock, if the filth be in doubt,
She needs but once puff, and her candle is out:
Now I, sir, knowing of every door the pin,
Came nicely,* and said no words, till time I was   *cautiously*
    within;   20
And there I saw the neele, even with these two eyes;
Whoever say the contrary, I will swear he lies.
    RAT. O Diccon, that I was not there then in thy
        stead!
    DICCON. Well, if ye will be ordered, and do by my
        rede,
I will bring you to a place, as the house stands,
Where ye shall take the drab with the neele in her
    hands.
    RAT. For God's sake do so, Diccon, and I will 'gage
        my gown
To give thee a full pot of the best ale in the town.
    DICCON. Follow me but a little, and mark what I
        will say;
Lay down your gown beside you; go to, come on
    your way!   30
See ye not what is here? A hole wherein ye may
    creep

Into the house, and suddenly unawares among them
    leap;
There shall ye find the bitchfox and the neele together.
Do as I bid you, man, come on your ways hither!
    RAT. Art thou sure, Diccon, the swill-tub stands
        not hereabout?
    DICCON. I was within myself, man, even now, there
        is no doubt.
Go softly, make no noise; give me your foot, Sir John.
    (*He helps* DOCTOR RAT *up.*)
Here will I wait upon you, till you come out anon.
    RAT. Help, Diccon! Out, alas! I shall be slain
        among them!
    DICCON. If they give you not the needle, tell them
        that ye will hang them.   40
'Ware that! How, my wenches! Have ye caught the
    Fox
That used to make revel among your hens and cocks?
Save his life yet for his order, though he sustain some
    pain.
Gog's bread I am afraid they will beat out his brain.
    (DICCON *runs away, and* DOCTOR RAT *reappears,*
    badly battered.)
    RAT. Woe worth the hour that I came here!
And woe worth him that wrought this gear!
A sort of drabs and queans have me blessed*—   wounded
Was ever creature half so evil dressed?*   treated
Whoever it wrought, and first did invent it
He shall, I warrant him, ere long repent it!   50
I will spend all I have without my skin
But he shall be brought to the plight I am in!
Master Bayly,* I trow, an he be worth his ears,   Master Bailiff
Will snaffle these murderers and all that them
    bears.*   support
I will surely neither bite nor sup
Till I fetch him hither, this matter to take up.
                                  (*Exit.*)

ACT V

SCENE 1

(*Enter* DOCTOR RAT, MASTER BAYLY, *and his assistant,* SCAPETHRIFT.)
    BAYLY. I can perceive none other, I speak it from
        my heart,

But either ye are in all the fault, or else in the
    greatest part.
    RAT. If it be counted his fault, besides all his
    grieves,
When a poor man is spoiled and beaten among
    thieves,
Then I confess my fault herein, at this season;
But I hope you will not judge so much against reason.
    BAYLY. And, methinks, by your own tale, of all that
    ye name.
If any played the thief, you were the very same.
The women they did nothing, as your words make
    probation.
But stoutly withstood your forcible invasion.   10
If that a thief at your window to enter should begin,
Would you hold forth your hand and help to pull
    him in?
Or you would keep him out? I pray you answer me.
    RAT. Marry, keep him out, and a good cause why!
But I am no thief, sir, but an honest learned clark.
    BAYLY. Yea, but who knoweth that, when he meets
    you in the dark?
I am sure your learning shines not out at your nose!
Was it any marvel though the poor woman arose
And start up, being afraid of that[36] was in her purse?
Methink you may be glad that your luck was no
    worse.   20
    RAT. Is not this evil enough, I pray you, as you
    think?
    (Showing his broken head.)
    BAYLY. Yea, but a man in the dark, if chances do
    wink,[37]
As soon he smites his father as any other man,
Because for lack of light discern him he ne can.*   cannot
Might it not have been your luck with a spit to have
    been slain?
    RAT. I think I am little better,[38] my scalp is cloven
    to the brain.
If there be all the remedy, I know who bears the
    knocks.

[36] "Worried about what."
[37] "If luck is blind."
[38] "Hardly better off."

BAYLY. By my troth, and well worthy besides to kiss
the stocks!
To come in on the back side when ye might go
about![39]
I know none such, unless they long to have their
brains knocked out.   30
    RAT. Well, will you be so good, sir, as talk with
Dame Chat,
And know what she intended? I ask no more but
that.
    BAYLY (*To* SCAPETHRIFT). Let her be called, fellow,
because of Master Doctor,
I warrant in this case she will be her own proctor;
She will tell her own tale in metre or in prose,
And bid you seek your remedy, and so go wipe your
nose.

SCENE 2

(MASTER BAYLY *and* DOCTOR RAT. *Enter* SCAPE-
THRIFT *with* DAME CHAT.)
    BAYLY. Dame Chat, Master Doctor upon you here
complained
That you and your maids should him much misorder,
And taketh many an oath, that no word he feigned,
Laying to your charge, how you thought him to
murder;
And on his part again, that same man saith furder*   **further**
He never offended you in word nor intent.
To hear you answer hereto, we have now for you sent.
    CHAT. That I would have murdered him? Fie on
him, wretch,
And evil mought he thee for it,[40] our Lord I beseech.
I will swear on all the books that opens and shuts,   10
He faineth* this tale out of his own guts;   **feigns**
For this seven weeks with me I am sure he sat not
down.
Nay, ye have other minions,* in the other end of the   **favorites**
town,
Where ye were liker to catch such a blow,
Than anywhere else, as far as I know!

[39] "Go in through the front."
[40] "Ill may he thrive for it."

BAYLY. Belike, then, Master Doctor, yon stripe
  there ye got not!
RAT. Think you I am so mad that where I was beat
  I wot not?
Will ye believe this quean, before she hath tried* it?   proved
It is not the first deed she hath done and afterwards
  denied it.
  CHAT. What, man, will you say I broke your head?   20
  RAT. How canst thou prove the contrary?
  CHAT. Nay, how provest thou that I did the dead*?   deed
  RAT. Too plainly, by St. Mary,
This proof I trow may serve, though I no word spoke!
  (*Showing his broken head.*)
  CHAT. Because thy head is broken, was it I that it
  broke?
I saw thee, Rat, I tell thee, not once within this
  fortnight.
  RAT. No, marry, thou sawest me not, for why thou
  hadst no light;
But I felt thee for all the dark, beshrew thy smooth
  cheeks!
And thou groped* me, this will declare any day this   seized
  six weeks.
  (*Showing his head.*)
  BAYLY. Answer me to this, Mast Rat: when caught
  you this harm of yours?   30
  RAT. A while ago, sir, God he knoweth, within less
  than these two hours.
  BAYLY. Dame Chat, was there none with you
  (confess, i'faith) about that season?
What, woman? Let it be what it will, 'tis neither
  felony nor treason.
  CHAT. Yea, by my faith, Master Bayly, there was a
  knave not far
Who caught one good fillip on the brow with a
  door-bar,
And well was he worthy, as it seemed to me;
But what is that to this man, since this was not he?
  BAYLY. Who was it then? Let's hear!
  RAT.   Alas, sir, ask you that?
Is it not made plain enough by the own mouth of
  Dame Chat?
The time agreeth, my head is broken, her tongue
  cannot lie,   40

Only upon a bare nay she saith it was not I.

    CHAT. No, marry, was it not indeed! Ye shall hear
      by this one thing:

This afternoon a friend of mine for goodwill gave
    me warning,

And bade me well look to my roost, and all my
    capons' pens,

For if I took not better heed, a knave would have my
    hens.

Then I, to save my goods, took so much pains as him
    to watch;

And as good fortune served me, it was my chance him
    for to catch.

What strokes he bare away, or other what was his
    gains,

I wot not, but sure I am he had something for his
    pains!

    BAYLY. Yet tells thou not who it was.

    CHAT.   Who it was? A false thief,   50

That came like a false fox my pullain* to kill and   poultry
    mischief!

    BAYLY. But knowest thou not his name?

    CHAT.   I know it; but what than*?   then

It was that crafty cullion,* Hodge, my Gammer   rascal
    Gurton's man.

    BAYLY. Call me the knave hither, he shall sure kiss
    the stocks.

I shall teach him a lesson for filching hens or cocks!

    RAT. I marvel, Master Bayly, so bleared be your
    eyes;

An egg is not so full of meat, as she is full of lies:

When she hath played this prank, to excuse all this
    gear,

She layeth the fault in such a one as I know was not
    there.

    CHAT. Was he not there? Look on his pate, that
    shall be his witness!   60

    RAT. I would my head were half so whole; I would
    seek no redress!

    (*Enter* GAMMER GURTON.)

    BAYLY. God bless you, Gammer Gurton!

    GAMMER.   God dild* you, master mine!   reward

    BAYLY. Thou hast a knave within thy house—
    Hodge, a servant of thine;

They tell me that busy knave is such a filching one,
That hen, pig, goose or capon, thy neighbour can
    have none.
  GAMMER. By God, cham much amoved, to hear
    any such report!
Hodge was not wont, ich trow, to 'have* him in   behave himself
    that sort.
  CHAT. A thievisher knave is not alive, more filching,
    nor more false;
Many a truer man than he has hanged up by the
    halse;*   neck
And thou, his dame—of all his theft thou art the sole
    receiver;   70
For Hodge to catch, and thou to keep, I never knew
    none better!
  GAMMER. Sir-reverence[41] of your masterdom, an
    you were out adoor,
Chould be so bold, for all her brags, to call her
    arrant whore;
An ich knew Hodge as bad as thou, ich wish me
    endless sorrow
And chould not take the pains to hang up before
    to-morrow!
  CHAT. What have I stolen from thee or thine, thou
    ill-favoured old trot?
  GAMMER. A great deal more, by God's blest, than
    chever* by thee got!   I ever
That thou knowest well, I need not say it.
  BAYLY.   Stop there, I say,
And tell me here, I pray you, this matter by the way,
How chance Hodge is not here? Him would I fain
    have had.   80
  GAMMER. Alas, sir, he'll be here anon; ha be
    handled too bad.
  CHAT (*thinking that* HODGE's *head was broke, and
    that* GAMMER *would not let him come before
    them*). Master Bayly, sir, ye be not such a fool, well
    I know,
But ye perceive by this lingering there is a pad* in   toad
    the straw.[42]
  GAMMER. Chill show you his face, ich warrant thee;
    lo, now where he is!

[41] "With all respect to your position."
[42] That is, concealed wrongdoing.

(Enter HODGE.*)*

BAYLY. Come on, fellow, it is told me thou
    art a shrew,* iwis.*   villain/certainly
Thy neighbour's hens thou takest and playest the
    two-legged fox;
Their chickens and their capons too, and now and
    then their cocks.

    HODGE. Ich defy them all that dare it say, cham as
    true* as the best!   honest

    BAYLY. Wert not thou take within this hour in
    Dame Chat's hens' nest?

    HODGE. Take there? No, master; should not do't
    for a house full of gold!   90

    CHAT. Thou or the devil in thy coat—swear this I
    dare be bold.

    RAT. Swear me no swearing, quean, the devil he
    give thee sorrow!
All is not worth a gnat thou canst swear till
    tomorrow.
Where is the harm he hath? Show it, by God's bread!
Ye beat him with a witness, but the stripes light on
    my head!

    HODGE. Beat me? Gog's blessed body, chould first,
    ich trow, have burst thee!
Ich think an chad my hands loose, callet, chould
    have crust* thee!   crushed

    CHAT. Thou shitten knave, I trow thou knowest the
    full weight of my fist;
I am fouly deceived unless thy head and my door-bar
    kist.

    HODGE. Hold thy chat, whore, thou criest so
    loud, can no man else be hard.*   heard/100

    CHAT. Well, knave, and I had thee alone, I would
    surely rap thy costard!*   head

    BAYLY. Sir, answer me to this: is thy head whole or
    broken?

    HODGE. Yea, Master Bayly, blest be every good
    token,
Is my hear whole! Ich warrant you, 'tis neither scurvy
    nor scald!
What, you foul beast, does think 'tis either piled* or   hairless
    bald?
Nay, ich thank God, chill not for all that thou mayst
    spend

That chad one scab on my narse as broad as thy
    finger's end.
  BAYLY. Come nearer here!
  HODGE.   Yes, that I dare.
  BAYLY.   By our Lady, here is no harm,
Hodge's head is whole enough, for all Dame Chat's
    charm.
  CHAT. By Gog's blest, however the thing he
    cloaks or smoulders,*   conceals/110
I know the blows he bare away, either with
    head or shoulders.
Camest thou not, knave,˙ within this hour, creeping
    into my pens,
And there was caught within my house groping
    among my hens?
  HODGE. A plague both on the hens and thee! A cart,
    whore, a cart!
Chould* I were hanged as high as a tree an chwere   I wish
    as false as thou art!
Give my gammer again her washical[43] thou stole away
    in thy lap!
  GAMMER. Yea, Master Bayly, there is a thing you
    know not on, mayhap;
This drab, she keeps away my good, the devil he
    might her snare!
Ich pray you that ich might have a right action on
    her.
  CHAT. Have I thy good, old filth, or any such old
    sows?   120
I am as true, I would thou knew, as skin between thy
    brows!
  GAMMER. Many a truer hath been hanged, though
    you escape the danger!
  CHAT. Thou shalt answer, by God's pity, for this
    thy foul slander!
  BAYLY. Why, what can ye charge her withal? To
    say so ye do not well.
  GAMMER. Marry, a vengeance to her heart! That
    whore has stolen my neele!
  CHAT. Thy needle, old witch? How so? It were alms
    thy soul to knock!
So didst thou say the other day that I had stolen thy
    cock,

[43] "What shall I call it."

And roasted him to my breakfast, which shall not be
    forgotten;
The devil pull out thy lying tongue and teeth that be
    so rotten!

    GAMMER. Give me my neele! As for my cock,
        could* be very loth   I should/130
That chould hear tell he should hang on thy false
    faith and troth.

    BAYLY. Your talk is such, I can scarce learn who
        should be most in fault.

    GAMMER. Yet shall be find no other wight,* save   person
        she, by bread and salt!

    BAYLY. Keep ye content* awhile, see that your   quiet
        tongues ye hold.
Methinks you should remember this is no place to
    scold.
How knowest thou, Gammer Gurton, Dame Chat thy
    needle had?

    GAMMER. To name you, sir, the party, could not
        be very glad.

    BAYLY. Yea, but we must needs hear it, and
        therefore say it boldly.

    GAMMER. Such one as told the tale fully soberly
        and coldly,
Even he that looked on—will swear on a book—
What time this drunken gossip my fair long neele
    uptook,   141
Diccon, master, the Bedlam, cham very sure ye know
    him.

    BAYLY. A false knave, by God's pity! Ye were but a
        fool to trow him.
I durst adventure* well the price of my best cape,   wager
That when the end is known, all will turn to a jape.*   trick
Told he not you that besides she stole your cock that
    tide?*   time

    GAMMER. No, master, no indeed; for then he should
        have lied.
My cock is, I thank Christ, safe and well a-fine.*   in the end

    CHAT. Yea, but that ragged colt, that whore, that
        Tib of thine,
Said plainly thy cock was stolen, and in my house
    was eaten.   150
That lying cut* is lost that she is not swinged and   harlot
    beaten,

And yet for all my good name, it were a small
   amends!
I pick not this gear,* hearest thou, out of my finger's   matter
   ends;
But he that heard it told me, who thou of late didst
   name,
Diccon, whom all men knows, it was the very same.
   BAYLY. This is the case: you lost your needle about
   the doors,
And she answers again, she has no cock of yours;
Thus in your talk and action, from that* you do   what
   intend,[44]
She is whole five mile wide, from that she doth
   defend.
Will you say she hath your cock?
   GAMMER.   No, marry, sir, that chill not,   160
   BAYLY. Will you confess her neele?
   CHAT.   Will I? No sir, will I not.
   BAYLY. Then there lieth all the matter.
   GAMMER.   Soft, master, by the way!
Ye know she could do little an she could not say nay.
   BAYLY. Yea, but he that made one lie about your
   cock stealing,
Will not stick to make another, what time lies be in
   dealing.[45]
I ween* the end will prove this brawl did first arise   believe
Upon no other ground but only Diccon's lies.
   CHAT. Though some be lies, as you belike have
   espied* them,   discovered
Yet other some be true, by proof I have well tried
   them.
   BAYLY. What other thing beside this, Dame Chat?
   CHAT.   Marry, sir, even this.   170
The tale I told before, the self same tale it was his;
He gave me, like a friend, warning against my loss,
Else had my hens be stolen each one, by God's cross!
He told me Hodge would come, and in he came
   indeed,
But as the matter chanced, with greater haste than
   speed.
This truth was said, and true was found, as truly I
   report.

[44] "From what you mean."
[45] "When he is bent on lying."

BAYLY. If Doctor Rat be not deceived, it was of
    another sort.
RAT. By God's mother, thou and he be a couple of
    subtle foxes!
Between you and Hodge, I bear away the boxes.*   blows
Did not Diccon appoint the place, where thou
    shouldst stand to meet him?   180
    CHAT. Yes, by the Mass, and if he came, bade me
    not stick to speet* him.   spit at
    RAT. God's sacrament! The villain knave hath
    dressed us round about!
He is the cause of all this brawl, that dirty shitten
    lout!
When Gammer Gurton here complained and made
    a rueful moan,
I heard him swear that you had gotten her needle
    that was gone;
And this to try, he further said, he was full loth;
    howbeit
He was content with small ado to bring me where to
    see it.
And where ye sat, he said full certain, if I would
    follow his rede,
Into your house a privy way he would me guide and
    lead,
And where ye had it in your hands, sewing about a
    clout,   190
And set me in the back hole, thereby to find you out:
And whilst I sought a quietness, creeping upon my
    knees,
I found the weight of your door bar for my reward
    and fees.
Such is the luck that some men gets while they begin
    to mell*   meddle
In setting at one such as were out,[46] minding* to   intending
    make all well.
    HODGE. Was not well blest, Gammer, to scape that
    stour?* And chad been there,   fight
Then chad been dressed,[47] belike, as ill, by the Mass,
    as Gaffer Vicar.[48]

[46] "In making peace between those who have a falling out."
[47] "I would have been treated."
[48] He means Master Doctor Rat, the vicar.

BAYLY. Marry, sir, here is a sport alone; I looked
    for such an end.
If Diccon had not played the knave, this had been
    soon amend.*   amended
My Gammer here he made a fool, and dressed* her   treated
    as she was;   200
And Goodwife Chat he set to school till both parts*   parties
    cried alas!
And Doctor Rat was not behind, whilst Chat his
    crown did pare.⁴⁹
I would the knave had been stark blind, if Hodge
    had not his share.
    HODGE. Cham meetly well sped already
    amongs,* cham dressed like a colt!   all this while
An chad not had the better wit, chad been made
    a dolt
    BAYLY (To SCAPETHRIFT). Sir knave, make haste
    Diccon were here, fetch him, wherever he be!
                            (Exit SCAPETHRIFT.)
    CHAT. Fie on the villain, fie, fie! that makes us thus
    agree!
    GAMMER. Fie on him, knave, with all my heart!
    Now fie! and fie again!
    RAT. Now 'fie on him!' may I best say, whom he
    hath almost slain.
(SCAPETHRIFT returns with DICCON.)
    BAYLY. Lo where he cometh at hand, belike he was
    not fare!*   far/210
Diccon, here be two or three thy company cannot
    spare.
    DICCON. God bless you, an you may be blest, so
    many all at once.
    CHAT. Come knave, it were a good deed to geld
    thee, by Cock's bones!
Seest not thy handiwork? Sir Rat, can ye forbear*   forgive
    him?
    DICCON. A vengeance on those hands light, for my
    hands came not near him.
The whoreson priest hath lift the pot in some of
    these alewives' chairs

⁴⁹ "While Chat pounded his head."

That his head would not serve him, belike, to come
  down the stairs.[50]
  BAYLY. Nay, soft! Thou mayest not play the knave,
  and have this language too!
If thou thy tongue bridle a while, the better mayest
  thou do.[51]
Confess the truth, as I shall ask, and cease awhile to
  fable;*   lie/220
And for thy fault I promise thee thy handling shall
  be reasonable.
Hast thou not made a lie or two, to set these two by
  the ears?
  DICCON. What if I have? Five hundred such have I
  seen within these seven years:
I am sorry for nothing else but that I see not the
  sport
Which was between them when they met, as they
  themselves report.
  BAYLY. The greatest thing—Master Rat, ye see how
  he is drest!
  DICCON. What devil need he be groping so deep,
  in Goodwife Chat's hens' nest?
  BAYLY. Yea, but it was thy drift to bring him into
  the briars.
  DICCON. God's bread! Hath not such an old fool
  wit to save his ears?
He showeth himself herein, ye see, so very a cox,*   fool/230
The cat was not so madly allured by the fox
To run into the snares was set for him, doubtless;
For he leapt in for mice, and this Sir John* for   priest
  madness.
  RAT. Well, an ye shift no better, ye losel,*   rogue
  lither,* and lazy,   sluggard
I will go near for this to make ye leap at a daisy.*   be hanged
In the king's name, Master Bayly, I charge you set
  him fast.*   arrest him
  DICCON. What, fast at cards, or fast on sleep? It is
  the thing I did last.
  RAT. Nay, fast in fetters, false varlet, according
  to thy deeds.

---

[50] That is, "if the priest's head is cracked, he must have fallen down the
stairs in an ale-house while drunk."
[51] "You would do well to bridle your tongue" after all your knavery.

BAYLY. Master Doctor, there is no remedy, I must   require
    entreat you needs*
Some other kind of punishment.

RAT.   Nay by all hallows[52]   240
His punishment, if I may judge, shall be naught else
    but the gallows.

BAYLY. That were too sore, a spiritual man to be so
    extreme!

RAT. Is he worthy any better, sir? How do ye judge
    and deem?

BAYLY. I grant him worthy punishment, but in no
    wise so great.

GAMMER. It is a shame, ich tell you plain, for such
    false knaves entreat!
He has almost undone us all—that is as true as steel—
And yet for all this great ado cham never the ne'er
    my neele![53]

BAYLY. Canst thou not say anything to that, Diccon,
    with least or most?

DICCON. Yea, marry, sir, this much I can say well,
    the needle is lost.

BAYLY. Nay, canst not thou tell which way that
    needle may be found?   250

DICCON. No, by my fay, sir, though I might have an
    hundred pound.

HODGE. Thou liar, lickdish, didst not say the neele
    would be gitten?*   gotten

DICCON. No, Hodge, by the same token, you were
    that time beshitten*   frightened
For fear of Hobgoblin*—you wot well what I mean;   the devil
As long as it is since, I fear me yet ye be scarce clean.

BAYLY. Well, Master Rat, you must both learn and
    teach us to forgive.
Since Diccon hath confession made, and is so clean
    shrive;*   shrived
If ye to me consent, to amend this heavy chance,*   ill luck
I will enjoin him here some open kind of penance,
Of this condition (where ye know my fee is twenty
    pence):   260
For the bloodshed, I am agreed with you here to
    dispense;

---

[52] "By all the saints."
[53] "I am no nearer to finding my needle."

Ye shall go quit, so that ye grant the matter now to
    run
To end with mirth among us all, even as it was
        begun.
 CHAT. Say yea, Master Vicar, and he shall sure
  confess to be your debtor,
And all we that be here present will love you much
        the better.
 RAT. My part is the worst; but since you all
  hereon agree,
Go even to, Master Bayly! Let it be so for me!
 BAYLY. How sayest thou, Diccon? Art content this
  shall on me depend?
 DICCON. Go to, Master Bayly, say on your
  mind,* I know ye are my friend.   *what you think*
 BAYLY (*jovially giving mock judgement*). Then
  mark ye well: To recompense this thy former
  action—   270
Because thou hast offended all, to make them
        satisfaction,
Before their faces here kneel down, and, as I shall
        thee teach—
For thou shalt take an oath of Hodge's leather
        breech:
First, for Master Doctor, upon pain of his curse,
Where he will pay for all, thou never draw thy
        purse;
And when ye meet at one pot he shall have the first
        pull,
And thou shalt never offer him the cup but it be full.
To Goodwife Chat thou shalt be sworn, even on the
        same wise,
If she refuse thy money once, never to offer it twice.
Thou shalt be bound by the same, here as thou dost
        take it,   280
When thou mayest drink of free cost, thou never
        forsake it.
For Gammer Gurton's sake, again sworn shalt thou
        be,
To help her to her needle again if it do lie in thee;[54]
And likewise be bound, by the virtue of that,

----

[54] "To help her find her needle if you can."

To be of good abearing to Gib her great cat.
Last of all, for Hodge the oath to scan,
Thou shalt never take him for fine gentleman.

HODGE. Come on, fellow Diccon, chall* be even   I shall
    with thee now![55]

BAYLY. Thou wilt not stick to do this, Diccon, I   refuse
    trow?

DICCON. Now, by my father's skin! My hand down
    down I lay it!   290
Look, as I have promised, I will not denay* it.   deny
But, Hodge, take good heed now, thou do not beshite
    me!

    (*He gives him a good blow on the buttocks, and
    HODGE gives a shriek, as if he were stabbed.*)

HODGE. Gog's heart! Thou false villain, dost thou
    bite me?

BAYLY. What, Hodge, doth he hurt thee ere ever
    he begin?

HODGE. He thrust me into the buttock with a
    bodkin* or a pin!   dagger
I say, Gammer! Gammer!

GAMMER.   How now Hodge, how now?

HODGE (*pulling something out of his trousers from
    behind*). God's malt, Gammer Gurton!

GAMMER.   Thou art mad, ich trow!

HODGE. Will you see the devil, Gammer?

GAMMER.   The devil, son! God bless us!

HODGE. Chould ich were hanged, Gammer——

GAMMER.   Marry, see, ye might dress us——

HODGE (*holding up the needle*). Chave* it, by the   I have
    mass, Gammer!

GAMMER.   What? Not my neele, Hodge?   300

HODGE. Your neele, Gammer! Your neele!

GAMMER.   No, fie, dost but dodge!

HODGE. Cha* found your neele, Gammer, here in   I have
    my hand be it!

GAMMER. For all the loves on earth, Hodge, let me
    see it!

HODGE (*showing her the needle*). Soft, Gammer!

GAMMER.   Good Hodge!

HODGE.   Soft, ich say; tarry awhile!

---

[55] The idea is that Diccon is ordered to take an oath by laying his hand on
Hodge's buttocks.

GAMMER. Nay, sweet Hodge, say truth, and do not
    me beguile!

HODGE. Cham sure on it, ich warrant you; it goes
    no more astray.

GAMMER. Hodge, when I speak so fair; wilt still say
    me nay?

HODGE. Go near the light, Gammer, this—well, in
    faith, good luck!—

Chwas almost undone, 'twas so far in my buttock!

GAMMER. 'Tis mine owne dear neele, Hodge,
    sickerly* I wot!   surely/310

HODGE. Cham I not a good son, Gammer, cham I
    not?

GAMMER. Christ's blessing light on thee, hast made
    me for ever!

HODGE. Ich knew that ich must find it, else could
    a had it never![56]

CHAT. By my troth, gossip Gurton, I am even as
    glad

As though I mine own self as good a turn had!

BAYLY. And I, by my conscience, to see it so come
    forth,

Rejoice so much at it as three needles be worth.

D. RAT. I am no whit sorry to see you so rejoice.

DICCON. Nor I much the gladder for all this noise;

Yet say "Gramercy, Diccon," for springing* of the   ferreting out
    game.   320

GAMMER. Gramercy, Diccon, twenty times! O how
    glad cham!

If that should do so much, your Masterdom to come
    hether,

    (*To* MASTER BAYLY.)

Master Rat, Goodwife Chat, and Diccon together,

Cha but one halfpenny, as far as ich know it,

And chill not rest this night till ich bestow it.

If ever ye love me, let us go in and drink.

BAYLY. I am content, if the rest think as I think.

Master Rat, it shall be best for you if we so do;

Then shall you warm you and dress yourself too.

DICCON (*to the audience*). Soft, sirs, take us with
    you, the company shall be the more!   330

---

[56] "Else I wish I never had it."

As proud comes behind, they say, as any goes before!
But now, my good masters, since we must be gone,
And leave you behind us here all alone,
Since at our last ending thus merry we be,
For Gammer Gurton's needle's sake, let us have a
    *plaudite!**   applause

Tudor Tragedy

Early Tudor tragedy was associated with the literary efforts of the law students of the Inns of Court in London. It reflected the interest in great events, history and politics the young men of the Inns of Court would be expected to entertain. Tragedy during the Renaissance was, in fact, more or less identified with history, and history with the political ambitions which involved highly placed individuals in struggles for power that culminated in crime and disaster. *Gorboduc* (1561–1562), the most famous of the Inns of Court plays, is characteristically a tragedy of considerable historical range and conveys appropriate lessons of a moral and political nature.

Early Tudor tragedy followed classical models, and the dramatic work of Seneca was the one international model recognized wherever the influence of the Renaissance was felt in Europe. In *Gorboduc*, the five-act dramatic form, the choruses, and the reports of off-stage action by a *Nuntius*, or Messenger, as well as the general theme of revenge, are Senecan features. To these were added allegorical pantomimes or "dumb shows" derived from Italian pageants known as *intermedii*; and a general influence from Italian Renaissance tragedy, itself patterned after Seneca's works, is to be found in the play. It was written by authors who were naturally responsive to classical and renaissance example: Thomas Sackville (1536–1608), a barrister of the Inner Temple, later the Earl of Dorset and Lord High Treasurer of England, and Thomas Norton (1532–1584), who became a distinguished lawyer.

Sackville was a poet of some distinction and contributed the best poems, *Induction* and *The Complaint of Buckingham*, to the 1563 edition of *A Mirror for Magistrates*, a collection of narrative poems dealing with the tragedies of famous persons, first licensed for publication in 1559. It was no doubt Sackville's facility in verse writing that accounted for the most important feature of *Gorboduc*, the substitution of blank verse for rhymed verse in the English drama. Blank verse, consisting of unrhymed iambic pentameter (introduced into English versification by the Earl of Surrey's translation of

Books II and III of Virgil's epic poem, the *Aeneid*), displaced the doggerel of the native drama and provided a suit-
ably sonorous yet also "natural" medium for the writing of
tragedy. It became the standard form of versification for plays
within a quarter of a century and developed into the great
poetic medium of Christopher Marlowe, William Shakespeare,
Ben Jonson, and John Webster. Also important in the history
of English drama is the fact that the young authors of this
work, although consciously Senecan in technique and classi-
cists by intention, took for their subject British legendary
material.

Gorboduc proved so successful after its premiere in the Hall
of the Inner Temple, where both authors were students, that
it was repeated before Queen Elizabeth as a command performance. It set the fashion for other Senecan tragedies. No
less than five young law students of the Inner Temple col-
laborated on another Senecan tragedy, *Gismonde of Salerne,*
which was presented before the Queen in 1566. Although
romantic in substance, dealing with a love story first related
by Boccaccio, it had all the formal Senecan features, including
a moralizing Chorus. Originally written in rhymed couplets,
it was rewritten in blank verse many years later by one of the
authors, Robert Wilmot, in 1591, and published under a new
title, *Tancred and Gismunda.* Another Senecan tragedy, *The
Misfortunes of Arthur,* was written by Thomas Hughes and
other law students of Gray's Inn in London as late as 1588
and performed for the Queen with dumb-shows conceived by
the young Francis Bacon among others. King Arthur was the
protagonist, but his story had none of the idealization of
knighthood associated with that celebrated name in romance;
the Arthur of this play commits incest with his sister and is
killed by their illegitimate son Mordred, who not only rebels
against Arthur but seduces the latter's Queen, Guinevere. A
Ghost calling for vengeance, a *Nuntius* reporting unseen action, a Chorus, several confidants, sententious passages, and
indeed direct quotations from Seneca's tragedies make this
play one of the most Senecan to be written in the period. It
marks the culmination and end of this type of pseudo-classic
drama already beginning to be supplanted by typically Elizabethan drama which presented the action of a play to the
audience instead of relegating it to narration by the Messenger.

No early work of tragic character was, however, as impressive as *Gorboduc.* Its very action, presented with a typically
British disregard of the unities of time and place, and its very

rhetoric had force and relevance for the times since it dealt with the dangers of civil war. This was becoming a subject of grave concern to Elizabeth's subjects, since problems of the succession would arise if their Virgin Queen should fail to marry and die without leaving an heir to the throne. No doubt both authors of the work, who became members of the Queen's first Parliament, thought of themselves chiefly as statesmen enforcing a warning against divided rule in the kingdom rather than as professional playwrights.

Imitations of Senecan drama had a vogue among the educated, Renaissance-influenced gentlemen of London. They could read the plays in Latin, of course; and five of Seneca's plays were separately translated as well as possibly performed between 1559 and 1566 before the famous complete translation, the *Ten Tragedies,* was published in 1581. But the tragedy of Gorboduc, the ancient king who abdicated in favor of his two sons and so allowed his kingdom to fall to pieces, was no academic exercise for Sackville and Norton. The uninterrupted seriousness of their play, its semi-abstractness that links it with the medieval morality plays, its stiffness and maxim-hurling rhetoric, and the symmetrical organization of the action into parallel situations—all these features serve the authors' high intention of instructing their times. And a high intention, a striving to achieve significant art and give meaning to fatality, is an indispensable ferment in the production of tragedy. It so happened, then, that the extraliterary interest of the two young authors of *Gorboduc* prefigured the greatest literary achievement of the Elizabethan Age—the creation of high tragedy by Marlowe, Shakespeare and the latter's contemporaries.

Gorboduc

By Thomas Norton and Thomas Sackville

THE ARGUMENT

Gorboduc, King of Britain, divided his realm in his life time to his sons, Ferrex and Porrex. The sons fell to dissension. The younger killed the elder. The mother, that more dearly loved the elder, for revenge killed the younger. The people, moved with the cruelty of the fact, rose in rebellion, and slew both father and mother. The nobility assembled, and most terribly destroyed the rebels; and afterwards, for want of issue of the Prince, whereby the succession of the crown became uncertain, they fell to civil war, in which both they and many of their issues were slain, and the land for a long time almost desolate and miserably wasted.

Characters

GORBODUC, King of Great Britain.

VIDENA, Queen, and wife to King Gorboduc.

FERREX, Elder son to King Gorboduc.

PORREX, Younger son to King Gorboduc.

CLOTYN, Duke of Cornwall.

FERGUS, Duke of Albany.

MANDUD, Duke of Loegris.

GWENARD, Duke of Cumberland.

EUBULUS, Secretary to the King.

AROSTUS, a Counsellor to the King.

DORDAN, a Counsellor assigned by the King to his eldest son Ferrex.

PHILANDER, a Counsellor assigned by the King to his youngest son, Porrex.
Both being of the old king's council before.

HERMON, a Parasite remaining with Ferrex.

TYNDAR, a Parasite remaining with Porrex.

NUNTIUS, a messenger of the elder brother's death.

NUNTIUS, a Messenger of Duke Fergus rising in arms.

MARCELLA, a Lady of the Queen's privy-chamber.

CHORUS, four ancient and sage men of Britain.

The Order of the Dumb Show Before the First Act, and the Signification Thereof.

First, the music of violins began to play, during which came in upon the stage six wild men, clothed in leaves. Of whom the first bare on his neck a fagot of small sticks, which they all, both severally and together, assayed with all their strength to break; but it could not be broken by them. At the length, one of them pulled out one of the sticks, and brake it: and the rest plucking out all the other sticks, one after another, did easily break them, the same being severed; which being conjoined, they had before attempted in vain. After they had this done, they departed the stage, and the music ceased. Hereby was signified, that a state knit in unity doth continue strong against all force, but being divided, is easily destroyed; as befell upon Duke [King] Gorboduc dividing his land to his two sons, which he before held in monarchy; and upon the dissension of the brethren, to whom it was divided.

ACT I

Scene 1

(*The palace of* King Gorboduc. *Enter the* Queen, Videna, *and her eldest son,* Ferrex.)

Videna. The silent night that brings the quiet pause,
From painful travails of the weary day,
Prolongs my careful thoughts, and makes me blame
The slow Aurore, that so for love or shame
Doth long delay to show her blushing face,
And now the day renews my grieffull plaint.

Ferrex. My gracious lady, and my mother dear,
Pardon my grief for your so grieved mind
To ask what cause tormenteth so your heart.

Videna. So great a wrong and so unjust despite,   10
Without all cause against all course of kind!*   nature

Ferrex. Such causeless wrong, and so unjust despite,
May have redress, or, at the least, revenge.

Videna. Neither, my son; such is the froward will,
The person such, such my mishap and thine.

Ferrex. Mine know I none, but grief for your distress.

VIDENA. Yes; mine for thine, my son. A father? no:
In kind a father, not in kindliness.
   FERREX. My Father? why, I know nothing at all,
Wherein I have misdone unto his grace.   20
   VIDENA. Therefore, the more unkind to thee and
     me.
For, knowing well, my son, the tender love
That I have ever borne, and bear to thee;
He grieved thereat, is not content alone
To spoil thee of my sight,[1] my chiefest joy,
But thee, of thy birth-right and heritage,
Causeless, unkindly, and in wrongful wise,
Against all law and right, he will bereave:
Half of his kingdom he will give away.
   FERREX. To whom?
   VIDENA.   Even to Porrex, his younger son;   30
Whose growing pride I do so sore suspect
That, being rais'd to equal rule with thee,
Methinks I see his envious heart to swell,
Fill'd with disdain and with ambitious hope.
The end the gods do know, whose altars I
Full oft have made in vain of cattle slain
To send the sacred smoke to Heaven's throne,
For thee, my son, if things do so succeed,*   come to pass
As now my jealous mind misdeemeth sore.
   FERREX. Madam, leave care and careful plaint
     for me.   40
Just hath my father been to every wight.*   person
His first injustice he will not extend
To me, I trust, that give no cause thereof;
My brother's pride shall hurt himself, not me.
   VIDENA. So grant the gods! But yet, thy father so
Hath firmly fixed his unmoved mind,
That plaints and prayers can no whit avail;
For those have I assay'd, but even this day
He will endeavour to procure assent
Of all his council to his fond* devise.   foolish/50
   FERREX. Their ancestors from race to race have
     borne
True faith to my forefathers and their seed:
I trust they eke* will bear the like to me.   also
   VIDENA. There resteth all. But if they fail thereof,

---

[1] Or "To spoil [despoil] me of thy sight," (Manly).

And if the end bring forth an ill success,
On them and theirs the mischief shall befall,
And so I pray the gods requite it them;
And so they will, for so is wont to be,
When lords and trusted rulers under kings,
To please the present fancy of the prince,   60
With wrong transpose the course of governance,
Murders, mischief, and civil sword at length,
Or mutual treason, or a just revenge,
When right succeeding line returns again,
By Jove's just judgment and deserved wrath,
Brings them to cruel and reproachful death,
And roots their names and kindreds from the earth.
    FERREX. Mother, content you, you shall see the end.
    VIDENA. The end! thy end I fear: Jove end me first!

SCENE 2

(The Court of KING GORBODUC. *Enter the* KING *and
his counsellors* AROSTUS *and* PHILANDER; *also his sec-
retary,* EUBULUS.)
    GORBODUC. My lords, whose grave advice and faith-
        ful aid   70
Have long upheld my honour and my realm,
And brought me to this age from tender years,
Guiding so great estate with great renown:
Now more importeth me, than erst* to use   formerly
Your faith and wisdom, whereby yet I reign;
That when by death my life and rule shall cease,
The kingdom yet may with unbroken course
Have certain prince, by whose undoubted right
Your wealth and peace may stand in quiet stay;*   condition
And eke that they, whom nature hath prepared,   80
In time to take my place in princely seat,
While in their father's time their pliant youth
Yields to the frame of skilful governance,
May so be taught and trained in noble arts,
As what their fathers, which have reigned before,
Have with great fame derived down to them,
With honour they may leave unto their seed;
And not be thought, for their unworthy life,
And for their lawless swerving out of kind,*   nature
Worthy to lose what law and kind them gave;   90
But that they may preserve the common peace,

The cause that first began and still maintains
The lineal course of kings' inheritance,
For me, for mine, for you, and for the state
Whereof both I and you have charge and care.
Thus do I mean to use your wonted faith
To me and mine, and to your native land.
My lords, be plain without all wry respect,
Or poisonous craft to speak in pleasing wise,
Lest as the blame of ill-succeeding things   100
Shall light on you, so light the harms also.

    AROSTUS. Your good acceptance so, most noble king,
Of such our faithfulness, as heretofore
We have employed in duties to your grace,
And to this realm, whose worthy head you are,
Well proves, that neither you mistrust at all,
Nor we shall need in boasting wise to show
Our truth to you, nor yet our wakeful care
For you, for yours, and for our native land.
Wherefore, O king, I speak as one for all,   110
Sith all as one do bear you equal faith:
Doubt not to use our counsels and our aids,
Whose honours, goods, and lives are whole avow'd,
To serve, to aid, and to defend your grace.

    GORBODUC. My lords, I thank you all. This is the
      case:
Ye know, the gods, who have the sovereign care
For kings, for kingdoms, and for common weals,
Gave me two sons in my more lusty age,
Who now, in my decaying years, are grown
Well towards riper state of mind and strength   120
To take in hand some greater princely charge.
As yet they live and spend their hopeful days
With me, and with their mother, here in court.
Their age now asketh other place and trade,
And mine also doth ask another change,
Theirs to more travail,* mine to greater ease.   painful labor
When fatal death shall end my mortal life,
My purpose is to leave unto them twain,
The realm divided in two sundry parts:
The one, Ferrex, mine elder son, shall have,   130
The other, shall the younger, Porrex, rule.
That both my purpose may more firmly stand,
And eke that they may better rule their charge,
I mean forthwith to place them in the same;

That in my life they may both learn to rule,
And I may joy to see their ruling well.
This is, in sum, what I would have you weigh:
First, whether ye allow my whole devise,
And think it good for me, for them, for you,
And for our country, mother of us all: 140
And if ye like it and allow it well,
Then, for their guiding and their governance,
Show forth such means of circumstance
As ye think meet to be both known and kept.
Lo, this is all; now tell me your advice.

    Arostus. And this is much, and asketh great advice:
But for my part, my sovereign lord and king,
This do I think: Your majesty doth know
How under you, in justice and in peace,
Great wealth and honour long we have enjoy'd: 150
So as we cannot seem with greedy minds
To wish for change of prince or governance:
But if we like your purpose and devise,
Our liking must be deemed to proceed
Of rightful reason, and of heedful care,
Not for ourselves, but for the common state,
Sith* our own state doth need no better change.   since
I think in all as erst your grace hath said:
First, when you shall unload your aged mind
Of heavy care and troubles manifold,   160
And lay the same upon my lords, your sons,
Whose growing years may bear the burden long,
(And long I pray the gods to grant it so)
And in your life, while you shall so behold
Their rule, their virtues, and their noble deeds,
Such as their kind behigheth* to us all,   promises[2]
Great be the profits that shall grow thereof;
Your age in quiet shall the longer last,
Your lasting age shall be their longer stay.
For cares of kings, that rule as you have rul'd,   170
For public wealth, and not for private joy,
Do waste man's life and hasten crooked age,
With furrowed face, and with enfeebled limbs,
To draw on creeping death a swifter pace.
They two, yet young, shall bear the parted reign
With greater ease than one, now old, alone

[2] Such as their nature promises.

Can wield the whole, for whom much harder is
With lessened strength the double weight to bear.
Your eye, your counsel, and the grave regard
Of father, yea, of such a father's name,   180
Now at beginning of their sundred* reign,   divided
When is the hazard of their whole success,
Shall bridle so their force of youthful heats,
And so restrain the rage of insolence,
Which most assails the young and noble minds,
And so shall guide and train in temper'd stay
Their yet green bending wits with reverend awe,
As now inured with virtues at the first,
Custom, O king, shall bring delightfulness,
By use of virtue, vice shall grow in hate.   190
But if you so dispose it, that the day
Which ends your life, shall first begin their reign,
Great is the peril, what will be the end,
When such beginning of such liberties,
Void of such stays as in your life do lie,
Shall leave them free to random of their will,
An open prey to traitorous flattery,
The greatest pestilence of noble youth:
Which peril shall be past, if in your life
Their temper'd youth with aged father's awe   200
Be brought in ure* of skilful stayedness;   practice
And in your life, their lives disposed so
Shall length your noble life in joyfulness.
Thus think I that your grace hath wisely thought,
And that your tender care of common weal*   welfare
Hath bred this thought, so to divide your land,
And plant your sons to bear the present rule,
While you yet live to see their ruling well,
That you may longer live by joy therein.
What further means behooveful are and meet   210
At greater leisure may your grace devise,
When all have said, and when we be agreed
If this be best, to part the realm in twain,
And place your sons in present government:
Whereof, as I have plainly said my mind,
So would I hear the rest of all my lords.
　　PHILANDER. In part I think as hath been said
　　　　before;
In part, again, my mind is otherwise.
As for dividing of this realm in twain,

And lotting out the same in equal parts   220
To either of my lords, your grace's sons,
That think I best for this your realm's behoof,
For profit and advancement of your sons,
And for your comfort and your honour eke:
But so to place them while your life do last,
To yield to them your royal governance,
To be above them only in the name
Of father, not in kingly state also,
I think not good for you, for them, nor us.
This kingdom, since the bloody civil field   230
Where Morgan slain did yield his conquer'd part
Unto his cousin's sword in Camberland,
Containeth all that whilom did suffice
Three noble sons of your forefather Brute;
So your two sons it may suffice also,
The moe* the stronger, if they 'gree* in one.   more/agree
The smaller compass that the realm doth hold,
The easier is the sway thereof to wield,
The nearer justice to the wronged poor,
The smaller charge, and yet enough for one.   240
And when the region is divided so
That brethren be the lords of either part,
Such strength doth nature knit between them both,
In sundry bodies by conjoined love,
That, not as two, but one of doubled force,
Each it to other as a sure defence:
The nobleness and glory of the one
Doth sharp the courage of the other's mind,
With virtuous envy to contend for praise.
And such an equalness hath nature made   250
Between the brethren of one father's seed,
As an unkindly wrong it seems to be
To throw the brother subject under feet
Of him whose peer he is by course of kind;
And Nature, that did make this equalness,
Oft so repineth at so great a wrong
That oft she raiseth up a grudging grief
In younger brethren at the elder's state:
Whereby both towns and kingdoms have been rased,
And famous stocks of royal blood destroyed: 260
The brother, that should be the brother's aid,
And have a wakeful care for his defence,
Gapes for his death, and blames the lingering years

That draw not forth his end with faster course;
And, oft impatient of so long delays,
With hateful slaughter he prevents the fates,
And heaps a just reward for brother's blood,
With endless vengeance on his stock for aye.
Such mischiefs here are wisely met withal;
If equal state may nourish equal love,   270
Where none hath cause to grudge at other's good.
But now the head to stoop beneath them both,
Ne kind, ne reason, ne good order bears.
And oft it hath been seen, where nature's course
Hath been perverted in disordered wise,
When fathers cease to know that they should rule,
The children cease to know they should obey;
And often over kindly tenderness
Is mother of unkindly stubbornness.
I speak not this in envy or reproach,   280
As if I grudg'd the glory of your sons,
Whose honour I beseech the gods increase:
Nor yet as if I thought there did remain
So filthy cankers in their noble breasts,
Whom I esteem (which is their greatest praise)
Undoubted children of so good a king.
Only I mean to show by certain rules,
Which kind hath graft within the mind of man,
That Nature hath her order and her course,
Which (being broken) doth corrupt the state   290
Of minds and things, ev'n in the best of all.
My lords, your sons, may learn to rule of you,
Your own example in your noble court
Is fittest guider of their youthful years.
If you desire to see some present joy
By sight of their well ruling in your life,
See them obey, so shall you see them rule:
Who so obeyeth not with humbleness
Will rule with outrage and with insolence.
Long may they rule, I do beseech the gods,   300
Long may they learn, ere they begin to rule.
If kind and fates would suffer, I would wish
Them aged princes, and immortal kings.
Wherefore, most noble king, I well assent
Between your sons that you divide your realm,
And as in kind, so match them in degree.
But while the gods prolong your royal life,

Prolong your reign; for thereto live you here,
And therefore have the gods so long forborne   310
To join you to themselves, that still you might
Be prince and father of our common weal.
They, when they see your children ripe to rule,
Will make them room, and will remove you hence,
That yours, in right ensuing of your life,
May rightly honor your immortal name.
    EUBULUS. Your wonted true regard of faithful hearts
Makes me, O king, the bolder to presume
To speak what I conceive within my breast;
Although the same do not agree at all   320
With that which other here my lords have said,
Nor which yourself have seemed best to like.
Pardon I crave, and that my words be deem'd
To flow from hearty zeal unto your grace,
And to the safety of your common weal.
To part your realm unto my lords, your sons,
I think not good for you, ne yet for them,
But worst of all for this our native land.
Within one land, one single rule is best:
Divided reigns do make divided hearts;   330
But peace preserves the country and the prince.
Such is in man the greedy mind to reign,
So great is his desire to climb aloft,
In worldly stage the stateliest parts to bear,
That faith and justice, and all kindly love,
Do yield unto desire of sovereignty,
Where equal state doth raise an equal hope
To win the thing that either would attain.
Your grace remembereth how in passed years,
The mighty Brute, first prince of all this land,[3]   340
Possess'd the same, and rul'd it well in one:
He, thinking that the compass did suffice
For his three sons three kingdoms eke to make,
Cut it in three, as you would now in twain.
But how much British blood hath since been split,
To join again the sunder'd unity!
What princes slain before their timely hour!
What waste of towns and people in the land!
What treasons heap'd on murders and on spoils!
Whose just revenge ev'n yet is scarcely ceas'd,   350

[3] The legendary founder of the royal line of England.

Ruthful remembrance is yet raw in mind.
The gods forbid the like to chance again:
And you, O king, give not the cause thereof.
My lord Ferrex, your elder son, perhaps
(Whom kind and custom gives a rightful hope
To be your heir, and to succeed your reign)
Shall think that he doth suffer greater wrong
Than he perchance will bear, if power serve.
Porrex, the younger, so uprais'd in state,
Perhaps in courage will be rais'd also.   360
If flattery then, which fails not to assail
The tender minds of yet unskilful youth,
In one shall kindle and increase disdain,
And envy in the other's heart inflame,
This fire shall waste their love, their lives, their land,
And ruthful ruin shall destroy them both.
I wish not this, O king, so to befall,
But fear the thing, that I do most abhor.
Give no beginning to so dreadful end,
Keep them in order and obedience,   370
And let them both by now obeying you,
Learn such behaviour as beseems their state;
The elder, mildness in his governance,
The younger, a yielding contentedness.
And keep them near unto your presence still,
That they, restrained by the awe of you,
May live in compass of well temper'd stay,*   control
And pass the perils of their youthful years.
Your aged life draws on to feebler time,
Wherein you shall less able be to bear   380
The travails that in youth you have sustain'd,
Both in your person's and your realm's defence.
If planting now your sons in further parts,
You send them further from your present reach,
Less shall you know how they themselves demean:
Traitorous corrupters of their pliant youth
Shall have unspied a much more free access;
And if ambition and inflam'd disdain
Shall arm the one, the other, or them both,
To civil war, or to usurping pride,   390
Late shall you rue that you ne recked* before.   not heeded
Good is I grant of all to hope the best,
But not to live still dreadless of the worst.
So trust the one that th' other be foreseen.

Arm not unskilfulness with princely power.
But you that long have wisely ruled the reins
Of royalty within your noble realm,
So hold them, while the gods, for our avails,
Shall stretch the thread of your prolonged days.
Too soon he clomb into the flaming car,   400
Whose want of skill did set the earth on fire.
Time, and example of your noble Grace,
Shall teach your sons both to obey and rule.
When time hath taught them, time shall make them
    place,
The place that now is full: and so I pray
Long it remain, to comfort of us all.
    GORBODUC. I take your faithful hearts in thankful
    part:
But sith I see no cause to draw my mind,
To fear the nature of my loving sons,
Or to misdeem that envy or disdain   410
Can there work hate, where nature planteth love;
In one self purpose do I still abide.
My love extendeth equally to both,
My land sufficeth for them both also.
Humber shall part the marches* of their realms: boundaries
The southern part the elder shall possess,
The northern shall Porrex, the younger, rule.
In quiet I will pass mine aged days,
Free from the travail, and the painful cares,
That hasten age upon the worthiest kings.   420
But lest the fraud, that ye do seem to fear,
Of flattering tongues, corrupt their tender youth,
And writhe them to the ways of youthful lust,
To climbing pride, or to revenging hate,
Or to neglecting of their careful charge
Lewdly to live in wanton recklessness,
Or to oppressing of the rightful cause,
Or not to wreak the wrongs done to the poor,
To tread down truth, or favour false deceit;
I mean to join to either of my sons   430
Some one of those, whose long approved faith
And wisdom tried, may well assure my heart,
That mining fraud shall find no way to creep
Into their fenced ears with grave advice.
This is the end; and so I pray you all
To bear my sons the love and loyalty

That I have found within your faithful breasts.
   AROSTUS. You, nor your sons, my sovereign lord,
     shall want
Our faith and service, while our hearts do last.
                          (Exeunt.)

CHORUS.

When settled stay* doth hold the royal throne   rule/440
   In steadfast place, by known and doubtless right,
And chiefly when descent* on one alone   inheritance
   Makes single and unparted reign to light;
Each change of course unjoints the whole estate,
And yields it thrall* to ruin by debate.*   slave/strife

The strength that knit by fast accord in one,
   Again all foreign power of mighty foes,
Could of itself defend itself alone,
   Disjoined once, the former force doth lose.
The sticks, that sunder'd brake so soon in twain,   450
In fagot bound attempted were in vain.

Oft tender mind that leads the partial eye
   Of erring parents in their children's love
Destroys the wrongly loved child thereby.
   This doth the proud son of Apollo[4] prove,
Who, rashly set in chariot of his sire,
Inflam'd the parched earth with heaven's fire.

And this great king that doth divide his land,
   And change the course of his descending crown,
And yields the reign into his children's hand,   460
   From blissful state of joy and great renown,
A mirror shall become to princes all,
To learn to shun the cause of such a fall.

THE ORDER AND SIGNIFICATION OF THE DUMB SHOW BEFORE THE SECOND ACT.

First, the music of cornets began to play, during which
   came in upon the stage a king accompanied with a
   number of his nobility and gentlemen. And after he
   had placed himself in a chair of estate prepared for
   him, there came and kneeled before him a grave

---

[4] The reference is to the myth of Phaeton, or Phaëthon, which the
authors of *Gorboduc* would have read in Ovid's *Metamorphoses*.

and aged gentleman, and offered up unto him a cup of wine in a glass, which the king refused. After him comes a brave* and lusty young gentleman, and presents the king with a cup of gold filled with poison, which the king accepted, and drinking the same, immediately fell down dead upon the stage, and so was carried thence away by his lords and gentlemen, and then the music ceased. Hereby was signified, that as glass by nature holdeth no poison, but is clear and may easily be seen through, ne boweth* by any art; so a faithful counsellor holdeth no treason, but is plain and open, ne* yieldeth to any indiscreet affection, but giveth wholesome counsel, which the ill advised prince refuseth. The delightful gold filled with poison betokeneth flattery, which under fair seeming of pleasant words beareth deadly poison, which destroyeth the prince that receiveth it. As befel in* the two brethren, Ferrex and Porrex, who, refusing the wholesome advice of grave counsellors, credited these young parasites, and brought to themselves death and destruction thereby.

well dressed

nor bendeth nor

befell

ACT II

Scene 1

(*The Court of* Ferrex. *Enter* Ferrex *attended by* Hermon *the parasite and* Dordan *the wise counsellor.*)

Ferrex. I marvel much what reason led the king,
My father, thus, without all my desert,
To reave* me half the kingdom, which by course   *rob*
Of law and nature should remain to me.

Hermon. If you with stubborn and untamed pride
Had stood against him in rebelling wise;
Or if, with grudging mind, you had envied
So slow a sliding of his aged years;
Or sought before your time to haste the course
Of fatal death upon his royal head;   10
Or stain'd your stock with murder of your kin;
Some face of reason might perhaps have seem'd
To yield some likely cause to spoil ye thus.

Ferrex. The wreakful* gods pour on my cursed   *avenging*
head

Eternal plagues and never-dying woes,
The hellish prince adjudge my damned ghost
To Tantale's thirst,⁵ or proud Ixion's wheel,⁶
Or cruel Gripe* to gnaw my growing heart,   griffin
To during torments and unquenched flames,
If ever I conceiv'd so foul a thought,   20
To wish his end of life, or yet of reign.

   DORDAN. Ne yet your father, O most noble prince,
Did ever think so foul a thing of you;
For he, with more than father's tender love,
While yet the fates do lend him life to rule,
(Who long might live to see your ruling well)
To you, my lord, and to his other son,
Lo, he resigns his realm and royalty;
Which never would so wise a prince have done,
If he had once misdeem'd* that in your heart   misjudged/30
There ever lodged so unkind a thought.
But tender love, my lord, and settled trust
Of your good nature, and your noble mind,
Made him to place you thus in royal throne,
And now to give you half this realm to guide;
Yea, and that half which, in abounding store
Of things that serve to make a wealthy realm,
In stately cities, and in fruitful soil,
In temperate breathing of the milder heaven,
In things of needful use, which friendly sea   40
Transports by traffic from the foreign parts,
In flowing wealth, in honour, and in force,
Doth pass the double value of the part
That Porrex hath allotted to his reign.
Such is your case, such is your father's love.

   FERREX. Ah love, my friends! Love wrongs not
     whom he loves.

   DORDAN. Ne yet he wrongeth you, that giveth you
So large a reign ere that the course of time
Bring you to kingdom by descended right,
Which time perhaps might end your time before.   50

   FERREX. Is this no wrong, say you, to reave from me
My native right of half so great a realm,
And thus to match his younger son with me

---

⁵ Tantalus is punished in the Greek underworld of Tartarus with thirst he
cannot quench with water just beyond his reach.
⁶ Ixion was fastened to a ceaselessly revolving wheel in the Greek underworld.

In equal pow'r, and in as great degree?
Yea, and what son? The son whose swelling pride
Would never yield one point of reverence,
When I the elder and apparent heir
Stood in the likelihood to possess the whole;
Yea, and that son which from his childish age
Envieth mine honour and doth hate my life.   60
What will he now do, when his pride, his rage,
The mindful malice of his grudging heart
Is arm'd with force, with wealth, and kingly state?

   HERMON. Was this not wrong? yea, ill advised wrong,
To give so mad a man so sharp a sword,
To so great peril of so great mishap,
Wide open thus to set so large a way?

   DORDAN. Alas, my lord, what grieffull* thing is this,   *grievous*
That of your brother you can think so ill?
I never saw him utter likely sign,   70
Whereby a man might see or once misdeem
Such hate of you, ne such unyielding pride.
Ill is their counsel, shameful be their end,
That raising such mistrustful fear in you,
Sowing the seed of such unkindly hate,
Travail* by treason to destroy you both.   *labor*
Wise is your brother, and of noble hope,
Worthy to wield a large and mighty realm.
So much a stronger friend have you thereby,
Whose strength is your strength if you 'gree in one.   80

   HERMON. If Nature and the Gods had pinched so
Their flowing bounty, and their noble gifts
Of princely qualities, from you, my lord,
And pour'd them all at once in wasteful wise
Upon your father's younger son alone;
Perhaps there be, that in your prejudice
Would say that birth should yield to worthiness.
But sith in each good gift and princely art
Ye are his match, and in the chief of all
In mildness and in sober governance   90
Ye far surmount; and sith there is in you
Sufficing skill and hopeful towardness
To wield the whole, and match your elder's praise;
I see no cause why ye should lose the half,
Ne would I wish you yield to such a loss:
Lest your mild sufferance of so great a wrong,
Be deemed cowardice and simple dread,

Which shall give courage to the fiery head
Of your young brother to invade the whole.
While yet therefore sticks in the people's mind   100
The loathed wrong of your disheritance;
And ere your brother have, by settled power,
By guileful cloak of an alluring show,
Got him some force and favour in the realm;
And while the noble queen, your mother, lives,
To work and practise all for your avail;
Attempt redress by arms, and wreak yourself
Upon his life that gaineth by your loss,
Who now to shame of you, and grief of us,
In your own kingdom triumphs over you.   110
Show now your courage meet for kingly state,
That they which have avow'd to spend their goods,
Their lands, their lives and honours in your cause,
May be the bolder to maintain your part,
When they do see that coward fear in you
Shall not betray, ne* fail their faithful hearts.   nor
If once the death of Porrex end the strife,
And pay the price of his usurped reign,
Your mother shall persuade the angry king,
The lords, your friends, eke shall appease his rage.   120
For they be wise, and well they can foresee,
That ere long time your aged father's death
Will bring a time when you shall well requite
Their friendly favour, or their hateful spite,
Yea, or their slackness to advance your cause.
"Wise men do not so hang on passing state
Of present princes, chiefly in their age,
But they will further cast their reaching eye,
To view and weigh the times and reigns to come."[7]
Ne* is it likely, though the king be wroth,   Nor/130
That he yet will, or that the realm will bear,
Extreme revenge upon his only son:
Or, if he would, what one is he that dare
Be minister to such an enterprise?
And here you be now placed in your own,
Amid your friends, your vassals, and your strength:
We shall defend and keep your person safe,
Till either counsel turn his tender mind,
Or age or sorrow end his weary days.

[7] The quotation marks were used to lend emphasis to sententious or
moralizing lines.

But if the fear of gods, and secret grudge 140
Of nature's law, repining at the fact,
Withhold your courage from so great attempt,
Know ye, that lust of kingdoms hath no law.
The gods do bear, and well allow in kings,
The things that they abhor in rascal routs.
"When kings on slender quarrels run to wars,
And then in cruel and unkindly wise,
Command thefts, rapes, murders of innocents,
The spoil of towns, ruins of mighty realms;
Think you such princes do suppose themselves 150
Subject to laws of kind, and fear of gods?"
Murders and violent thefts in private men
Are heinous crimes, and full of foul reproach;
Yet none offence, but decked with glorious name
Of noble conquests in the hands of kings.
But if you like not yet so hot devise,
Ne list* to take such vantage of the time,   nor desire
But, though with peril of your own estate,
You will not be the first that shall invade;
Assemble yet your force for your defence, 160
And for your safety stand upon your guard.
    DORDAN. O heaven! was there ever heard or known,
So wicked counsel to a noble prince?
Let me, my lord, disclose unto your grace
This heinous tale, what mischief it contains;
Your father's death, your brother's, and your own,
Your present murder, and eternal shame.
Hear me, O king, and suffer not to sink
So high a treason in your princely breast.
    FERREX. The mighty gods forbid that ever I 170
Should once conceive such mischief in my heart.
Although my brother hath bereft my realm,
And bear, perhaps, to me an hateful mind,
Shall I revenge it with his death therefore?
Or shall I so destroy my father's life
That gave me life? The gods forbid, I say:
Cease you to speak so any more to me;
Ne you, my friend, with answer once repeat
So foul a tale. In silence let it die.
What lord or subject shall have hope at all, 180
That under me they safely shall enjoy
Their goods, their honours, lands, and liberties,
With whom, neither one only brother dear,

Ne father dearer, could enjoy their lives?
But, sith I fear my younger brother's rage,
And sith, perhaps, some other man may give
Some like advice, to move his grudging head
At mine estate; which counsel may perchance
Take greater force with him, than this with me;
I will in secret so prepare myself,   190
As, if his malice or his lust to reign
Break forth in arms or sudden violence,
I may withstand his rage and keep mine own.

       (*Exeunt* FERREX *and* HERMON.)

 DORDAN. I fear the fatal time now draweth on
When civil hate shall end the noble line
Of famous Brute, and of his royal seed.
Great Jove, defend the mischiefs now at hand!
O that the secretary's wise advice
Had erst been heard when he besought the king
Not to divide his land, nor send his sons   200
To further parts, from presence of his court,
Ne yet to yield to them his governance.
Lo, such are they now in the royal throne
As was rash Phaeton in Phœbus'[8] car;
Ne then the fiery steeds did draw the flame
With wilder random through the kindled skies,
Than traitorous counsel now will whirl about
The youthful heads of these unskilful kings.
But I hereof their father will inform;
The reverence of him perhaps shall stay   210
The growing mischiefs, while they yet are green.
If this help not, then woe unto themselves,
The prince, the people, the divided land!

           (*Exit.*)

SCENE 2

(*The Court of* PORREX. *Enter* PORREX *attended by*
TYNDAR *the parasite and by* PHILANDER *the wise
counsellor.*)

 PORREX. And is it thus? and doth he so prepare
Against his brother as his mortal foe?
And now, while yet his aged father lives?
Neither regards he him? nor fears he me?
War would he have? and he shall have it so.

---

[8] "Phoebus' car" is, of course, Apollo's golden chariot of the sun.

TYNDAR. I saw, myself, the great prepared store
Of horse, of armour, and of weapons there: 220
Ne bring I to my lord reported tales,
Without the ground of seen and searched truth.
Lo, secret quarrels run about his court,
To bring the name of you, my lord, in hate.
Each man, almost, can now debate the cause,
And ask a reason of so great a wrong,
Why he, so noble and so wise a prince,
Is, as unworthy, reft his heritage?
And why the king, misled by crafty means,
Divided thus his land from course of right?   230
The wiser sort hold down their griefful* heads;   grieving
Each man withdraws from talk and company
Of those that have been known to favour you:
To hide the mischief of their meaning there,
Rumours are spread of your preparing here.
The rascal numbers of unskilful sort
Are filled with monstrous tales of you and yours.
In secret, I was counsell'd by my friends
To haste me thence, and brought you, as you know,
Letters from those that both can truly tell,   240
And would not write unless they knew it well.
   PHILANDER. My lord, yet ere you move unkindly
      war,
Send to your brother, to demand the cause.
Perhaps some traitorous tales have filled his ears
With false reports against your noble grace;
Which, once disclos'd, shall end the growing strife,
That else, not stay'd with wise foresight in time,
Shall hazard both your kingdoms and your lives.
Send to your father eke, he shall appease
Your kindled minds, and rid you of this fear.   250
   PORREX. Rid me of fear! I fear him not at all;
Ne will to him, ne to my father send.
If danger were for one to tarry there,
Think ye it safety to return again?
In mischiefs, such as Ferrex now intends,
The wonted courteous laws to messengers
Are not observ'd, which in just war they use.
Shall I so hazard any one of mine?
Shall I betray my trusty friends to him,
That have disclosed his treason unto me?   260
Let him entreat that fears; I fear him not.

Or shall I to the king, my father, send?
Yea, and send now, while such a mother lives,
That loves my brother, and that hateth me?
Shall I give leisure, by my fond delays,
To Ferrex to oppress me all unware?
I will not; but I will invade his realm,
And seek the traitor prince within his court.
Mischief for mischief is a due reward.
His wretched head shall pay the worthy price   270
Of this his treason and his hate to me.
Shall I abide, and treat, and send, and pray,
And hold my yielding throat to traitor's knife,
While I, with valiant mind and conquering force,
Might rid myself of foes and win a realm?
Yet rather, when I have the wretch's head,
Then to the king, my father, will I send.
The bootless case may yet appease his wrath:
If not, I will defend me as I may.
                    (*Exeunt* PORREX *and* TYNDAR.)
   PHILANDER. Lo, here the end of these two youthful
       kings!   280
The father's death! the ruin of their realms!
"O most unhappy state of counsellors,
That light on so unhappy lords and times,
That neither can their good advice be heard,
Yet must they bear the blames of ill success."
But I will to the king, their father, haste,
Ere this mischief come to the likely end;
That, if the mindful wrath of wreakful gods
(Since mighty Ilion's fall not yet appeas'd
With these poor remnants of the Trojan name)   290
Have not determin'd by unmoved fate,
Out of this realm to raze the British line,*   royal line
By good advice, by awe of father's name,
By force of wiser lords, this kindled hate
May yet be quench'd ere it consume us all.
                                          (*Exit.*)

CHORUS

When youth, not bridled with a guiding stay,
    Is left to random of their own delight,
And wields whole realms by force of sovereign sway,
    Great is the danger of unmaster'd might,
Lest skilless rage throw down, with headlong fall, 300

Their lands, their states, their lives, themselves and
   all.

When growing pride doth fill the swelling breast,
   And greedy lust doth raise the climbing mind,
Oh, hardly may the peril be repress'd.
   Ne fear of angry gods, ne lawes kind,
Ne country's care can fired hearts restrain,
When force hath armed envy and disdain.

When kings of foresight will neglect the rede*   counsel
   Of best advice, and yield to pleasing tales
That do their fancies' noisome humour* feed,   disposition/310
   Ne reason nor regard of right avails.
Succeeding heaps of plagues shall teach, too late,
To learn the mischiefs of misguided state.

Foul fall the traitor false, that undermines
   The love of brethren, to destroy them both.
Woe to the prince, that pliant ear inclines,
   And yields his mind to poisonous tale that floweth
From flattering mouth! And woe to wretched land
That wastes itself with civil sword in hand!
   Lo thus it is poison in gold to take   320
   And wholesome drink in homely cup forsake.

The Order and Signification of the Dumb Show Before the Third Act.

First, the music of flutes began to play, during which came in
upon the stage, a company of mourners, all clad in black,
betokening death and sorrow to ensue upon the ill-advised
misgovernment and dissension of brethren, as befell upon
the murderer of Ferrex by his younger brother. After the
mourners had passed thrice about the stage, they departed,
and then the music ceased.

ACT III

Scene 1

(*The Court of* King Gorboduc. *Enter the* King *with*
Eubulus, *his secretary, and his counsellor* Arostus.)
Gorboduc. O cruel fates, O mindful wrath of gods,
Whose vengeance, neither Simois' stained streams
Flowing with blood of Trojan princes slain,
Nor Phrygian* fields made rank with corpses dead   Trojan

Of Asian kings and lords, can yet appease;
Ne slaughter of unhappy Priam's race,*   Trojans
Nor Ilion's fall,9 made level with the soil,
Can yet suffice: but still continued rage
Pursues our lives, and from the farthest seas
Doth chase the issues of destroyed Troy.   10
"Oh, no man happy till his end be seen."
If any flowing wealth and seeming joy
In present years might make a happy wight,*   person
Happy was Hecuba,10 the woefull'st wretch
That ever lived to make a mirror of;
And happy Priam, with his noble sons;
And happy I, till now, alas! I see
And feel my most unhappy wretchedness.
Behold, my lords, read ye this letter here;
Lo, it contains the ruin of our realm,   20
If timely speed provide not hasty help.
Yet, O ye gods, if ever woeful king
Might move ye, kings of kings, wreak it on me
And on my sons, not on this guiltless realm:
Send down your wasting flames from wrathful skies,
To reave me and my sons the hateful breath.
Read, read, my lords; this is the matter why
I call'd ye now, to have your good advice.
      (*The letter from* DORDAN, *the Counsellor of the*
      elder Prince. EUBULUS *readeth the letter.*)
My sovereign lord, what I am loath to write,
But loathest am to see, that I am forc'd   30
By letters now to make you understand.
My lord Ferrex, your eldest son, misled
By traitorous fraud of young untemper'd wits,
Assembleth force against your younger son,
Ne can my counsel yet withdraw the heat
And furious pangs of his inflamed head.
Disdain, saith he, of his disheritance
Arms him to wreak the great pretended wrong,
With civil sword upon his brother's life.
If present help do not restrain this rage,   40
This flame will waste your sons, your land, and you.
            Your Majesty's faithful,
                  and most humble subject,
                        DORDAN.

9 The fall of Troy.
10 The queen of Troy.

AROSTUS. O king, appease your grief, and stay your
    plaint;
Great is the matter, and a woeful case:
But timely knowledge may bring timely help.
Send for them both unto your presence here:
The reverence of your honour, age, and state,
Your grave advice, the awe of father's name,   50
Shall quickly knit again this broken peace.
And if in either of my lords, your sons,
Be such untamed and unyielding pride
As will not bend unto your noble hests;*   commands
If Ferrex, the elder son, can bear no peer,
Or Porrex, not content, aspires to more
Than you him gave above his native right;
Join with the juster side, so shall you force
Them to agree, and hold the land in stay.
    EUBULUS. What meaneth this? Lo ,yonder comes in
        haste   60
Philander from my lord, your younger son.
    (*Enter* PHILANDER.)
    GORBODUC. The gods send joyful news!
    PHILANDER.   The mighty
    Jove
Preserve your majesty, O noble king.
    GORBODUC. Philander, welcome: but how doth my
        son?
    PHILANDER. Your son, sir, lives, and healthy I him
        left.
But yet, O king, the want of lustful health
Could not be half so griefful to your grace,
As these most wretched tidings that I bring.
    GORBODUC. O heavens, yet more? no end of woes to
        me?
    PHILANDER. Tyndar, O king, came lately from the
        court   70
Of Ferrex, to my lord your younger son,
And made report of great prepared store
For war, and saith that it is wholly meant
Against Porrex, for high disdain that he
Lives now a king, and equal in degree
With him that claimeth to succeed the whole,
As by due title of descending right.
Porrex is now so set on flaming fire,
Partly with kindled rage of cruel wrath,

Partly with hope to gain a realm thereby,   80
That he in haste prepareth to invade
His brother's land, and with unkindly war
Threatens the murder of your elder son;
Ne could I him persuade, that first he should
Send to his brother to demand the cause;
Nor yet to you to stay this hateful strife.
Wherefore sith there no more I can be heard,
I come myself now to inform your grace,
And to beseech you, as you love the life
And safety of your children and your realm,   90
Now to employ your wisdom and your force
To stay this mischief ere it be to late.
    GORBODUC. Are they in arms? would he not send to
      me?
Is this the honour of a father's name?
In vain we travail to assuage their minds,
As if their hearts, whom neither brother's love,
Nor father's awe, nor kingdom's cares, can move,
Our counsels could withdraw from raging heat.
Jove slay them both, and end the cursed line.
For though perhaps fear of such mighty force   100
As I, my lords, joined with your noble aids,
May yet raise, shall repress their present heat,
The secret grudge and malice will remain,
The fire not quench'd, but kept in close restraint,
Fed still within, breaks forth with double flame.
Their death and mine must 'pease* the angry gods.   appease
    PHILANDER. Yield not, O king, so much to weak
      despair:
Your sons yet live, and long, I trust, they shall.
If fates had taken you from earthly life,
Before beginning of this civil strife,   110
Perhaps your sons in their unmaster'd youth,
Lose from regard of any living wight,
Would run on headlong, with unbridled race,
To their own death and ruin of this realm.
But sith the gods, that have the care for kings,
Of things and times dispose the order so,
That in your life this kindled flame breaks forth,
While yet your life, your wisdom, and your power,
May stay the growing mischief and repress
The fiery blaze of their enkindled heat;   120
It seems, and so ye ought to deem thereof,

That loving Jove hath temper'd so the time
Of this debate to happen in your days,
That you yet living may the same appease,
And add it to the glory of your age,
And they your sons may learn to live in peace.
Beware, O king, the greatest harm of all,
Lest, by your wailful plaints, your hastened death
Yield larger room unto their growing rage.
Preserve your life, the only hope of stay.   130
And if your highness herein list to use
Wisdom or force, counsel or knightly aid,
Lo we, our persons, powers, and lives are yours;
Use us till death, O king, we are your own.
    EUBULUS. Lo, here the peril that was erst foreseen,
When you, O king, did first divide your land,
And yield your present reign unto your sons.
But now, O noble prince, now is no time
To wail and plain, and waste your woeful life;
Now is the time for present good advice.   140
Sorrow doth dark the judgment of the wit.
"The heart unbroken, and the courage free
From feeble faintness of bootless despair,
Doth either rise to safety or renown
By noble valour of unvanquish'd mind,
Or yet doth perish in more happy sort."
Your grace may send to either of your sons
Some one both wise and noble personage,
Which with good counsel, and with weighty name
Of father, shall present before their eyes   150
Your hest, your life, your safety, and their own,
The present mischief of their deadly strife.
And in the while, assemble you the force
Which your commandment and the speedy haste
Of all my lords here present can prepare.
The terror of your mighty power shall stay
The rage of both, or yet of one at least.
    (*Enter* NUNTIUS [MESSENGER].)
    NUNTIUS. O king, the greatest grief that ever prince
        did hear,
That ever woeful messenger did tell,
That ever wretched land hath seen before,   160
I bring to you: Porrex your younger son
With sudden force invaded hath the land
That you to Ferrex did allot to rule;

And with his own most bloody hand he hath
His brother slain, and doth possess his realm.
   GORBODUC. O heavens, send down the flames of your
     revenge!
Destroy, I say, with flash of wreakful fire
The traitor son, and then the wretched sire!
But let us go, that yet perhaps I may
Die with revenge, and 'pease the hateful gods.

(Exeunt.)

CHORUS.

The lust of kingdom knows no sacred faith,   171
  No rule of reason, no regard of right,
No kindly love, no fear of heaven's wrath;
  But with contempt of gods, and man's despite,
Through bloody slaughter doth prepare the ways
  To fatal sceptre and accursed reign.
The son so loathes the father's lingering days,
  Ne dreads his hand in brother's blood to stain.
O wretched prince, ne dost thou yet record
  The yet fresh murders done within the land   180
Of thy forefathers, when the cruel sword
  Bereft Morgan his life with cousin's hand?
Thus fatal plagues pursue the guilty race,
  Whose murderous hand, imbru'd with guiltless blood.
Asks vengeance still before the heaven's face
  With endless mischiefs on the cursed brood.
The wicked child thus brings to woeful sire
  The mournful plaints to waste his very life.
Thus do the cruel flames of civil fire
  Destroy the parted reign with hateful strife.   190
And hence doth spring the well from which doth
    flow
The dead black streams of mourning, plaints, and
    woe.

THE ORDER AND SIGNIFICATION OF THE DUMB SHOW BEFORE THE FOURTH ACT.

First, the music of hautboys began to play, during which there
came forth from under the stage, as though out of hell, three
furies, Alecto, Megæra, and Tisiphone, clad in black garments sprinkled with blood and flames, their bodies girt with
snakes, their heads spread with serpents instead of hair, the

one bearing in her hand a snake, the other a whip, and the third a burning firebrand: each driving before them a king and a queen; which, moved by furies, unnaturally had slain their own children. The names of the kings and queens were these, Tantalus, Medea, Athamas, Ino, Cambyses, Althea; after that the furies and these had passed about the stage thrice, they departed, and then the music ceased. Hereby was signified the unnatural murders to follow; that is to say, Porrex slain by his own mother, and of King Gorboduc and Queen Videna, killed by their own subjects.

ACT IV

Scene 1

(King Gorboduc's *Palace. Enter* Queen Videna.)
Videna (*solo*[11]). Why should I live, and linger forth
    my time
In longer life to double my distress?
O me, most woeful wight, whom no mishap
Long ere this day could have bereaved hence.
Might not these hands, by fortune or by fate,
Have pierc'd this breast, and life with iron reft?
Or in this palace here, where I so long
Have spent by days, could not that happy hour
Once, once have happ'd, in which these hugy frames
With death by fall might have oppressed me?   10
Or should not this most hard and cruel soil,
So oft where I have press'd my wretched steps,
Sometime had ruth of mine accursed life
To rend in twain, and swallow me therein?
So had my bones possessed now in peace
Their happy grave within the closed ground,
And greedy worms had gnawn* this pined*   gnawed/wasted
    heart
Without my feeling pain: so should not now
This living breast remain the ruthful tomb,
Wherein my heart yielden to death is graved;   20
Nor dreary thoughts, with pangs of pinning grief,
My doeful mind had not afflicted thus.
O my beloved son! O my sweet child!
My dear Ferrex, my joy, my life's delight!
Is my beloved son, is my sweet child,

[11] Alone; Videna delivers a soliloquy here.

My dear Ferrex, my joy, my life's delight,
Murder'd with cruel death? O hateful wretch!
O heinous traitor both to heaven and earth!
Thou, Porrex, thou this damned deed hast wrought;
Thou, Porrex, thou shalt dearly bye* the same.   suffer/30
Traitor to kin and kind, to sire and me,
To thine own flesh, and traitor to thyself:
To gods on thee in hell shall wreak their wrath,
And here in earth this hand shall take revenge
On thee, Porrex, thou false and caitiff* wight.   villain
If after blood so eager were thy thirst,
And murd'rous mind has so possessed thee,
If such hard heart of rock and stony flint
Lived in thy breast, that nothing else could like
Thy cruel tyrant's thought but death and blood: 40
Wild savage beasts, might not their slaughter serve
To feed thy greedy will, and in the midst
Of their entrails to stain thy deadly hands
With blood deserv'd, and drink thereof thy fill?
Or if nought else but death and blood of man
Might please thy lust, could none in Britain land,
Whose heart betorn out of his panting breast
With thine own hand, or work what death thou
        would'st,
Suffice to make a sacrifice to 'pease*   appease
That deadly mind and murderous thought in thee,   50
But he who in the selfsame womb was wrapp'd,
Where thou in dismal hour receivedst life?
Or if needs, needs thy hand must slaughter make,
Mightest thou not have reach'd a mortal wound,
And with thy sword have pierc'd this cursed womb
That the accursed Porrex brought to light,
And given me a just reward therefore?
So Ferrex yet sweet life might have enjoyed,
And to his aged father comfort brought,
With some young son in whom they both might live.   60
But whereunto waste I this ruthful speech,
To thee that hast thy brother's blood thus shed?
Shall I still think that from this womb thou sprung?
That I thee bare? or take thee for my son?
No, traitor, no; I thee refuse for mine:
Murderer, I thee renounce; thou are not mine.
Never, O wretch, this womb conceived thee;
Nor never bode I painful throws for thee.

Changeling[12] to me thou art, and not my child,
Nor to no wight* that spark of pity knew.   person/70
Ruthless, unkind, monster of nature's work,
Thou never suck'd the milk of woman's breast;
But, from thy birth, the cruel tiger's teats
Have nursed thee; nor yet of flesh and blood
Form'd is thy heart, but of hard iron wrought;
And wild and desert woods bred thee to life.
But canst thou hope to 'scape my just revenge?
Or that these hands will not be wroke on thee?
Dost thou not know that Ferrex' mother lives,
That loved him more dearly than herself?   80
And doth she live, and is not veng'd on thee?   avenged

(*Exit.*)

SCENE 2

(*The Court of* KING GORBODUC. *Enter the* KING *attended by*
AROSTUS, *his Counsellor.*)

GORBODUC. We marvel much, whereto this ling'ring
      stay
Falls out so long: Porrex unto our court,
By order of our letters, is return'd;
And Eubulus receiv'd from us behest,
At his arrival here, to give him charge
Before our presence straight to make repair,
And yet we have no word whereof he stays.

AROSTUS. Lo where he comes, and Eubulus with him.

(*Enter the* KING's *Secretary* EUBULUS *with* PORREX.)

EUBULUS. According to your highness' hest to me,   90
Here have I Porrex brought, even in such sort
As from his wearied horse he did alight,
For that your grace did will such haste therein.

GORBODUC. We like and praise this speedy will in
      you,
To work the thing that to your charge we gave.
Porrex, if we so far should swerve from kind,
And from those bounds which law of nature sets,
As thou hast done by vile and wretched deed,
In cruel murder of thy brother's life;
Our present hand could stay no longer time,   100
But straight should bathe this blade in blood of thee,
As just revenge of thy detested crime.

---

[12] A child substituted by the fairies for a child they have stolen.

No; we should not offend the law of kind,
If now this sword of ours did slay thee here:
For thou hast murder'd him, whose heinous death
Even nature's force doth move us to revenge
By bloo dagain; and justice forceth us
To measure death for death, thy due desert.
Yet since thou art our child, and sith as yet
In this hard case what word thou canst allege   110
For thy defence, bu us hath not been heard,
We are content to stay our will for that
Which justice bids us presently to work,
And give thee leave to us thy speech at full,
If ought thou have to lay for thine excuse.
   PORREX. Neither, O king, I can or will deny
But that this hand from Ferrex life hath reft:
Which fact how much my doleful heart doth wail,
Oh! would it might as full appear to sight,
As inward grief doth pour it forth to me.   120
So yet, perhaps, if ever ruthful heart
Melting in tears within a manly breast,
Through deep repentance of his bloody fact;
If ever grief, if ever woeful man
Might move regret with sorrow of his fault,
I think the torment of my mournful case,
Known to your grace, as I do feel the same,
Would force even Wrath herself to pity me.
But as the water, troubled with the mud,
Shows not the face which else the eye should see;   130
Even so your ireful mind with stirred thought
Cannot so perfectly discern my cause.
But this unhap, amongst so many haps,
I must content me with, most wretched man,
That to myself I must reserve my woe,
In pining thoughts of mine accursed fact;
Since I may not show here my smallest grief,
Such as it is, and as my breast endures,
Which I esteem the greatest misery
Of all mishaps that fortune now can send.   140
Not that I rest in hope with plaint and tears
To purchase life; for to the gods I clepe*   call
For true record of this my faithful speech;
Never this heart shall have the thoughtful dread
To die the death that by your grace's doom,
By just desert, shall be pronounced to me:

Nor never shall this tongue once spend the speech,
Pardon to crave, or seek by suit to live.
I mean not this as though I were not touch'd
With care of dreadful death, or that I held   150
Life in contempt: but that I know the mind
Stoops to no dread, although the flesh be frail.
And for my guilt, I yield the same so great
As in myself I find a fear to sue
For grant of life.
    GORBODUC.   In vain, O wretch, thou showest
A woeful heart: Ferrex now lies in grave,
Slain by thy hand.
    PORREX.   Yet this, O father, hear;
And then I end. Your majesty well knows,
That when my brother Ferrex and myself
By your own hest were join'd in governance   160
Of this your grace's realm of Britain land,
I never sought nor travail'd for the same;
Nor by myself, nor by no friend I wrought,
But from your highness' will alone it sprung,
Of your most gracious goodness bent to me.
But how my brother's heart even then repin'd
With swollen disdain against mine equal rule,
Seeing that realm, which by descent should grow
Wholly to him, allotted half to me;
Even in your highness' court he now remains,   170
And with my brother then in nearest place,
Who can record what proof thereof was show'd,
And how my brother's envious heart appear'd.
Yet I that judged it my part to seek
His favour and good will, and loath to make
Your highness know the thing which should have
    brought
Grief to your grace, and your offence to him;
Hoping my earnest suit should have won
A loving heart within a brother's breast,
Wrought in that sort, that, for a pledge of love   180
And faithful heart, he gave to me his hand.
This made me think that he had banish'd quite
All rancour from his thought, and bare to me
Such hearty love as I did owe to him.
But after once we left your grace's court,
And from your highness' presence liv'd apart,
This equal rule still, still did grudge him so,

That now those envious sparks which ers* lay raked   before
In living cinders of dissembling breast,
Kindled so far within his heart disdain,   190
That longer could he not refrain from proof
Of secret practice to deprive me life
By poison's force; and had bereft me so,
If mine own servant hired to this fact,
And mov'd by truth with hate to work the same,
In time had not bewray'd* unto me.   betrayed
When thus I saw the knot of love unknit,
All honest league and faithful promise broke,
The law of kind and truth thus rent in twain,
His heart on mischief set, and in his breast   200
Black treason hid; then, then did I despair
That ever time could win him friend to me;
Then saw I how he smiled with slaying knife
Wrapp'd under cloak, then saw I deep deceit
Lurk in his face and death prepar'd for me:
Even nature moved me then to hold my life
More dear to me than his, and bade this hand,
Since by his life my death must needs ensue,
And by his death my life to be preserved,
To shed his blood, and seek my safety so.   210
And wisdom willed me without protract
In speedy wise to put the same in ure.
Thus have I told the cause that moved me
To work my brother's death; and so I yield
My life, my death, to judgment of your grace.
   GORBODUC. Oh cruel wight, should any cause prevail
To make thee stain thy hands with brother's blood?
But what of thee we will resolve to do
Shall yet remain unknown. Thou in the mean
Shalt from our royal presence banish'd be,   220
Until our princely pleasure further shall
To thee be show'd. Depart therefore our sight,
Accursed child! [Exit PORREX.] What cruel destiny,
What froward fate hath sorted us this chance,
That even in those, where we should comfort find,
Where our delight now in our aged days
Should rest and be, even there our only grief
And deepest sorrows to abridge our life,
Most pining cares and deadly thoughts do grow.
   AROSTUS. Your grace should now, in these grave
      years of yours,   230

Have found ere this the price of mortal joys;
How short they be, fading here in earth,
How full of change, how brittle our estate,
Of nothing sure, save only of the death,
To whom both man and all the world doth owe
Their end at last; neither shall nature's power
In other sort against your heart prevail,
Than as the naked hand whose stroke assays
The armed* breast where force doth light in vain.   armored
   GORBODUC. Many can yield right sage and grave
     advice   240
Of patient spirit to others wrapp'd in woe,
And can in speech both rule and conquer kind;
Who, if by proof they might feel nature's force,
Would show themselves men as they are indeed,
Which now will needs be gods. But what doth mean
The sorry cheer of her that here doth come?
   (*Enter the Queen's waiting lady* MARCELLA.)
   MARCELLA. Oh where is ruth?* or where is pity now?   remorse
Whither is gentle heart and mercy fled?
Are they exiled out of our stony breasts,
Never to make return? is all the world   250
Drowned in blood, and sunk in cruelty?
If not in women mercy may be found,
If not, alas, within the mother's breast,
To her own child, to her own flesh and blood;
If ruth be banish'd thence, if pity there
May have no place, if there no gentle heart
Do live and dwell, where should we seek it then?
   GORBODUC. Madam, alas, what means your woeful
     tale?
   MARCELLA. O silly woman I! why to this hour
Have kind and fortune thus deferr'd my breath,   260
That I should live to see this doleful day?
Will ever wight believe that such hard heart
Could rest within the cruel mother's breast,
With her own hand to slay her only son?
But out, alas! these eyes beheld the same:
They saw the dreary sight, and are become
Most ruthful records of the bloody fact.
Porrex, alas, is by his mother slain,
And with her hand, a woeful thing to tell,
While slumbering on his careful bed he rests,   270
His heart stabb'd in with knife is reft of life.

GORBODUC. O Eubulus, oh draw this sword of ours,
And pierce this heart with speed! O hateful light,
O loathesome life, O sweet and welcome death!
Dear Eubulous, work this we thee beseech!

 EUBULUS. Patient your grace; perhaps he liveth yet,
With wound receiv'd, but not of certain death.

 GORBODUC. O let us then repair unto the place,
And see if Porrex live, or thus be slain.

      (*Exeunt* GORBODUC *and* EUBULUS.)

 MARCELLA. Alas, he liveth not! it is too true,   280
That with these eyes, of him a peerless prince,
Son to a king, and in the flower of youth,
Even with a twink a senseless stock I saw.

 AROSTUS. O damned deed!

 MARCELLA.   But hear his ruthful end:
The noble prince, pierc'd with the sudden wound,
Out of his wretched slumber hastely start,
Whose strength now failing straight he overthrew,
When in the fall his eyes, ev'n new unclos'd,
Beheld the queen, and cried to her for help.
We then, alas, the ladies which that time   290
Did there attend, seeing that heinous deed,
And hearing him oft call the wretched name
Of mother, and to cry to her for aid,
Whose direful hand gave him the mortal wound,
Pitying, alas, (for nought else could we do)
His ruthful end, ran to the woeful bed,
Despoiled straight his breast, and all we might
Wiped in vain with napkins* next at hand,   handkerchiefs
The sudden streams of blood that flushed fast
Out of the gaping wound. O what a look,   300
O what a ruthful* steadfast eye methought   pitiful
He fix'd upon my face, which to my death
Will never part from me, when with a braid*   start
A deep-fetch'd sigh he gave, and therewithal
Clasping his hands, to heaven he cast his sight;
And straight pale death pressing within his face,
The flying ghost his mortal corpse forsook.

 AROSTUS. Never did age bring forth so vile a fact.

 MARCELLA. O hard and cruel hap,* that thus assign'd fate
Unto so worthy a wight so wretched end: 310
But most hard cruel heart that could consent
To lend the hateful destinies that hand,
By which, alas, so heinous crime was wrought.

O queen of adamant*! O marble breast!   hard-hearted
If not the favour of his comely face,
If not his princely cheer and countenance,
His valiant active arms, his manly breast,
If not his fair and seemly personage,
His noble limbs in such proportion cast
As would have wrapt a silly woman's thought;   320
If this might not have mov'd thy bloody heart,
And that most cruel hand the wretched weapon
Ev'n to let fall, and kiss'd him in the face,
With tears for ruth to reave* such one by death;   bereave
Should nature yet consent to slay her son?
O mother, thou to murder thus thy child!
Even Jove[13] with justice must with lightening flames
From heaven send down some strange revenge on
     thee.
Ah, noble prince, how oft have I beheld
Thee mounted on thy fierce and trampling steed,   330
Shining in armour bright before the tilt,
And with thy mistress' sleeve tied on thy helm,
And charge thy staff, to please thy lady's eye,
That bow'd the head-piece of thy friendly foe!
How oft in arms on horse to bend the mace,
How oft in arms on foot to break the sword,
Which never now these eyes may see again!
     AROSTUS. Madam, alas, in vain these plaints are
     shed;
Rather with me depart, and help to 'swage
The thoughtful griefs that in the aged king   340
Must needs by nature grow by death of this
His only son, whom he did hold so dear.
     MARCELLA. What wight is that which saw that I
     did see,
And could refrain to wail with plaint and tears?
Not I, alas! that heart is not in me:
But let us go, for I am griev'd anew,
To call to mind the wretched father's woe.

                                             (*Exeunt.*)

                              CHORUS.

When greedy lust in royal seat to reign
     Hath reft all care of gods and eke of men;
And cruel heart, wrath, treason, and disdain,   350

[13] The ·supreme Roman deity.

Within ambitious breast are lodged, then
Behold how mischief wide herself displays,
And with the brother's hand the brother slays.

When blood thus shed doth stain the heaven's face,
   Crying to Jove for vengeance of the deed,
The mighty god ev'n moveth from his place,
   With wrath to wreak: then sends he forth with
     speed
The dreadful Furies, daughters of the night,
   With serpents girt, carrying the whip of ire,
With hair of stinging snakes, and shining bright   360
   With flames and blood, and with a brand of fire,
These, for revenge of wretched murder done,
Do make the mother kill her only son.

Blood asketh blood, and death must death requite:
   Jove,* by his just and everlasting doom,   God
Justly hath ever so requited it.
   The times before record, and times to come
Shall find it true, and so doth present proof
Present before our eyes for our behoof.

O happy wight, that suffers not the snare   370
   Of murderous mind to tangle him in blood;
And happy he, that can in time beware
   By other's harms, and turn it to his good.
But woe to him that, fearing not to offend,
Doth serve his lust and will not see the end.

The Order and Signification of the Dumb Show Before the Fifth Act.

First, the drums and flutes began to sound, during which there
came forth upon the stage a company of harquebussiers, and
of armed men, all in order of battle. These, after their pieces
discharged, and that the armed men had three times marched
about the stage, departed, and then the drums and flutes did
cease. Hereby was signified tumults, rebellions, arms, and
civil wars to follow, as fell in the realm of Great Britain,
which, by the space of fifty years and more, continued in
civil war between the nobility after the death of king Gorboduc and of his issues, for want of certain limitation in the
succession of the crown, till the time of Dunwallo Mol-
mutius, who reduced the land to monarchy.

ACT V

Scene 1

(The Court of King Gorboduc. *Enter* Clotyn,
Duke of Cornwall, Mandud, *Duke of Loegris,*
Gwenard, *Duke of Cumberland,* Fergus, *Duke of
Albany, and the king's Secretary,* Eubulus.)

Clotyn. Did ever age bring forth such tyrant
    hearts?
The brother hath bereft the brother's life,
The mother, she hath dyed her cruel hands
In blood of her own son; and now at last
The people, lo, forgetting truth and love,
Contemning quite both law and loyal heart,
Ev'n they have slain their sovereign lord and queen.
    Mandud. Shall this their traitorous crime unpunish'd
    rest?
Ev'n yet they cease not, carried on with rage,
In their rebellious routs, to threaten still   10
A new bloodshed unto the prince's kin,
To slay them all, and to uproot the race
Both of the king and queen; so are they mov'd
With Porrex' death, wherein they falsely charge
The guiltless king, without desert at all;
And traitorously have murder'd him therefore,
And eke the queen.
    Gwenard.   Shall subjects dare with force
To work revenge upon their prince's fact*?   deed
Admit the worst that may, as sure in this
The deed was foul, the queen to slay her son,   20
Shall yet the subject seek to take the sword,
Arise against his lord and slay his king?
O wretched state, where those rebellious hearts
Are not rent out ev'n from their living breasts,
And with the body thrown unto the fowls,
As carrion food, for terror of the rest.
    Fergus. There can no punishment be thought too
    great
For this so grievous crime: let speed therefore
Be used therein, for it behooveth so.
    Eubulus. Ye all, my lords, I see, consent in one,   30
And I as one consent with ye in all.
I hold it more than need, with sharpest law

To punish this tumultuous bloody rage.
For nothing more may shake the common state
Than sufferance of uproars without redress;
Whereby how some kingdoms of mighty power,
After great conquests made, and flourishing
In fame and wealth, have been to ruin brought:
I pray to Jove, that we may rather wail
Such hap in them than witness in ourselves.   40
Eke fully with the duke my mind agrees,
[That no cause serves, whereby the subject may
Call to account the doings of his prince,
Much less in blood by sword to work revenge,
No more than may the hand cut off the head;
In act nor speech, no not in secret thought
The subject may rebel against his lord,
Or judge of him that sits in Cæsar's seat,
With grudging mind to damn those he mislikes.]14
Though kings forget to govern as they ought,
Yet subjects must obey as they are bound.
But now, my lords, before ye farther wade,
Or spend your speech, what sharp revenge shall fall
By justice' plague on these rebellious wights;
Methinks ye rather should first search the way,
By which in time the rage of this uproar
Might be repress'd, and these great tumults ceas'd.
Even yet the life of Britain land doth hang   50
In traitors' balance of unequal weight.
Think not, my lords, the death of Gorboduc,
Nor yet Videna's blood, will cease their rage:
Ev'n our own lives, our wives, and children dear,
Our country, dear'st of all, in danger stands,
Now to be spoil'd, now, now made desolate,
And by ourselves a conquest to ensue.
For, give once sway unto the people's lusts,
To rush forth on, and stay them not in time,
And as the stream that rolleth down the hill,   60
So will they headlong run with raging thoughts
From blood to blood, from mischief unto more,
To ruin of the realm, themselves, and all:
So giddy are the common people's minds,
So glad of change, more wavering than the sea.
Ye see, my lords, what strength these rebels have,

---

14 This passage was inserted into the 1565 edition of the play.

What hugy number is assembled still:
For though the traitorous fact, for which they rose,
Be wrought and done, yet lodge they still in field;
So that, how far their furies yet will stretch,   70
Great cause we have to dread. That we may seek
By present battle to repress their power,
Speed must we use to levy force therefore;
For either they forthwith will mischief work,
Or their rebellious roars forthwith will cease.
These violent things may have no lasting long
Let us, therefore, use this for present help;
Persuade by gentle speech, and offer grace
With gift of pardon, save unto the chief;
And that upon condition that forthwith   80
They yield the captains of their enterprise,
To bear such guerdon* of their traitorous fact   payment
As may be both due vengeance to themselves,
And wholesome terrour to posterity.
This shall, I think, scatter the greatest part
That now are holden with desire of home,
Wearied in field with cold of winter's nights,
And some, no doubt, stricken with dread of law.
When this is once proclaimed, it shall make
The captains to mistrust the multitude,
Whose safety bids them to betray their heads;*   90
                                                         rulers
And so much more, because the rascal routs,
In things of great and perilous attempts,
Are never trusty to the noble race.
And while we treat, and stand on terms of grace,
We shall both stay their furious rage the while,
And eke gain time, whose only help sufficeth
Withouten war to vanquish rebels' power.
In the meanwhile, make you in readiness
Such band of horsemen as ye may prepare.   100
Horsemen, you know, are not the commons' strength,
But are the force and store of noble men;
Whereby the unchosen and unarmèd sort
Of skilless rebels, whom none other power
But number makes to be of dreadful force,
With sudden brunt may quickly be oppress'd.
And if this gentle men of proffer'd grace
With stubborn hearts cannot so far avail
As to assuage their desp'rate courages;
Then do I wish such slaughter to be made,   110

As present age, and eke posterity,
May be adrad* with horrour of revenge   afraid
That justly then shall on these rebels fall.
This is, my lords, the sum of mine advice.
   CLOTYN. Neither this case admits debate at large;
And though it did, this speech that hath been said,
Hath well abridged the tale I would have told.
Fully with Eubulus do I consent
In all that he hath said: and if the same
To you, my lords, may seem for best advice,   120
I wish that it should straight be put in use.
   MANDUD. My lords, then let us presently depart,
And follow this that liketh us so well.
   (*Exteunt* CLOTYN, MANDUD, GWENARD, *and* EUBULUS.
   FERGUS, *Duke of Albany, alone on the stage.*)
   FERGUS. If ever time to gain a kingdom here
Were offered man, now it is offered me.
The realm is reft both of their king and queen,
The offspring of the prince is slain and dead,
No issue now remains, the heir unknown,
The people are in arms and mutinies,
The nobles, they are busied how to cease   130
These great rebellious tumults and uproars;
And Britain land, now desert left alone
Amid these broils uncertain where to rest,
Offers herself unto that noble heart
That will or dare pursue to bear her crown.
Shall I, that am the Duke of Albany,
Descended from that line of noble blood,
Which hath so long flourish'd in worthy fame
Of valiant hearts, such as in noble breasts
Of right should rest above the baser sort,   140
Refuse to venture life to win a crown?
Whom shall I find enemies that will withstand
My fact herein, if I attempt by arms
To seek the same now in these times of broil?
These dukes' power can hardly well appease
The people that already are in arms.
But if, perhaps, my force be once in field,
Is not my strength in power above the best
Of all these lords now left in Britain land?
And though they should match me with power of
    men,   150
Yet doubtful is the chance of battles joined.

If victors of the field we may depart,
Ours is the sceptre then of Great Britain;
If slain amid the plain this body lie,
Mine enemies yet shall not deny me this,
But that I died giving the noble charge
To hazard life for conquest of a crown.
Forthwith, therefore, will I in post* depart   hastily
To Albany, and raise in armour there
All power I can[15]: and here my secret friends,   160
By secret practice shall solicit still
To seek to win to me the people's hearts.

                                        (*Exit.*)

Scene 2

(*The Court. Enter the Secretary* Eubulus.)
  Eubulus (*solus*). O Jove, how are these people's
      hearts abused!
What blind fury thus headlong carries them?
That though so many books, so many rolls
Of ancient time, record what grievous plagues
Light on these rebels aye, and though so oft
Their ears have heard their aged fathers tell
What just reward these traitors still receive;
Yea, though themselves have seen deep death and
      blood,   170
By strangling cord, and slaughter of the sword,
To such assign'd, yet can they not beware,
Yet cannot stay their lewd* rebellious hands;   base
But suffering, lo, foul treason to distain
Their wretched minds, forget their loyal heart,
Reject all truth, and rise against their prince.
A ruthful* case, that those, whom duty's bond,   pitiful
Whom grafted law, by nature, truth, and faith,
Bound to preserve their country and their king,
Born to defend their commonwealth and prince,   180
Ev'n they should give consent thus to subvert
Thee, Britain land, and from thy womb should
      spring,
O native soil, those that will needs destroy
And ruin thee, and eke themselves in fine.
For lo, when once the dukes had offer'd grace
Of pardon sweet, the multitude, misled

---

[15] He will raise an army.

By traitorous fraud of their ungracious heads,
One sort that saw the dangerous success
Of stubborn standing in rebellious war,
And knew the difference of prince's power   190
From headless number of tumultuous routs,
Whom common country's care, and private fear
Taught to repent the error of their rage,
Laid hands upon the captains of their band,
And brought them bound unto the mighty dukes:
And other sort, not trusting yet so well
The truth of pardon, or mistrusting more
Their own offence than that they could conceive
Such hope of pardon for so foul misdeed,
Or for that they their captains could not yield,   200
Who, fearing to be yielded, fled before,
Stole home by silence of the secret night:
The third unhappy and enraged sort
Of desp'rate hearts, who, stain'd in princes' blood,
From traitorous furor could not be withdrawn
By love, by law, by grace, ne yet by fear,
By proffer'd life, ne yet by threaten'd death,
With minds hopeless of life, dreadless of death,
Careless of country, and aweless of God,
Stood bent to fight, as furies did them move,   210
With violent death to close their traitorous life.
These all by power of horsemen were oppress'd,
And with revenging sword slain in the field,
Or with the strangling cord hang'd on the trees,
Where yet their carrion carcases to preach
The fruits that rebels reap of their uproars,
And of the murder of their sacred prince.
But lo, where do approach the noble dukes
By whom these tumults have been thus appeas'd.
       (*Enter* CLOTYN, MANDUD, GWENARD, *and* AROSTUS.)
       CLOTYN. I think the world will now at length
          beware   220
And fear to put on arms against their prince.
       MANDUD. If not, those traitorous hearts that dare
          rebel,
Let them behold the wide and hugy fields
With blood and bodies spread of rebels slain;
The lofty trees cloth'd with the corpses dead,
That, strangled with the cord, do hang thereon.
       AROSTUS. A just reward; such as all times before

Have ever lotted* to those wretched folks.   allotted
    GWENARD. But what means he that cometh here so
      fast?
    (*Enter* NUNTIUS.)
    NUNTIUS. My lords, as duty and my troth* doth   loyalty
      move,   230
And of my country work a care in me,
That, if the spending of my breath availed
To do the service that my heart desires,
I would not shun to embrace a present death;
So have I now, in that wherein I thought
My travail might perform some good effect,
Ventur'd my life to bring these tidings here.
Fergus, the mighty duke of Albany,
Is now in arms, and lodgeth in the field
With twenty thousand men: hither he bends   240
His speedy march, and minds to invade the crown.
Daily he gathereth strength, and spreads abroad,
That to this realm no certain heir remains,
That Britain land is left without a guide,
That he the sceptre seeks, for nothing else
But to preserve the people and the land,
Which now remain as ship without a stern.
Lo, this is that which I have here to say.
    CLOTYN. Is this his faith? and shall he falsely thus
Abuse the vantage of unhappy times?   250
O wretched land, if his outrageous pride,
His cruel and untemper'd wilfulness,
His deep dissembling shows of false pretence,
Should once attain the crown of Britain land!
Let us, my lords, with timely force resist
The new attempt of this our common foe,
As we would quench the flames of common fire.
    MANDUD. Though we remain without a certain
      prince,
To wield the realm, or guide the wand'ring rule,
Yet now the common mother of us all,   260
Our native land, our country, that contains
Our wives, children, kindred, ourselves, and all
That ever is or may be dear to man,
Cries unto us to help ourselves and her.
Let us advance our powers to repress
This growing foe of all our liberties.
    GWENARD. Yea, let us so, my lords, with hasty speed.

And ye, O gods, send us the welcome death,
To shed our blood in field, and leave us not
In loathsome life to linger out our days,   270
To see the hugy* heaps of these unhaps,*   huge/unfortunates
That now roll down upon the wretched land,
Where empty place of princely governance,*   rule
No certain stay now left of doubtless heir,
Thus leave this guideless realm an open prey
To endless storms and waste of civil war.
   AROSTUS. That ye, my lords, do so agree in one,
To save your country from the violent reign
And wrongfully usurped tyranny
Of him that threatens conquest of you all,   280
To save your realm, and in this realm yourselves,
From foreign thraldom of so proud a prince,
Much do I praise; and I beseech the gods,
With happy honour to requite it you.
But, O my lords, sith* now the heaven's wrath   since
Hath reft this land the issue of their prince;
Sith of the body of our late sovereign lord
Remains no more, since the young kings be slain,
And of the title of descended crown
Uncertainly the divers* minds do think   various/290
Even of the learned sort, and more uncertainly
Will partial fancy and affection deem;
But most uncertainly will climbing pride
And hope of reign withdraw to sundry parts
The doubtful right and hopeful lust to reign.
When once this noble service is achiev'd
For Britain land, the mother of ye all,
When once ye have with armed force repress'd
The proud attempts of this Albanian prince,
That threatens thraldom* to your native land,   slavery/300
When ye shall vanquishers return from field
And find the princely state an open prey
To greedy lust and to usurping power,
Then, then, my lords, if ever kindly care
Of ancient honour of your ancestors,
Of present wealth and nobless of your stocks,
Yea of the lives and safety yet to come
Of your dear wives, your children, and yourselves,
Might move your noble hearts with gentle ruth,
Then, then, have pity on the torn estate;   310
Then help to salve the well-near hopeless sore;

Which ye shall do, if ye yourselves withhold
The slaying knife from your own mother's throat.
Her shall you save, and you, and yours in her,
In ye shall all with one assent forbear
Once to lay hand or take unto yourselves
The crown, by colour* of pretended right,   pretense
Or by what other means soe'er it be,
Till first by common counsel of you all
In parliament, the regal diadem   320
Be set in certain place of governance;
In which your parliament, and in your choice,
Prefer the right, my lords, without respect
Of strength or friends, or whatsoever cause
That may set forward any other's part.
For right will last, and wrong cannot endure.
Right mean I his or hers, upon whose name
The people rest by mean of native line,
Or by the virtue of some former law,
Already made their title to advance.   330
Such one, my lords, let be your chosen king,
Such one so born within your native land;
Such one prefer, and in no wise admit
The heavy yoke of foreign governance:
Let foreign titles yield to public wealth.
And with that heart wherewith ye now prepare
Thus to withstand the proud invading foe,
With that same heart, my lords, keep out also
Unnatural thraldom of stranger's reign;
Ne suffer you, against the rules of kind,   340
Your mother land to serve a foreign prince.
　　EUBULUS. Lo, here the end of Brutus' royal line,
And lo, the entry to the woeful wreck
And utter ruin of this noble realm.
The royal king and eke his sons are slain;
No ruler rests within the regal seat;
The heir, to whom the sceptre 'longs,* unknown;   belongs
That to each force of foreign princes' power,
Whom vantage of our wretched state may move
By sudden arms to gain so rich a realm,   350
And to the proud and greedy mind at home,
Whom blinded lust to reign leads to aspire,
Lo, Britain* realm is left an open prey,   Britain's
A present spoil by conquest to ensue.
Who seeth not now how many rising minds

Do feed their thoughts with hope to reach a realm?
And who will not by force attempt to win
So great a gain, that hope persuades to have?
A simple colour shall for title serve.
Who wins the royal crown will want* no right,   lack/360
Nor such as shall display by long descent
A lineal race to prove him lawful king.
In the meanwhile these civil arms* shall rage,   wars
And thus a thousand mischiefs shall unfold,
And far and near spread thee, O Britain land;
All right and law shall cease, and he that had
Nothing today, tomorrow shall enjoy
Great heaps of gold, and he that flow'd in wealth,
Lo, he shall be bereft of life and all;
And happiest he that then possesseth least.   370
The wives shall suffer rape, the maids deflour'd,
And children fatherless shall weep and wail;
With fire and sword thy native folk shall perish,
One kinsman shall bereave another life,
The father shall unwitting slay the son,
The son shall slay the sire and know it not.
Women and maids the cruel soldier's sword
Shall pierce to death, and silly children lo,
That playing in the streets and fields are found,
By violent hands shall close their latter day.   380
Whom shall the fierce and bloody soldier
Reserve to life? whom shall he spare from death?
Ev'n thou, O wretched mother, half alive,
Thou shalt behold thy dear and only child
Slain with the sword while he yet sucks thy breast.
Lo, guiltless blood shall thus each where be shed.
Thus shall the wasted soil yield forth no fruit,
But dearth and famine shall possess the land.
The towns shall be consum'd and burnt with fire,
The peopled cities shall wax desolate;   390
And thou, O Britain, whilom in renown,
Whilom in wealth and fame, shalt thus be torn,
Dismember'd thus, and thus be rent in twain,
Thus wasted and defaced, spoil'd and destroyed.
These be the fruits your civil wars will bring.
Hereto it comes when kings will not consent
To grave advice, but follow wilful will.
This is the end, when in fond princes' hearts
Flattery prevails, and sage rede* hath no place: counsel

These are the plagues, when murder is the mean   400
To make new heirs unto the royal crown.
Thus wreak* the gods, when that the mother's wrath   *punish*
Nought but the blood of her own child may swage,*   *assuage*
These mischiefs spring when rebels will arise
To work revenge and judge their prince's fact.
This, this ensues, when noble men do fail
In loyal truth, and subjects will be kings.
And this doth grow, when lo, unto the prince,
Whom death or sudden hap* of life bereaves,   *chance*
No certain heir remains, such certain heir,   410
As not all only is the rightful heir,
But to the realm is so made known to be;
And troth* thereby vested in subjects' hearts,   *trust*
To owe faith there where right is known to rest.
Alas, in parliament what hope can be,
When is of parliament no hope at all,
Which, though it be assembled by consent,
Yet is not likely with consent to end;
While each one for himself, or for his friend,
Against his foe, shall travail what he may;
While now the state, left open to the man
That shall with greatest force invade the same,
Shall fill ambitious minds with gaping hope;
When will they once with yielding hearts agree?
Or in the while, how shall the realm be used?
No, no: then parliament should have been holden,
And certain heirs appointed to the crown,
To stay the title of established right,
And in the people plant obedience,
While yet the prince did live, whose name and power   430
By lawful summons and authority
Might make a parliament to be of force,
And might have set the state in quiet stay.
But now, O happy man, whom speedy death
Deprives of life, ne is enforc'd to see
These hugy* mischiefs, and these miseries,   *huge*
These civil wars, these murders, and these wrongs.
Of justice, yet must God in fine restore
This noble crown unto the lawful heir:
For right will always live, and rise at length,
But wrong can never take deep root to last.

A SELECTIVE BIBLIOGRAPHY

Adams, Joseph Quincy (ed.), *Chief Pre-Shakespearean Drama*, Boston, 1924.

Baker, Howard, *Induction to Tragedy: A Study in a Development of Form in Gorboduc, The Spanish Tragedy, and Titus Andronicus*, Baton Rouge (La.), 1939.

Baugh, Albert C. (ed.), *A Literary History of England*, New York, 1948.

Block, K. S. (ed.), *Ludus Coventriæ* (Early English Text Society, Extra Series, 120), London, 1922.

Boas, Frederick Samuel, *An Introduction to Tudor Drama*, Oxford, 1933.

Bolwell, R. G., *The Life and Works of John Heywood*, New York, 1921.

Bridges-Adams, W., *The Irresistible Theatre*, Cleveland and New York, 1957.

Bullen, A. H. (ed.), *A Collection of Old Plays*, London, 1882–1888.

Butler, Sister Mary Marguerite, *Hrotsvitha: The Theatricality of Her Plays*, New York, 1960.

Cargill, Oscar, *Drama and Liturgy*, New York, 1930.

Chambers, Edmund K., *English Folk-play*, Oxford, 1933.

———, *English Literature at the Close of the Middle Ages*, Oxford, 1945.

———, *The Elizabethan Stage* (4 vols.), Oxford, 1933.

———, *The Medieval Stage* (2 vols.), London, 1903.

Clark, W. S., *The Early Irish Stage*, Oxford, 1955.

Cohen, Gustave, *Anthologie du drame liturgique en France au moyen-âge*, Paris, 1955.

———, *Etudes d'histoire du théâtre en France au moyen-âge et à la renaissance*, Paris, 1956.

———, *Histoire de la mise en scène dans le théâtre réligieux français du moyen-âge*, Paris, 1926.

———, *Le théâtre en France en moyen-âge*, Paris, 1948.

Clarke, Sidney W., *The Miracle Play in England*, London, 1897.

Craig, Hardin, *English Religious Drama of the Middle Ages*, Oxford, 1955.

Craig, Hardin (ed.), *Two Coventry Corpus Christi Plays* (Early English Text Society, Extra Series, 87), London, 1902, 1931.

Craik, Thomas Wallace, *The Tudor Interlude*, Leicester, 1958.

Creizenach, W., *Geschichte des neueren Dramas*, Halle, 1911–1923.

Cunliffe, John William, *Early English Classical Dramas*, Oxford, 1912.

Cushman, L. W., *The Devil and the Vice in English Dramatic Before Shakespeare*, Halle, 1900.

Deimling, H., and Matthews, G. W. (eds.), *The Chester Plays* (Early English Text Society, Extra Series, 62 and 115), London, 1892, 1916.

England, G., and Pollard, A. W. (eds.), *The Towneley Plays* (Early English Text Society, Extra Series 71), London, 1897, 1952.

Farmer, John Stephen (ed.), *Six Anonymous Plays. First Series* (1510–1537), London, 1905.

Farmer, John Stephen (ed.), *Tudor Facsimile Texts*, London, 1907, 1908, 1912.

Farnham, W., *The Medieval Heritage of Elizabethan Tragedy*, Boston, 1936.

Frank, Grace, *The Medieval French Drama*, Oxford, 1954.

Furnivall, F. J. (ed.), *The Digby Plays* (Early English Text Society, Extra Series, 91), London, 1896, 1930.

Furnivall, F. J., and Pollard, A. W. (eds.), *The Macro Plays* (Early English Text Society, Extra Series, 91), London, 1904, 1924.

Gardiner, Harold C., *Mysteries' End*, New Haven, 1946.

Gassner, John, *Masters of the Drama*, New York, 1940, 1954.

Gautier, Léon, *Histoire de la poèsie liturgique: les tropes*, Paris, 1886.

Gayley, Charles Mills, *Plays of Our Forefathers*, New York, 1907.

Greg, W. W., *Bibliographical and Textual Problems of the English Miracle Cycles* (in *The Library*, Third Series, v. 1), 1914.

Gregor, Joseph, *Weltgeschichte des Theaters*, Zurich, 1933.

———, *Das Theater des Mittelalters*, München, 1929.

Hartl, Eduard, *Das Drama des Mittelalters*, Leipzig, 1937.

Hrotsvithae Opera (Latin text of the works of Hrotsvitha), Edited by Karl Strecker, Leipzig, 1906. Also see: *Plays of Roswitha*, translated by H. J. W. Tillyard, London, 1923; *The Plays of Roswitha*, translated by Christopher St. John, London, 1923.

Hunningher, Benjamin, *The Origin of the Theatre*, New York, 1955.

Hussey, Maurice (ed.), *The Chester Plays*, New York, 1957. (See introduction.)

James, E. O., *Christian Myth and Ritual*, London, 1933.

Kindermann, Heinz, *Theatergeschichte Europas*, vol. 1, Salzburg, 1957, pp. 207–450.

Kirwan, Patrick, *The Dawn of English Drama*, London, 1920.

Kopke, Ernst Rudolf, *Hrotsvitha von Gandersheim*, Berlin, 1869.

Loomis, Roger Sherman, *Representative Medieval and Tudor Plays* (Translated and modernized with an introduction by Roger S. Loomis and Henry W. Wells), New York, 1942.

Magnin, Charles, *Théâtre de Hrotsvitha*, Paris, 1845.

Manly, John Matthews (ed.), *Specimens of Pre-Shakespearean Drama*, Boston, 1897, 1900.

Mill, A. J., *Medieval Plays in Scotland* (St. Andrews University Publications, xxiv), Edinburgh, 1927.

Nicoll, Allardyce, *Masks, Mimes, and Miracles*, London, 1931.

———, *The Development of the Theatre*, London, 1937.

Norris, A., *The Ancient Cornish Drama* (2 vols.), Oxford, 1859.

Parks, Ed Winfield (ed.), *The English Drama, an Anthology*, New York, 1935.

Parrott, Thomas Marc, and Ball, Robert Hamilton, *A Short View of Elizabethan Drama*, New York, 1943.

Pollard, Alfred W. (ed.), *The Towneley Plays* (Re-edited), London, 1897.

———, *English Miracle Plays, Moralities and Interludes*, London, 1890, 1927.

Prouty, Charles T., *George Gascoigne*, New York, 1942.

Purvis, Rev. J. S., *The York Cycle of Mystery Plays*, London, 1951. (Text prepared for presentation in York.)

———, *The York Cycle of Mystery Plays, A Complete Version*, London, 1957.

Reed, A. W., *Early Tudor Drama*, 1926.

Reich, Hermann, *Der Mimus*, Berlin, 1903. (See criticism by Philip S. Allen in *Modern Philology* VII and VIII.)

Rossiter, Arthur Percival, *English Drama from Early Times to the Elizabethans*, London, 1950.

Salter, Frederick Millet, *Medieval Drama in Chester*, Toronto, 1955.

Smith, Lucy Toulmin (ed.), *York Plays*, Oxford, 1885.

Southern, Richard, *The Medieval Theatre in the Round*, London, 1957.

Stratman, Carl J., *Bibliography of Medieval Drama*, Berkeley, 1954.

Studer, Paul (ed.), *Mystère d'Adam*, Manchester, 1918.

Thompson, E. N. S., *The English Moral Plays* (*Transactions of the Connecticut Academy of Arts and Sciences*, XIV), 1910.

Townsend, Walter, *Mystery and Miracle Plays in England*, London, 1931.

Waterhouse, O. (ed.), *The Non-Cycle Mystery Plays* (Early English Text Society, Extra Series, 104), London, 1909.

Wickham, Glynne, *Early English Stages, 1300–1660*, London and New York, 1959.

Williams, Arnold, *The Drama of Medieval England*, Ann Arbor (Mich.), 1961.

Young, Karl, *The Drama of the Medieval Church* (2 vols.), Oxford, 1933.

NOTE: For an extensive bibliography on the Middle Ages, see *Bibliography of Medieval Drama*, compiled by Carl J. Stratman, University of California Press, Berkeley.

SOLILOQUY!
The Shakespeare Monologues
Edited by Michael Earley and Philippa Keil

At last, over 175 of Shakespeare's finest and most performable monologues taken from all 37 plays are here in two easy-to-use volumes (MEN and WOMEN). Selections travel the entire spectrum of the great dramatist's vision, from comedies and romances to tragedies, pathos and histories.

"SOLILOQUY *is an excellent and comprehensive collection of Shakespeare's speeches. Not only are the monologues wide-ranging and varied, but they are superbly annotated. Each volume is prefaced by an informative and reassuring introduction, which explains the signals and signposts by which Shakespeare helps the actor on his journey through the text. It includes a very good explanation of blank verse, with excellent examples of irregularities which are specifically related to character and acting intentions. These two books are a must for any actor in search of a 'classical' audition piece.*"

ELIZABETH SMITH
Head of Voice & Speech
The Juilliard School

paper • MEN: ISBN 0-936839-78-3 • WOMEN: ISBN 0-936839-79-1

APPLAUSE

LIFE IS A DREAM
AND OTHER SPANISH CLASSICS
Edited by Eric Bentley
Translated by Roy Campbell

"The name of Eric Bentley is enough to guarantee the significance of any book of or about drama."

—Robert Penn Warren

LIFE IS A DREAM
by Calderon de la Barca

FUENTE OVEJUNA
by Lope de Vega

THE TRICKSTER OF SEVILLE
by Tirso de Molina

THE SIEGE OF NUMANTIA
by Miguel de Cervantes

paper • ISBN: 1-55783-006-1   cloth • ISBN: 1-55783-005-3

ELIZABETHAN DRAMA
Eight Plays
Edited and with Introductions by
John Gassner and William Green

Boisterous and unrestrained like the age itself, the Elizabethan theatre has long defended its place at the apex of English dramatic history. Shakespeare was but the brightest star in this extraordinary galaxy of playwrights. Led by a group of young playwrights dubbed "the university wits," the Elizabethan popular stage was imbued with a dynamic force never since equalled. The stage boasted a rich and varied repertoire from courtly and romantic comedy to domestic and high tragedy, melodrama, farce, and histories. The Gassner-Green anthology revives the whole range of this universal stage, offering us the unbounded theatrical inventiveness of the age.

Arden of Feversham, **Anonymous**

The Spanish Tragedy, by **Thomas Kyd**

Friar Bacon and Friar Bungay, by **Robert Greene**

Doctor Faustus, by **Christopher Marlowe**

Edward II, by **Christopher Marlowe**

Everyman in His Humour, by **Ben Jonson**

The Shoemaker's Holiday, by **Thomas Dekker**

A Woman Killed with Kindness, by **Thomas Heywood**

paper • ISBN: 1-55783-028-2

CLASSICAL TRAGEDY
GREEK AND ROMAN: Eight Plays

In Authoritative Modern Translations
Accompanied by Critical Essays

Edited by Robert W. Corrigan

AESCHYLUS   **PROMETHEUS BOUND**
translated by David Grene
ORESTEIA
translated by Tony Harrison

SOPHOCLES   **ANTIGONE**
translated by Dudley Fitts
and Robert Fitzgerald
OEDIPUS THE KING
translated by Kenneth Cavander

EURIPIDES   **MEDEA**
translated by Michael Townsend
THE BAKKHAI
translated by Robert Bagg

SENECA   **OEDIPUS**
translated by David Anthony Turner
MEDEA
translated by Frederick Ahl

paper • ISBN: 1-55783-046-0

CLASSICAL COMEDY
GREEK AND ROMAN: Six Plays
Edited by Robert W. Corrigan

The only book of its kind: for the first time Greek and Roman masters of comedy meet in this extraordinary new forum devised and edited by a master scholar of comedy himself, Robert Corrigan. Corrigan has enlisted six superb translations to create an unmatched Olympiad of classical comedy.

ARISTOPHANES	**LYSISTRATA** translated by Donald Sutherland **THE BIRDS** translated by Walter Kerr
MENANDER	**THE GROUCH** translated by Sheila D'Atri
PLAUTUS	**THE MENAECHMI** translated by Palmer Bovie **THE HAUNTED HOUSE** translated by Palmer Bovie
TERENCE	**THE SELF-TORMENTOR** translated by Palmer Bovie

paper • ISBN: 0-936839-85-6